ATTACK OF THE Deranged Mutant Killer Monster SNOW GOONS

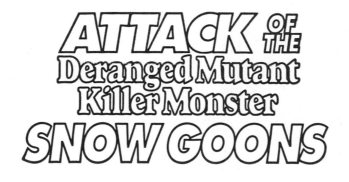

Other Books by Bill Watterson

Calvin and Hobbes
Something Under the Bed Is Drooling
Yukon Ho!
Weirdos From Another Planet!
The Revenge of the Baby-Sat
Scientific Progress Goes "Boink"

Treasury Collections

The Essential Calvin and Hobbes
The Calvin and Hobbes Lazy Sunday Book
The Authoritative Calvin and Hobbes

ATTACK OF THE Deranged Mutant Killer Monster SNOW GOONS

A Calvin and Hobbes Collection by Bill Watterson

Andrews and McMeel
A Universal Press Syndicate Company
Kansas City

Calvin and Hobbes is distributed internationally by Universal Press Syndicate.

ISBN: 0-8362-1883-3

Library of Congress Catalog Card Number: 91-73947

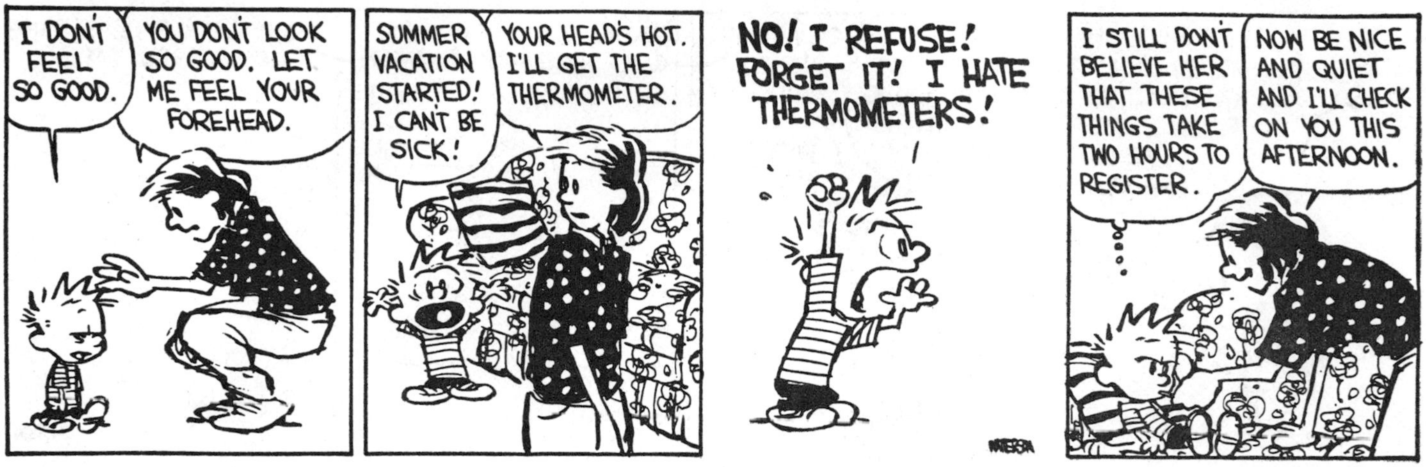
I DON'T FEEL SO GOOD.
YOU DON'T LOOK SO GOOD. LET ME FEEL YOUR FOREHEAD.
SUMMER VACATION STARTED! I CAN'T BE SICK!
YOUR HEAD'S HOT. I'LL GET THE THERMOMETER.
NO! I REFUSE! FORGET IT! I HATE THERMOMETERS!
I STILL DON'T BELIEVE HER THAT THESE THINGS TAKE TWO HOURS TO REGISTER.
NOW BE NICE AND QUIET AND I'LL CHECK ON YOU THIS AFTERNOON.

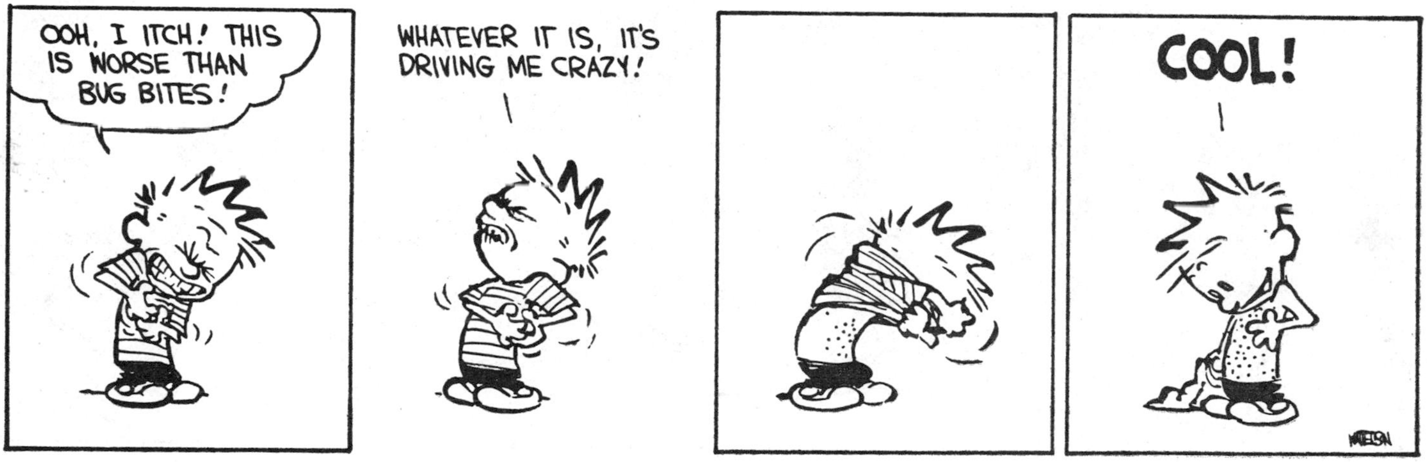
OOH, I ITCH! THIS IS WORSE THAN BUG BITES!
WHATEVER IT IS, IT'S DRIVING ME CRAZY!
COOL!

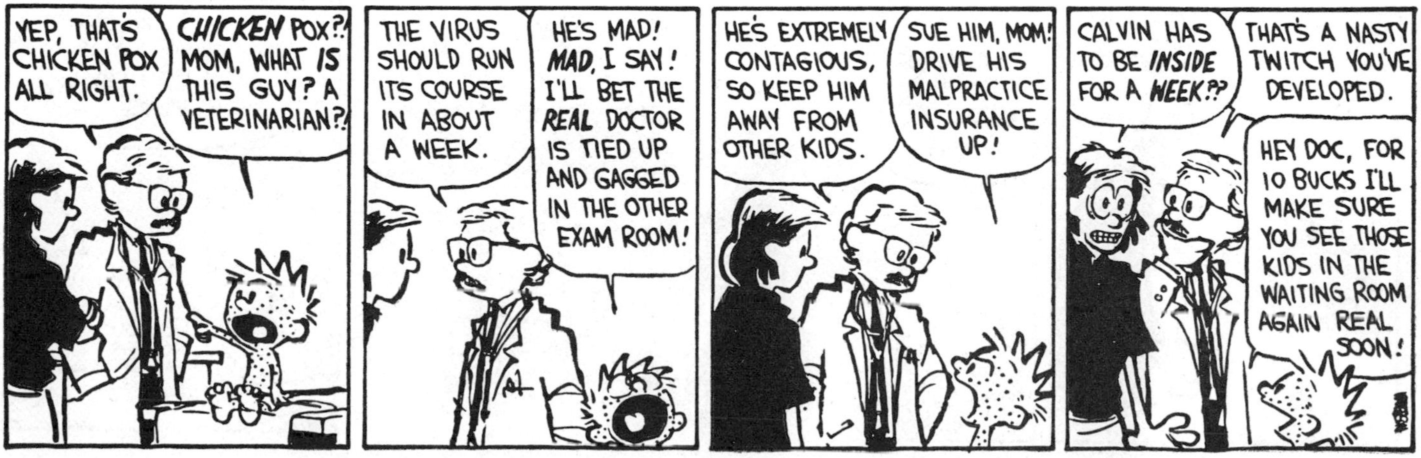
YEP, THAT'S CHICKEN POX ALL RIGHT.
CHICKEN POX?! MOM, WHAT IS THIS GUY? A VETERINARIAN?!
THE VIRUS SHOULD RUN ITS COURSE IN ABOUT A WEEK.
HE'S MAD! MAD, I SAY! I'LL BET THE REAL DOCTOR IS TIED UP AND GAGGED IN THE OTHER EXAM ROOM!
HE'S EXTREMELY CONTAGIOUS, SO KEEP HIM AWAY FROM OTHER KIDS.
SUE HIM, MOM! DRIVE HIS MALPRACTICE INSURANCE UP!
CALVIN HAS TO BE INSIDE FOR A WEEK?!
THAT'S A NASTY TWITCH YOU'VE DEVELOPED.
HEY DOC, FOR 10 BUCKS I'LL MAKE SURE YOU SEE THOSE KIDS IN THE WAITING ROOM AGAIN REAL SOON!

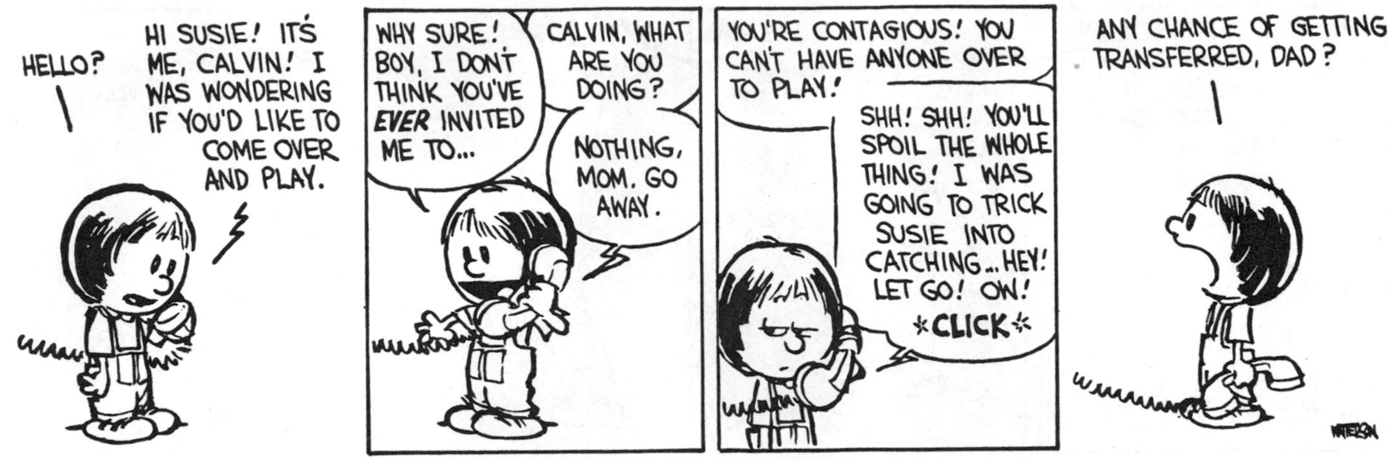
HELLO?
HI SUSIE! IT'S ME, CALVIN! I WAS WONDERING IF YOU'D LIKE TO COME OVER AND PLAY.
WHY SURE! BOY, I DON'T THINK YOU'VE *EVER* INVITED ME TO...
CALVIN, WHAT ARE YOU DOING?
NOTHING, MOM. GO AWAY.
YOU'RE CONTAGIOUS! YOU CAN'T HAVE ANYONE OVER TO PLAY!
SHH! SHH! YOU'LL SPOIL THE WHOLE THING! I WAS GOING TO TRICK SUSIE INTO CATCHING... HEY! LET GO! OW!
CLICK
ANY CHANCE OF GETTING TRANSFERRED, DAD?

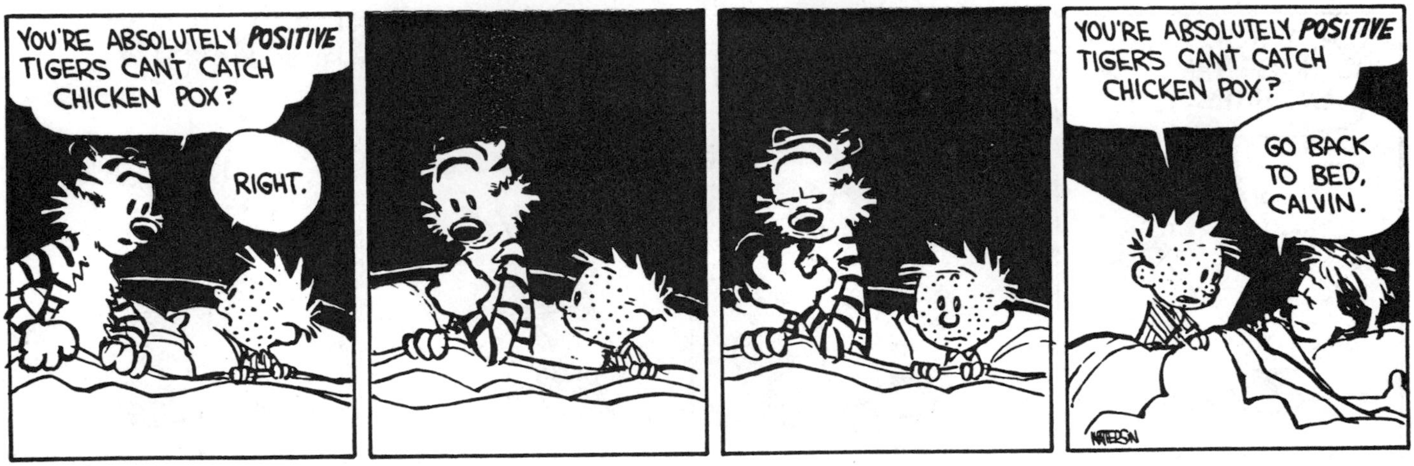
YOU'RE ABSOLUTELY *POSITIVE* TIGERS CAN'T CATCH CHICKEN POX?
RIGHT.
YOU'RE ABSOLUTELY *POSITIVE* TIGERS CAN'T CATCH CHICKEN POX?
GO BACK TO BED, CALVIN.

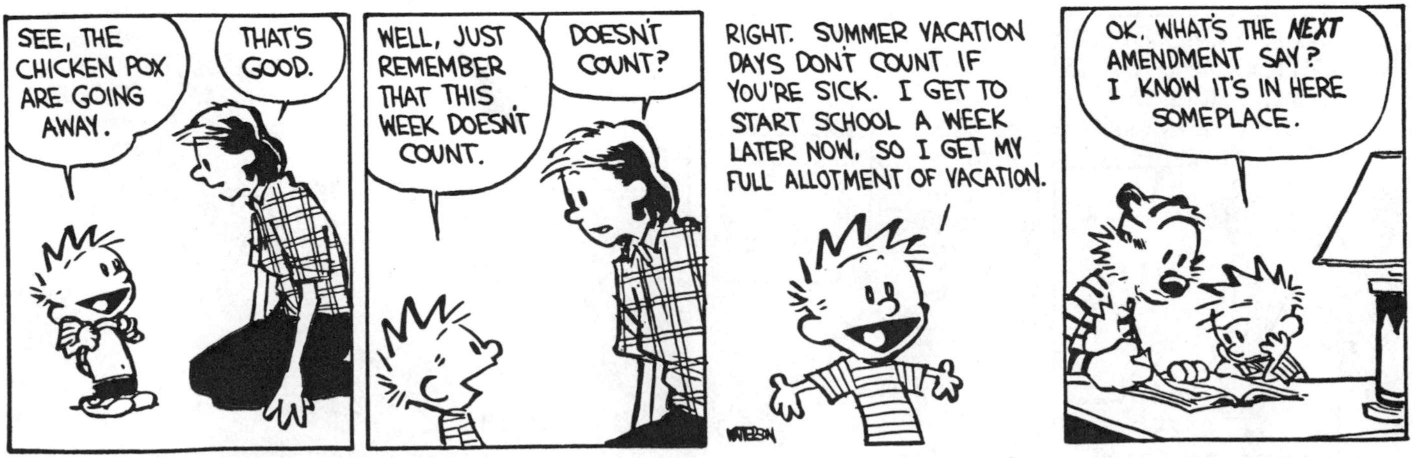
SEE, THE CHICKEN POX ARE GOING AWAY.
THAT'S GOOD.
WELL, JUST REMEMBER THAT THIS WEEK DOESN'T COUNT.
DOESN'T COUNT?
RIGHT. SUMMER VACATION DAYS DON'T COUNT IF YOU'RE SICK. I GET TO START SCHOOL A WEEK LATER NOW, SO I GET MY FULL ALLOTMENT OF VACATION.
OK, WHAT'S THE *NEXT* AMENDMENT SAY? I KNOW IT'S IN HERE SOMEPLACE.

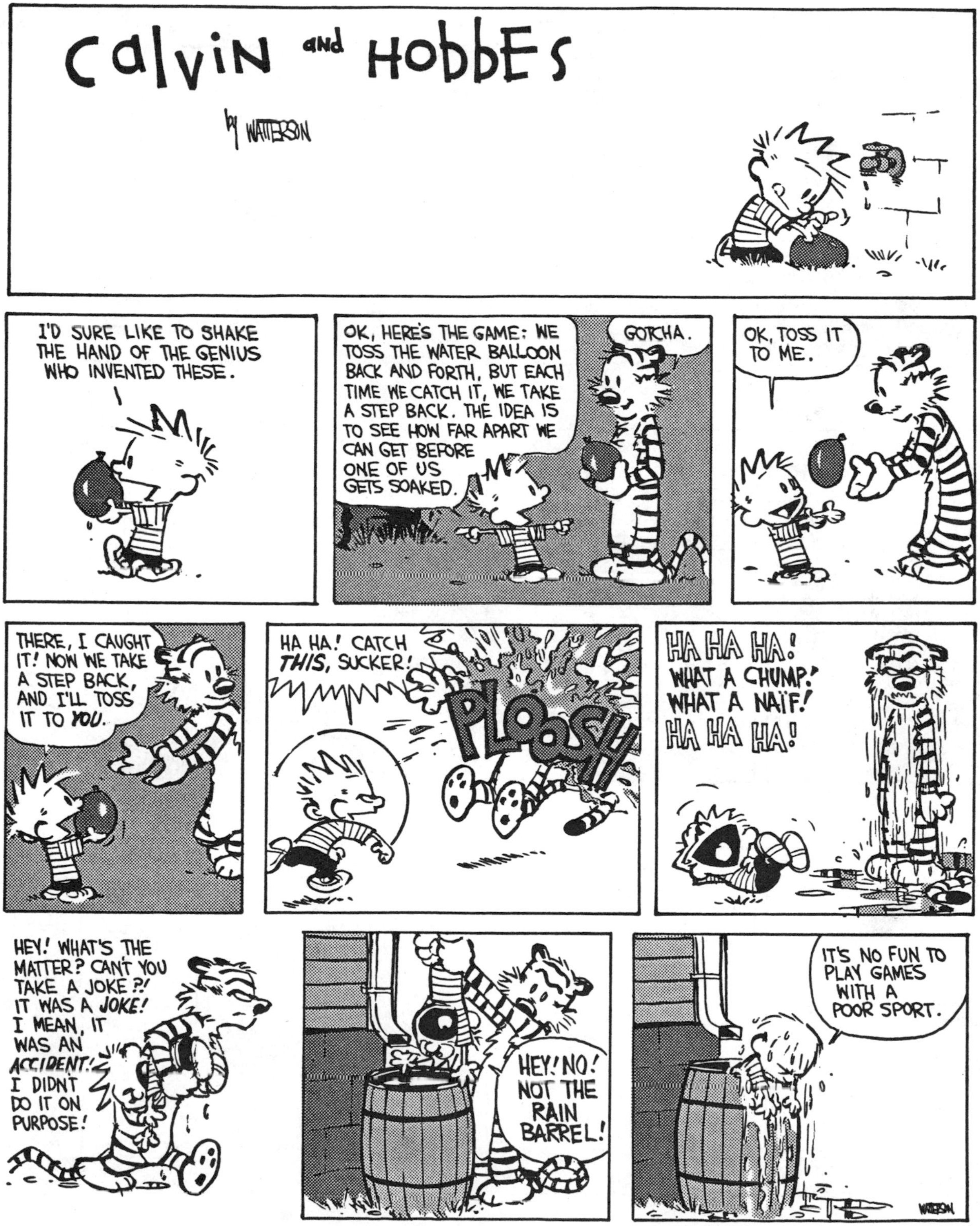
Calvin and Hobbes
by WATTERSON
I'D SURE LIKE TO SHAKE THE HAND OF THE GENIUS WHO INVENTED THESE.
OK, HERE'S THE GAME: WE TOSS THE WATER BALLOON BACK AND FORTH, BUT EACH TIME WE CATCH IT, WE TAKE A STEP BACK. THE IDEA IS TO SEE HOW FAR APART WE CAN GET BEFORE ONE OF US GETS SOAKED.
GOTCHA.
OK, TOSS IT TO ME.
THERE, I CAUGHT IT! NOW WE TAKE A STEP BACK, AND I'LL TOSS IT TO YOU.
HA HA! CATCH THIS, SUCKER!
PLOOSH
HA HA HA! WHAT A CHUMP! WHAT A NAÏF! HA HA HA!
HEY! WHAT'S THE MATTER? CAN'T YOU TAKE A JOKE?! IT WAS A JOKE! I MEAN, IT WAS AN ACCIDENT! I DIDN'T DO IT ON PURPOSE!
HEY! NO! NOT THE RAIN BARREL!
IT'S NO FUN TO PLAY GAMES WITH A POOR SPORT.
WATTERSON

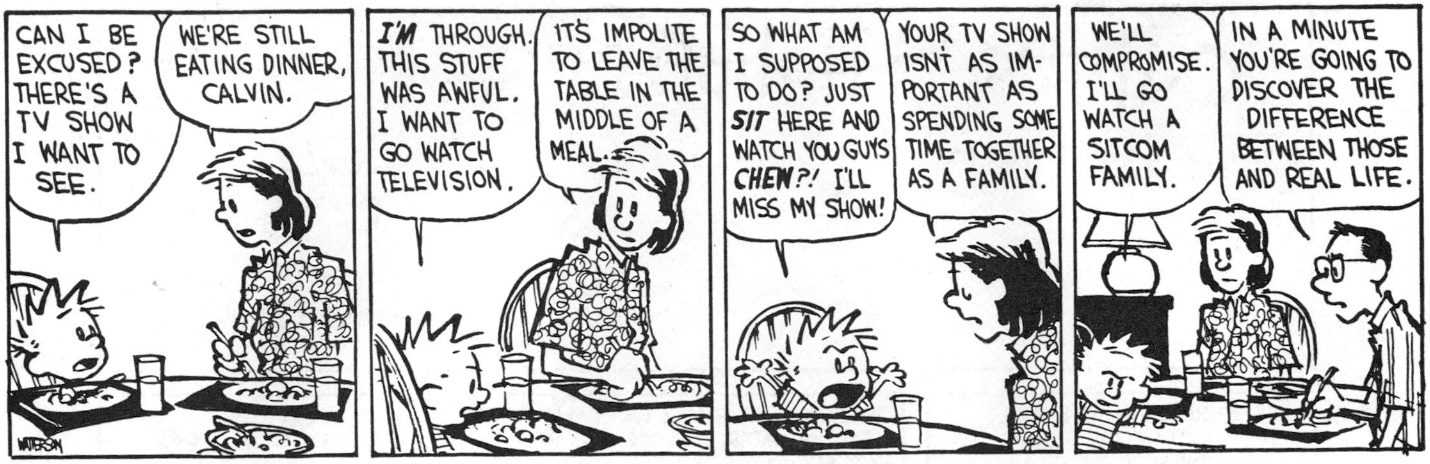
CAN I BE EXCUSED? THERE'S A TV SHOW I WANT TO SEE.
WE'RE STILL EATING DINNER, CALVIN.
I'M THROUGH. THIS STUFF WAS AWFUL. I WANT TO GO WATCH TELEVISION.
IT'S IMPOLITE TO LEAVE THE TABLE IN THE MIDDLE OF A MEAL.
SO WHAT AM I SUPPOSED TO DO? JUST SIT HERE AND WATCH YOU GUYS CHEW?! I'LL MISS MY SHOW!
YOUR TV SHOW ISN'T AS IMPORTANT AS SPENDING SOME TIME TOGETHER AS A FAMILY.
WE'LL COMPROMISE. I'LL GO WATCH A SITCOM FAMILY.
IN A MINUTE YOU'RE GOING TO DISCOVER THE DIFFERENCE BETWEEN THOSE AND REAL LIFE.

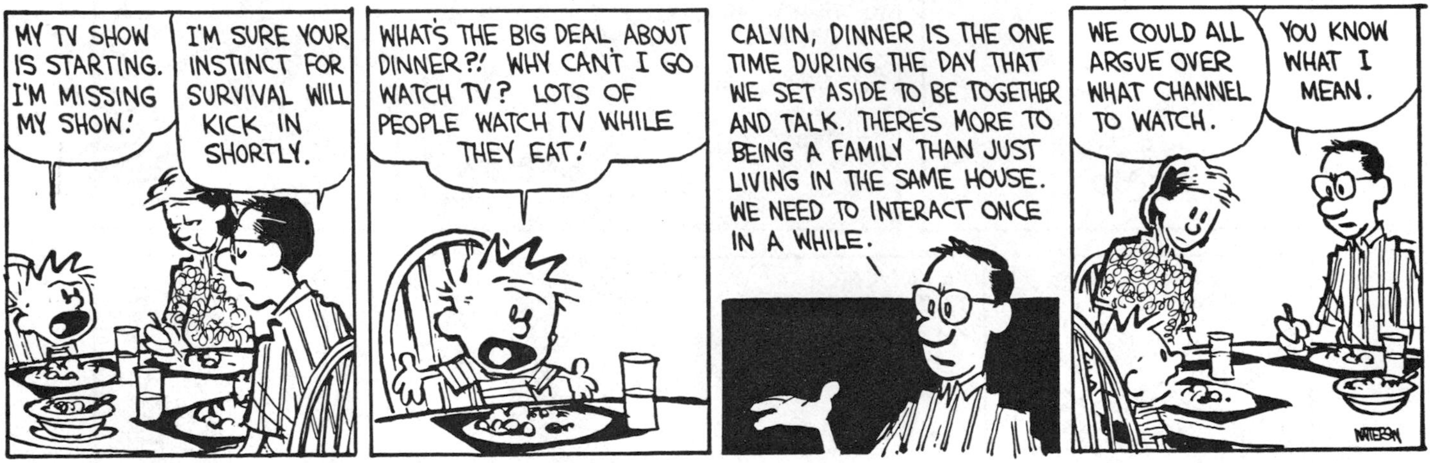
MY TV SHOW IS STARTING. I'M MISSING MY SHOW!
I'M SURE YOUR INSTINCT FOR SURVIVAL WILL KICK IN SHORTLY.
WHAT'S THE BIG DEAL ABOUT DINNER?! WHY CAN'T I GO WATCH TV? LOTS OF PEOPLE WATCH TV WHILE THEY EAT!
CALVIN, DINNER IS THE ONE TIME DURING THE DAY THAT WE SET ASIDE TO BE TOGETHER AND TALK. THERE'S MORE TO BEING A FAMILY THAN JUST LIVING IN THE SAME HOUSE. WE NEED TO INTERACT ONCE IN A WHILE.
WE COULD ALL ARGUE OVER WHAT CHANNEL TO WATCH.
YOU KNOW WHAT I MEAN.

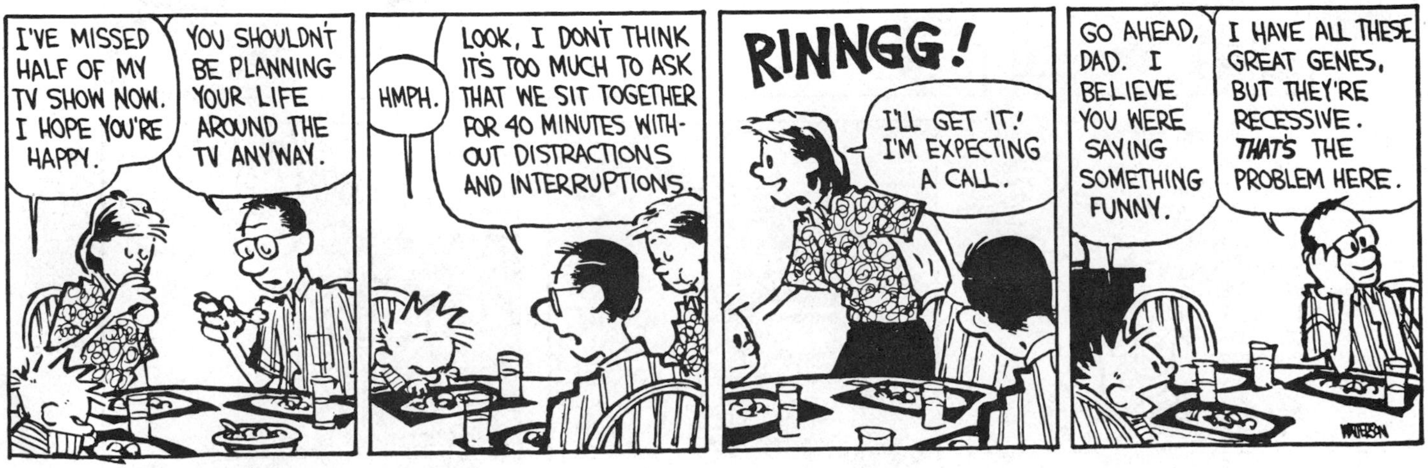
I'VE MISSED HALF OF MY TV SHOW NOW. I HOPE YOU'RE HAPPY.
YOU SHOULDN'T BE PLANNING YOUR LIFE AROUND THE TV ANYWAY.
HMPH.
LOOK, I DON'T THINK IT'S TOO MUCH TO ASK THAT WE SIT TOGETHER FOR 40 MINUTES WITHOUT DISTRACTIONS AND INTERRUPTIONS.
RINNGG!
I'LL GET IT! I'M EXPECTING A CALL.
GO AHEAD, DAD. I BELIEVE YOU WERE SAYING SOMETHING FUNNY.
I HAVE ALL THESE GREAT GENES, BUT THEY'RE RECESSIVE. THAT'S THE PROBLEM HERE.

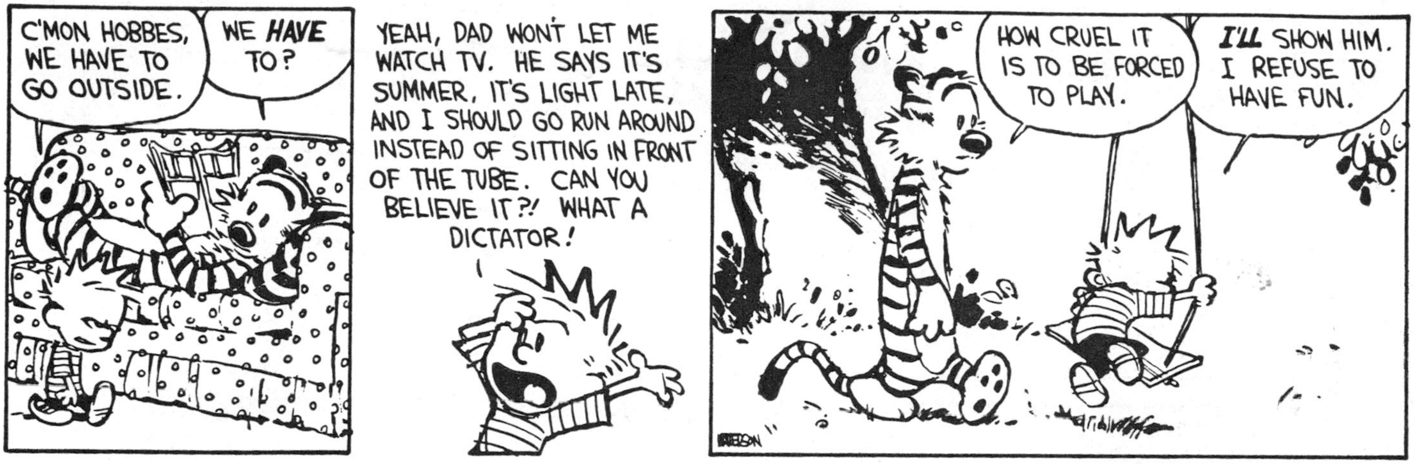
C'MON HOBBES, WE HAVE TO GO OUTSIDE.
WE **HAVE** TO?
YEAH, DAD WON'T LET ME WATCH TV. HE SAYS IT'S SUMMER, IT'S LIGHT LATE, AND I SHOULD GO RUN AROUND INSTEAD OF SITTING IN FRONT OF THE TUBE. CAN YOU BELIEVE IT?! WHAT A DICTATOR!
HOW CRUEL IT IS TO BE FORCED TO PLAY.
I'LL SHOW HIM. I REFUSE TO HAVE FUN.

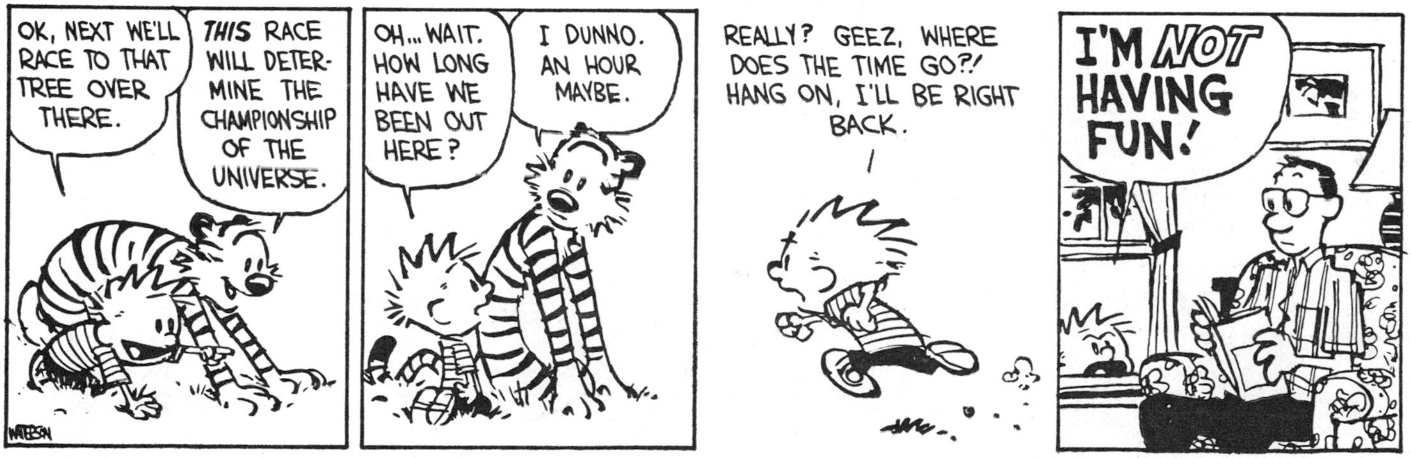
OK, NEXT WE'LL RACE TO THAT TREE OVER THERE.
THIS RACE WILL DETERMINE THE CHAMPIONSHIP OF THE UNIVERSE.
OH... WAIT. HOW LONG HAVE WE BEEN OUT HERE?
I DUNNO. AN HOUR MAYBE.
REALLY? GEEZ, WHERE DOES THE TIME GO?! HANG ON, I'LL BE RIGHT BACK.
I'M **NOT** HAVING FUN!

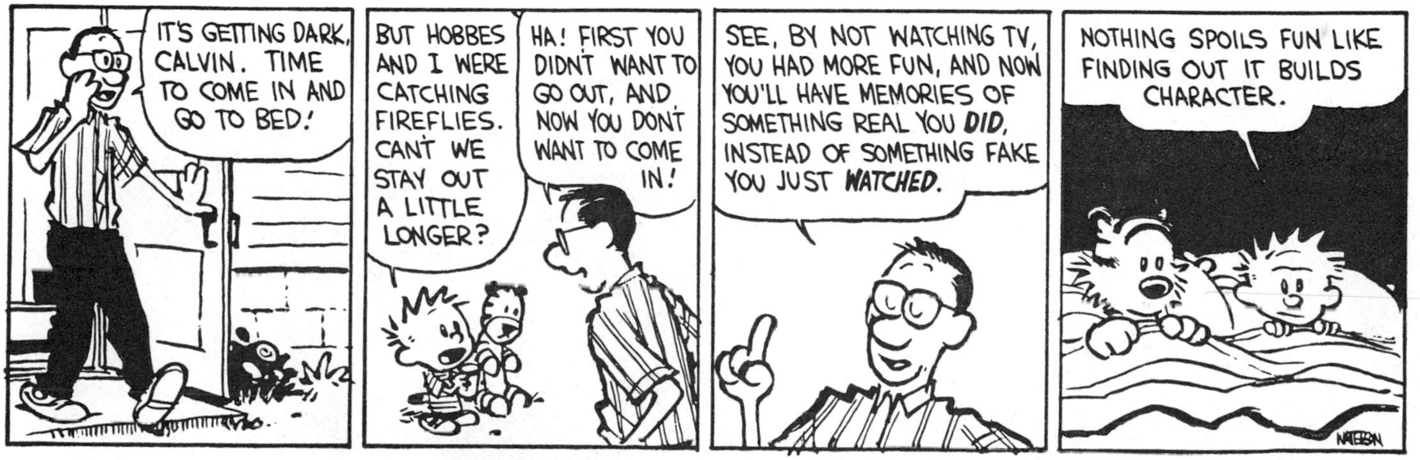
IT'S GETTING DARK, CALVIN. TIME TO COME IN AND GO TO BED!
BUT HOBBES AND I WERE CATCHING FIREFLIES. CAN'T WE STAY OUT A LITTLE LONGER?
HA! FIRST YOU DIDN'T WANT TO GO OUT, AND NOW YOU DON'T WANT TO COME IN!
SEE, BY NOT WATCHING TV, YOU HAD MORE FUN, AND NOW YOU'LL HAVE MEMORIES OF SOMETHING REAL YOU **DID**, INSTEAD OF SOMETHING FAKE YOU JUST **WATCHED**.
NOTHING SPOILS FUN LIKE FINDING OUT IT BUILDS CHARACTER.

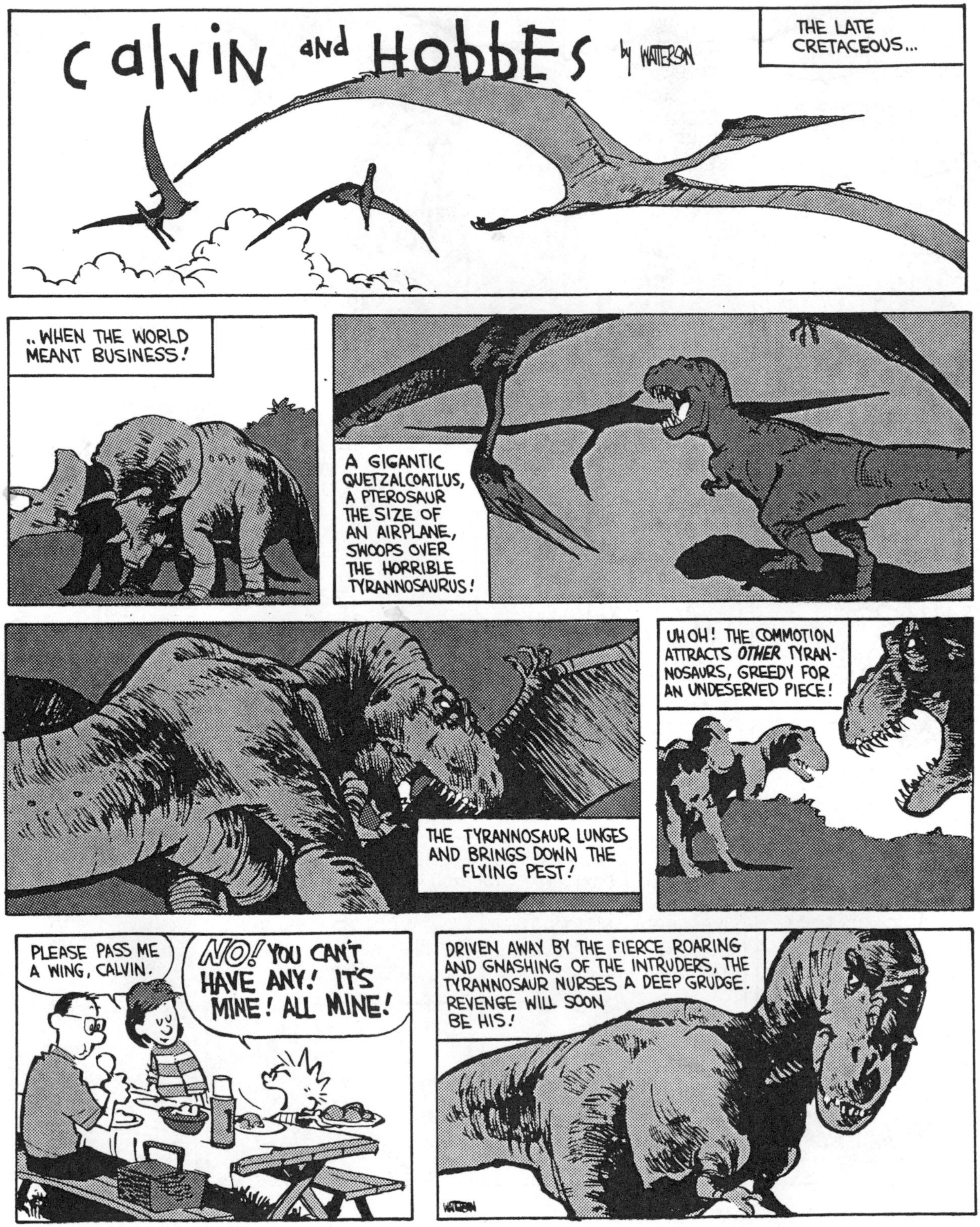
Calvin and HobbEs by WATTERSON
THE LATE CRETACEOUS...
..WHEN THE WORLD MEANT BUSINESS!
A GIGANTIC QUETZALCOATLUS, A PTEROSAUR THE SIZE OF AN AIRPLANE, SWOOPS OVER THE HORRIBLE TYRANNOSAURUS!
THE TYRANNOSAUR LUNGES AND BRINGS DOWN THE FLYING PEST!
UH OH! THE COMMOTION ATTRACTS OTHER TYRANNOSAURS, GREEDY FOR AN UNDESERVED PIECE!
DRIVEN AWAY BY THE FIERCE ROARING AND GNASHING OF THE INTRUDERS, THE TYRANNOSAUR NURSES A DEEP GRUDGE. REVENGE WILL SOON BE HIS!
PLEASE PASS ME A WING, CALVIN.
NO! YOU CAN'T HAVE ANY! IT'S MINE! ALL MINE!
WATTERSON

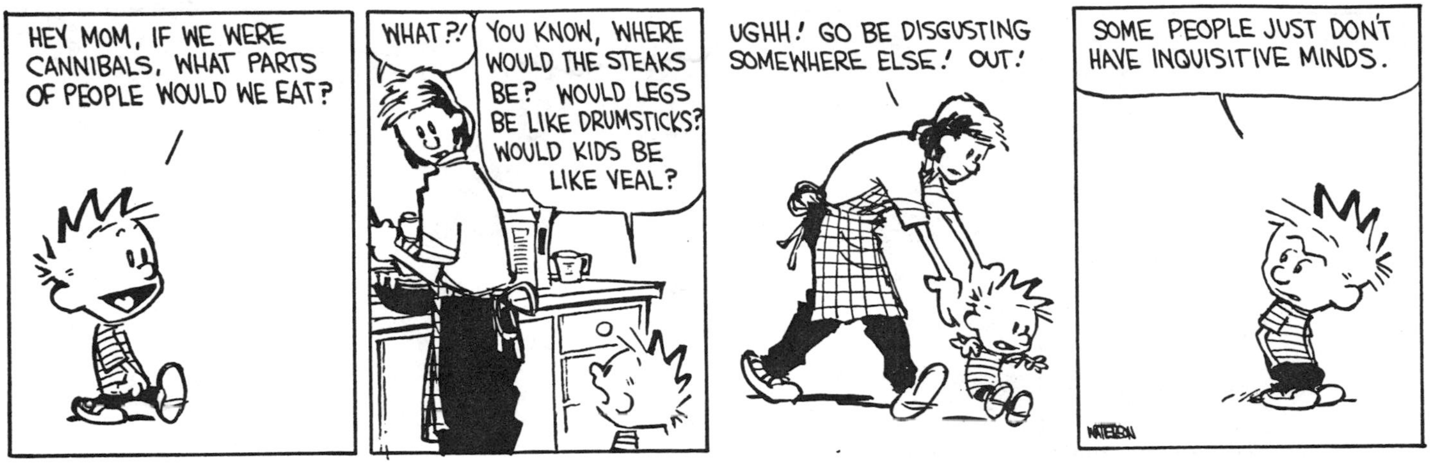
HEY MOM, IF WE WERE CANNIBALS, WHAT PARTS OF PEOPLE WOULD WE EAT?
WHAT?!
YOU KNOW, WHERE WOULD THE STEAKS BE? WOULD LEGS BE LIKE DRUMSTICKS? WOULD KIDS BE LIKE VEAL?
UGHH! GO BE DISGUSTING SOMEWHERE ELSE! OUT!
SOME PEOPLE JUST DON'T HAVE INQUISITIVE MINDS.

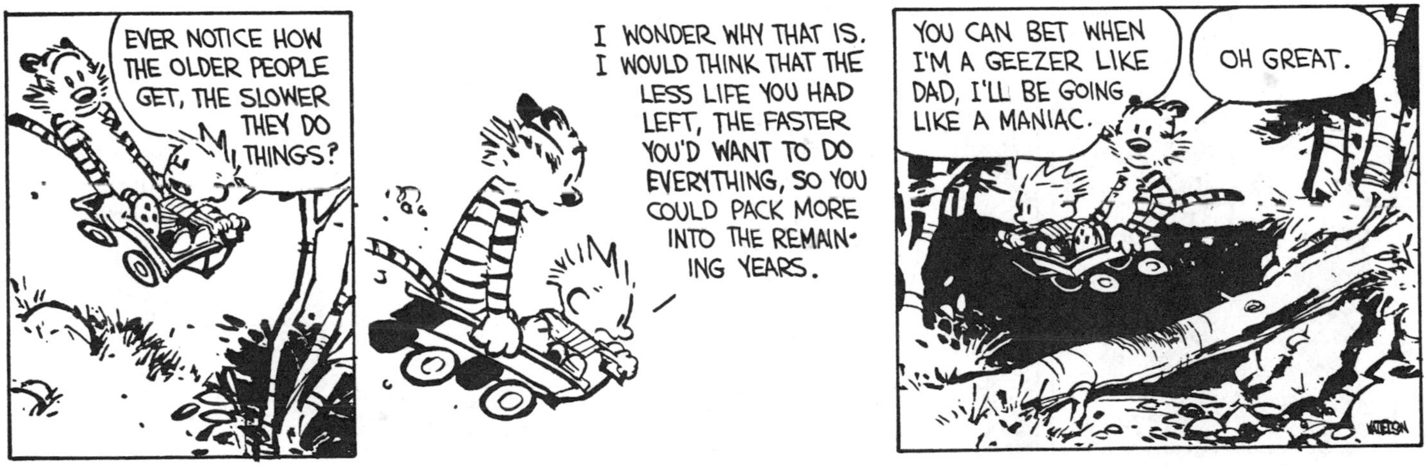
EVER NOTICE HOW THE OLDER PEOPLE GET, THE SLOWER THEY DO THINGS?
I WONDER WHY THAT IS. I WOULD THINK THAT THE LESS LIFE YOU HAD LEFT, THE FASTER YOU'D WANT TO DO EVERYTHING, SO YOU COULD PACK MORE INTO THE REMAINING YEARS.
YOU CAN BET WHEN I'M A GEEZER LIKE DAD, I'LL BE GOING LIKE A MANIAC.
OH GREAT.

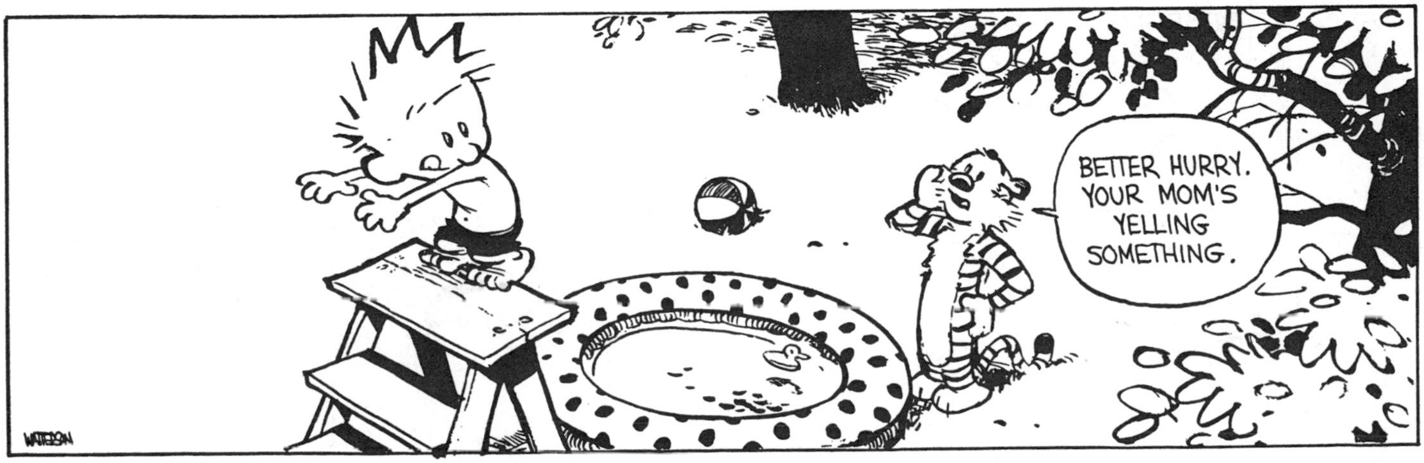
BETTER HURRY. YOUR MOM'S YELLING SOMETHING.

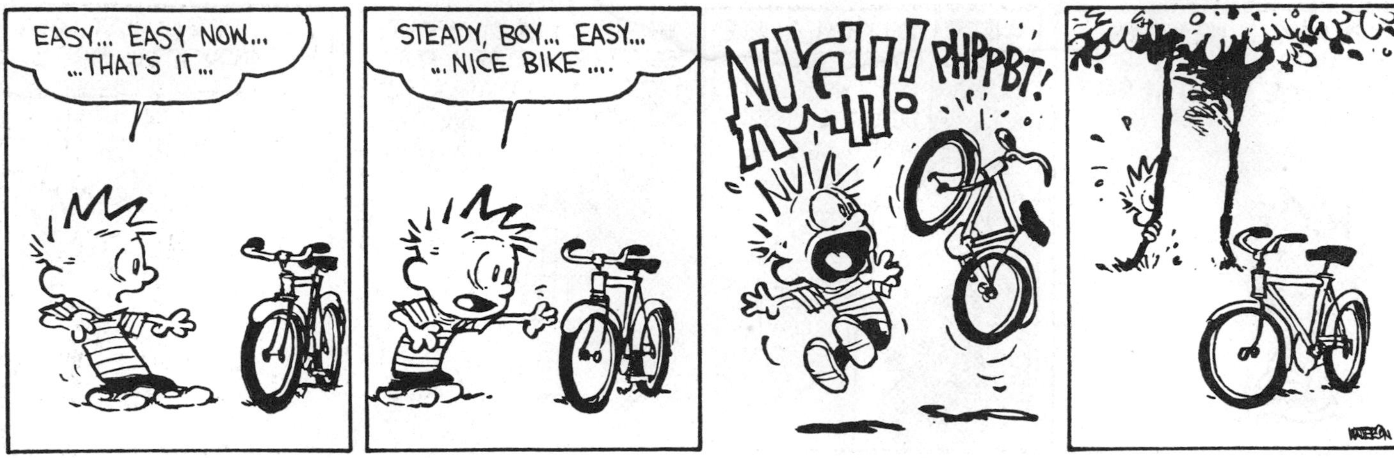
EASY... EASY NOW... ...THAT'S IT...
STEADY, BOY... EASY... ...NICE BIKE....
AUGH!
PHPPBT!

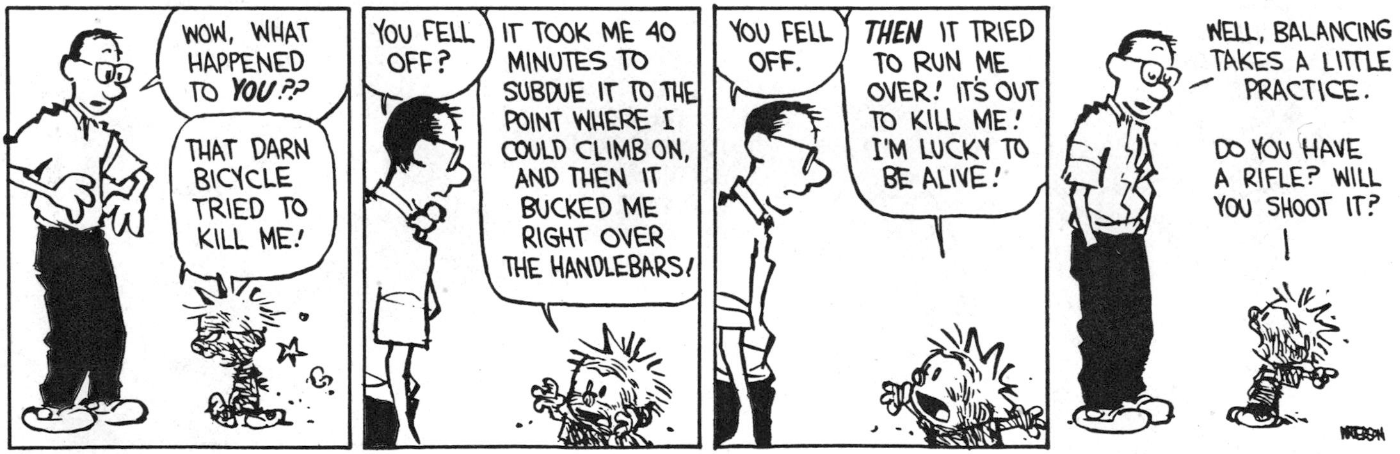
WOW, WHAT HAPPENED TO *YOU*??
THAT DARN BICYCLE TRIED TO KILL ME!
YOU FELL OFF?
IT TOOK ME 40 MINUTES TO SUBDUE IT TO THE POINT WHERE I COULD CLIMB ON, AND THEN IT BUCKED ME RIGHT OVER THE HANDLEBARS!
YOU FELL OFF.
THEN IT TRIED TO RUN ME OVER! IT'S OUT TO KILL ME! I'M LUCKY TO BE ALIVE!
WELL, BALANCING TAKES A LITTLE PRACTICE.
DO YOU HAVE A RIFLE? WILL YOU SHOOT IT?

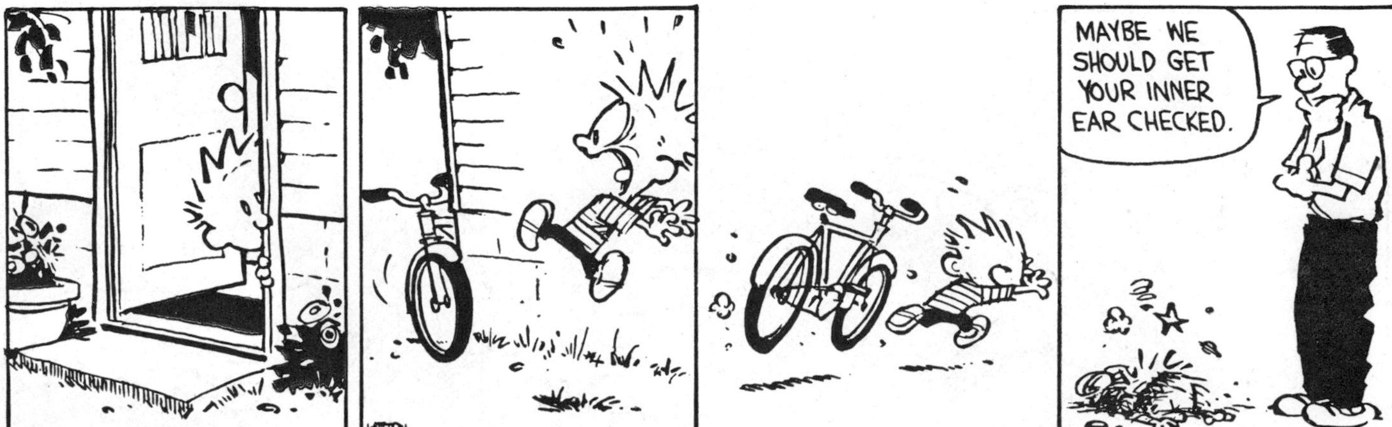
MAYBE WE SHOULD GET YOUR INNER EAR CHECKED.

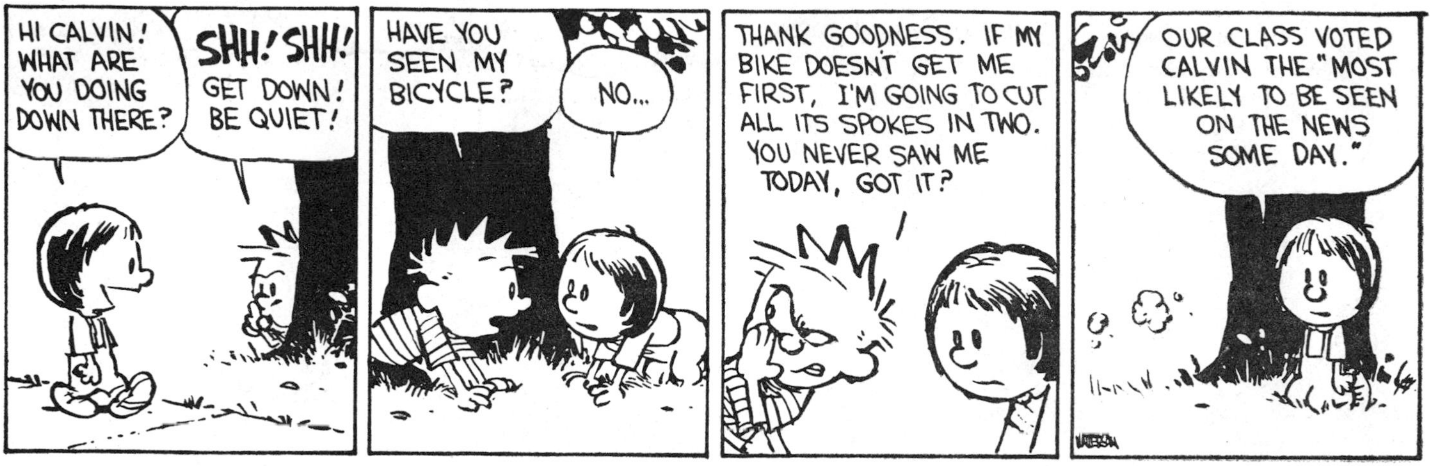
HI CALVIN! WHAT ARE YOU DOING DOWN THERE?
SHH! SHH! GET DOWN! BE QUIET!
HAVE YOU SEEN MY BICYCLE?
NO...
THANK GOODNESS. IF MY BIKE DOESN'T GET ME FIRST, I'M GOING TO CUT ALL ITS SPOKES IN TWO. YOU NEVER SAW ME TODAY, GOT IT?
OUR CLASS VOTED CALVIN THE "MOST LIKELY TO BE SEEN ON THE NEWS SOME DAY."

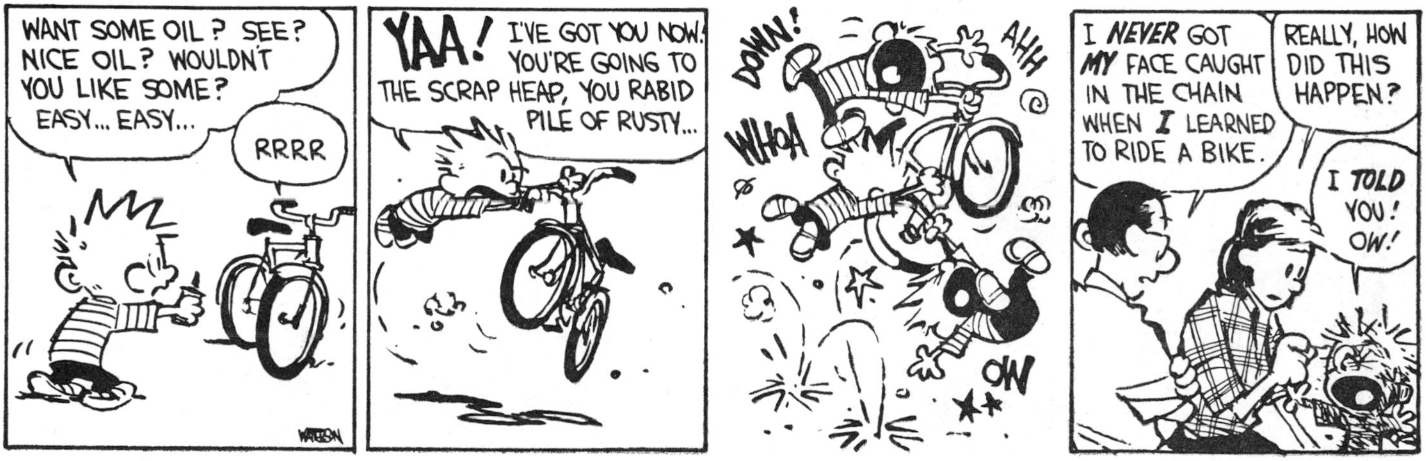
WANT SOME OIL? SEE? NICE OIL? WOULDN'T YOU LIKE SOME? EASY... EASY...
RRRR
YAA!
I'VE GOT YOU NOW! YOU'RE GOING TO THE SCRAP HEAP, YOU RABID PILE OF RUSTY...
DOWN!
AHH
WHOA
OW
I NEVER GOT MY FACE CAUGHT IN THE CHAIN WHEN I LEARNED TO RIDE A BIKE.
REALLY, HOW DID THIS HAPPEN?
I TOLD YOU! OW!

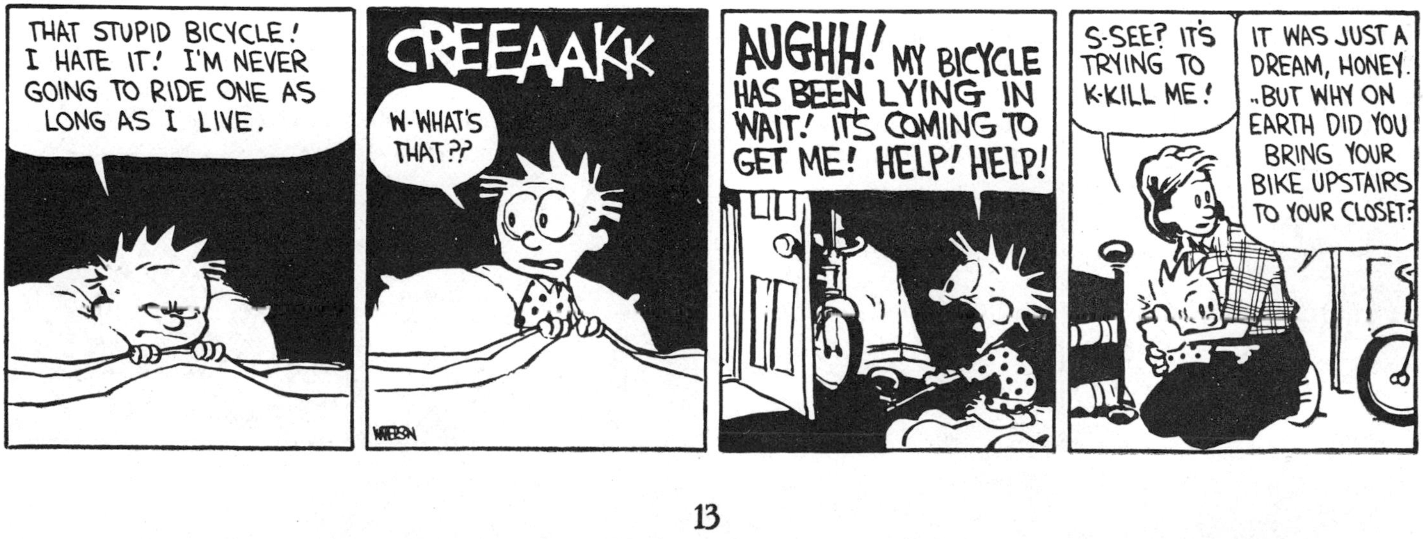
THAT STUPID BICYCLE! I HATE IT! I'M NEVER GOING TO RIDE ONE AS LONG AS I LIVE.
CREEAAKK
W-WHAT'S THAT??
AUGHH! MY BICYCLE HAS BEEN LYING IN WAIT! IT'S COMING TO GET ME! HELP! HELP!
S-SEE? IT'S TRYING TO K-KILL ME!
IT WAS JUST A DREAM, HONEY. ..BUT WHY ON EARTH DID YOU BRING YOUR BIKE UPSTAIRS TO YOUR CLOSET?

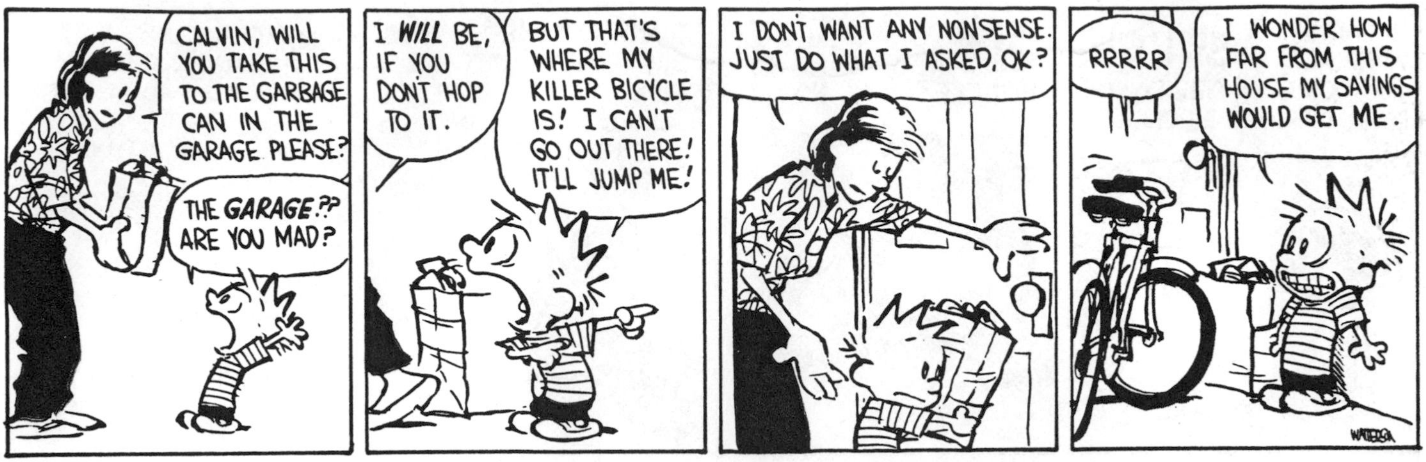
CALVIN, WILL YOU TAKE THIS TO THE GARBAGE CAN IN THE GARAGE PLEASE?
THE GARAGE?? ARE YOU MAD?
I WILL BE, IF YOU DON'T HOP TO IT.
BUT THAT'S WHERE MY KILLER BICYCLE IS! I CAN'T GO OUT THERE! IT'LL JUMP ME!
I DON'T WANT ANY NONSENSE. JUST DO WHAT I ASKED, OK?
RRRRR
I WONDER HOW FAR FROM THIS HOUSE MY SAVINGS WOULD GET ME.

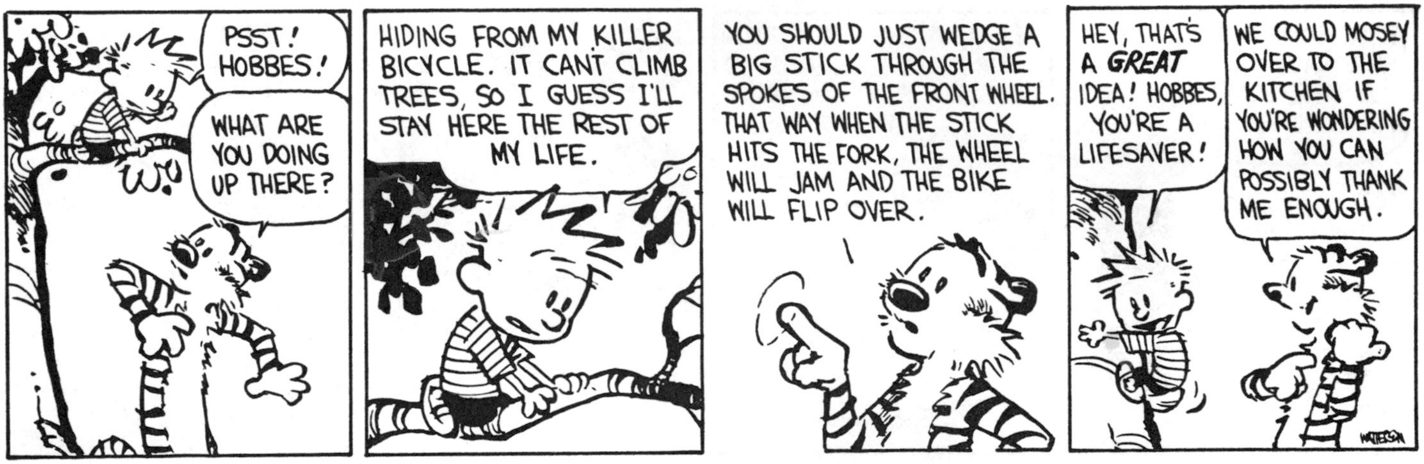
PSST! HOBBES!
WHAT ARE YOU DOING UP THERE?
HIDING FROM MY KILLER BICYCLE. IT CAN'T CLIMB TREES, SO I GUESS I'LL STAY HERE THE REST OF MY LIFE.
YOU SHOULD JUST WEDGE A BIG STICK THROUGH THE SPOKES OF THE FRONT WHEEL. THAT WAY WHEN THE STICK HITS THE FORK, THE WHEEL WILL JAM AND THE BIKE WILL FLIP OVER.
HEY, THAT'S A GREAT IDEA! HOBBES, YOU'RE A LIFESAVER!
WE COULD MOSEY OVER TO THE KITCHEN IF YOU'RE WONDERING HOW YOU CAN POSSIBLY THANK ME ENOUGH.

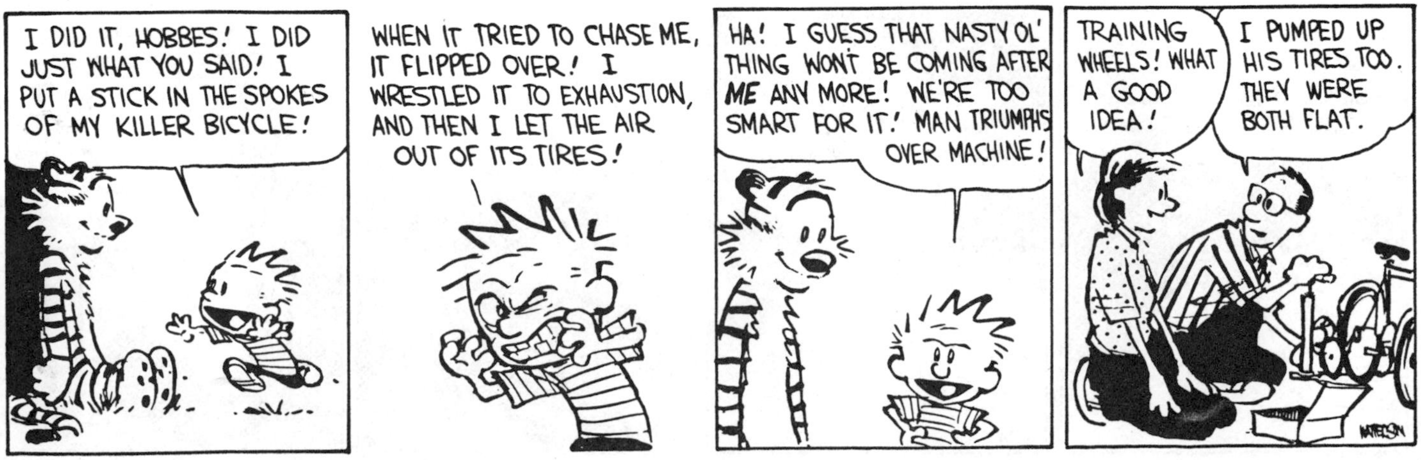
I DID IT, HOBBES! I DID JUST WHAT YOU SAID! I PUT A STICK IN THE SPOKES OF MY KILLER BICYCLE!
WHEN IT TRIED TO CHASE ME, IT FLIPPED OVER! I WRESTLED IT TO EXHAUSTION, AND THEN I LET THE AIR OUT OF ITS TIRES!
HA! I GUESS THAT NASTY OL' THING WON'T BE COMING AFTER ME ANY MORE! WE'RE TOO SMART FOR IT! MAN TRIUMPHS OVER MACHINE!
TRAINING WHEELS! WHAT A GOOD IDEA!
I PUMPED UP HIS TIRES TOO. THEY WERE BOTH FLAT.

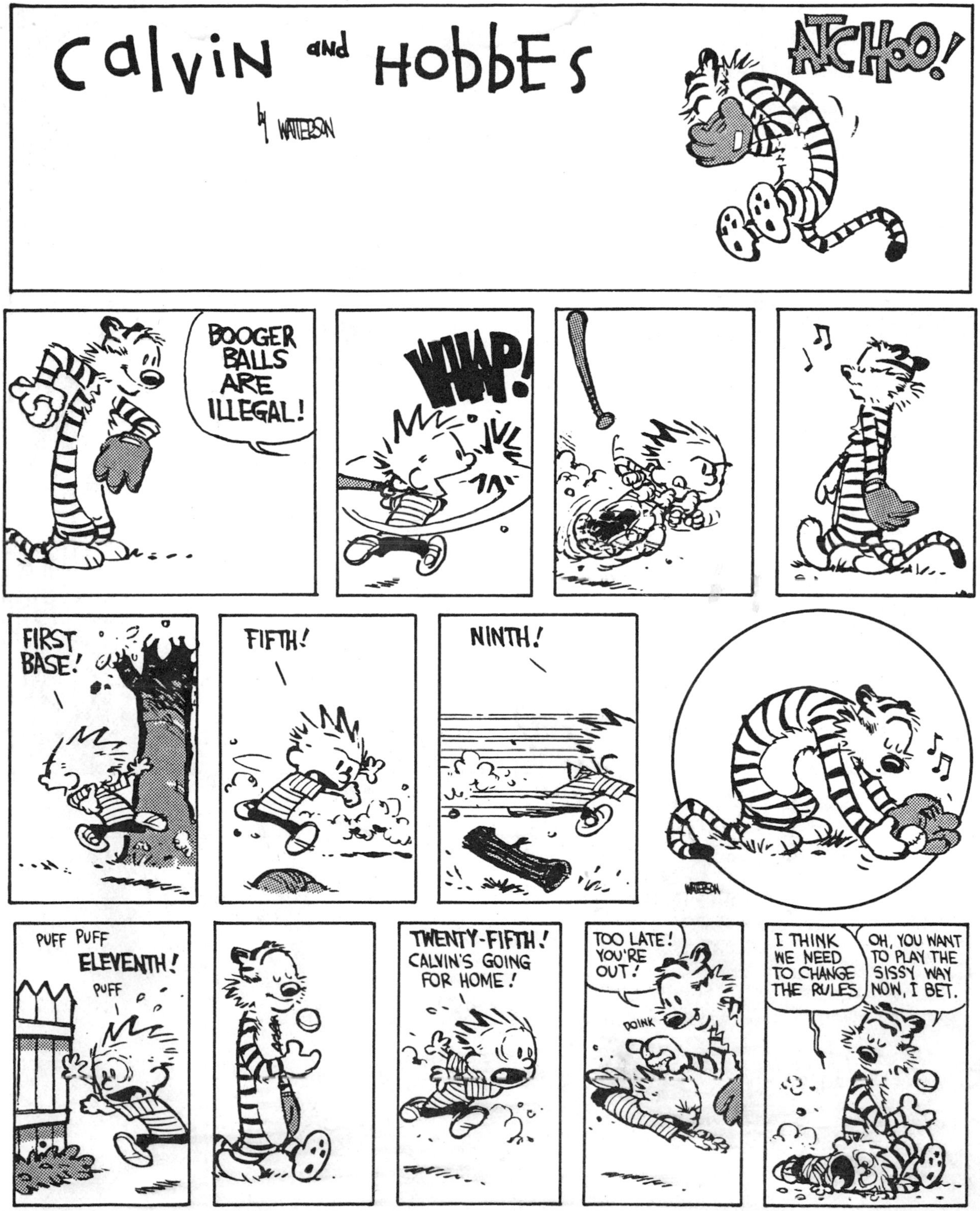
Calvin and HOBBES
by WATTERSON
ATCHOO!
BOOGER BALLS ARE ILLEGAL!
WHAP!
FIRST BASE!
FIFTH!
NINTH!
WATTERSON
PUFF PUFF
ELEVENTH!
PUFF
TWENTY-FIFTH! CALVIN'S GOING FOR HOME!
TOO LATE! YOU'RE OUT!
DOINK
I THINK WE NEED TO CHANGE THE RULES
OH, YOU WANT TO PLAY THE SISSY WAY NOW, I BET.

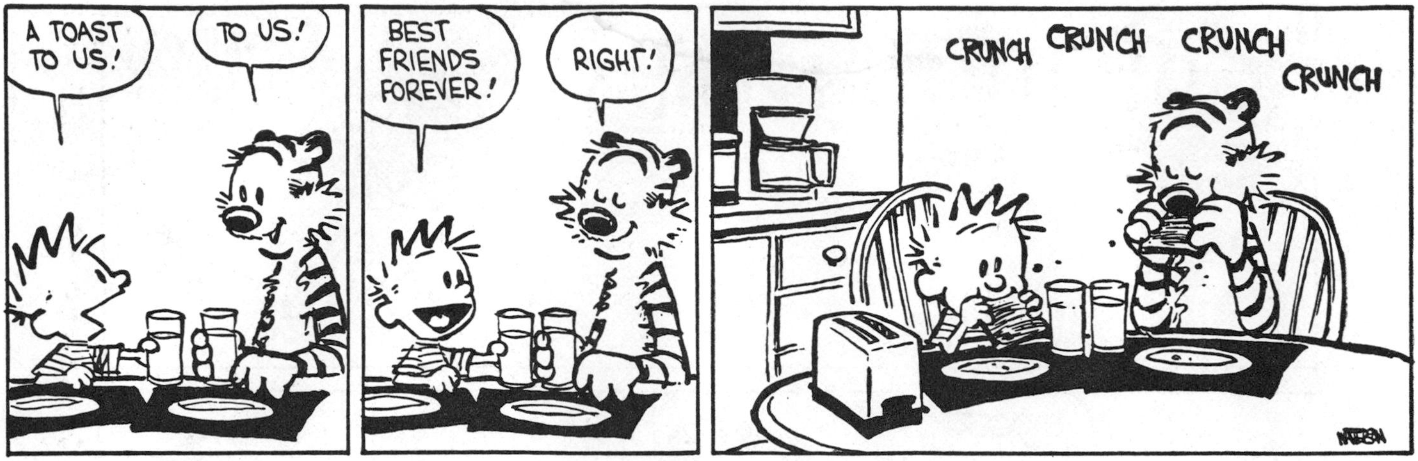
A TOAST TO US!
TO US!
BEST FRIENDS FOREVER!
RIGHT!
CRUNCH CRUNCH CRUNCH CRUNCH

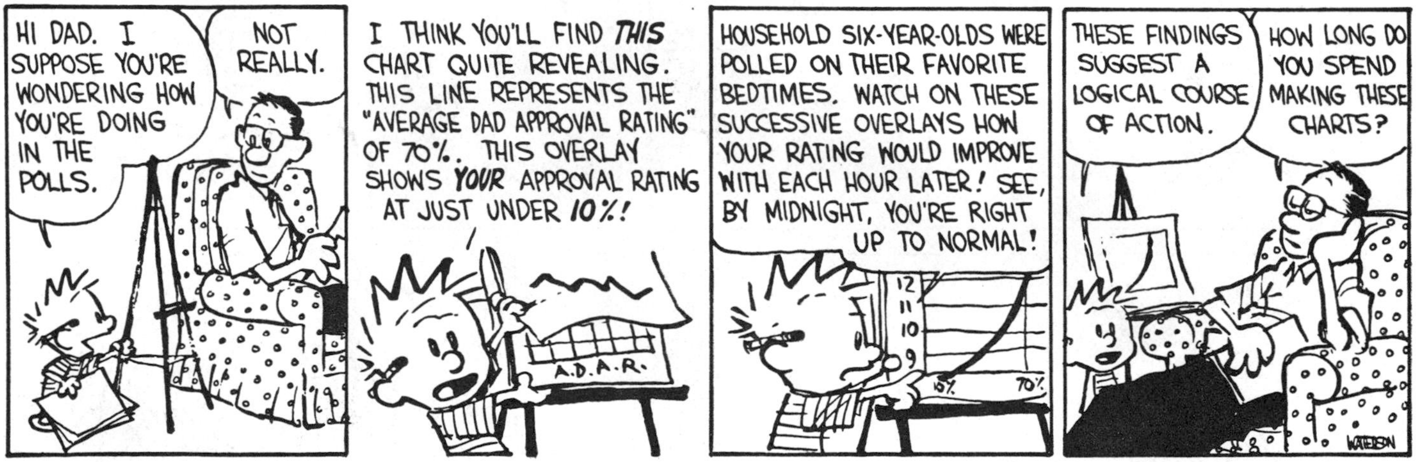
HI DAD. I SUPPOSE YOU'RE WONDERING HOW YOU'RE DOING IN THE POLLS.
NOT REALLY.
I THINK YOU'LL FIND **THIS** CHART QUITE REVEALING. THIS LINE REPRESENTS THE "AVERAGE DAD APPROVAL RATING" OF 70%. THIS OVERLAY SHOWS **YOUR** APPROVAL RATING AT JUST UNDER **10%**!
A.D.A.R.
HOUSEHOLD SIX-YEAR-OLDS WERE POLLED ON THEIR FAVORITE BEDTIMES. WATCH ON THESE SUCCESSIVE OVERLAYS HOW YOUR RATING WOULD IMPROVE WITH EACH HOUR LATER! SEE, BY MIDNIGHT, YOU'RE RIGHT UP TO NORMAL!
12
11
10
9
10%
70%
THESE FINDINGS SUGGEST A LOGICAL COURSE OF ACTION.
HOW LONG DO YOU SPEND MAKING THESE CHARTS?

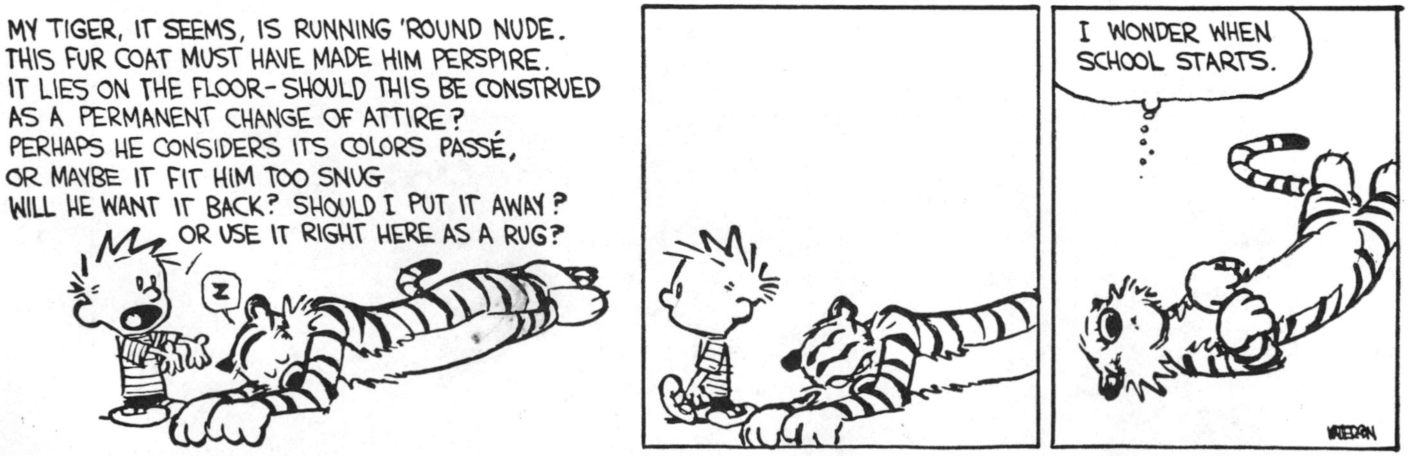
MY TIGER, IT SEEMS, IS RUNNING 'ROUND NUDE.
THIS FUR COAT MUST HAVE MADE HIM PERSPIRE.
IT LIES ON THE FLOOR- SHOULD THIS BE CONSTRUED
AS A PERMANENT CHANGE OF ATTIRE?
PERHAPS HE CONSIDERS ITS COLORS PASSÉ,
OR MAYBE IT FIT HIM TOO SNUG.
WILL HE WANT IT BACK? SHOULD I PUT IT AWAY?
OR USE IT RIGHT HERE AS A RUG?
Z
I WONDER WHEN SCHOOL STARTS.

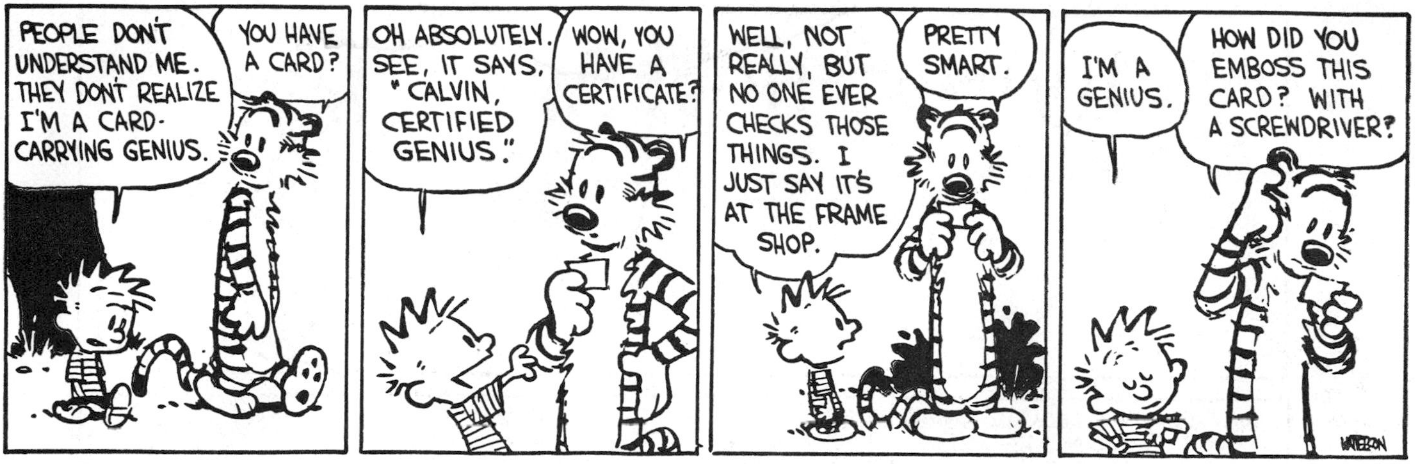
PEOPLE DON'T UNDERSTAND ME. THEY DON'T REALIZE I'M A CARD-CARRYING GENIUS.
YOU HAVE A CARD?
OH ABSOLUTELY. SEE, IT SAYS, "CALVIN, CERTIFIED GENIUS."
WOW, YOU HAVE A CERTIFICATE?
WELL, NOT REALLY, BUT NO ONE EVER CHECKS THOSE THINGS. I JUST SAY IT'S AT THE FRAME SHOP.
PRETTY SMART.
I'M A GENIUS.
HOW DID YOU EMBOSS THIS CARD? WITH A SCREWDRIVER?

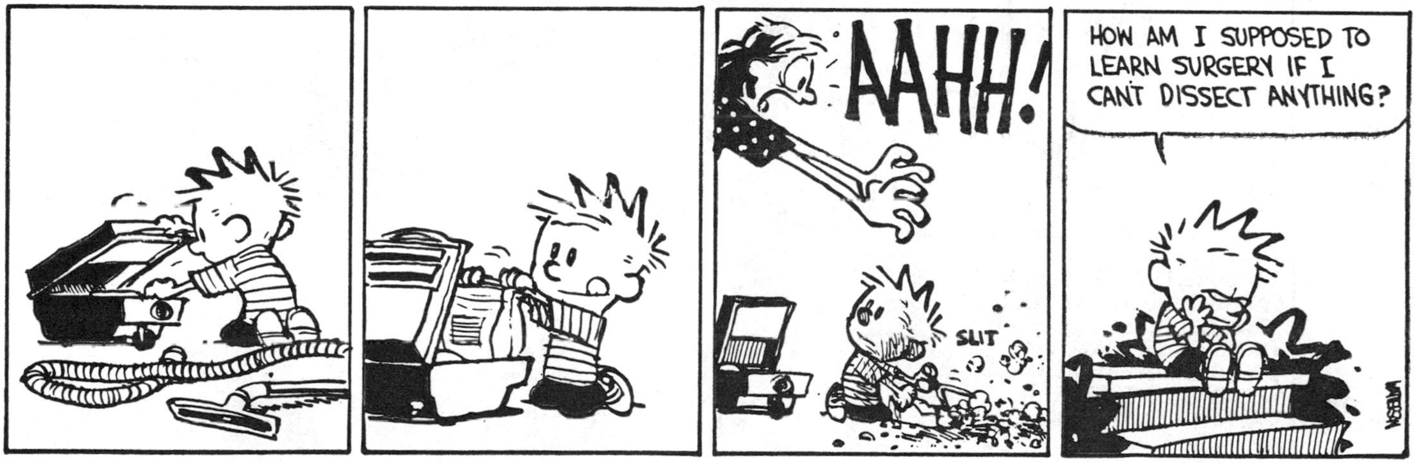
AAHH!
SLIT
HOW AM I SUPPOSED TO LEARN SURGERY IF I CAN'T DISSECT ANYTHING?

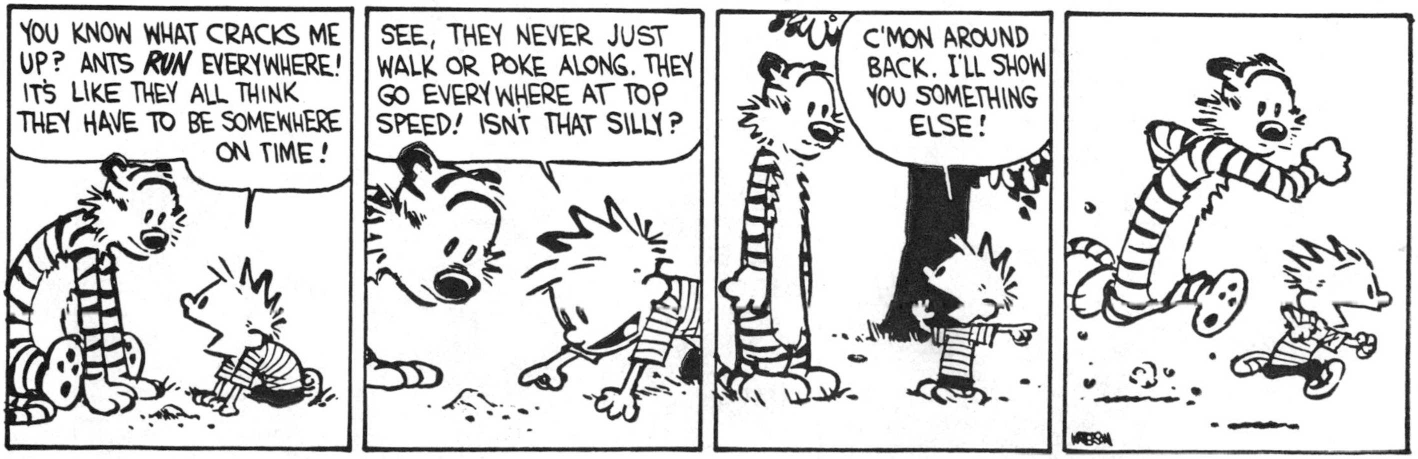
YOU KNOW WHAT CRACKS ME UP? ANTS RUN EVERYWHERE! IT'S LIKE THEY ALL THINK THEY HAVE TO BE SOMEWHERE ON TIME!
SEE, THEY NEVER JUST WALK OR POKE ALONG. THEY GO EVERYWHERE AT TOP SPEED! ISN'T THAT SILLY?
C'MON AROUND BACK. I'LL SHOW YOU SOMETHING ELSE!

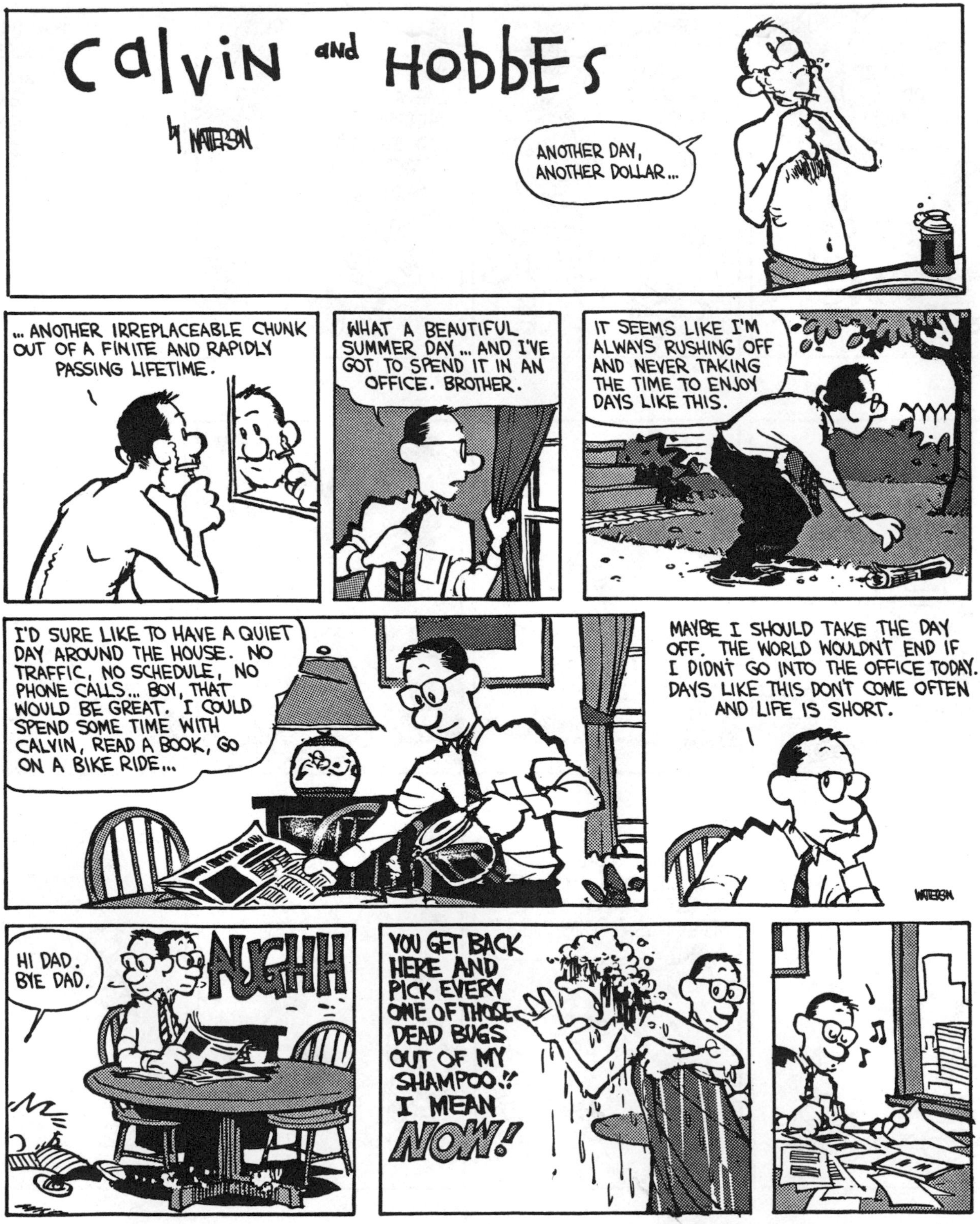
Calvin and HOBBES
by WATTERSON
ANOTHER DAY, ANOTHER DOLLAR...
... ANOTHER IRREPLACEABLE CHUNK OUT OF A FINITE AND RAPIDLY PASSING LIFETIME.
WHAT A BEAUTIFUL SUMMER DAY ... AND I'VE GOT TO SPEND IT IN AN OFFICE. BROTHER.
IT SEEMS LIKE I'M ALWAYS RUSHING OFF AND NEVER TAKING THE TIME TO ENJOY DAYS LIKE THIS.
I'D SURE LIKE TO HAVE A QUIET DAY AROUND THE HOUSE. NO TRAFFIC, NO SCHEDULE, NO PHONE CALLS... BOY, THAT WOULD BE GREAT. I COULD SPEND SOME TIME WITH CALVIN, READ A BOOK, GO ON A BIKE RIDE...
MAYBE I SHOULD TAKE THE DAY OFF. THE WORLD WOULDN'T END IF I DIDN'T GO INTO THE OFFICE TODAY. DAYS LIKE THIS DON'T COME OFTEN AND LIFE IS SHORT.
WATTERSON
HI DAD. BYE DAD.
NUGHH
YOU GET BACK HERE AND PICK EVERY ONE OF THOSE DEAD BUGS OUT OF MY SHAMPOO!! I MEAN NOW!

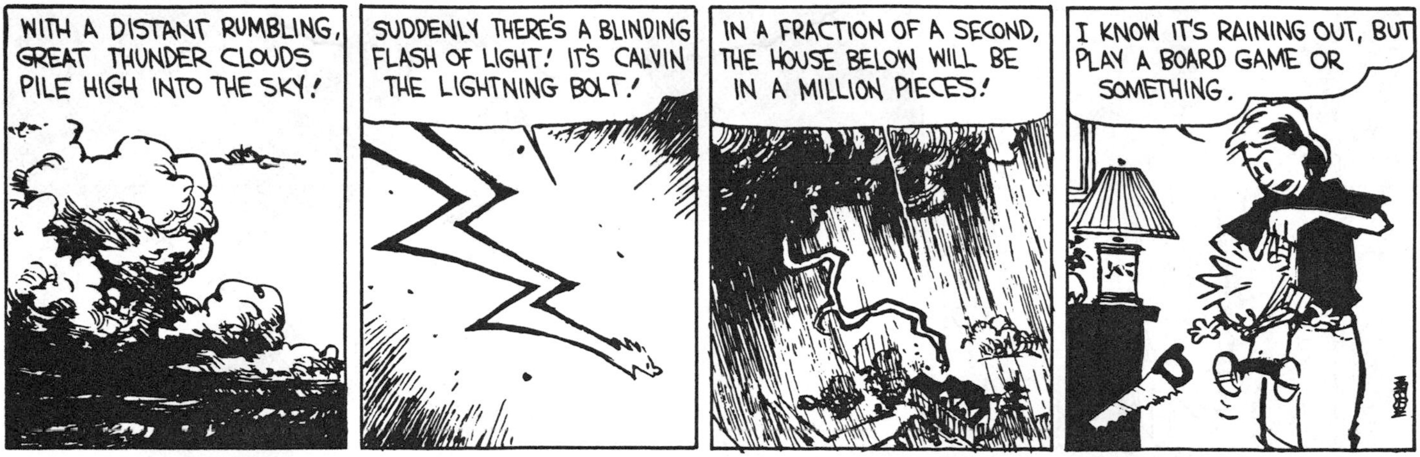
WITH A DISTANT RUMBLING, GREAT THUNDER CLOUDS PILE HIGH INTO THE SKY!
SUDDENLY THERE'S A BLINDING FLASH OF LIGHT! IT'S CALVIN THE LIGHTNING BOLT!
IN A FRACTION OF A SECOND, THE HOUSE BELOW WILL BE IN A MILLION PIECES!
I KNOW IT'S RAINING OUT, BUT PLAY A BOARD GAME OR SOMETHING.

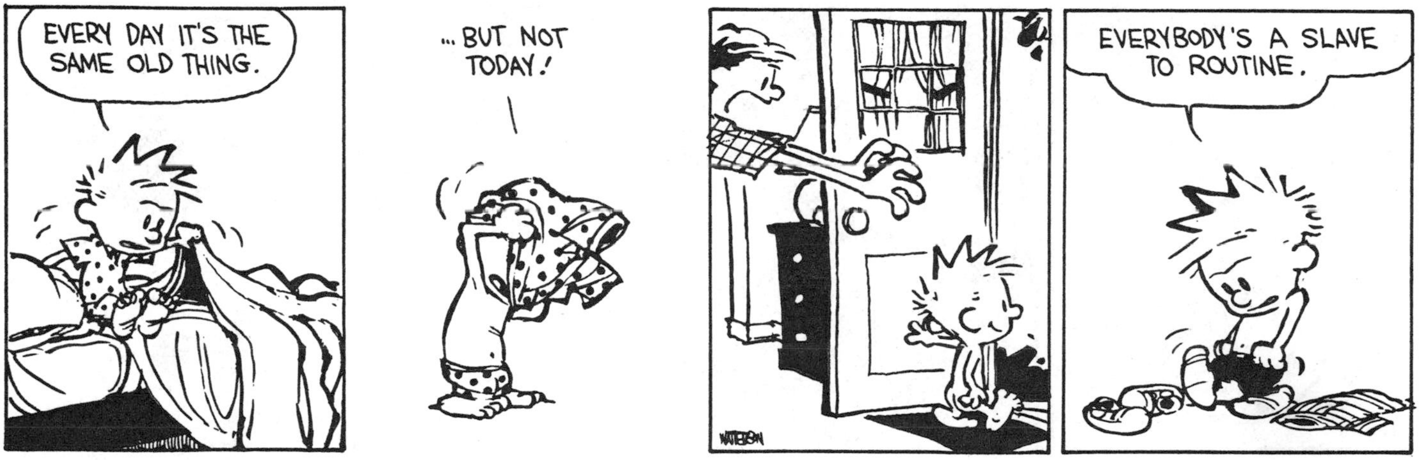
EVERY DAY IT'S THE SAME OLD THING.
... BUT NOT TODAY!
EVERYBODY'S A SLAVE TO ROUTINE.

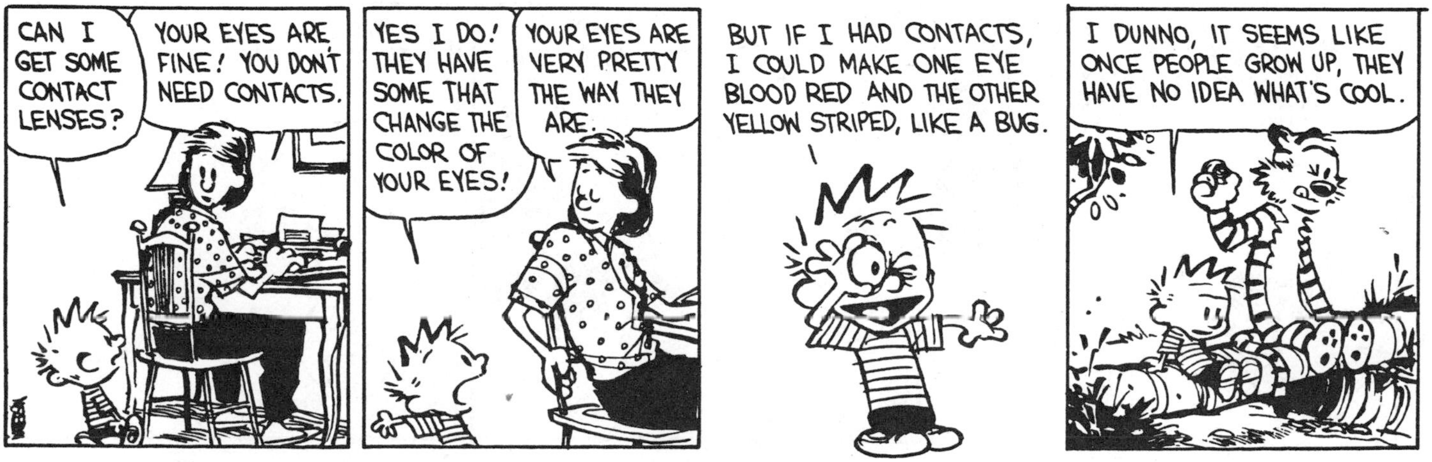
CAN I GET SOME CONTACT LENSES?
YOUR EYES ARE FINE! YOU DON'T NEED CONTACTS.
YES I DO! THEY HAVE SOME THAT CHANGE THE COLOR OF YOUR EYES!
YOUR EYES ARE VERY PRETTY THE WAY THEY ARE.
BUT IF I HAD CONTACTS, I COULD MAKE ONE EYE BLOOD RED AND THE OTHER YELLOW STRIPED, LIKE A BUG.
I DUNNO, IT SEEMS LIKE ONCE PEOPLE GROW UP, THEY HAVE NO IDEA WHAT'S COOL.

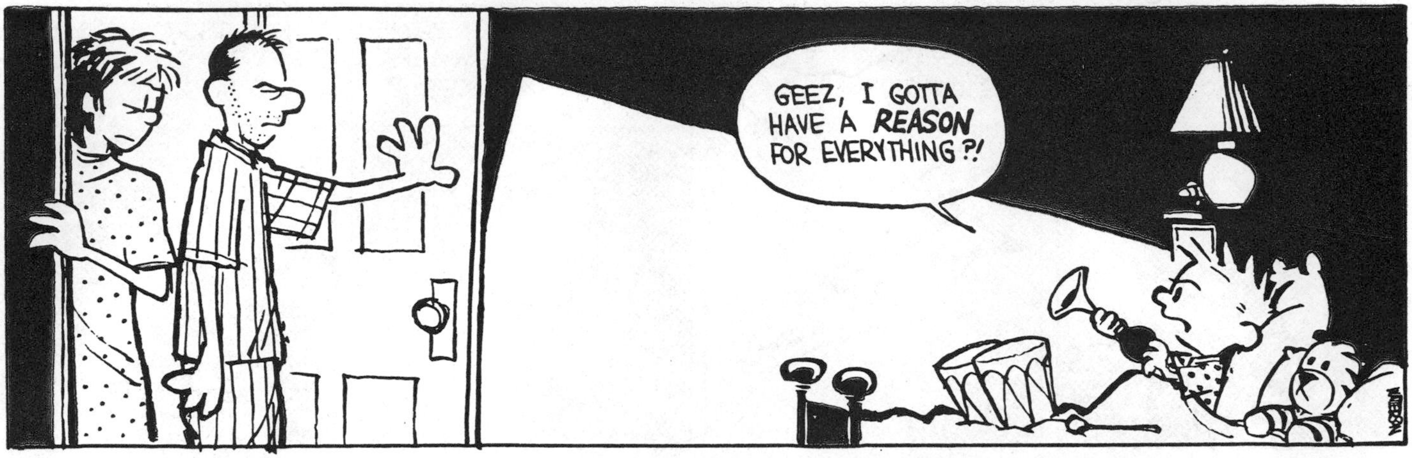
GEEZ, I GOTTA HAVE A REASON FOR EVERYTHING ?!

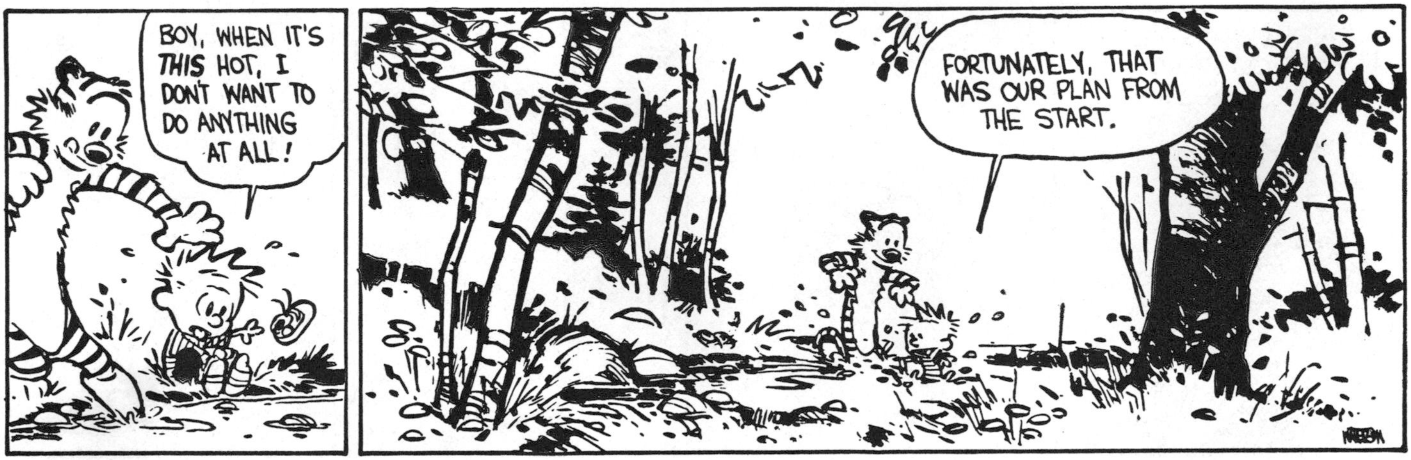
BOY, WHEN IT'S THIS HOT, I DON'T WANT TO DO ANYTHING AT ALL!
FORTUNATELY, THAT WAS OUR PLAN FROM THE START.

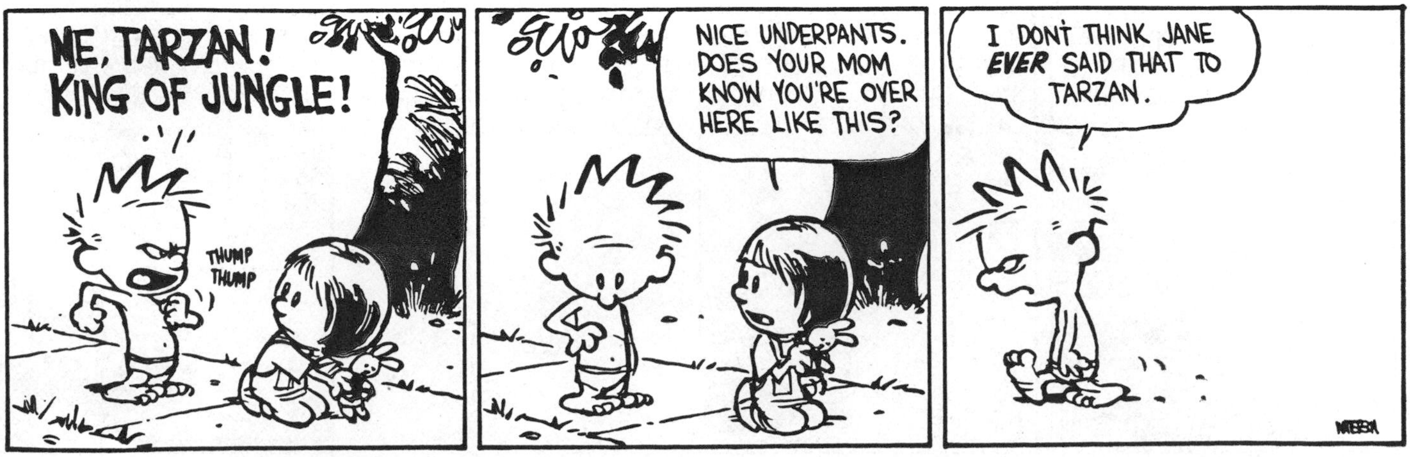
ME, TARZAN! KING OF JUNGLE!
THUMP THUMP
NICE UNDERPANTS. DOES YOUR MOM KNOW YOU'RE OVER HERE LIKE THIS?
I DON'T THINK JANE EVER SAID THAT TO TARZAN.

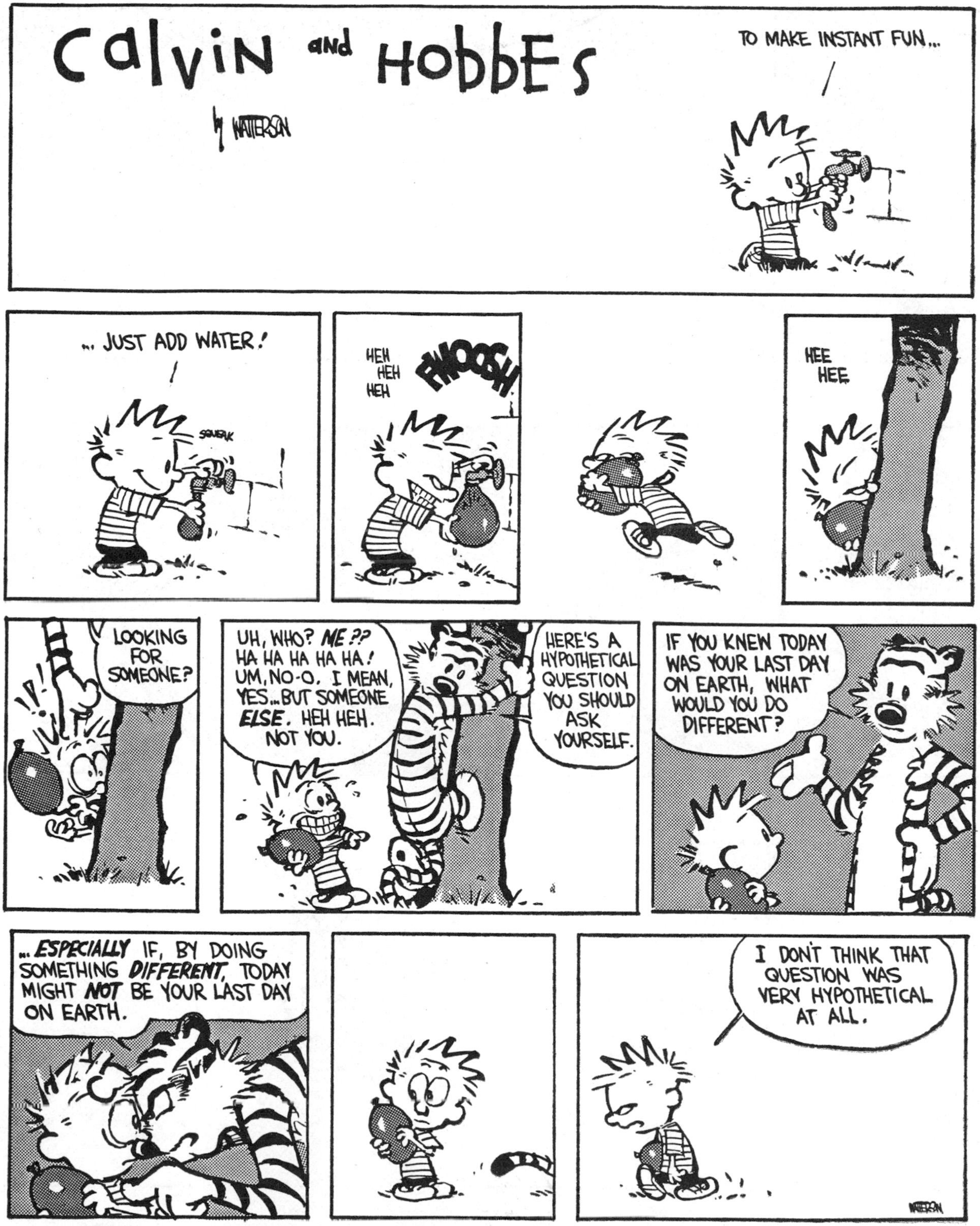
Calvin and HOBBES
by WATTERSON
TO MAKE INSTANT FUN...
... JUST ADD WATER!
SQUEAK
HEH HEH HEH
FWOOSH
HEE HEE
LOOKING FOR SOMEONE?
UH, WHO? ME?? HA HA HA HA HA! UM, NO-O. I MEAN, YES...BUT SOMEONE ELSE. HEH HEH. NOT YOU.
HERE'S A HYPOTHETICAL QUESTION YOU SHOULD ASK YOURSELF.
IF YOU KNEW TODAY WAS YOUR LAST DAY ON EARTH, WHAT WOULD YOU DO DIFFERENT?
... ESPECIALLY IF, BY DOING SOMETHING DIFFERENT, TODAY MIGHT NOT BE YOUR LAST DAY ON EARTH.
I DON'T THINK THAT QUESTION WAS VERY HYPOTHETICAL AT ALL.
WATTERSON

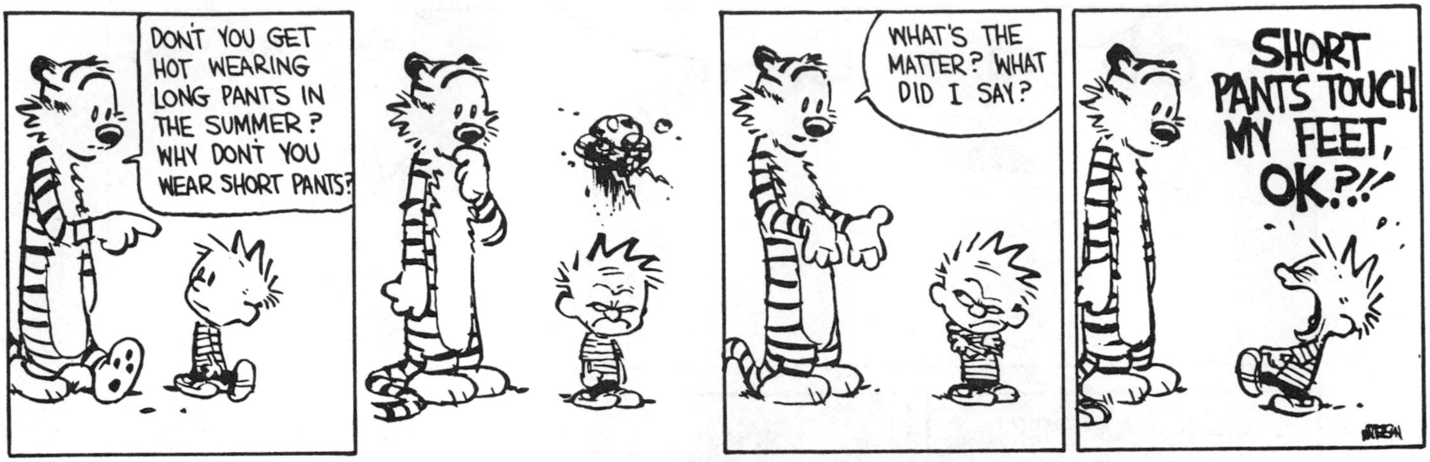
DON'T YOU GET HOT WEARING LONG PANTS IN THE SUMMER? WHY DON'T YOU WEAR SHORT PANTS?
WHAT'S THE MATTER? WHAT DID I SAY?
SHORT PANTS TOUCH MY FEET, OK?!!

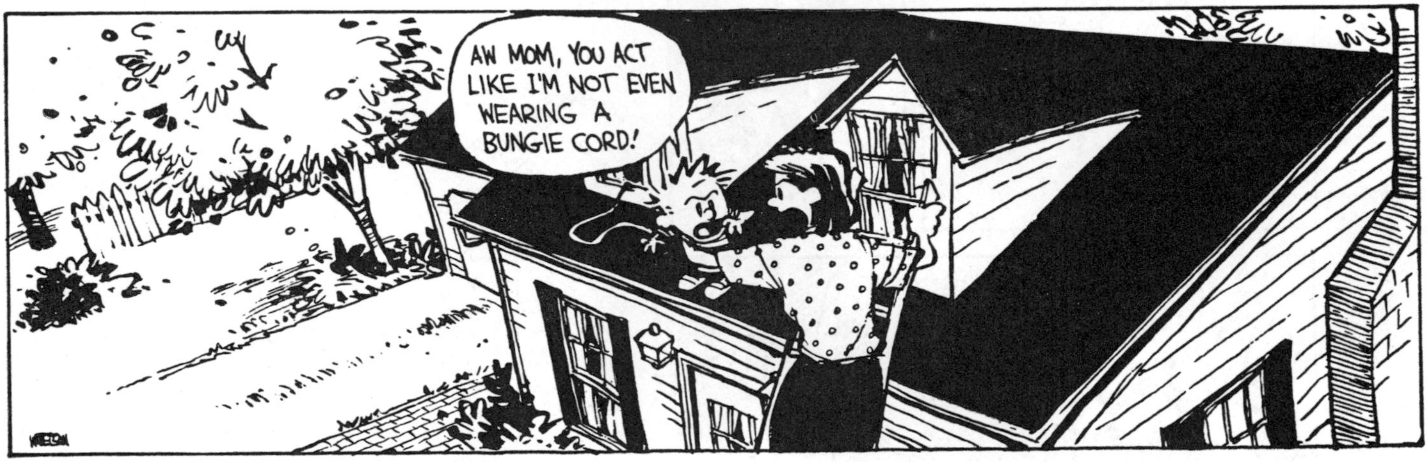
AW MOM, YOU ACT LIKE I'M NOT EVEN WEARING A BUNGIE CORD!

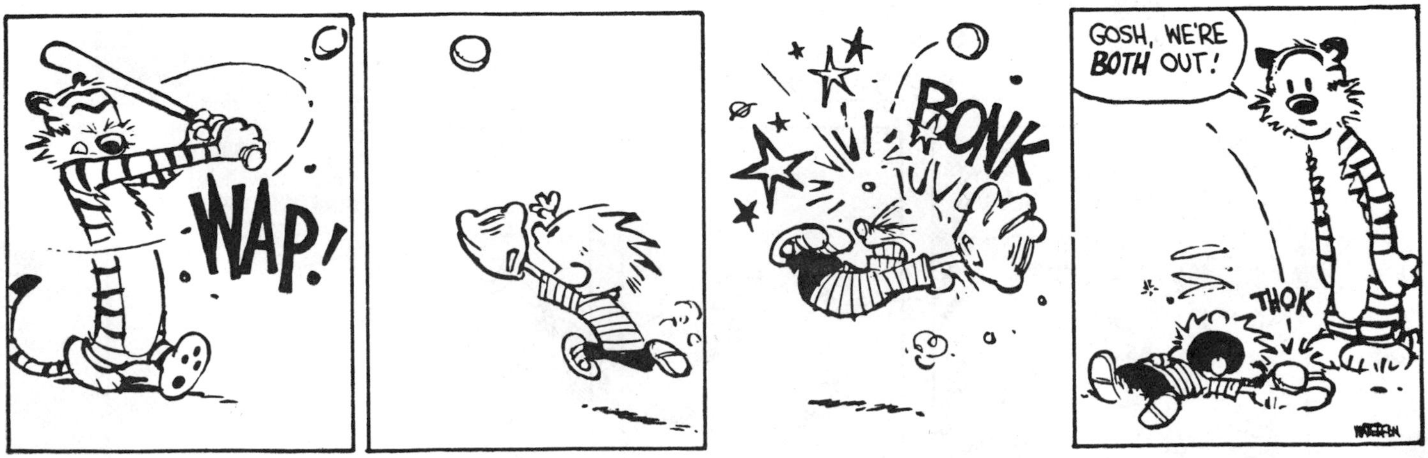
WAP!
BONK
GOSH, WE'RE *BOTH* OUT!
THOK

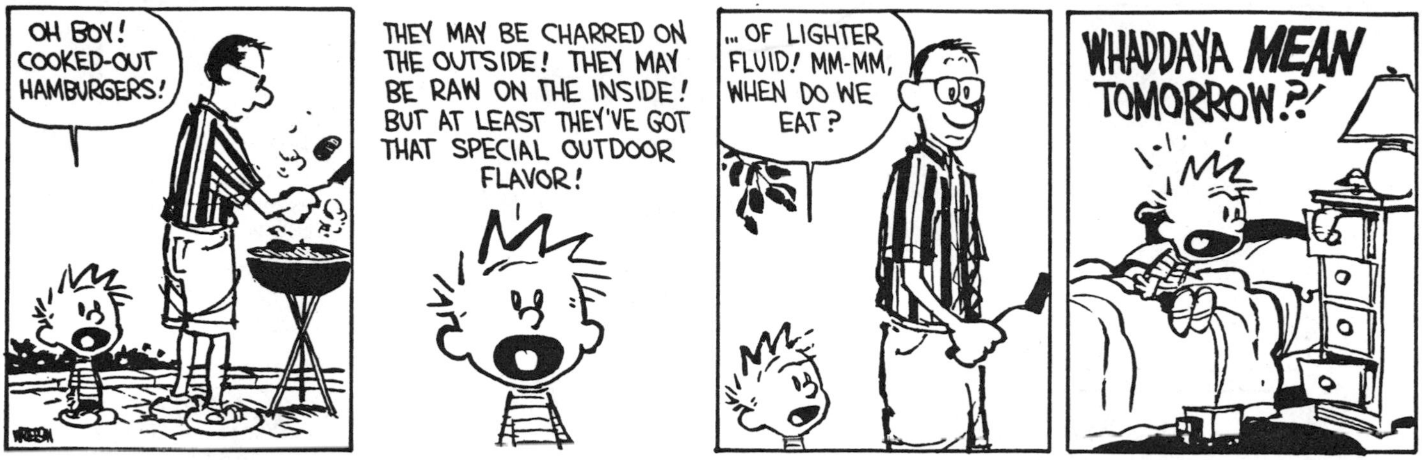
OH BOY! COOKED-OUT HAMBURGERS!
THEY MAY BE CHARRED ON THE OUTSIDE! THEY MAY BE RAW ON THE INSIDE! BUT AT LEAST THEY'VE GOT THAT SPECIAL OUTDOOR FLAVOR!
... OF LIGHTER FLUID! MM-MM, WHEN DO WE EAT?
WHADDAYA MEAN TOMORROW?!

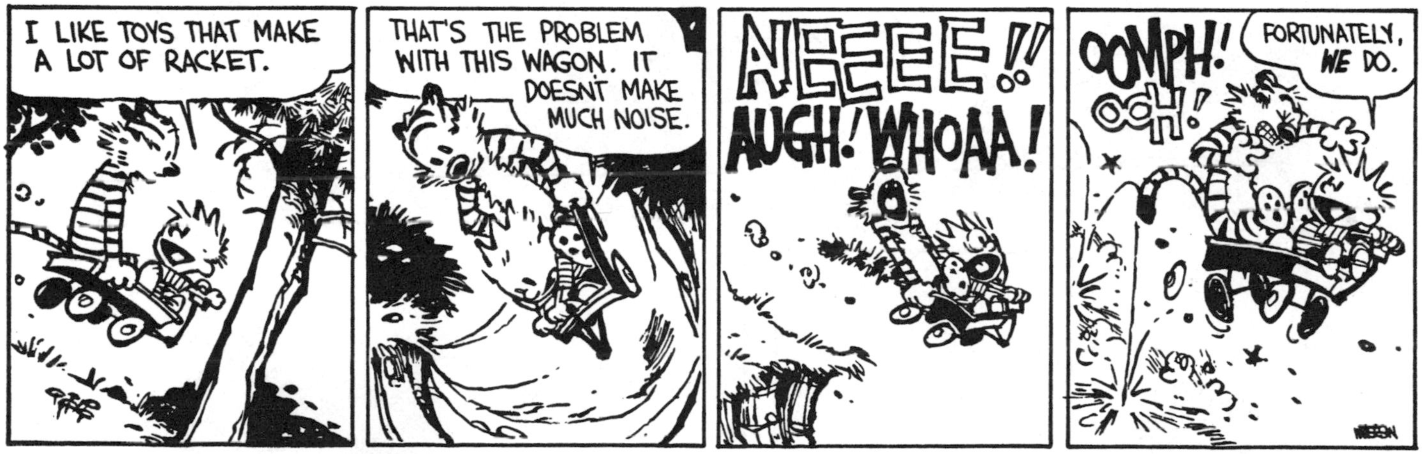
I LIKE TOYS THAT MAKE A LOT OF RACKET.
THAT'S THE PROBLEM WITH THIS WAGON. IT DOESN'T MAKE MUCH NOISE.
AEEEEE!!
AUGH! WHOAA!
OOMPH!
OOH!
FORTUNATELY, WE DO.

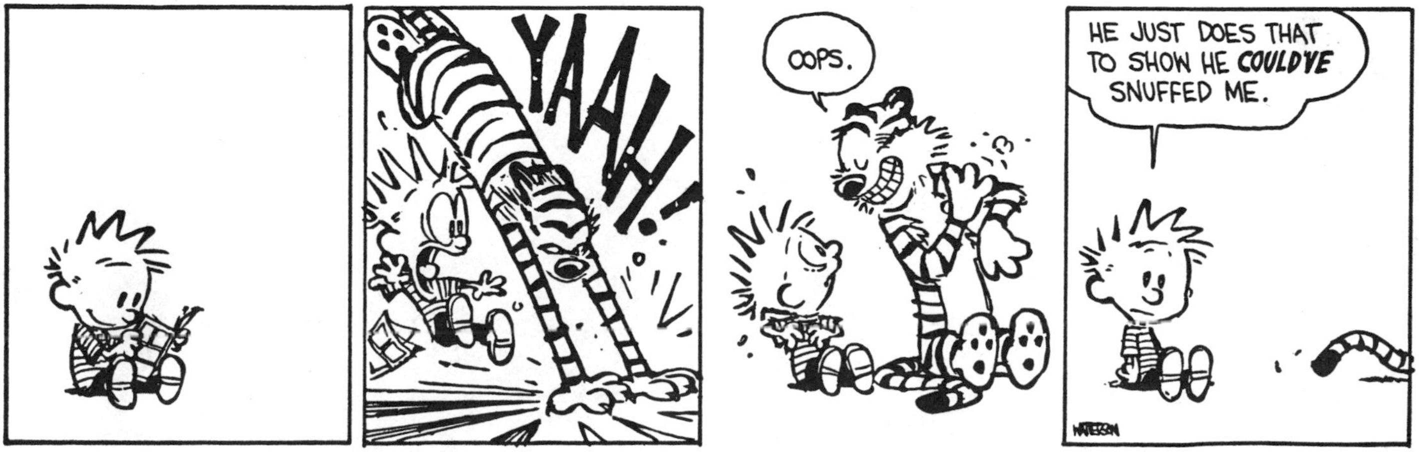
YAAH!
OOPS.
HE JUST DOES THAT TO SHOW HE COULD'VE SNUFFED ME.

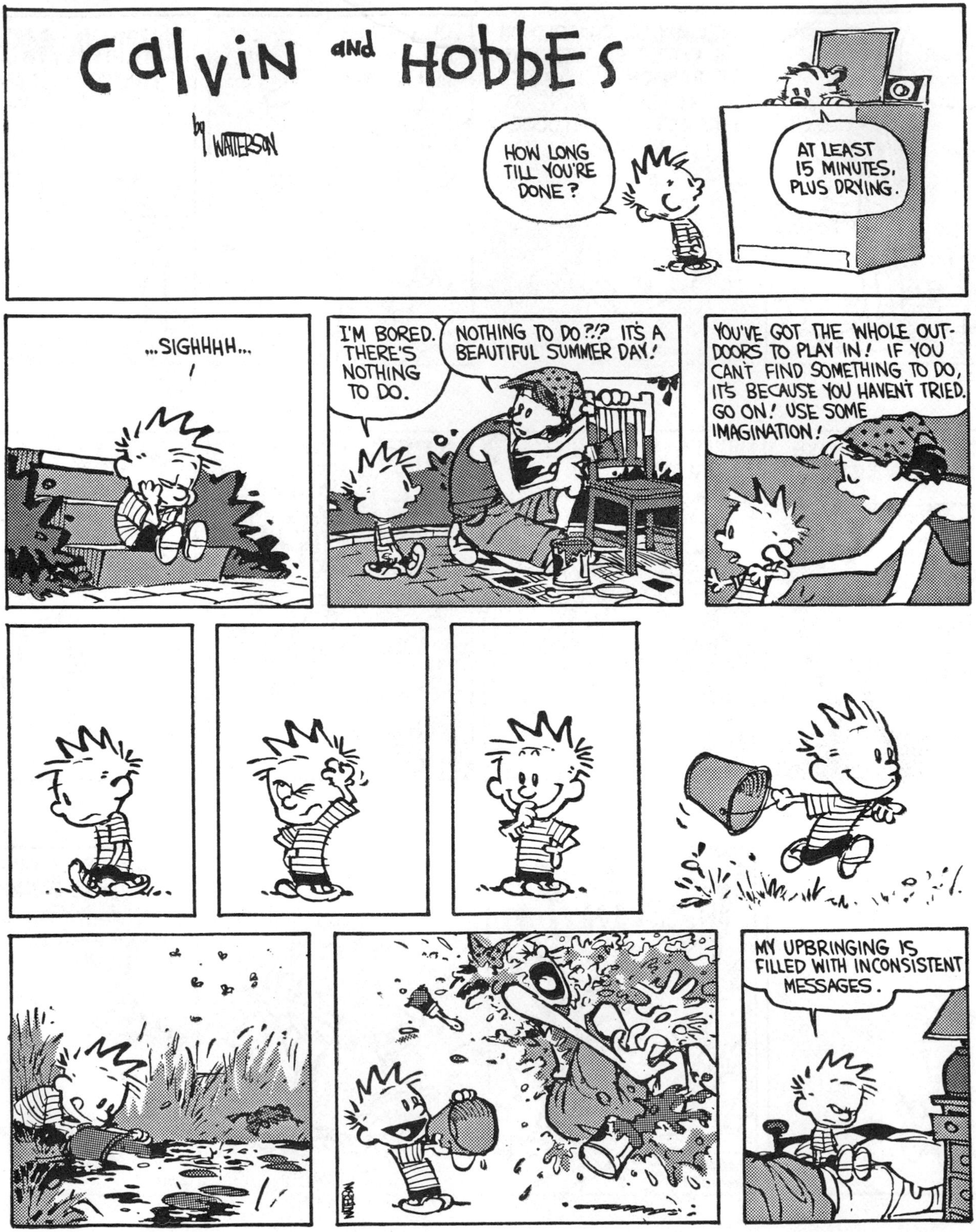
Calvin and HOBBES
by WATTERSON
HOW LONG TILL YOU'RE DONE?
AT LEAST 15 MINUTES, PLUS DRYING.
...SIGHHHH...
I'M BORED. THERE'S NOTHING TO DO.
NOTHING TO DO?!? IT'S A BEAUTIFUL SUMMER DAY!
YOU'VE GOT THE WHOLE OUT-DOORS TO PLAY IN! IF YOU CAN'T FIND SOMETHING TO DO, IT'S BECAUSE YOU HAVEN'T TRIED. GO ON! USE SOME IMAGINATION!
MY UPBRINGING IS FILLED WITH INCONSISTENT MESSAGES.

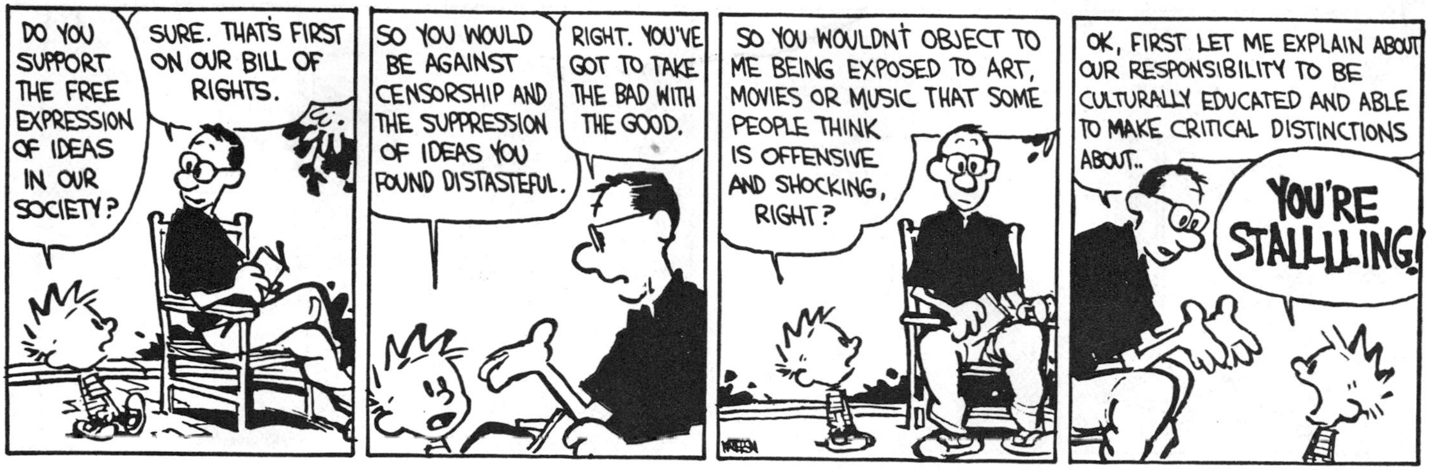
DO YOU SUPPORT THE FREE EXPRESSION OF IDEAS IN OUR SOCIETY?
SURE. THAT'S FIRST ON OUR BILL OF RIGHTS.
SO YOU WOULD BE AGAINST CENSORSHIP AND THE SUPPRESSION OF IDEAS YOU FOUND DISTASTEFUL.
RIGHT. YOU'VE GOT TO TAKE THE BAD WITH THE GOOD.
SO YOU WOULDN'T OBJECT TO ME BEING EXPOSED TO ART, MOVIES OR MUSIC THAT SOME PEOPLE THINK IS OFFENSIVE AND SHOCKING, RIGHT?
OK, FIRST LET ME EXPLAIN ABOUT OUR RESPONSIBILITY TO BE CULTURALLY EDUCATED AND ABLE TO MAKE CRITICAL DISTINCTIONS ABOUT..
YOU'RE STALLLLING!

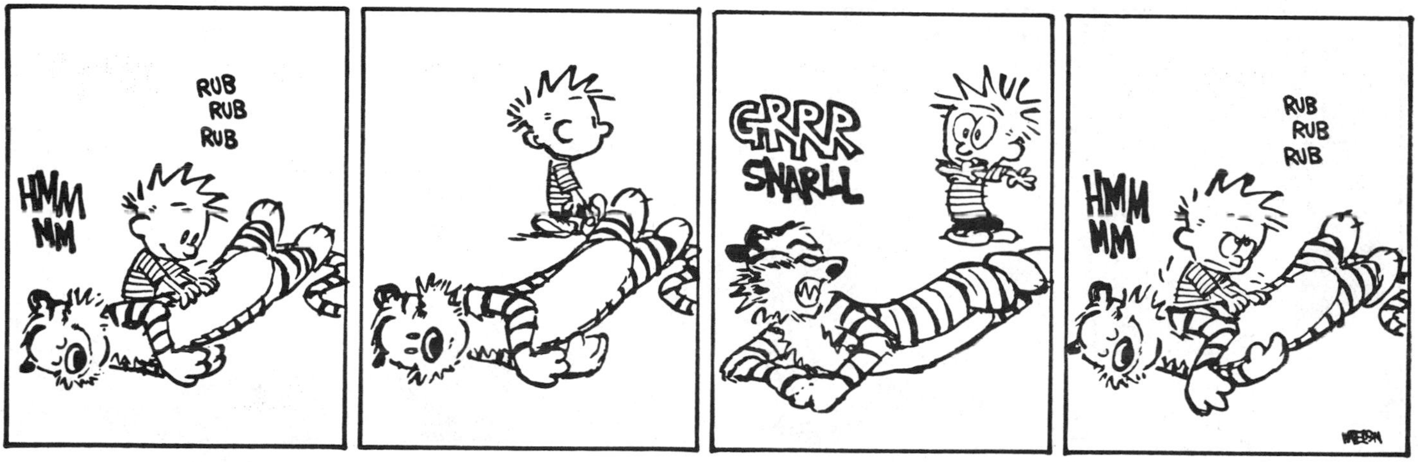
RUB RUB RUB
HMM MM
GRRR SNARLL
RUB RUB RUB
HMM MM

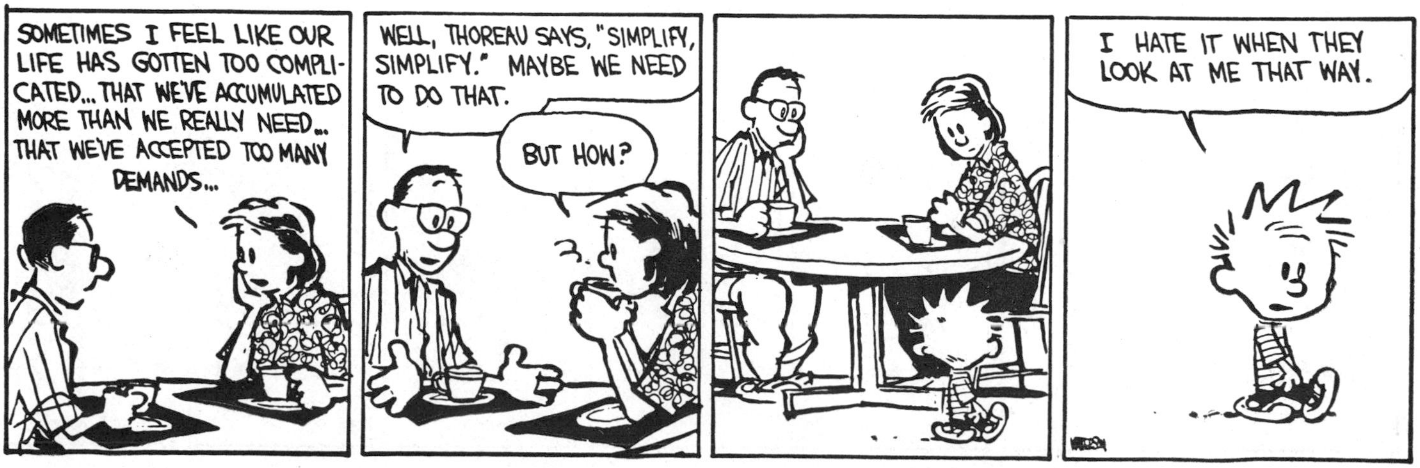
SOMETIMES I FEEL LIKE OUR LIFE HAS GOTTEN TOO COMPLICATED... THAT WE'VE ACCUMULATED MORE THAN WE REALLY NEED... THAT WE'VE ACCEPTED TOO MANY DEMANDS...
WELL, THOREAU SAYS, "SIMPLIFY, SIMPLIFY." MAYBE WE NEED TO DO THAT.
BUT HOW?
I HATE IT WHEN THEY LOOK AT ME THAT WAY.

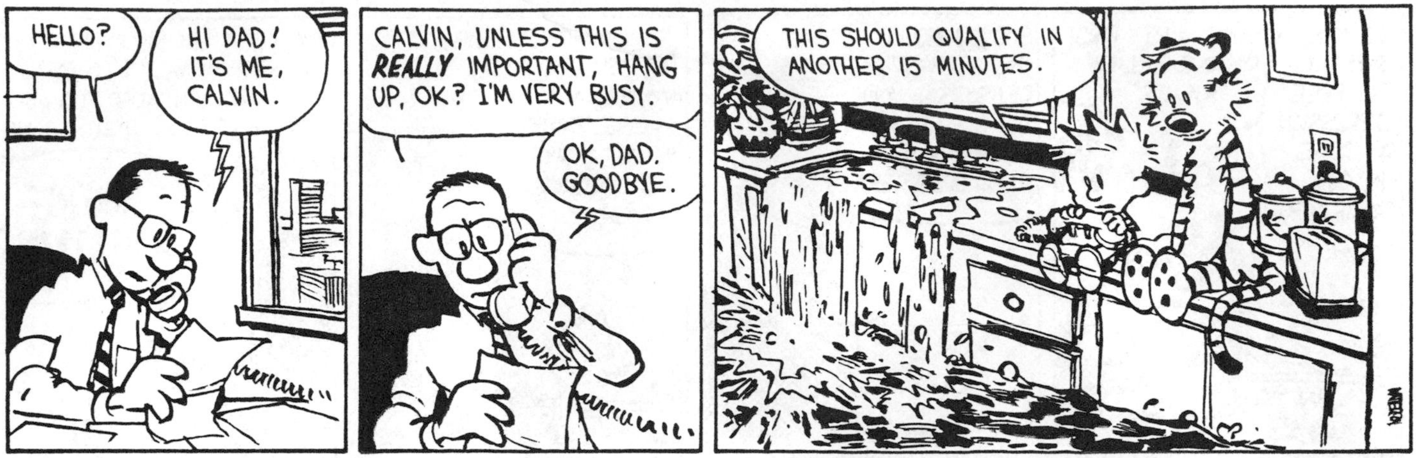
HELLO?
HI DAD! IT'S ME, CALVIN.
CALVIN, UNLESS THIS IS ***REALLY*** IMPORTANT, HANG UP, OK? I'M VERY BUSY.
OK, DAD. GOODBYE.
THIS SHOULD QUALIFY IN ANOTHER 15 MINUTES.

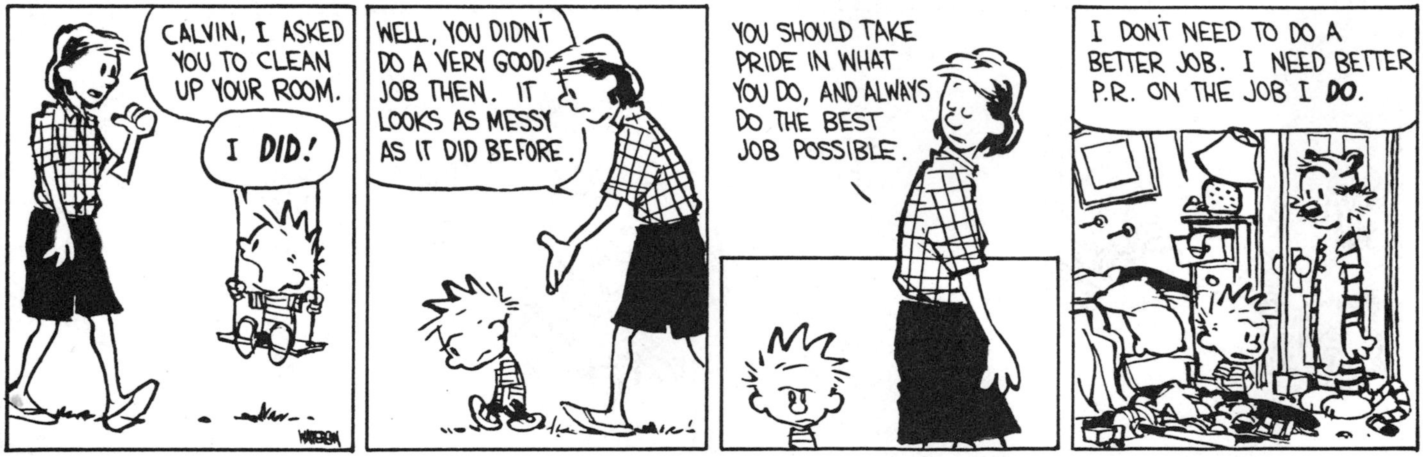
CALVIN, I ASKED YOU TO CLEAN UP YOUR ROOM.
I ***DID!***
WELL, YOU DIDN'T DO A VERY GOOD JOB THEN. IT LOOKS AS MESSY AS IT DID BEFORE.
YOU SHOULD TAKE PRIDE IN WHAT YOU DO, AND ALWAYS DO THE BEST JOB POSSIBLE.
I DON'T NEED TO DO A BETTER JOB. I NEED BETTER P.R. ON THE JOB I ***DO***.

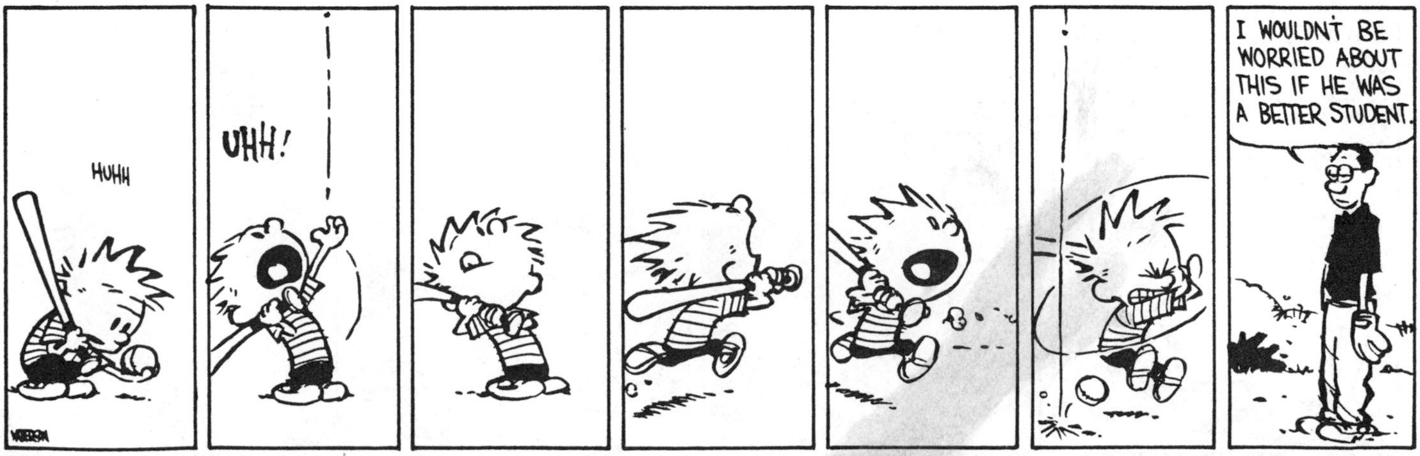
HUHH
UHH!
I WOULDN'T BE WORRIED ABOUT THIS IF HE WAS A BETTER STUDENT.

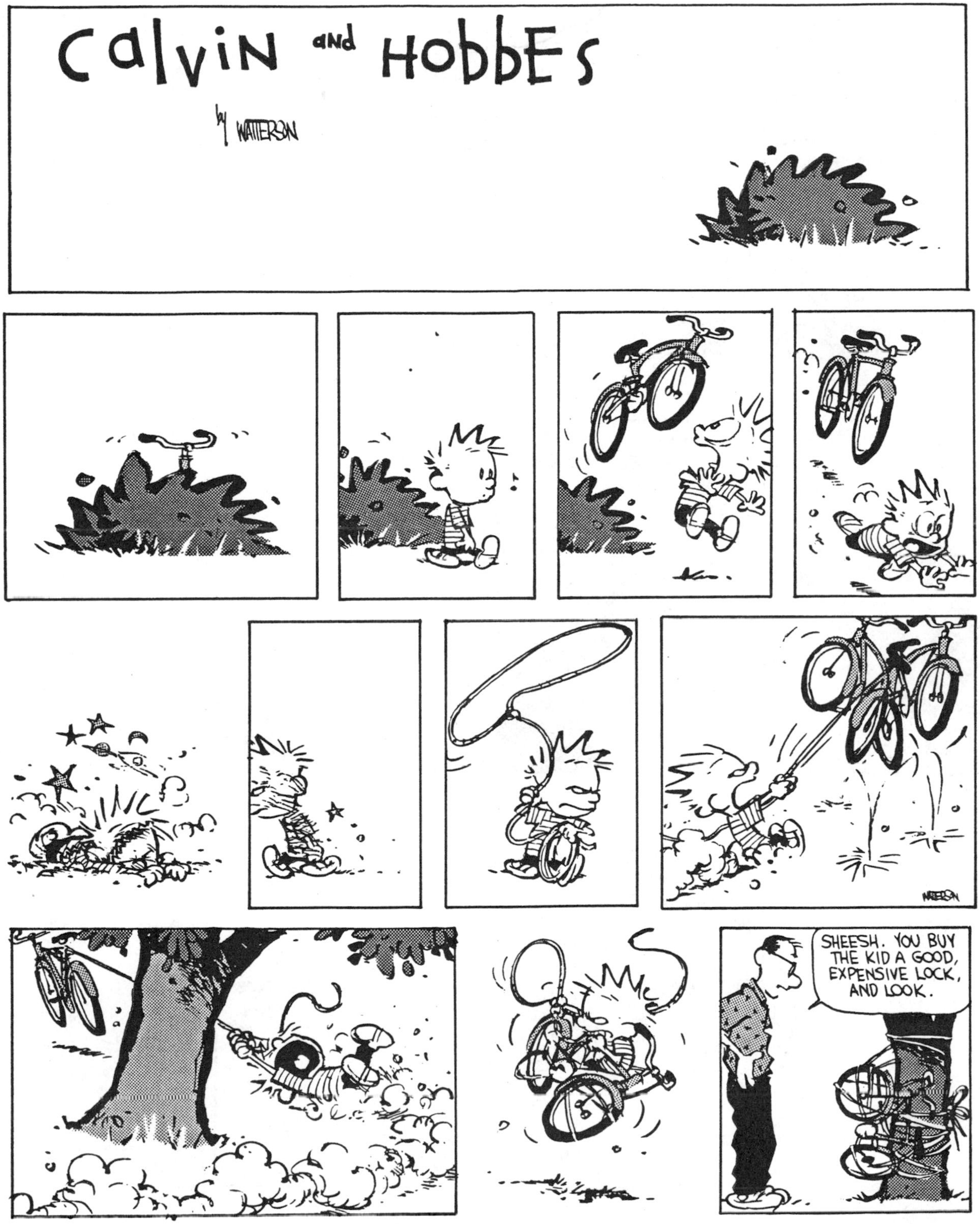
Calvin and HOBBES
by WATTERSON
WATTERSON
SHEESH. YOU BUY THE KID A GOOD, EXPENSIVE LOCK, AND LOOK.

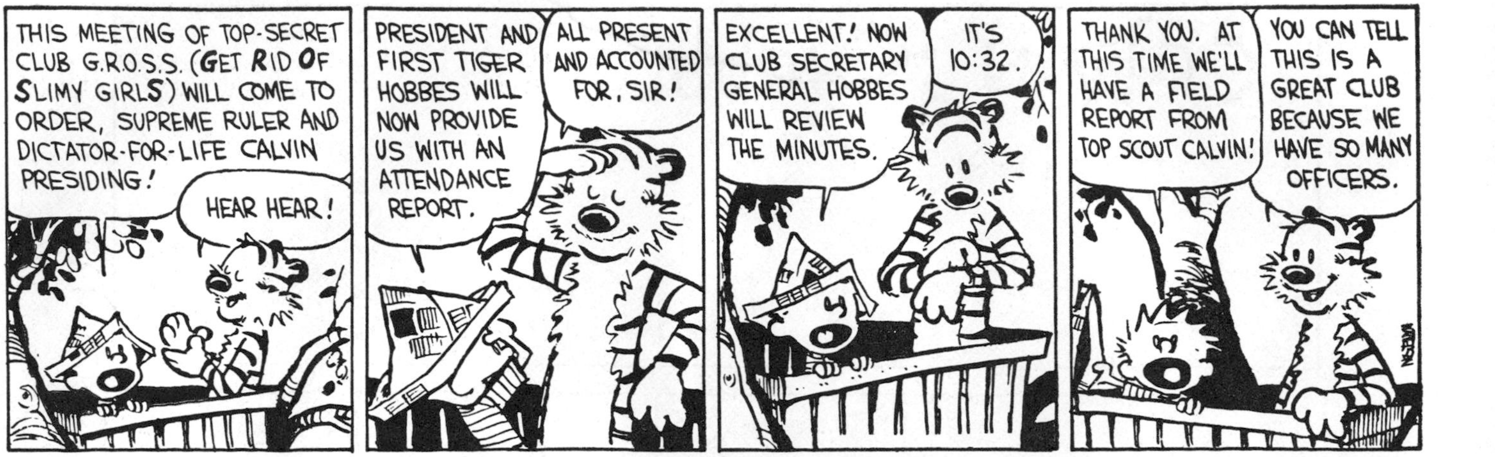
THIS MEETING OF TOP-SECRET CLUB G.R.O.S.S. (GET RID OF SLIMY GIRLS) WILL COME TO ORDER, SUPREME RULER AND DICTATOR-FOR-LIFE CALVIN PRESIDING!
HEAR HEAR!
PRESIDENT AND FIRST TIGER HOBBES WILL NOW PROVIDE US WITH AN ATTENDANCE REPORT.
ALL PRESENT AND ACCOUNTED FOR, SIR!
EXCELLENT! NOW CLUB SECRETARY GENERAL HOBBES WILL REVIEW THE MINUTES.
IT'S 10:32.
THANK YOU. AT THIS TIME WE'LL HAVE A FIELD REPORT FROM TOP SCOUT CALVIN!
YOU CAN TELL THIS IS A GREAT CLUB BECAUSE WE HAVE SO MANY OFFICERS.

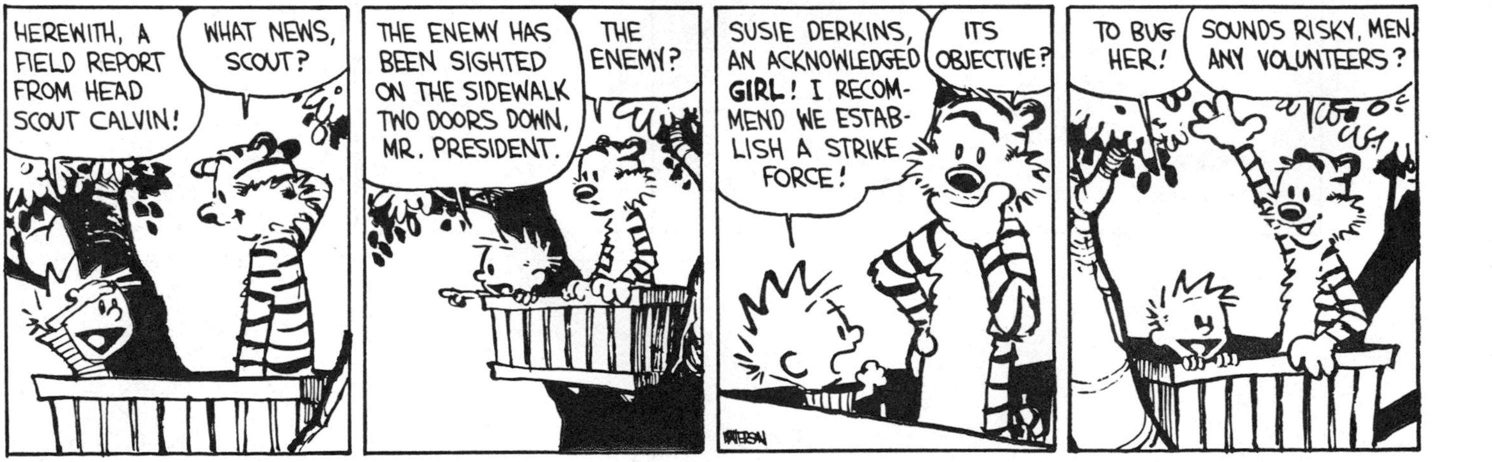
HEREWITH, A FIELD REPORT FROM HEAD SCOUT CALVIN!
WHAT NEWS, SCOUT?
THE ENEMY HAS BEEN SIGHTED ON THE SIDEWALK TWO DOORS DOWN, MR. PRESIDENT.
THE ENEMY?
SUSIE DERKINS, AN ACKNOWLEDGED GIRL! I RECOMMEND WE ESTABLISH A STRIKE FORCE!
ITS OBJECTIVE?
TO BUG HER!
SOUNDS RISKY, MEN. ANY VOLUNTEERS?

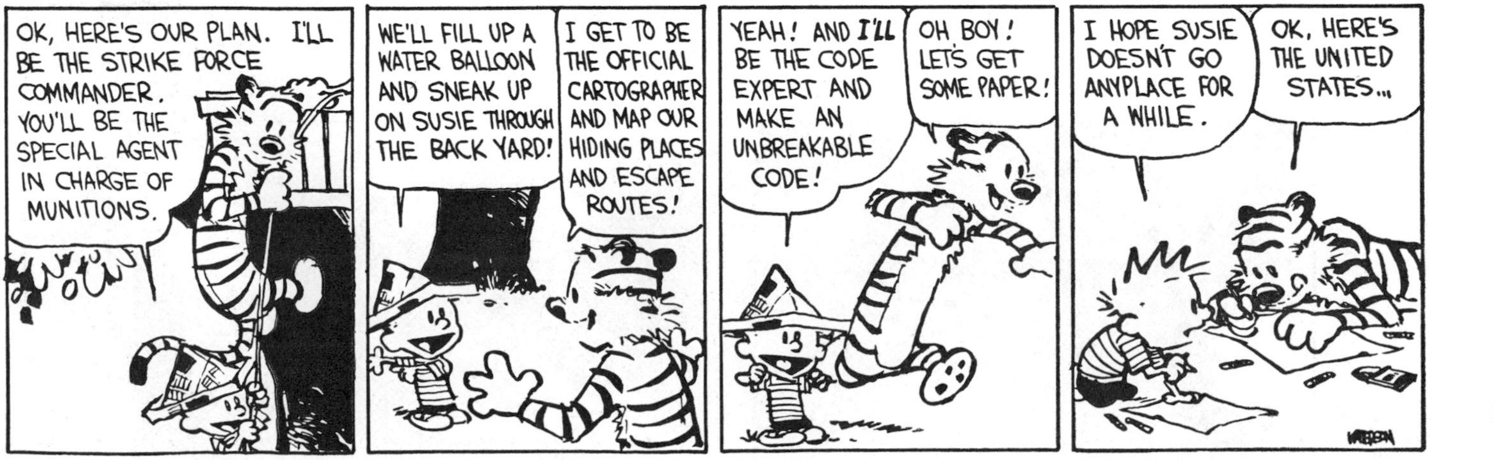
OK, HERE'S OUR PLAN. I'LL BE THE STRIKE FORCE COMMANDER. YOU'LL BE THE SPECIAL AGENT IN CHARGE OF MUNITIONS.
WE'LL FILL UP A WATER BALLOON AND SNEAK UP ON SUSIE THROUGH THE BACK YARD!
I GET TO BE THE OFFICIAL CARTOGRAPHER AND MAP OUR HIDING PLACES AND ESCAPE ROUTES!
YEAH! AND I'LL BE THE CODE EXPERT AND MAKE AN UNBREAKABLE CODE!
OH BOY! LET'S GET SOME PAPER!
I HOPE SUSIE DOESN'T GO ANYPLACE FOR A WHILE.
OK, HERE'S THE UNITED STATES...

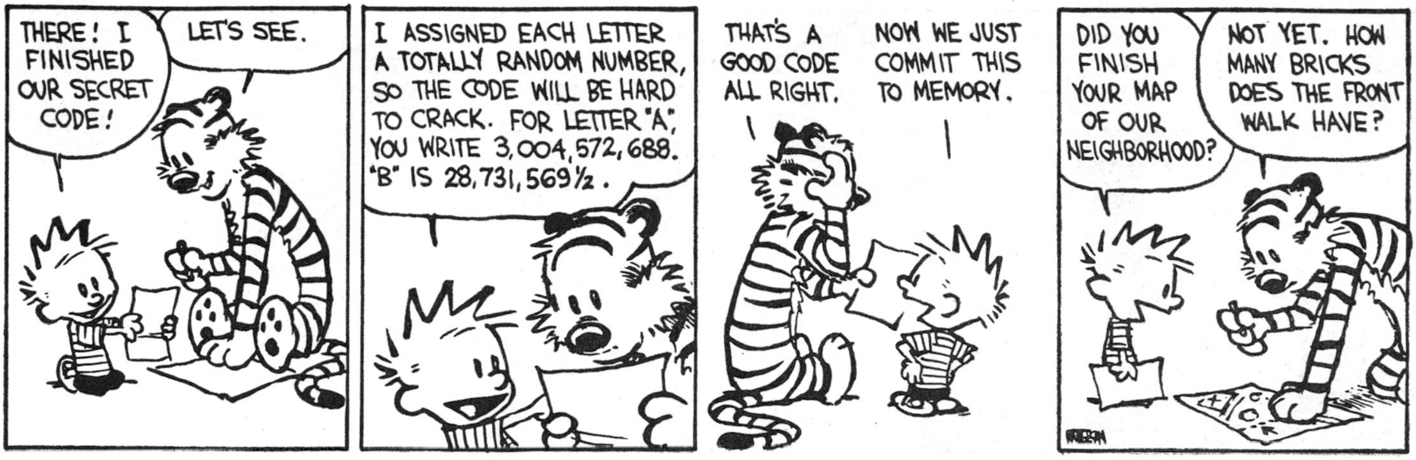
THERE! I FINISHED OUR SECRET CODE!
LET'S SEE.
I ASSIGNED EACH LETTER A TOTALLY RANDOM NUMBER, SO THE CODE WILL BE HARD TO CRACK. FOR LETTER "A", YOU WRITE 3,004,572,688. "B" IS 28,731,569½.
THAT'S A GOOD CODE ALL RIGHT.
NOW WE JUST COMMIT THIS TO MEMORY.
DID YOU FINISH YOUR MAP OF OUR NEIGHBORHOOD?
NOT YET. HOW MANY BRICKS DOES THE FRONT WALK HAVE?

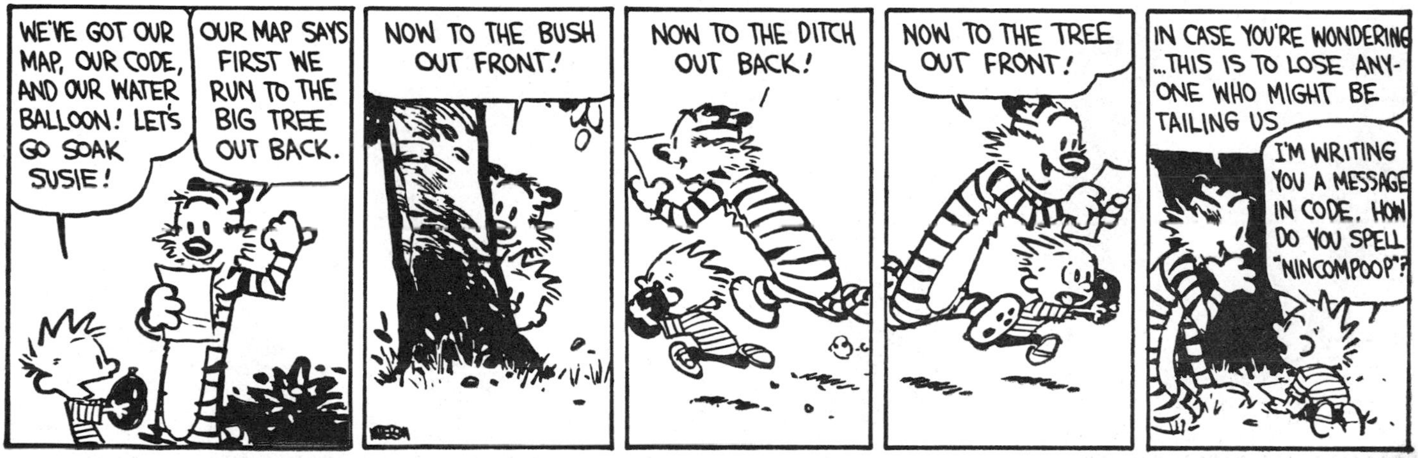
WE'VE GOT OUR MAP, OUR CODE, AND OUR WATER BALLOON! LET'S GO SOAK SUSIE!
OUR MAP SAYS FIRST WE RUN TO THE BIG TREE OUT BACK.
NOW TO THE BUSH OUT FRONT!
NOW TO THE DITCH OUT BACK!
NOW TO THE TREE OUT FRONT!
IN CASE YOU'RE WONDERING ...THIS IS TO LOSE ANYONE WHO MIGHT BE TAILING US.
I'M WRITING YOU A MESSAGE IN CODE. HOW DO YOU SPELL "NINCOMPOOP"?

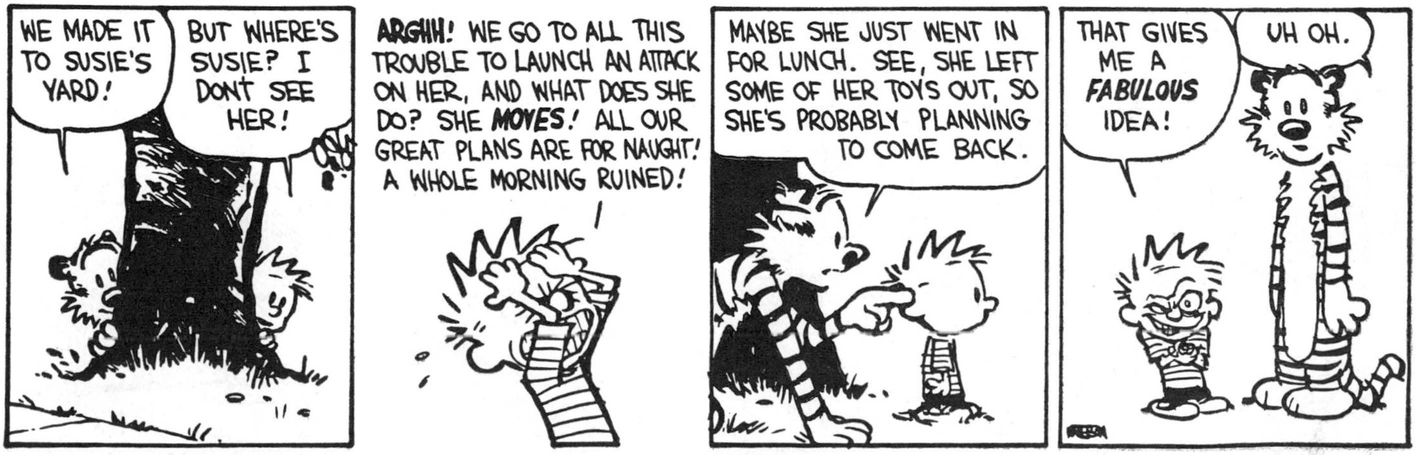
WE MADE IT TO SUSIE'S YARD!
BUT WHERE'S SUSIE? I DON'T SEE HER!
ARGHH! WE GO TO ALL THIS TROUBLE TO LAUNCH AN ATTACK ON HER, AND WHAT DOES SHE DO? SHE MOVES! ALL OUR GREAT PLANS ARE FOR NAUGHT! A WHOLE MORNING RUINED!
MAYBE SHE JUST WENT IN FOR LUNCH. SEE, SHE LEFT SOME OF HER TOYS OUT, SO SHE'S PROBABLY PLANNING TO COME BACK.
THAT GIVES ME A FABULOUS IDEA!
UH OH.

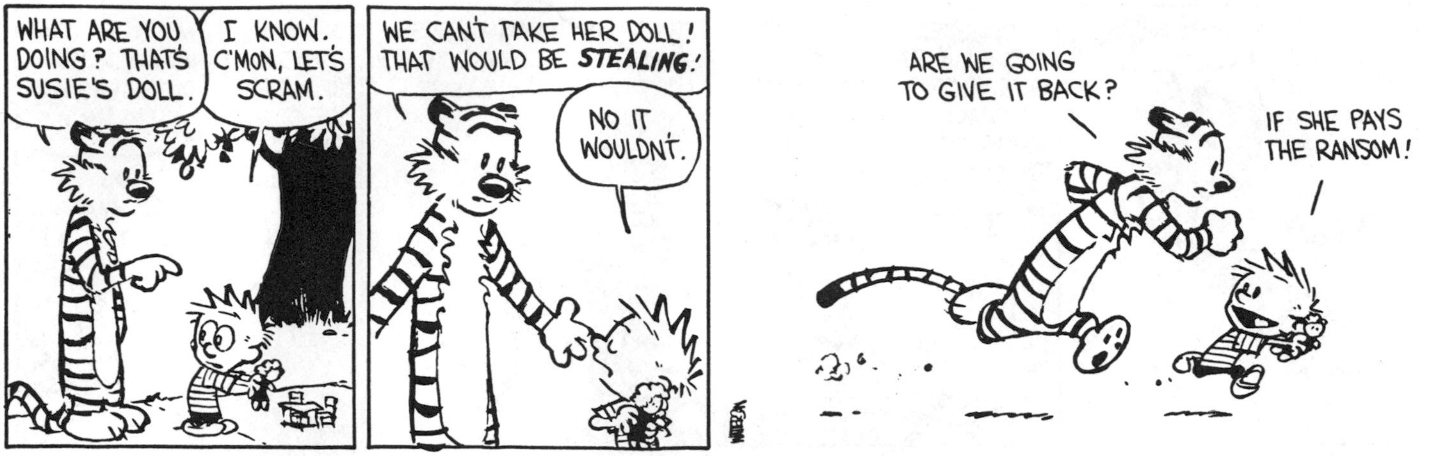
WHAT ARE YOU DOING? THAT'S SUSIE'S DOLL.
I KNOW. C'MON, LET'S SCRAM.
WE CAN'T TAKE HER DOLL! THAT WOULD BE **STEALING**!
NO IT WOULDN'T.
ARE WE GOING TO GIVE IT BACK?
IF SHE PAYS THE RANSOM!

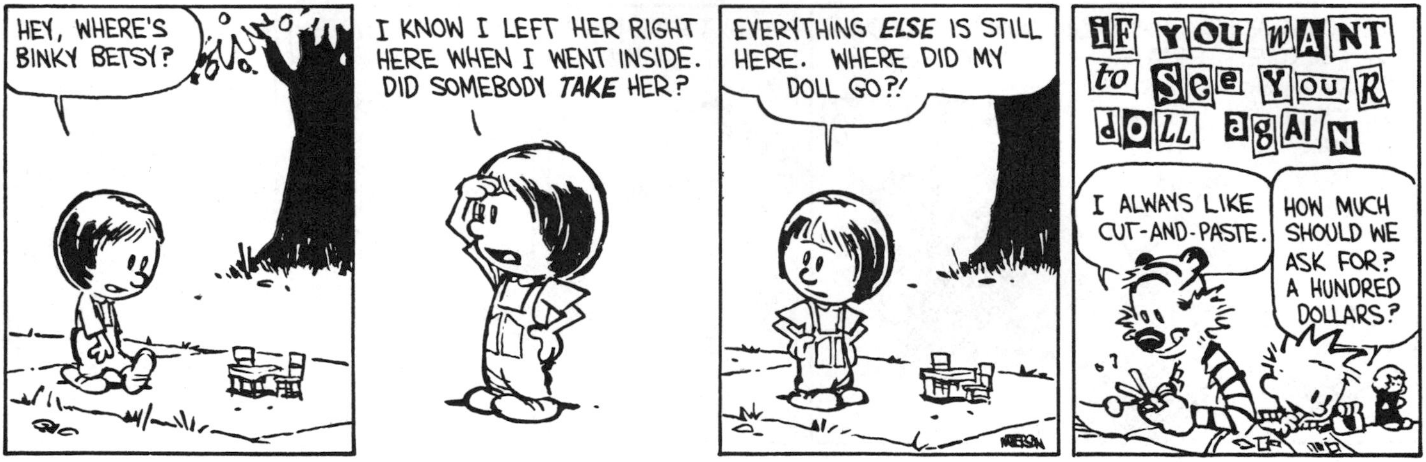
HEY, WHERE'S BINKY BETSY?
I KNOW I LEFT HER RIGHT HERE WHEN I WENT INSIDE. DID SOMEBODY **TAKE** HER?
EVERYTHING **ELSE** IS STILL HERE. WHERE DID MY DOLL GO?!
IF YOU WANT to SEE YOUR doll agAIN
I ALWAYS LIKE CUT-AND-PASTE.
HOW MUCH SHOULD WE ASK FOR? A HUNDRED DOLLARS?

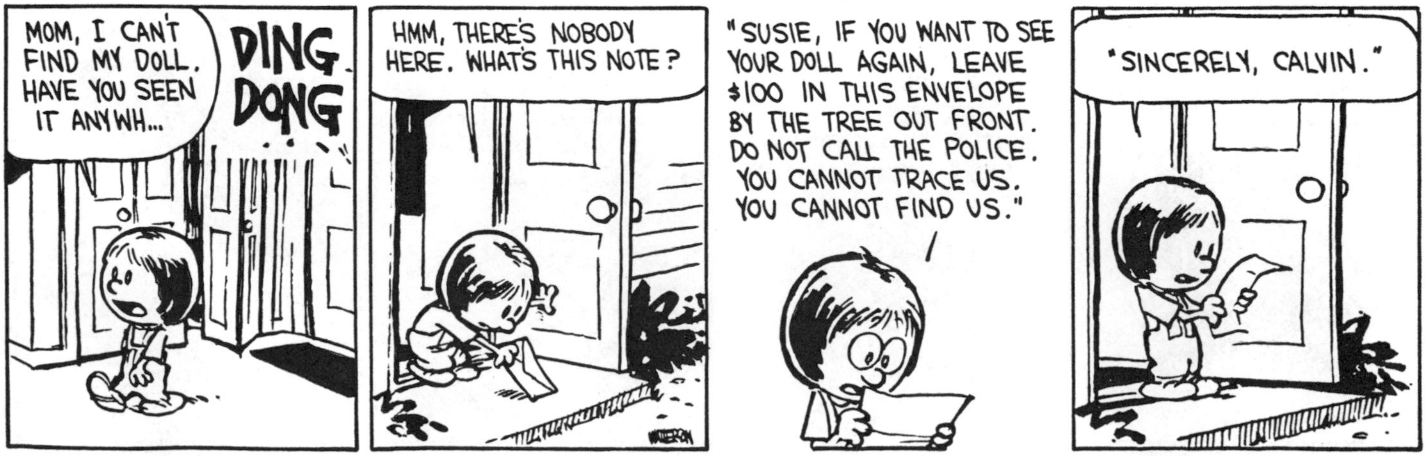
MOM, I CAN'T FIND MY DOLL. HAVE YOU SEEN IT ANYWH...
DING DONG
HMM, THERE'S NOBODY HERE. WHAT'S THIS NOTE?
"SUSIE, IF YOU WANT TO SEE YOUR DOLL AGAIN, LEAVE $100 IN THIS ENVELOPE BY THE TREE OUT FRONT. DO NOT CALL THE POLICE. YOU CANNOT TRACE US. YOU CANNOT FIND US."
"SINCERELY, CALVIN."

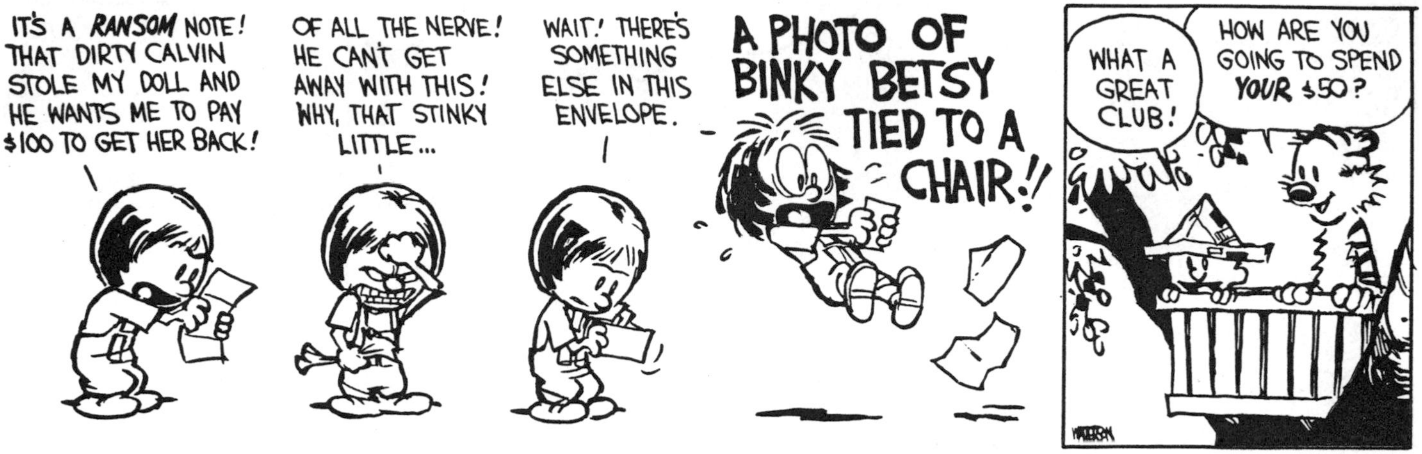
IT'S A RANSOM NOTE! THAT DIRTY CALVIN STOLE MY DOLL AND HE WANTS ME TO PAY $100 TO GET HER BACK!
OF ALL THE NERVE! HE CAN'T GET AWAY WITH THIS! WHY, THAT STINKY LITTLE...
WAIT! THERE'S SOMETHING ELSE IN THIS ENVELOPE.
A PHOTO OF BINKY BETSY TIED TO A CHAIR!!
WHAT A GREAT CLUB!
HOW ARE YOU GOING TO SPEND YOUR $50?

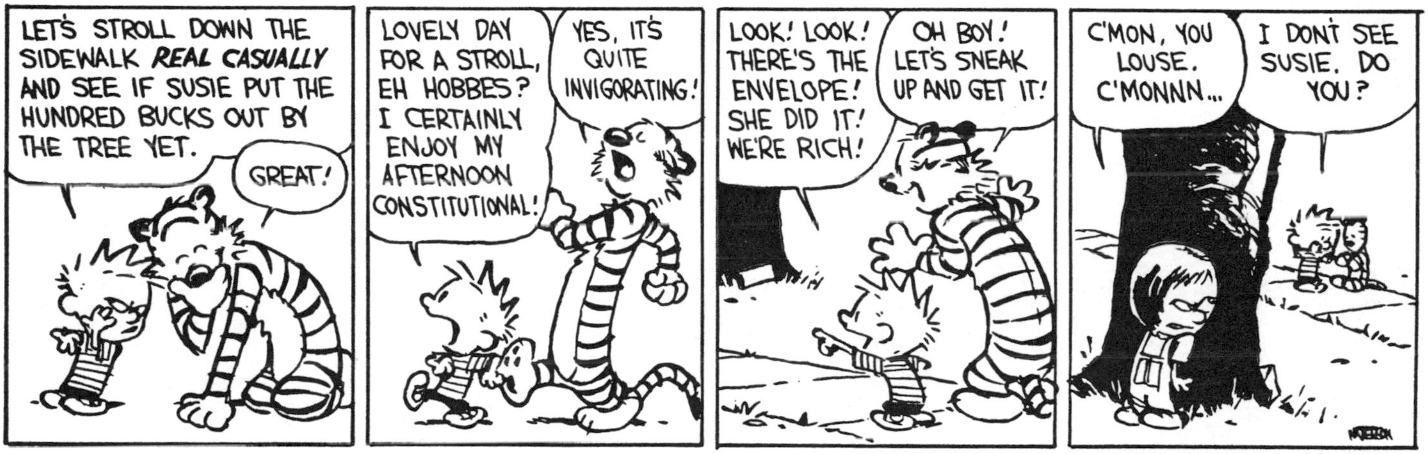
LET'S STROLL DOWN THE SIDEWALK REAL CASUALLY AND SEE IF SUSIE PUT THE HUNDRED BUCKS OUT BY THE TREE YET.
GREAT!
LOVELY DAY FOR A STROLL, EH HOBBES? I CERTAINLY ENJOY MY AFTERNOON CONSTITUTIONAL!
YES, IT'S QUITE INVIGORATING!
LOOK! LOOK! THERE'S THE ENVELOPE! SHE DID IT! WE'RE RICH!
OH BOY! LET'S SNEAK UP AND GET IT!
C'MON, YOU LOUSE. C'MONNN...
I DON'T SEE SUSIE. DO YOU?

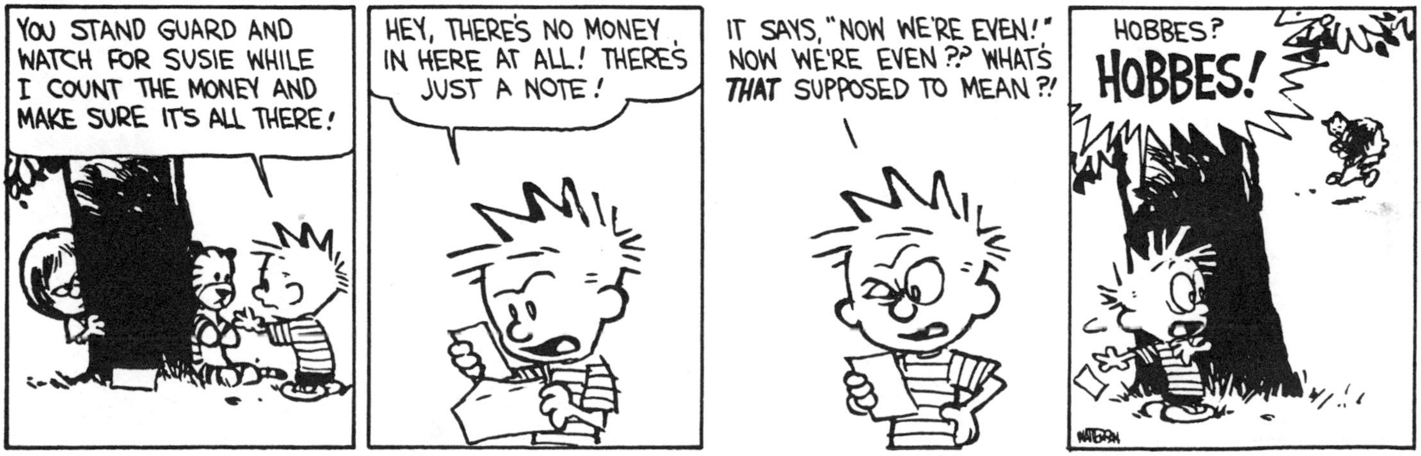
YOU STAND GUARD AND WATCH FOR SUSIE WHILE I COUNT THE MONEY AND MAKE SURE IT'S ALL THERE!
HEY, THERE'S NO MONEY IN HERE AT ALL! THERE'S JUST A NOTE!
IT SAYS, "NOW WE'RE EVEN!" NOW WE'RE EVEN?? WHAT'S THAT SUPPOSED TO MEAN?!
HOBBES?
HOBBES!

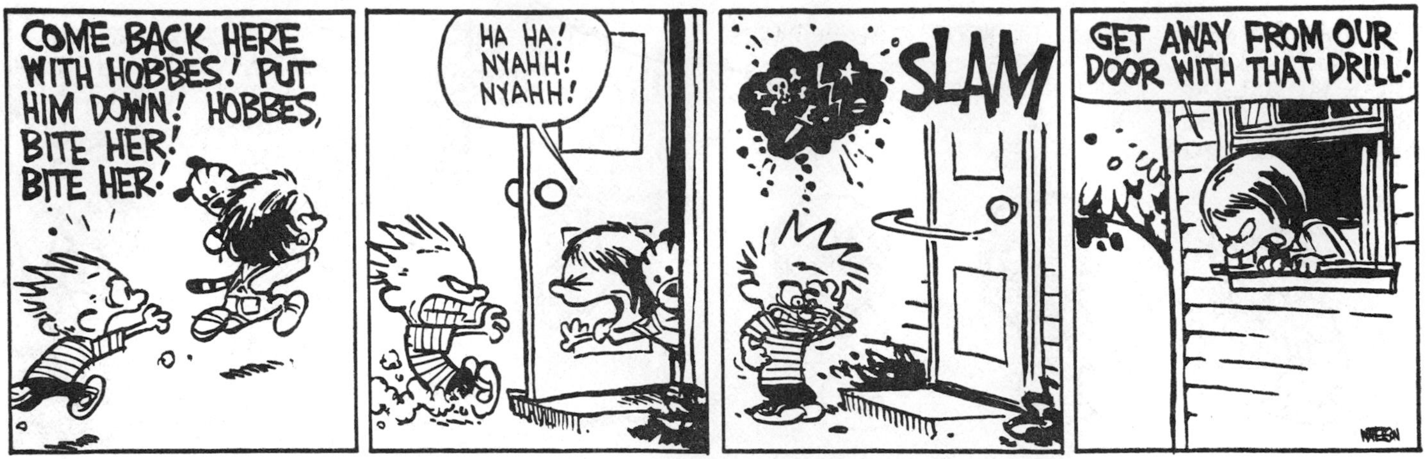
COME BACK HERE WITH HOBBES! PUT HIM DOWN! HOBBES, BITE HER! BITE HER!
HA HA! NYAHH! NYAHH!
SLAM
GET AWAY FROM OUR DOOR WITH THAT DRILL!

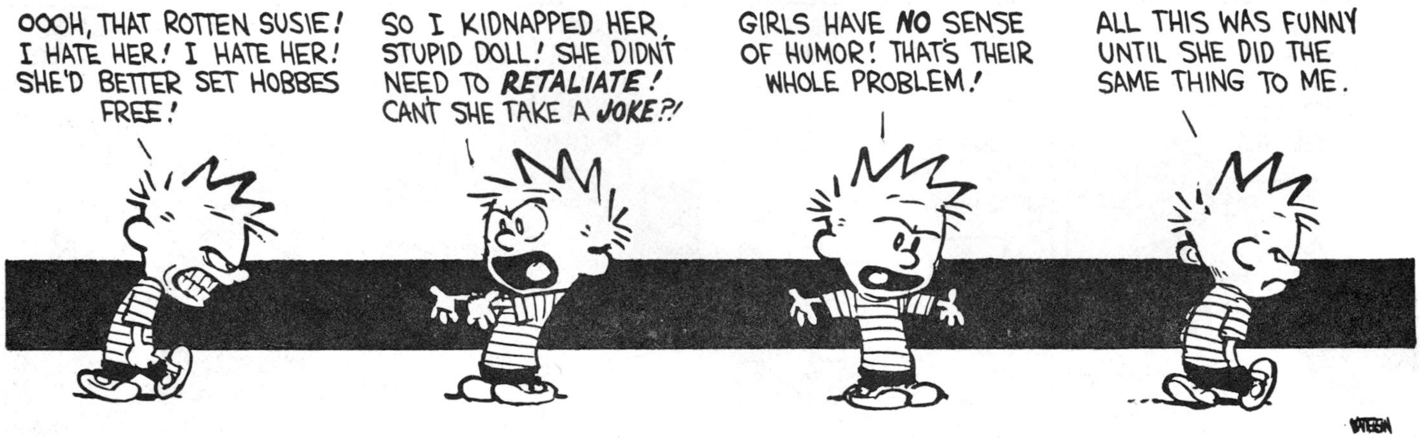
OOOH, THAT ROTTEN SUSIE! I HATE HER! I HATE HER! SHE'D BETTER SET HOBBES FREE!
SO I KIDNAPPED HER STUPID DOLL! SHE DIDN'T NEED TO RETALIATE! CAN'T SHE TAKE A JOKE?!
GIRLS HAVE NO SENSE OF HUMOR! THAT'S THEIR WHOLE PROBLEM!
ALL THIS WAS FUNNY UNTIL SHE DID THE SAME THING TO ME.

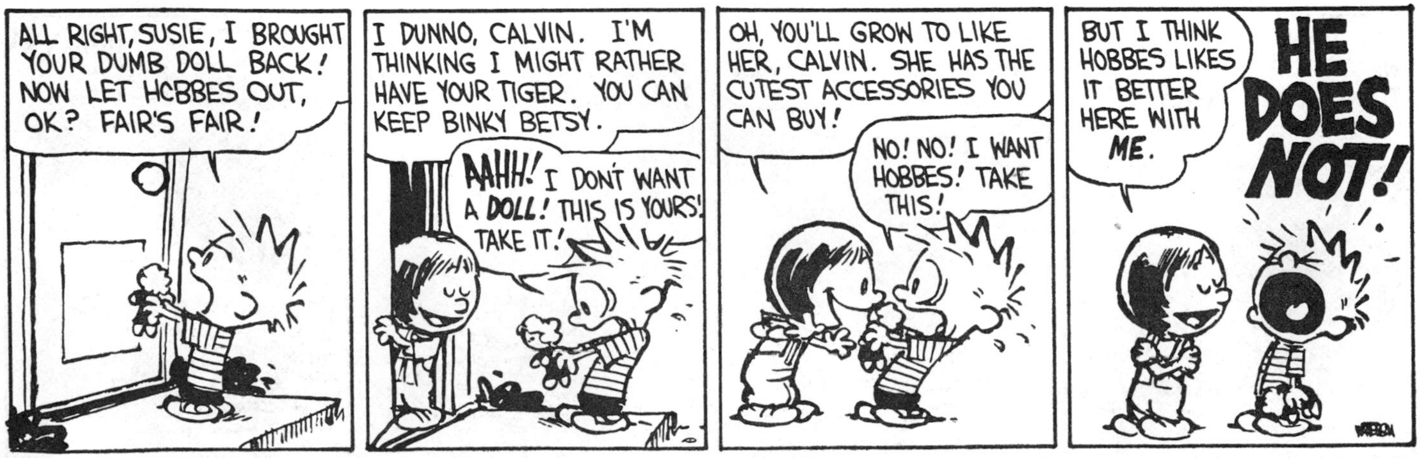
ALL RIGHT, SUSIE, I BROUGHT YOUR DUMB DOLL BACK! NOW LET HOBBES OUT, OK? FAIR'S FAIR!
I DUNNO, CALVIN. I'M THINKING I MIGHT RATHER HAVE YOUR TIGER. YOU CAN KEEP BINKY BETSY.
AAHH! I DON'T WANT A DOLL! THIS IS YOURS! TAKE IT!
OH, YOU'LL GROW TO LIKE HER, CALVIN. SHE HAS THE CUTEST ACCESSORIES YOU CAN BUY!
NO! NO! I WANT HOBBES! TAKE THIS!
BUT I THINK HOBBES LIKES IT BETTER HERE WITH ME.
HE DOES NOT!

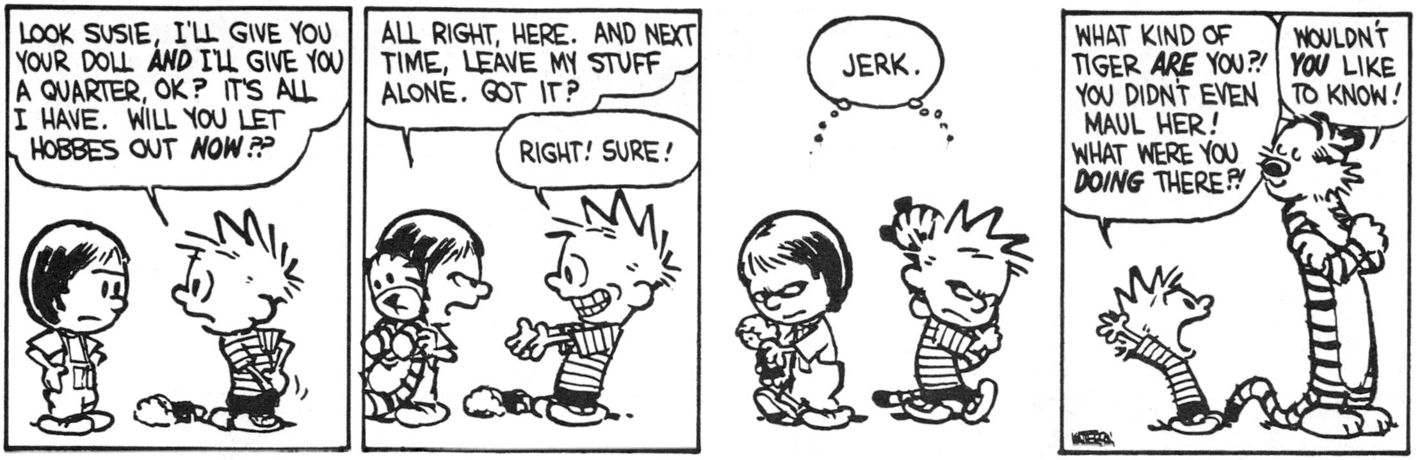
LOOK SUSIE, I'LL GIVE YOU YOUR DOLL AND I'LL GIVE YOU A QUARTER, OK? IT'S ALL I HAVE. WILL YOU LET HOBBES OUT NOW?!
ALL RIGHT, HERE. AND NEXT TIME, LEAVE MY STUFF ALONE. GOT IT?
RIGHT! SURE!
JERK.
WHAT KIND OF TIGER ARE YOU?! YOU DIDN'T EVEN MAUL HER! WHAT WERE YOU DOING THERE?!
WOULDN'T YOU LIKE TO KNOW!

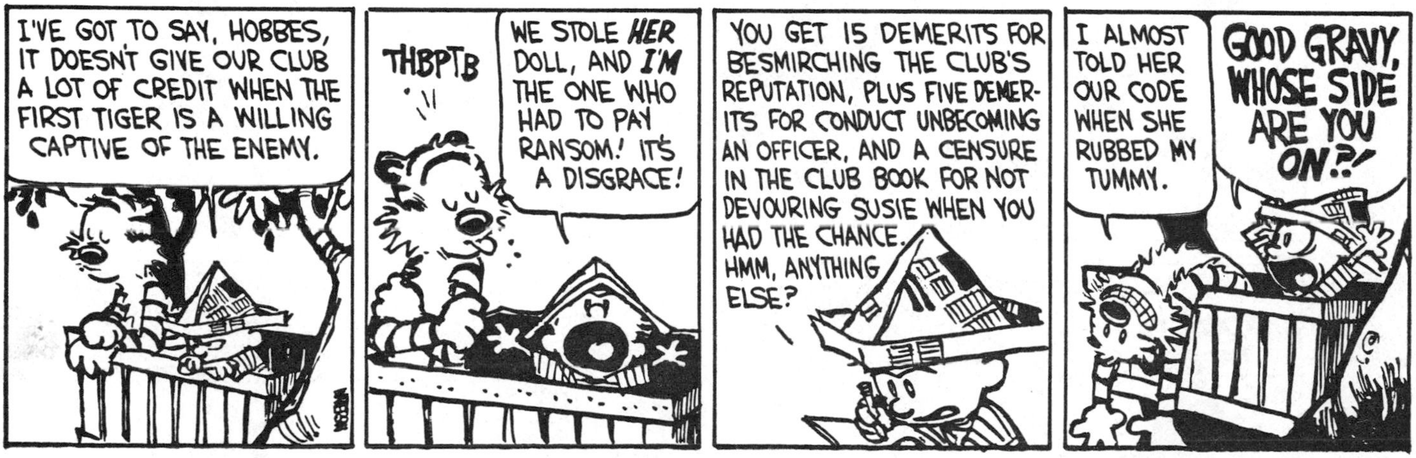
I'VE GOT TO SAY, HOBBES, IT DOESN'T GIVE OUR CLUB A LOT OF CREDIT WHEN THE FIRST TIGER IS A WILLING CAPTIVE OF THE ENEMY.
THBPTB
WE STOLE HER DOLL, AND I'M THE ONE WHO HAD TO PAY RANSOM! IT'S A DISGRACE!
YOU GET 15 DEMERITS FOR BESMIRCHING THE CLUB'S REPUTATION, PLUS FIVE DEMERITS FOR CONDUCT UNBECOMING AN OFFICER, AND A CENSURE IN THE CLUB BOOK FOR NOT DEVOURING SUSIE WHEN YOU HAD THE CHANCE.
HMM, ANYTHING ELSE?
I ALMOST TOLD HER OUR CODE WHEN SHE RUBBED MY TUMMY.
GOOD GRAVY, WHOSE SIDE ARE YOU ON?!

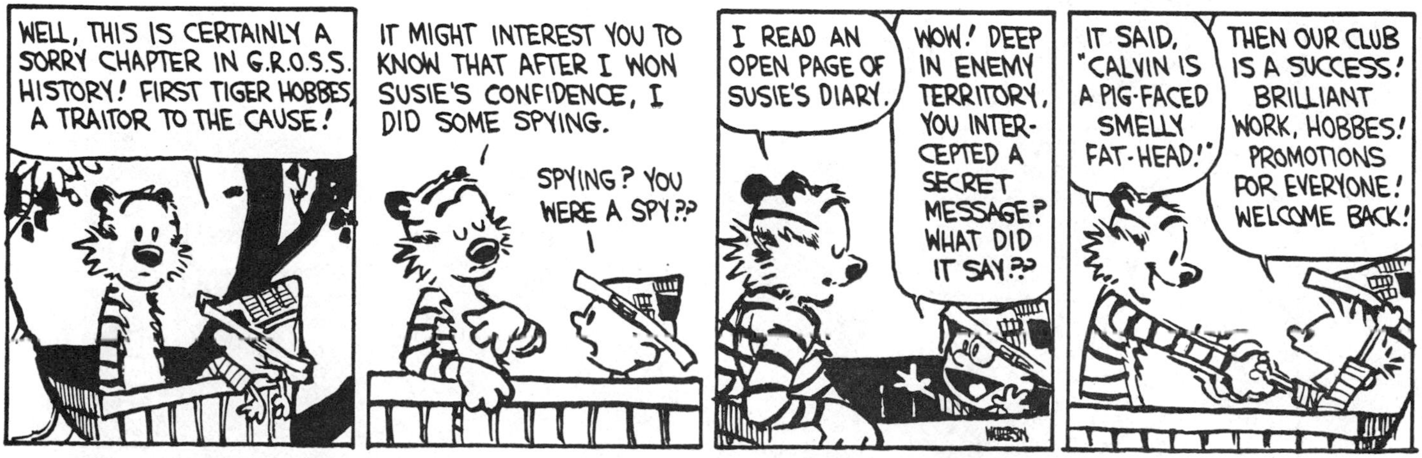
WELL, THIS IS CERTAINLY A SORRY CHAPTER IN G.R.O.S.S. HISTORY! FIRST TIGER HOBBES, A TRAITOR TO THE CAUSE!
IT MIGHT INTEREST YOU TO KNOW THAT AFTER I WON SUSIE'S CONFIDENCE, I DID SOME SPYING.
SPYING? YOU WERE A SPY?!
I READ AN OPEN PAGE OF SUSIE'S DIARY.
WOW! DEEP IN ENEMY TERRITORY, YOU INTERCEPTED A SECRET MESSAGE? WHAT DID IT SAY?!
IT SAID, "CALVIN IS A PIG-FACED SMELLY FAT-HEAD!"
THEN OUR CLUB IS A SUCCESS! BRILLIANT WORK, HOBBES! PROMOTIONS FOR EVERYONE! WELCOME BACK!

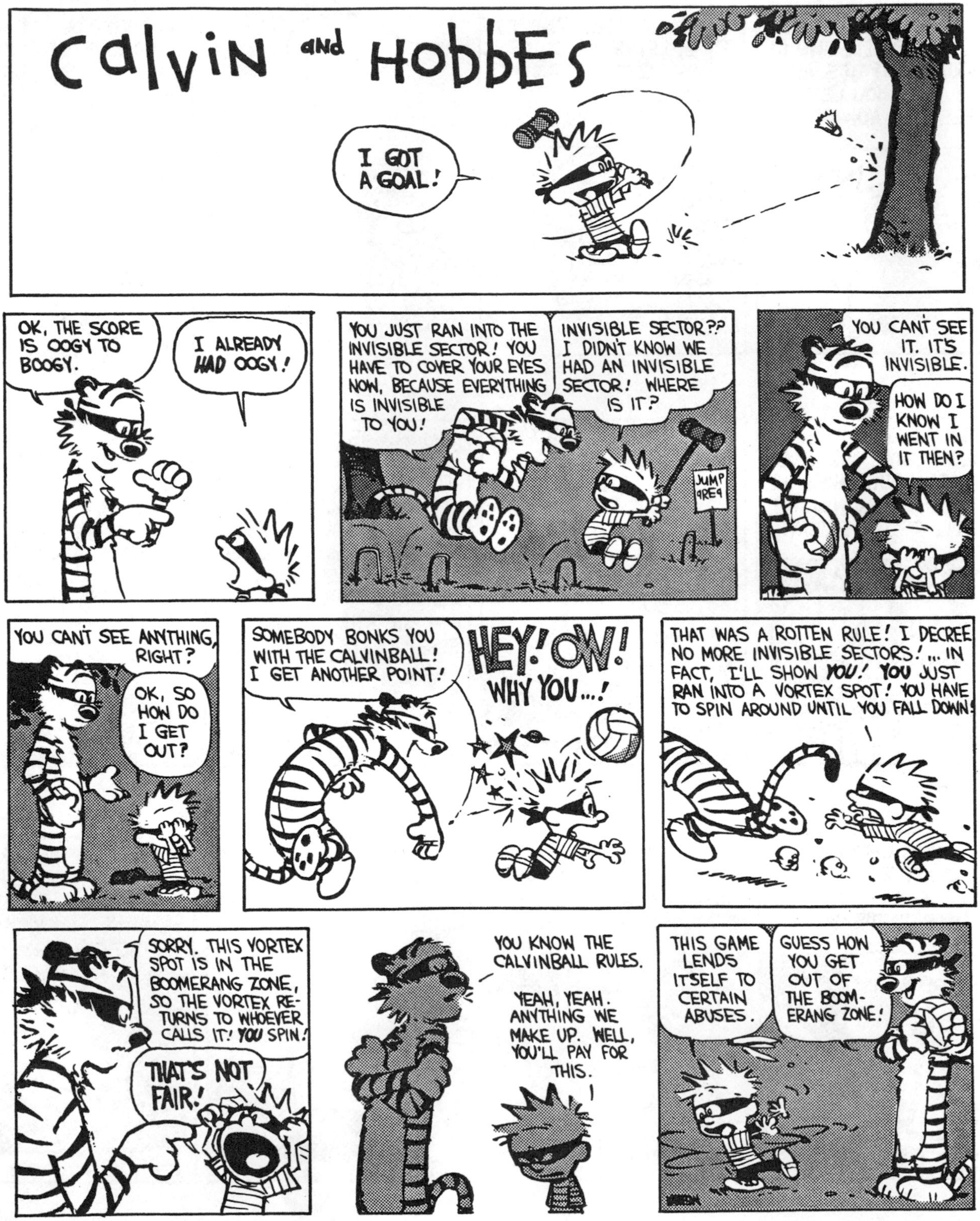
Calvin and HOBBES
I GOT A GOAL!
OK, THE SCORE IS OOGY TO BOOGY.
I ALREADY HAD OOGY!
YOU JUST RAN INTO THE INVISIBLE SECTOR! YOU HAVE TO COVER YOUR EYES NOW, BECAUSE EVERYTHING IS INVISIBLE TO YOU!
INVISIBLE SECTOR?? I DIDN'T KNOW WE HAD AN INVISIBLE SECTOR! WHERE IS IT?
JUMP 9RE9
YOU CAN'T SEE IT. IT'S INVISIBLE.
HOW DO I KNOW I WENT IN IT THEN?
YOU CAN'T SEE ANYTHING, RIGHT?
OK, SO HOW DO I GET OUT?
SOMEBODY BONKS YOU WITH THE CALVINBALL! I GET ANOTHER POINT!
HEY! OW!
WHY YOU...!
THAT WAS A ROTTEN RULE! I DECREE NO MORE INVISIBLE SECTORS! ... IN FACT, I'LL SHOW YOU! YOU JUST RAN INTO A VORTEX SPOT! YOU HAVE TO SPIN AROUND UNTIL YOU FALL DOWN!
SORRY. THIS VORTEX SPOT IS IN THE BOOMERANG ZONE, SO THE VORTEX RETURNS TO WHOEVER CALLS IT! YOU SPIN!
THAT'S NOT FAIR!
YOU KNOW THE CALVINBALL RULES.
YEAH, YEAH. ANYTHING WE MAKE UP. WELL, YOU'LL PAY FOR THIS.
THIS GAME LENDS ITSELF TO CERTAIN ABUSES.
GUESS HOW YOU GET OUT OF THE BOOMERANG ZONE!

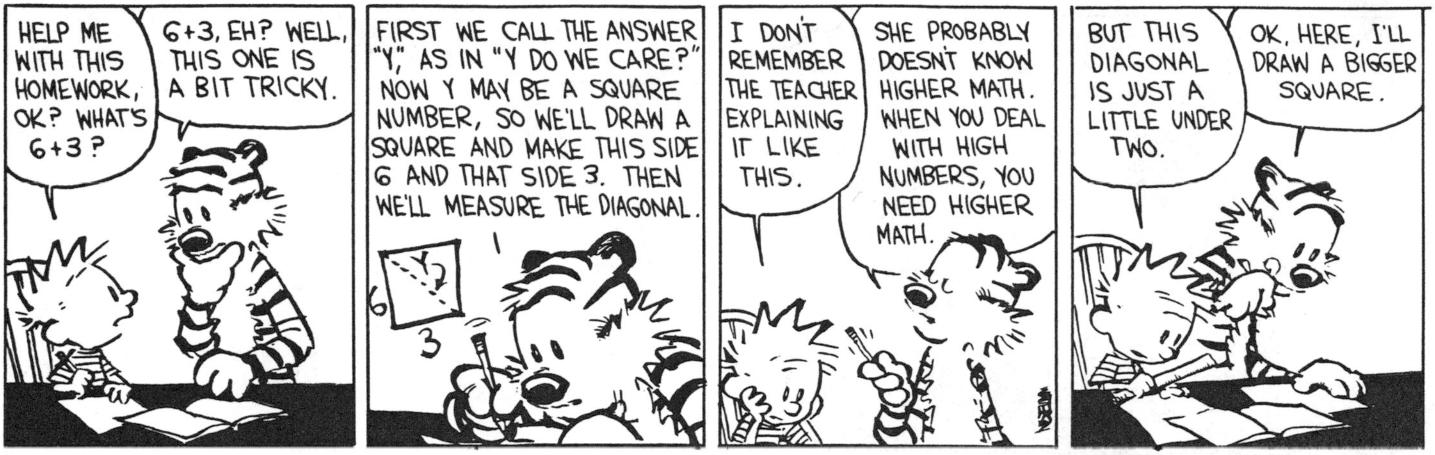
HELP ME WITH THIS HOMEWORK, OK? WHAT'S 6+3?
6+3, EH? WELL, THIS ONE IS A BIT TRICKY.
FIRST WE CALL THE ANSWER "Y," AS IN "Y DO WE CARE?" NOW Y MAY BE A SQUARE NUMBER, SO WE'LL DRAW A SQUARE AND MAKE THIS SIDE 6 AND THAT SIDE 3. THEN WE'LL MEASURE THE DIAGONAL.
Y
2
6
3
I DON'T REMEMBER THE TEACHER EXPLAINING IT LIKE THIS.
SHE PROBABLY DOESN'T KNOW HIGHER MATH. WHEN YOU DEAL WITH HIGH NUMBERS, YOU NEED HIGHER MATH.
BUT THIS DIAGONAL IS JUST A LITTLE UNDER TWO.
OK, HERE, I'LL DRAW A BIGGER SQUARE.

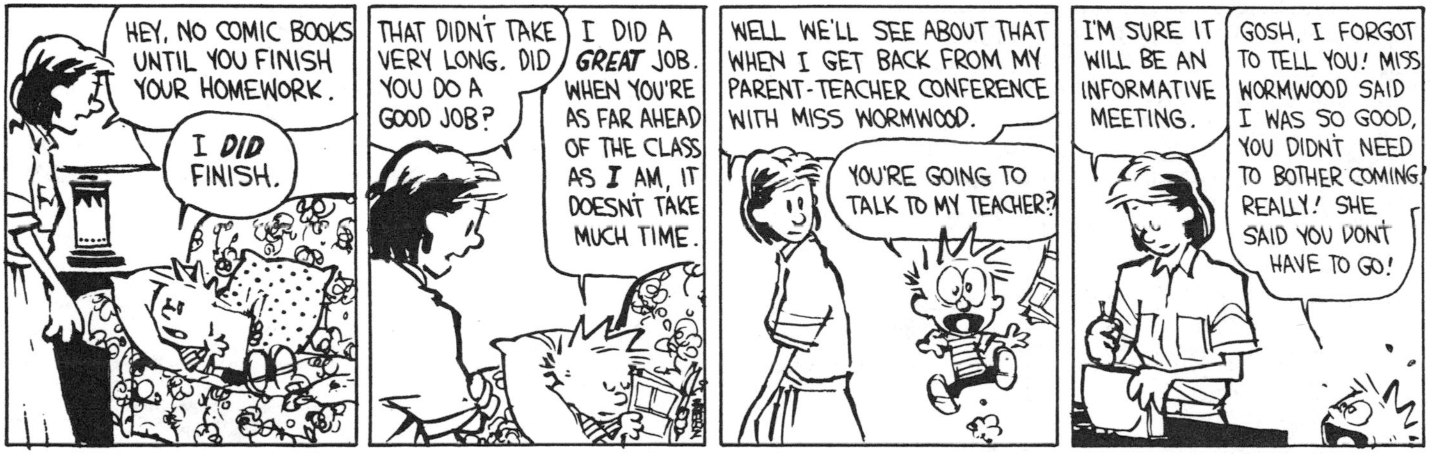
HEY, NO COMIC BOOKS UNTIL YOU FINISH YOUR HOMEWORK.
I **DID** FINISH.
THAT DIDN'T TAKE VERY LONG. DID YOU DO A GOOD JOB?
I DID A **GREAT** JOB. WHEN YOU'RE AS FAR AHEAD OF THE CLASS AS **I** AM, IT DOESN'T TAKE MUCH TIME.
WELL WE'LL SEE ABOUT THAT WHEN I GET BACK FROM MY PARENT-TEACHER CONFERENCE WITH MISS WORMWOOD.
YOU'RE GOING TO TALK TO MY TEACHER?!
I'M SURE IT WILL BE AN INFORMATIVE MEETING.
GOSH, I FORGOT TO TELL YOU! MISS WORMWOOD SAID I WAS SO GOOD, YOU DIDN'T NEED TO BOTHER COMING. REALLY! SHE SAID YOU DON'T HAVE TO GO!

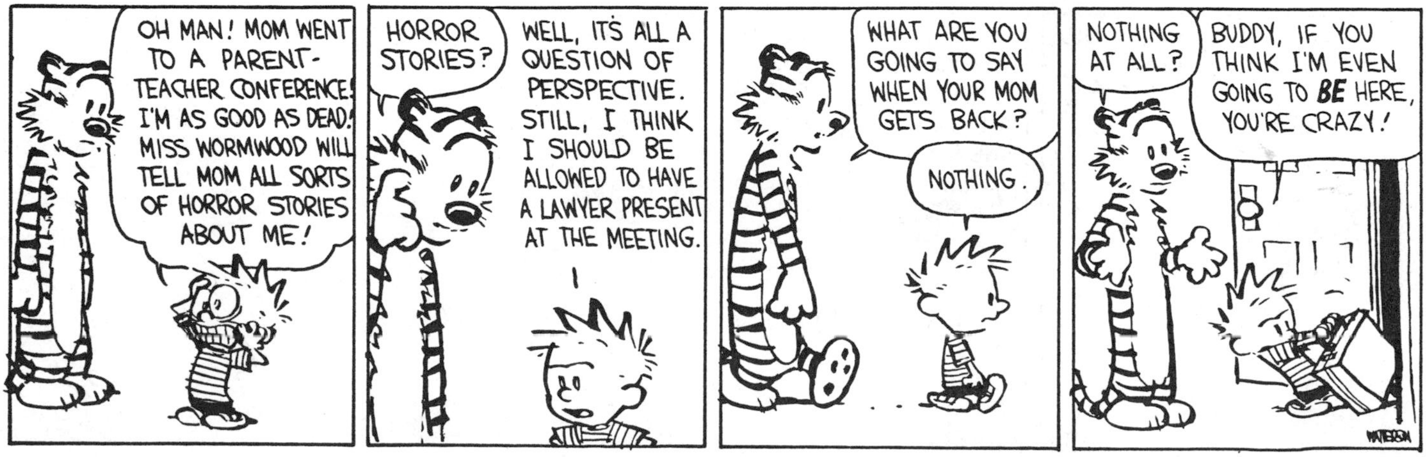
OH MAN! MOM WENT TO A PARENT-TEACHER CONFERENCE! I'M AS GOOD AS DEAD! MISS WORMWOOD WILL TELL MOM ALL SORTS OF HORROR STORIES ABOUT ME!
HORROR STORIES?
WELL, IT'S ALL A QUESTION OF PERSPECTIVE. STILL, I THINK I SHOULD BE ALLOWED TO HAVE A LAWYER PRESENT AT THE MEETING.
WHAT ARE YOU GOING TO SAY WHEN YOUR MOM GETS BACK?
NOTHING.
NOTHING AT ALL?
BUDDY, IF YOU THINK I'M EVEN GOING TO **BE** HERE, YOU'RE CRAZY!

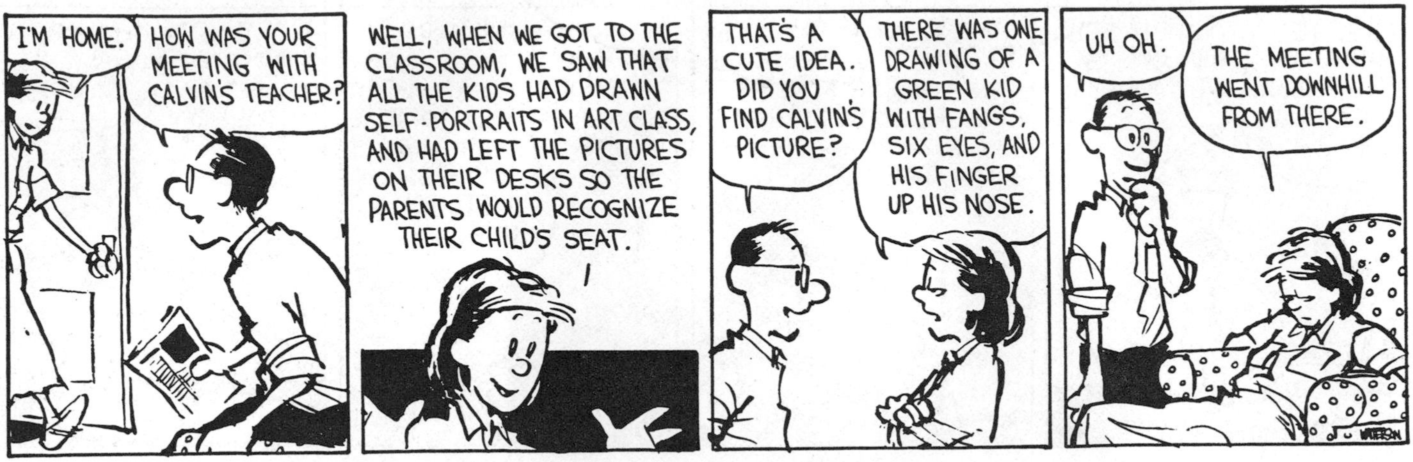
I'M HOME.
HOW WAS YOUR MEETING WITH CALVIN'S TEACHER?
WELL, WHEN WE GOT TO THE CLASSROOM, WE SAW THAT ALL THE KIDS HAD DRAWN SELF-PORTRAITS IN ART CLASS, AND HAD LEFT THE PICTURES ON THEIR DESKS SO THE PARENTS WOULD RECOGNIZE THEIR CHILD'S SEAT.
THAT'S A CUTE IDEA. DID YOU FIND CALVIN'S PICTURE?
THERE WAS ONE DRAWING OF A GREEN KID WITH FANGS, SIX EYES, AND HIS FINGER UP HIS NOSE.
UH OH.
THE MEETING WENT DOWNHILL FROM THERE.

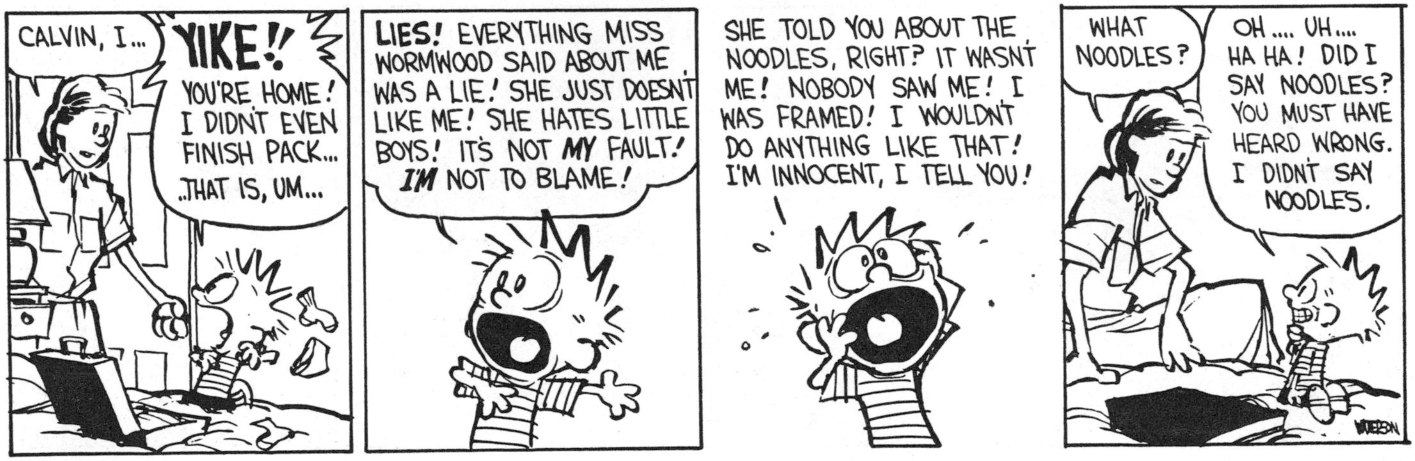
CALVIN, I...
YIKE!!
YOU'RE HOME! I DIDN'T EVEN FINISH PACK... ..THAT IS, UM...
LIES! EVERYTHING MISS WORMWOOD SAID ABOUT ME WAS A LIE! SHE JUST DOESN'T LIKE ME! SHE HATES LITTLE BOYS! IT'S NOT MY FAULT! I'M NOT TO BLAME!
SHE TOLD YOU ABOUT THE NOODLES, RIGHT? IT WASN'T ME! NOBODY SAW ME! I WAS FRAMED! I WOULDN'T DO ANYTHING LIKE THAT! I'M INNOCENT, I TELL YOU!
WHAT NOODLES?
OH .... UH.... HA HA! DID I SAY NOODLES? YOU MUST HAVE HEARD WRONG. I DIDN'T SAY NOODLES.

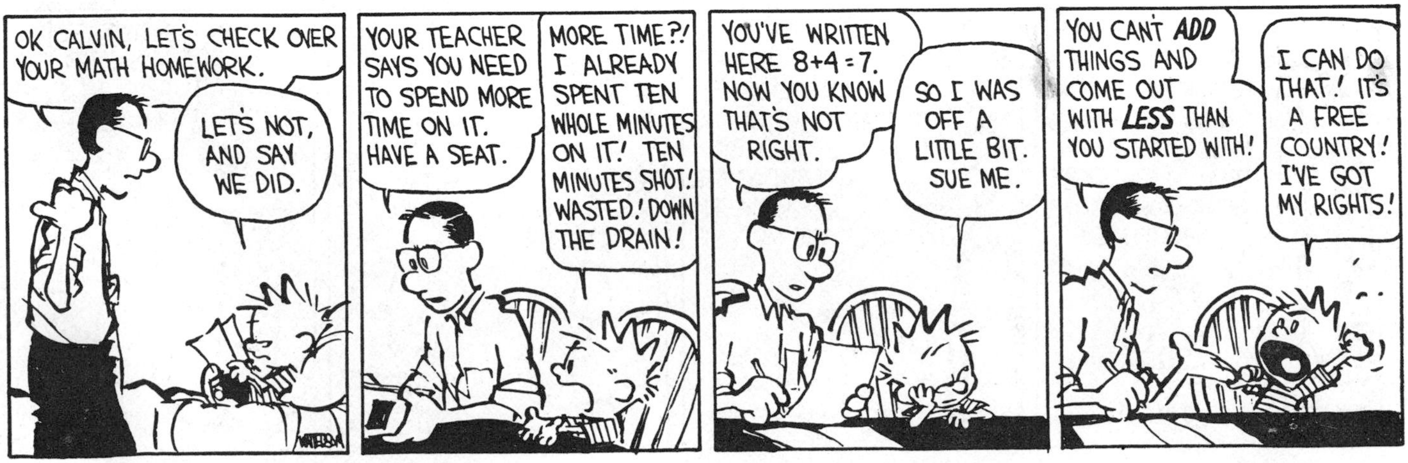
OK CALVIN, LET'S CHECK OVER YOUR MATH HOMEWORK.
LET'S NOT, AND SAY WE DID.
YOUR TEACHER SAYS YOU NEED TO SPEND MORE TIME ON IT. HAVE A SEAT.
MORE TIME?! I ALREADY SPENT TEN WHOLE MINUTES ON IT! TEN MINUTES SHOT! WASTED! DOWN THE DRAIN!
YOU'VE WRITTEN HERE 8+4=7. NOW YOU KNOW THAT'S NOT RIGHT.
SO I WAS OFF A LITTLE BIT. SUE ME.
YOU CAN'T ADD THINGS AND COME OUT WITH LESS THAN YOU STARTED WITH!
I CAN DO THAT! IT'S A FREE COUNTRY! I'VE GOT MY RIGHTS!

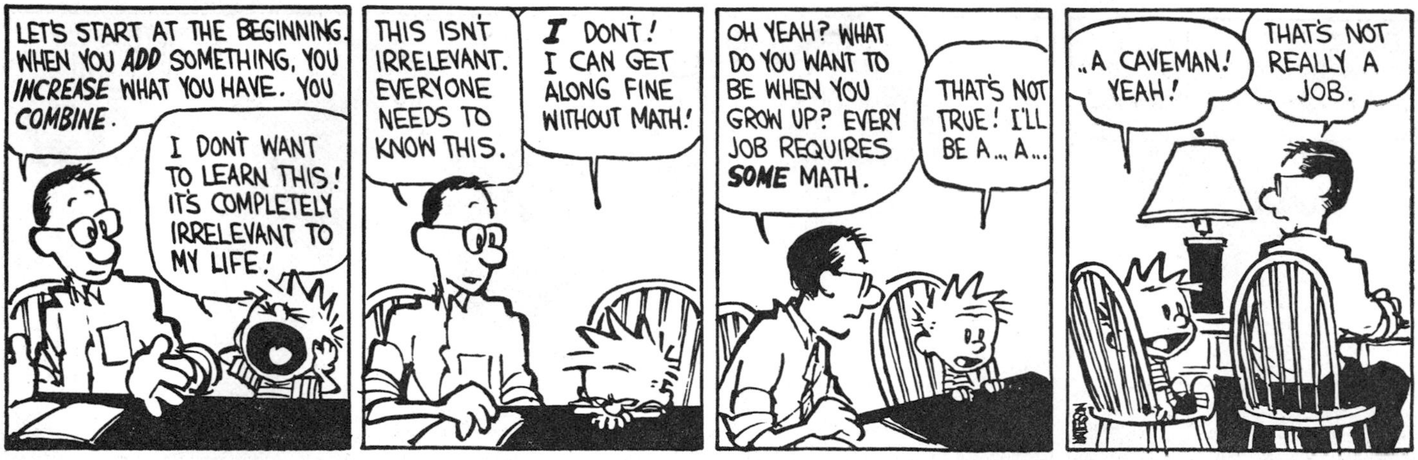
LET'S START AT THE BEGINNING. WHEN YOU **ADD** SOMETHING, YOU **INCREASE** WHAT YOU HAVE. YOU **COMBINE**.
I DON'T WANT TO LEARN THIS! IT'S COMPLETELY IRRELEVANT TO MY LIFE!
THIS ISN'T IRRELEVANT. EVERYONE NEEDS TO KNOW THIS.
I DON'T! I CAN GET ALONG FINE WITHOUT MATH!
OH YEAH? WHAT DO YOU WANT TO BE WHEN YOU GROW UP? EVERY JOB REQUIRES **SOME** MATH.
THAT'S NOT TRUE! I'LL BE A... A...
..A CAVEMAN! YEAH!
THAT'S NOT REALLY A JOB.

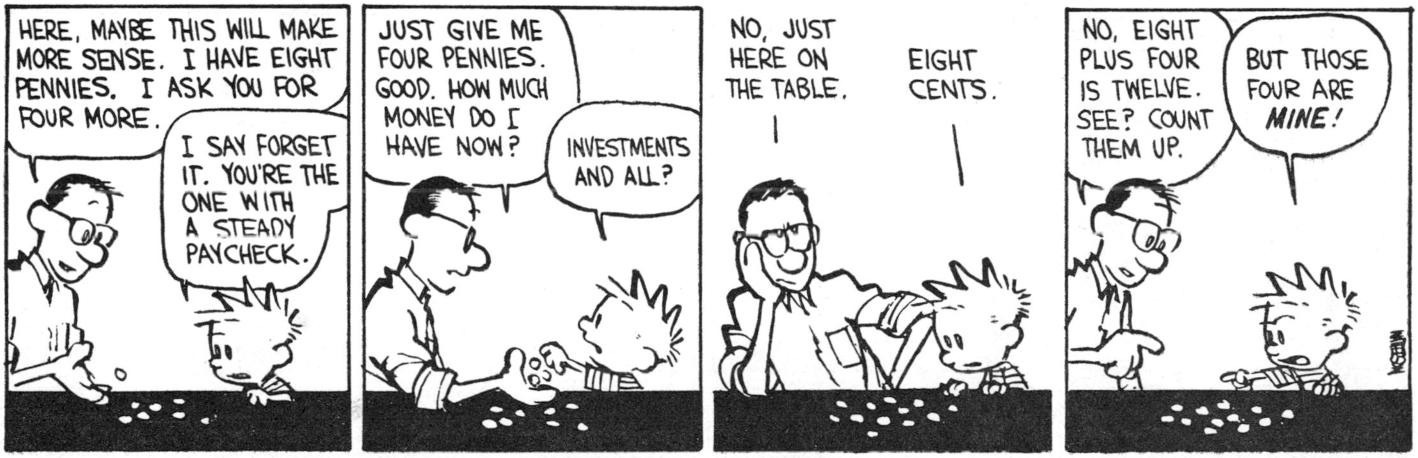
HERE, MAYBE THIS WILL MAKE MORE SENSE. I HAVE EIGHT PENNIES. I ASK YOU FOR FOUR MORE.
I SAY FORGET IT. YOU'RE THE ONE WITH A STEADY PAYCHECK.
JUST GIVE ME FOUR PENNIES. GOOD. HOW MUCH MONEY DO I HAVE NOW?
INVESTMENTS AND ALL?
NO, JUST HERE ON THE TABLE.
EIGHT CENTS.
NO, EIGHT PLUS FOUR IS TWELVE. SEE? COUNT THEM UP.
BUT THOSE FOUR ARE ***MINE!***

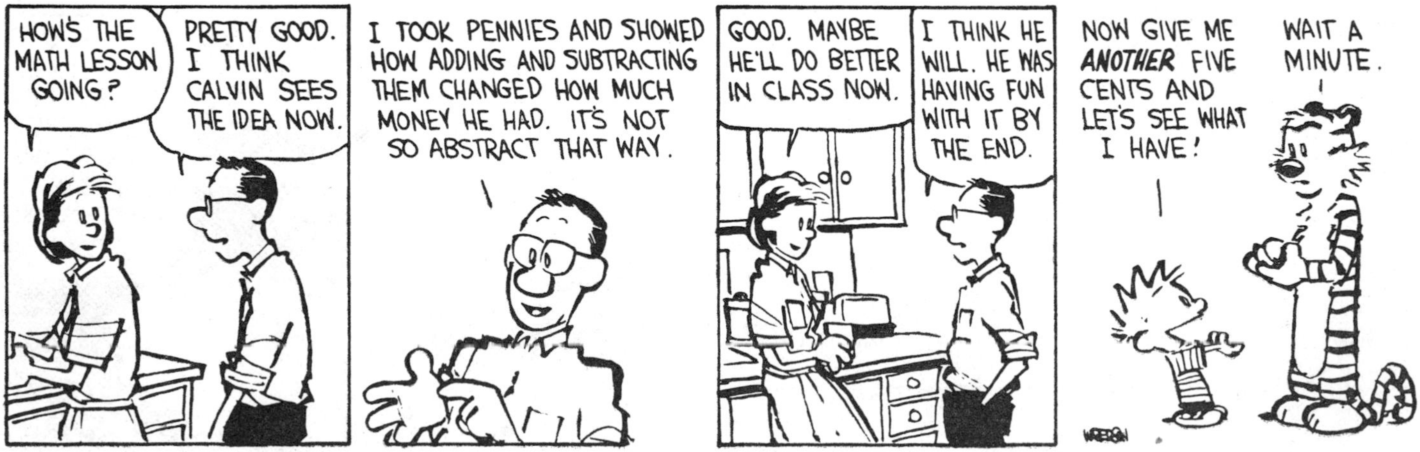
HOW'S THE MATH LESSON GOING?
PRETTY GOOD. I THINK CALVIN SEES THE IDEA NOW.
I TOOK PENNIES AND SHOWED HOW ADDING AND SUBTRACTING THEM CHANGED HOW MUCH MONEY HE HAD. IT'S NOT SO ABSTRACT THAT WAY.
GOOD. MAYBE HE'LL DO BETTER IN CLASS NOW.
I THINK HE WILL. HE WAS HAVING FUN WITH IT BY THE END.
NOW GIVE ME ***ANOTHER*** FIVE CENTS AND LET'S SEE WHAT I HAVE!
WAIT A MINUTE.

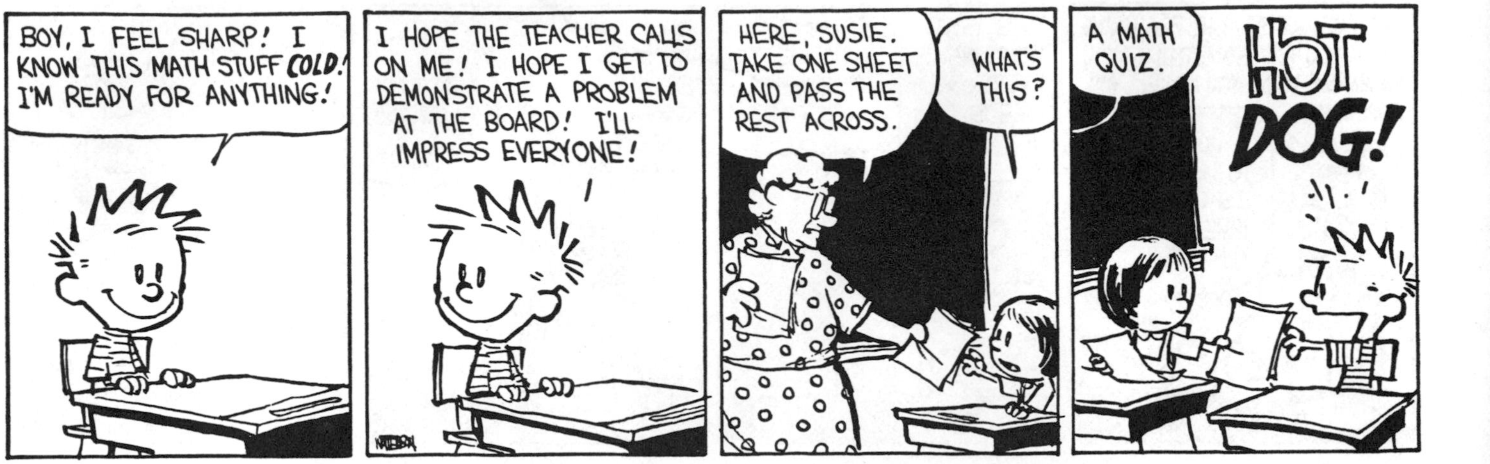
BOY, I FEEL SHARP! I KNOW THIS MATH STUFF COLD! I'M READY FOR ANYTHING!
I HOPE THE TEACHER CALLS ON ME! I HOPE I GET TO DEMONSTRATE A PROBLEM AT THE BOARD! I'LL IMPRESS EVERYONE!
HERE, SUSIE. TAKE ONE SHEET AND PASS THE REST ACROSS.
WHAT'S THIS?
A MATH QUIZ.
HOT DOG!

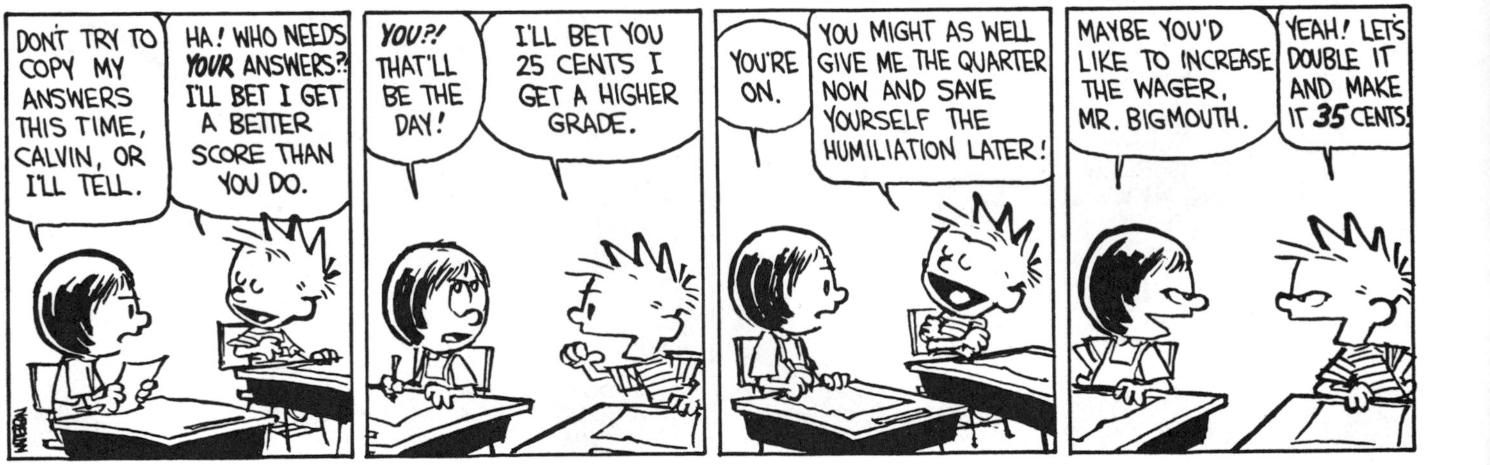
DON'T TRY TO COPY MY ANSWERS THIS TIME, CALVIN, OR I'LL TELL.
HA! WHO NEEDS YOUR ANSWERS?! I'LL BET I GET A BETTER SCORE THAN YOU DO.
YOU?!! THAT'LL BE THE DAY!
I'LL BET YOU 25 CENTS I GET A HIGHER GRADE.
YOU'RE ON.
YOU MIGHT AS WELL GIVE ME THE QUARTER NOW AND SAVE YOURSELF THE HUMILIATION LATER!
MAYBE YOU'D LIKE TO INCREASE THE WAGER, MR. BIGMOUTH.
YEAH! LET'S DOUBLE IT AND MAKE IT 35 CENTS!

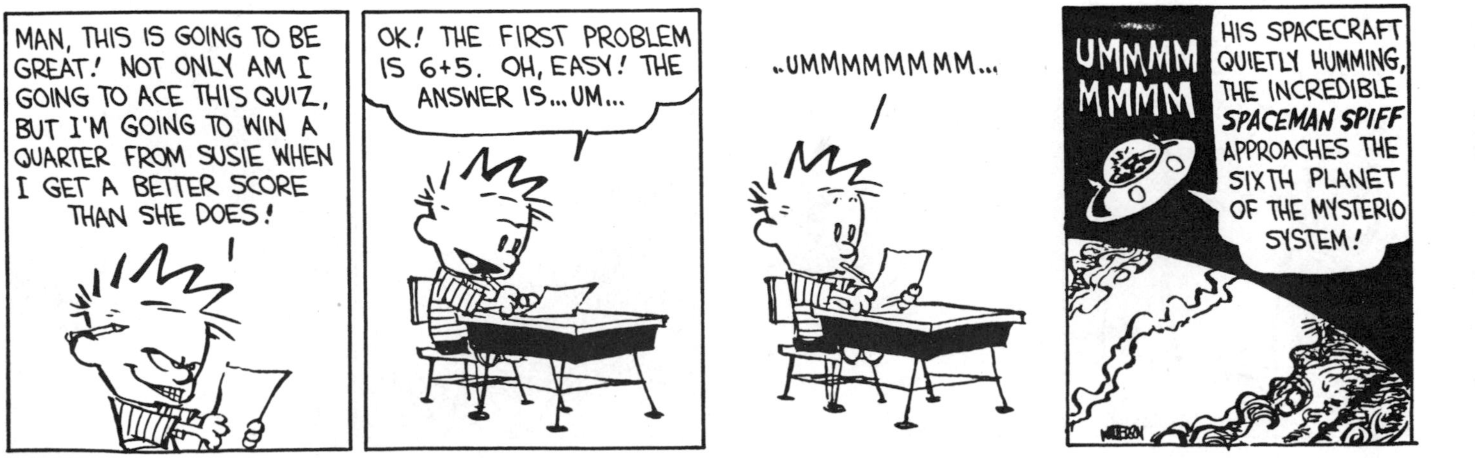
MAN, THIS IS GOING TO BE GREAT! NOT ONLY AM I GOING TO ACE THIS QUIZ, BUT I'M GOING TO WIN A QUARTER FROM SUSIE WHEN I GET A BETTER SCORE THAN SHE DOES!
OK! THE FIRST PROBLEM IS 6+5. OH, EASY! THE ANSWER IS...UM...
..UMMMMMMMMM...
UMMMM MMMM
HIS SPACECRAFT QUIETLY HUMMING, THE INCREDIBLE SPACEMAN SPIFF APPROACHES THE SIXTH PLANET OF THE MYSTERIO SYSTEM!

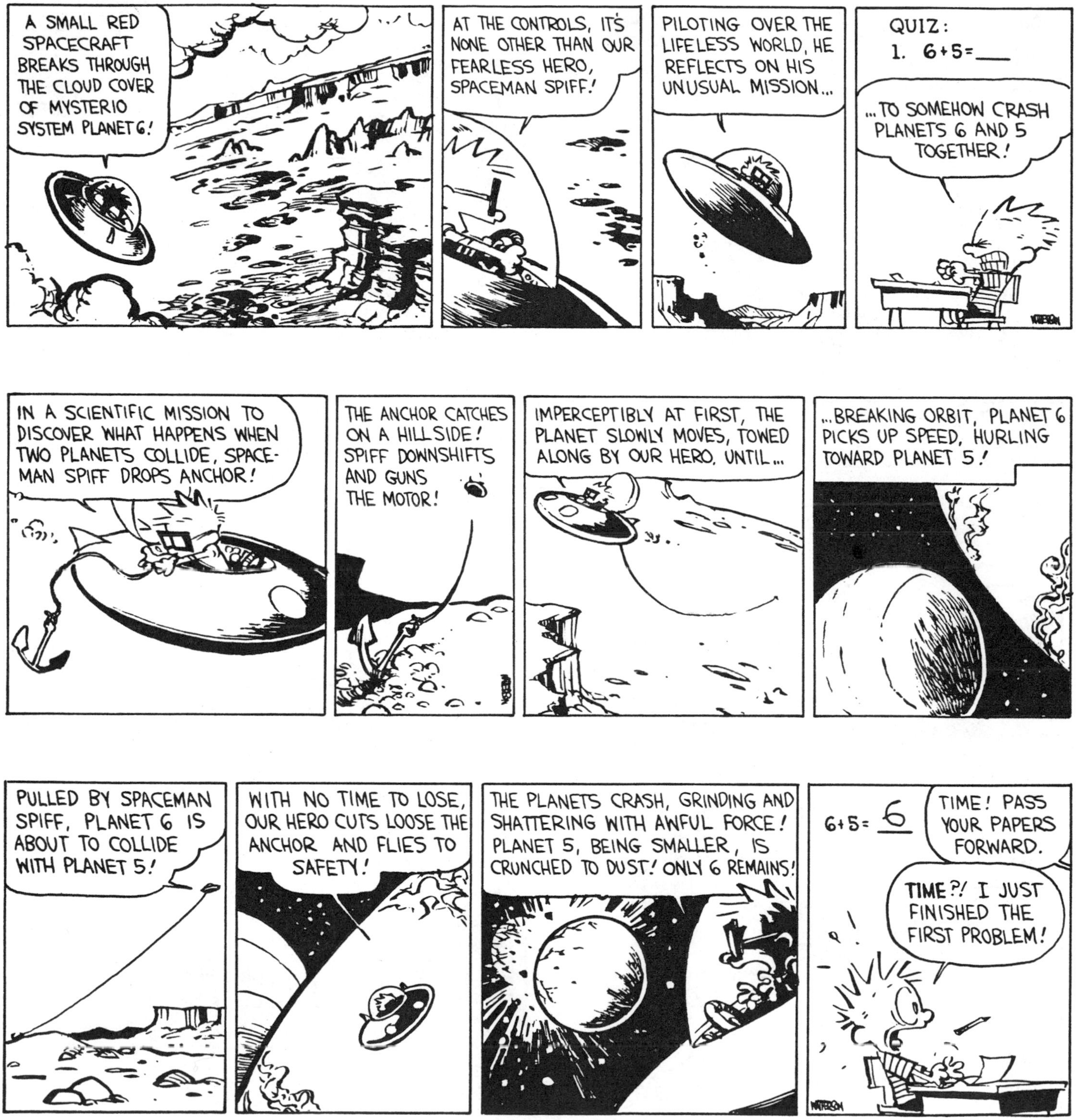
A SMALL RED SPACECRAFT BREAKS THROUGH THE CLOUD COVER OF MYSTERIO SYSTEM PLANET 6!
AT THE CONTROLS, IT'S NONE OTHER THAN OUR FEARLESS HERO, SPACEMAN SPIFF!
PILOTING OVER THE LIFELESS WORLD, HE REFLECTS ON HIS UNUSUAL MISSION...
QUIZ:
1. 6+5=___
...TO SOMEHOW CRASH PLANETS 6 AND 5 TOGETHER!
IN A SCIENTIFIC MISSION TO DISCOVER WHAT HAPPENS WHEN TWO PLANETS COLLIDE, SPACEMAN SPIFF DROPS ANCHOR!
THE ANCHOR CATCHES ON A HILLSIDE! SPIFF DOWNSHIFTS AND GUNS THE MOTOR!
IMPERCEPTIBLY AT FIRST, THE PLANET SLOWLY MOVES, TOWED ALONG BY OUR HERO, UNTIL...
...BREAKING ORBIT, PLANET 6 PICKS UP SPEED, HURLING TOWARD PLANET 5!
PULLED BY SPACEMAN SPIFF, PLANET 6 IS ABOUT TO COLLIDE WITH PLANET 5!
WITH NO TIME TO LOSE, OUR HERO CUTS LOOSE THE ANCHOR AND FLIES TO SAFETY!
THE PLANETS CRASH, GRINDING AND SHATTERING WITH AWFUL FORCE! PLANET 5, BEING SMALLER, IS CRUNCHED TO DUST! ONLY 6 REMAINS!
6+5= 6
TIME! PASS YOUR PAPERS FORWARD.
TIME?! I JUST FINISHED THE FIRST PROBLEM!

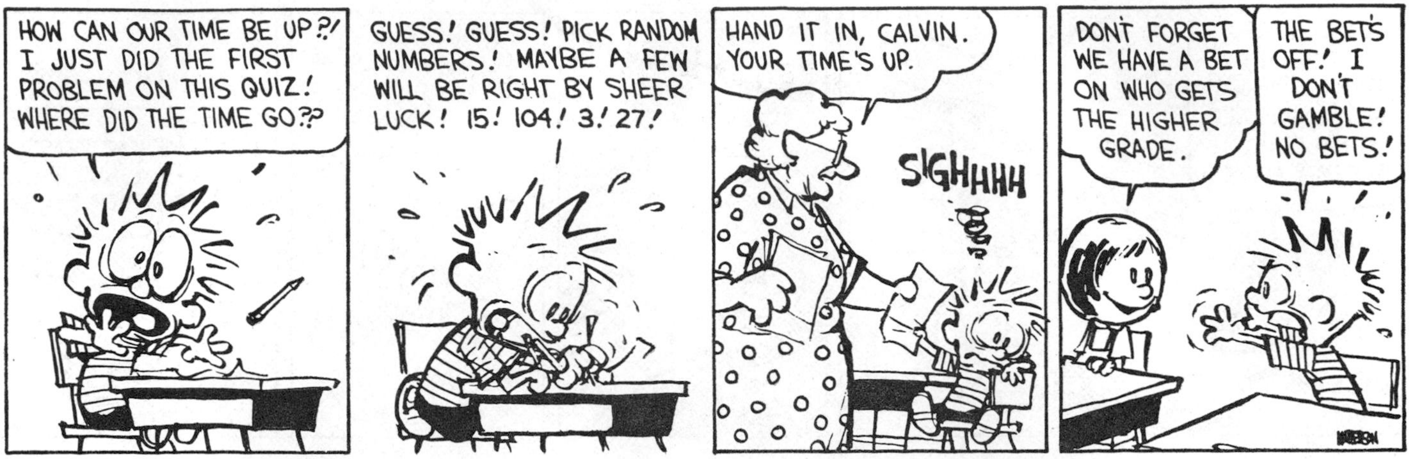
HOW CAN OUR TIME BE UP?! I JUST DID THE FIRST PROBLEM ON THIS QUIZ! WHERE DID THE TIME GO??
GUESS! GUESS! PICK RANDOM NUMBERS! MAYBE A FEW WILL BE RIGHT BY SHEER LUCK! 15! 104! 3! 27!
HAND IT IN, CALVIN. YOUR TIME'S UP.
SIGHHHH
DON'T FORGET WE HAVE A BET ON WHO GETS THE HIGHER GRADE.
THE BET'S OFF! I DON'T GAMBLE! NO BETS!

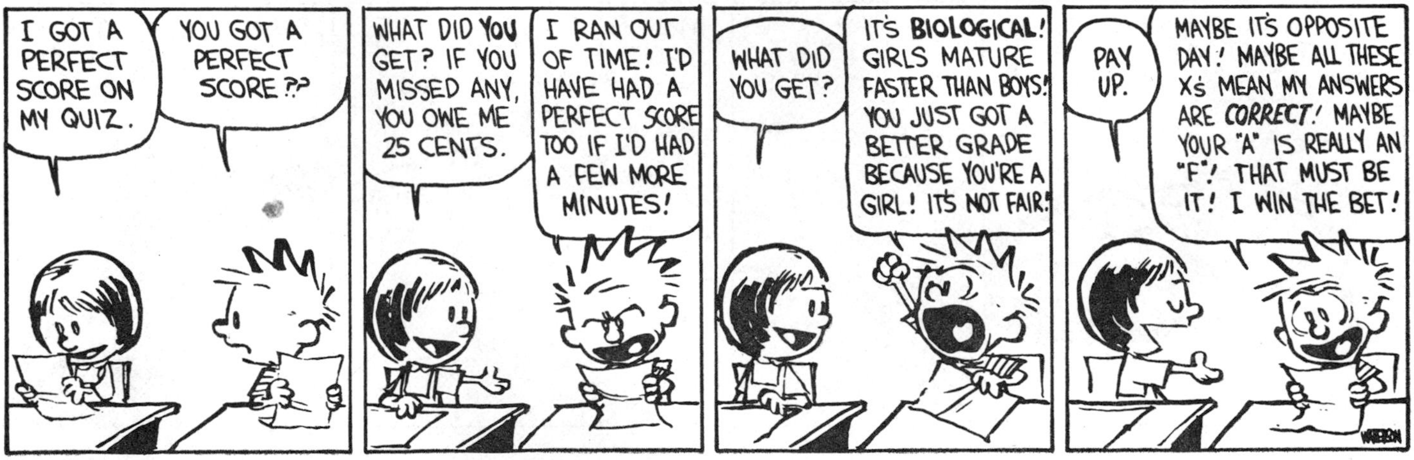
I GOT A PERFECT SCORE ON MY QUIZ.
YOU GOT A PERFECT SCORE??
WHAT DID YOU GET? IF YOU MISSED ANY, YOU OWE ME 25 CENTS.
I RAN OUT OF TIME! I'D HAVE HAD A PERFECT SCORE TOO IF I'D HAD A FEW MORE MINUTES!
WHAT DID YOU GET?
IT'S BIOLOGICAL! GIRLS MATURE FASTER THAN BOYS! YOU JUST GOT A BETTER GRADE BECAUSE YOU'RE A GIRL! IT'S NOT FAIR!
PAY UP.
MAYBE IT'S OPPOSITE DAY! MAYBE ALL THESE X's MEAN MY ANSWERS ARE CORRECT! MAYBE YOUR "A" IS REALLY AN "F"! THAT MUST BE IT! I WIN THE BET!

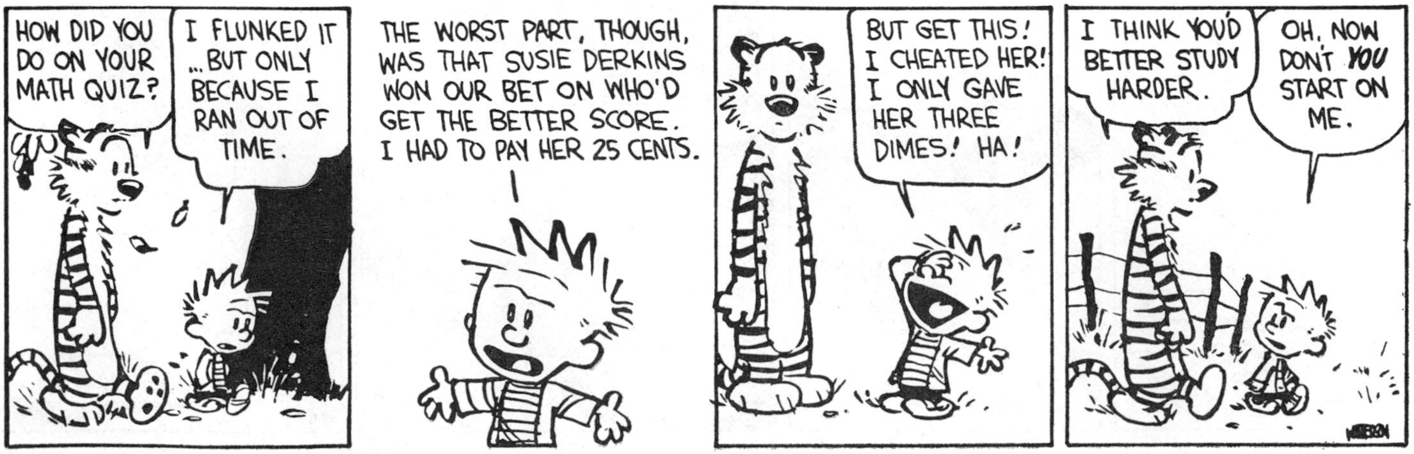
HOW DID YOU DO ON YOUR MATH QUIZ?
I FLUNKED IT ...BUT ONLY BECAUSE I RAN OUT OF TIME.
THE WORST PART, THOUGH, WAS THAT SUSIE DERKINS WON OUR BET ON WHO'D GET THE BETTER SCORE. I HAD TO PAY HER 25 CENTS.
BUT GET THIS! I CHEATED HER! I ONLY GAVE HER THREE DIMES! HA!
I THINK YOU'D BETTER STUDY HARDER.
OH, NOW DON'T YOU START ON ME.

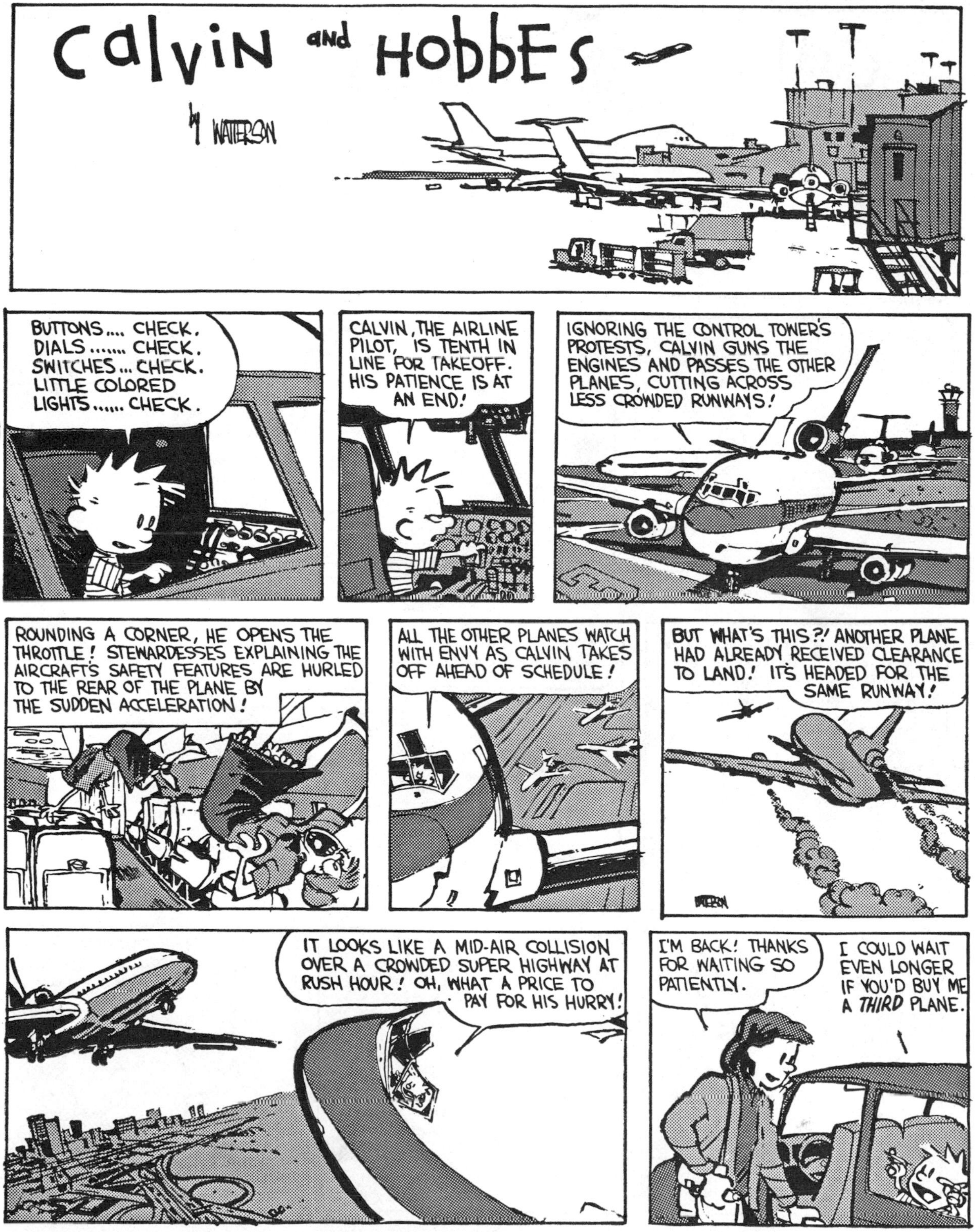
Calvin and HOBBES
by WATTERSON
BUTTONS.... CHECK. DIALS....... CHECK. SWITCHES... CHECK. LITTLE COLORED LIGHTS...... CHECK.
CALVIN, THE AIRLINE PILOT, IS TENTH IN LINE FOR TAKEOFF. HIS PATIENCE IS AT AN END!
IGNORING THE CONTROL TOWER'S PROTESTS, CALVIN GUNS THE ENGINES AND PASSES THE OTHER PLANES, CUTTING ACROSS LESS CROWDED RUNWAYS!
ROUNDING A CORNER, HE OPENS THE THROTTLE! STEWARDESSES EXPLAINING THE AIRCRAFT'S SAFETY FEATURES ARE HURLED TO THE REAR OF THE PLANE BY THE SUDDEN ACCELERATION!
ALL THE OTHER PLANES WATCH WITH ENVY AS CALVIN TAKES OFF AHEAD OF SCHEDULE!
BUT WHAT'S THIS?! ANOTHER PLANE HAD ALREADY RECEIVED CLEARANCE TO LAND! IT'S HEADED FOR THE SAME RUNWAY!
WATTERSON
IT LOOKS LIKE A MID-AIR COLLISION OVER A CROWDED SUPER HIGHWAY AT RUSH HOUR! OH, WHAT A PRICE TO PAY FOR HIS HURRY!
I'M BACK! THANKS FOR WAITING SO PATIENTLY.
I COULD WAIT EVEN LONGER IF YOU'D BUY ME A THIRD PLANE.

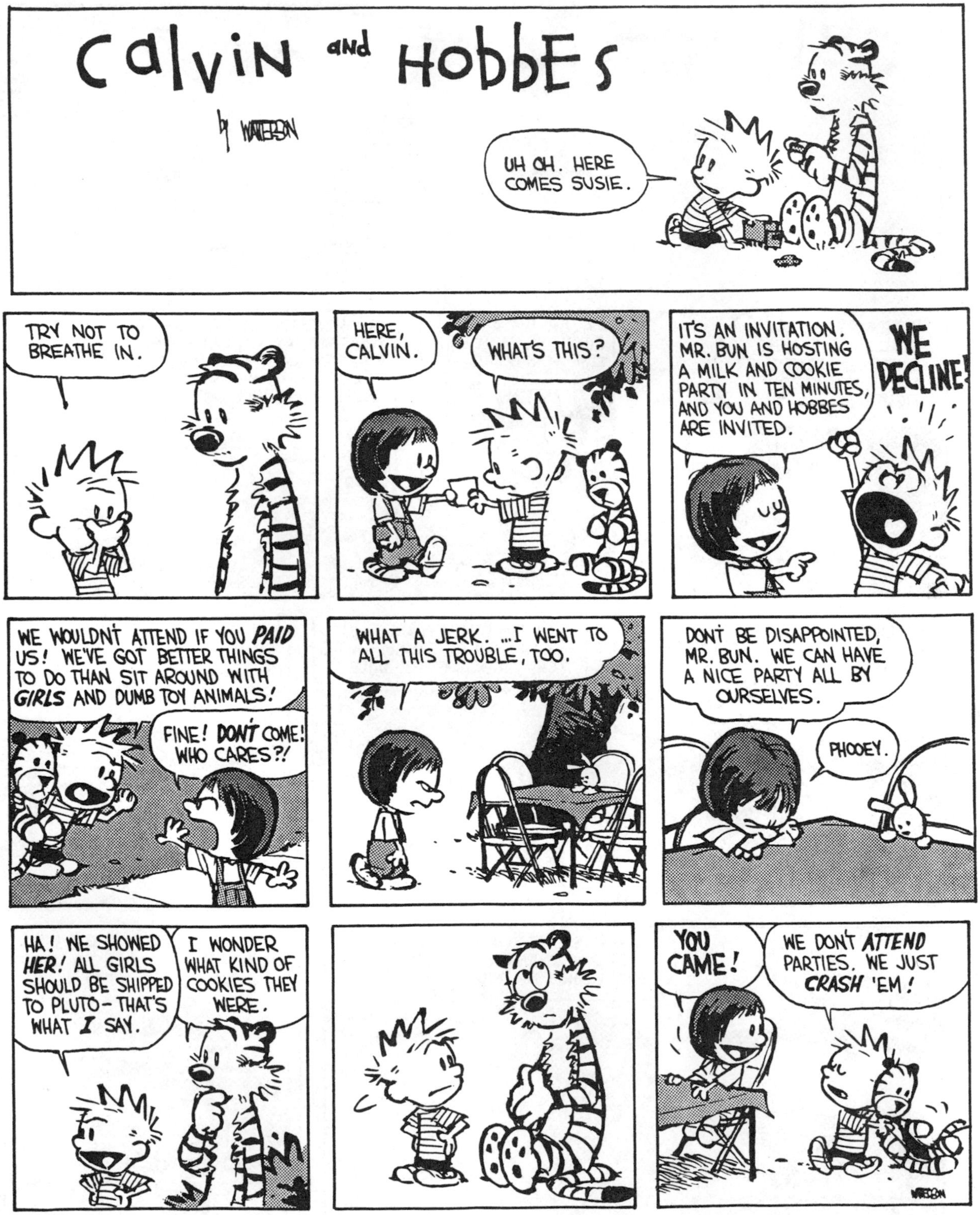
Calvin and HOBBES
by WATTERSON
UH OH. HERE COMES SUSIE.
TRY NOT TO BREATHE IN.
HERE, CALVIN.
WHAT'S THIS?
IT'S AN INVITATION. MR. BUN IS HOSTING A MILK AND COOKIE PARTY IN TEN MINUTES, AND YOU AND HOBBES ARE INVITED.
WE DECLINE!
WE WOULDN'T ATTEND IF YOU PAID US! WE'VE GOT BETTER THINGS TO DO THAN SIT AROUND WITH GIRLS AND DUMB TOY ANIMALS!
FINE! DON'T COME! WHO CARES?!
WHAT A JERK. ...I WENT TO ALL THIS TROUBLE, TOO.
DON'T BE DISAPPOINTED, MR. BUN. WE CAN HAVE A NICE PARTY ALL BY OURSELVES.
PHOOEY.
HA! WE SHOWED HER! ALL GIRLS SHOULD BE SHIPPED TO PLUTO - THAT'S WHAT I SAY.
I WONDER WHAT KIND OF COOKIES THEY WERE.
YOU CAME!
WE DON'T ATTEND PARTIES. WE JUST CRASH 'EM!
WATTERSON

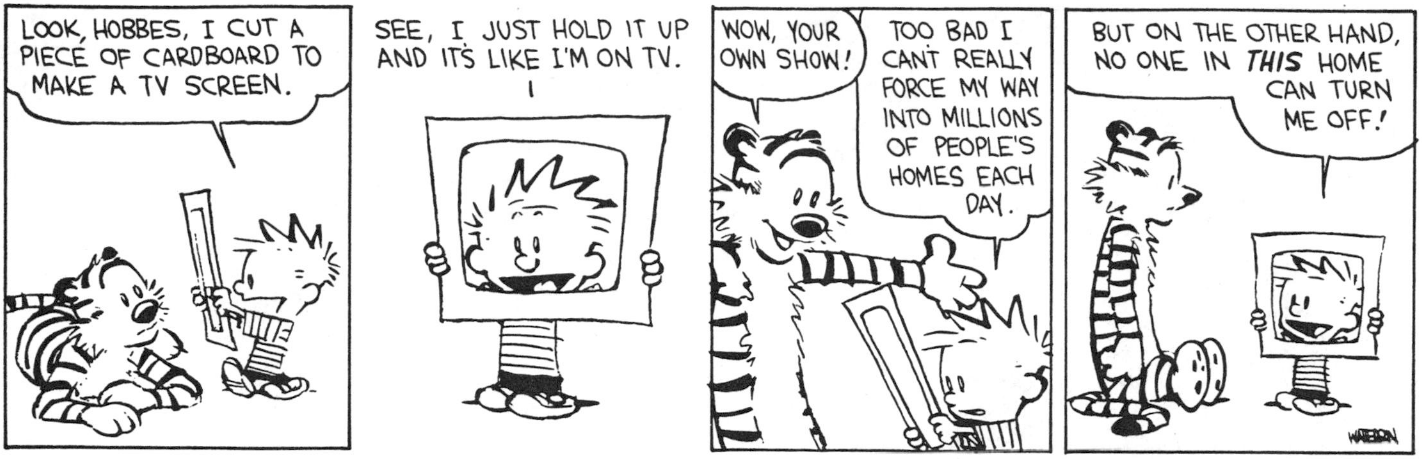
LOOK, HOBBES, I CUT A PIECE OF CARDBOARD TO MAKE A TV SCREEN.
SEE, I JUST HOLD IT UP AND IT'S LIKE I'M ON TV.
WOW, YOUR OWN SHOW!
TOO BAD I CAN'T REALLY FORCE MY WAY INTO MILLIONS OF PEOPLE'S HOMES EACH DAY.
BUT ON THE OTHER HAND, NO ONE IN THIS HOME CAN TURN ME OFF!

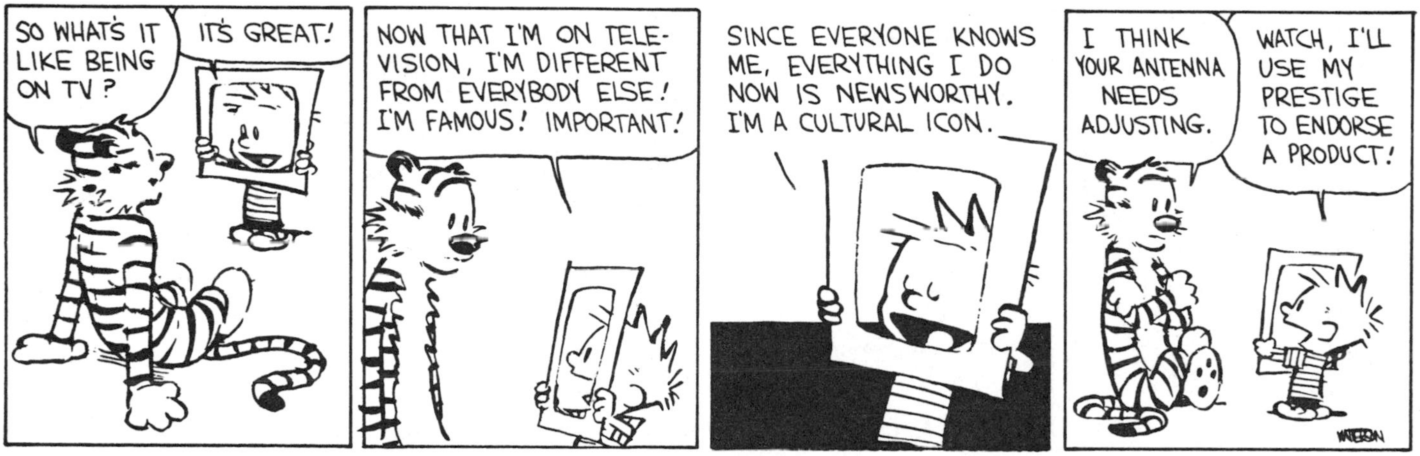
SO WHAT'S IT LIKE BEING ON TV?
IT'S GREAT!
NOW THAT I'M ON TELE-VISION, I'M DIFFERENT FROM EVERYBODY ELSE! I'M FAMOUS! IMPORTANT!
SINCE EVERYONE KNOWS ME, EVERYTHING I DO NOW IS NEWSWORTHY. I'M A CULTURAL ICON.
I THINK YOUR ANTENNA NEEDS ADJUSTING.
WATCH, I'LL USE MY PRESTIGE TO ENDORSE A PRODUCT!

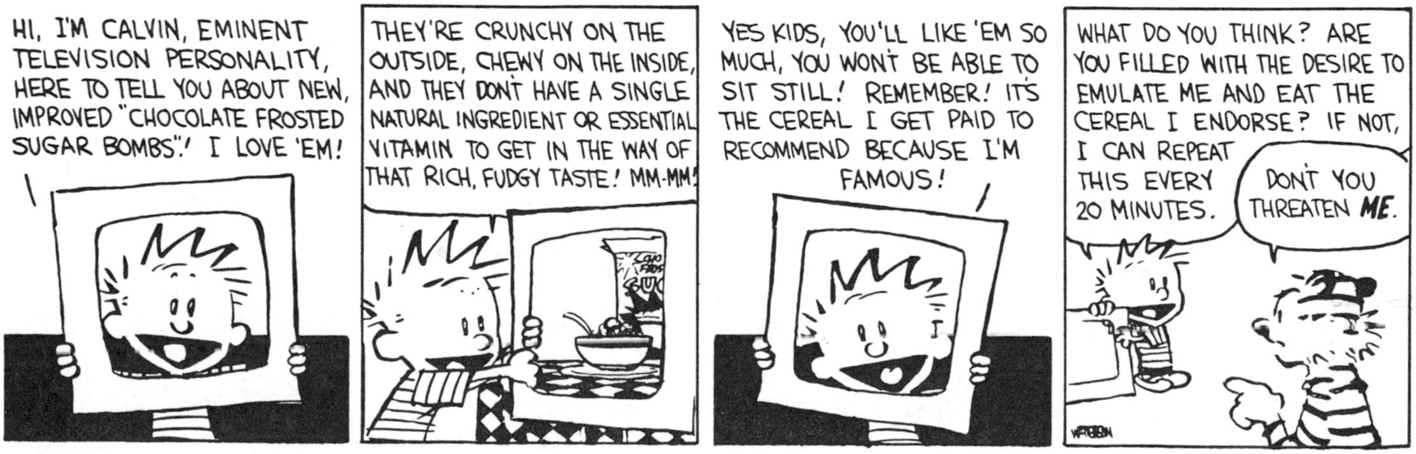
HI, I'M CALVIN, EMINENT TELEVISION PERSONALITY, HERE TO TELL YOU ABOUT NEW, IMPROVED "CHOCOLATE FROSTED SUGAR BOMBS"! I LOVE 'EM!
THEY'RE CRUNCHY ON THE OUTSIDE, CHEWY ON THE INSIDE, AND THEY DON'T HAVE A SINGLE NATURAL INGREDIENT OR ESSENTIAL VITAMIN TO GET IN THE WAY OF THAT RICH, FUDGY TASTE! MM-MM!
YES KIDS, YOU'LL LIKE 'EM SO MUCH, YOU WON'T BE ABLE TO SIT STILL! REMEMBER! IT'S THE CEREAL I GET PAID TO RECOMMEND BECAUSE I'M FAMOUS!
WHAT DO YOU THINK? ARE YOU FILLED WITH THE DESIRE TO EMULATE ME AND EAT THE CEREAL I ENDORSE? IF NOT, I CAN REPEAT THIS EVERY 20 MINUTES.
DON'T YOU THREATEN ME.

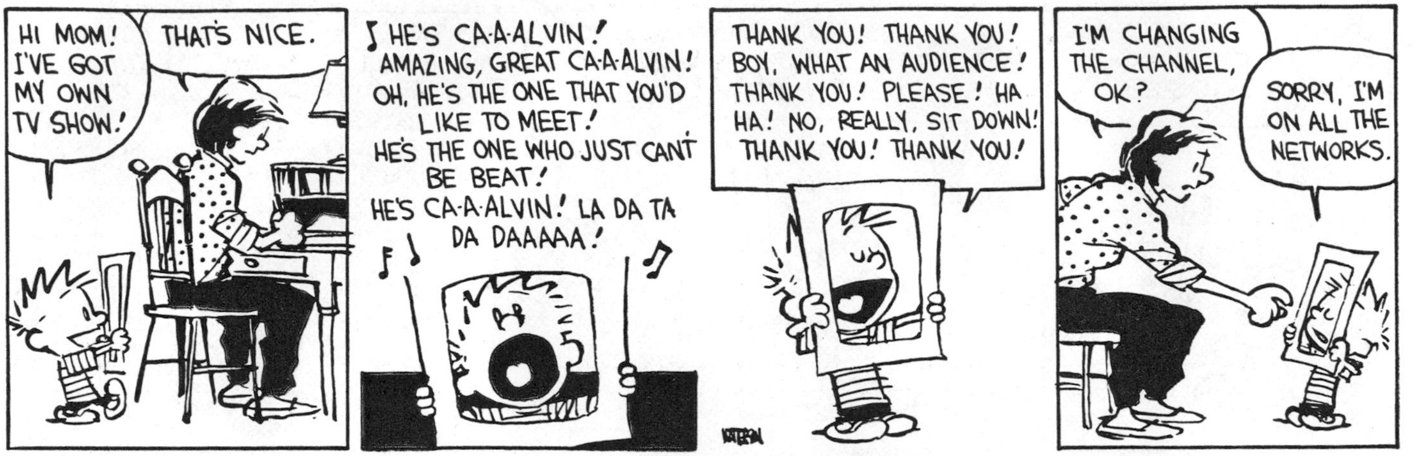
HI MOM! I'VE GOT MY OWN TV SHOW!
THAT'S NICE.
HE'S CA-A-ALVIN! AMAZING, GREAT CA-A-ALVIN! OH, HE'S THE ONE THAT YOU'D LIKE TO MEET! HE'S THE ONE WHO JUST CAN'T BE BEAT! HE'S CA-A-ALVIN! LA DA TA DA DAAAAA!
THANK YOU! THANK YOU! BOY, WHAT AN AUDIENCE! THANK YOU! PLEASE! HA HA! NO, REALLY, SIT DOWN! THANK YOU! THANK YOU!
I'M CHANGING THE CHANNEL, OK?
SORRY, I'M ON ALL THE NETWORKS.

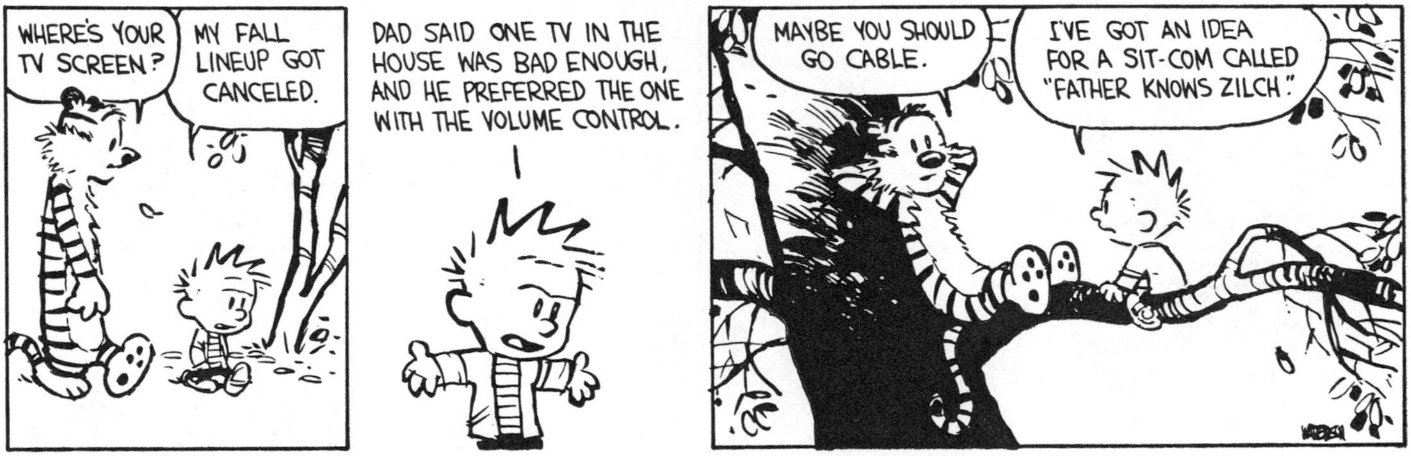
WHERE'S YOUR TV SCREEN?
MY FALL LINEUP GOT CANCELED.
DAD SAID ONE TV IN THE HOUSE WAS BAD ENOUGH, AND HE PREFERRED THE ONE WITH THE VOLUME CONTROL.
MAYBE YOU SHOULD GO CABLE.
I'VE GOT AN IDEA FOR A SIT-COM CALLED "FATHER KNOWS ZILCH."

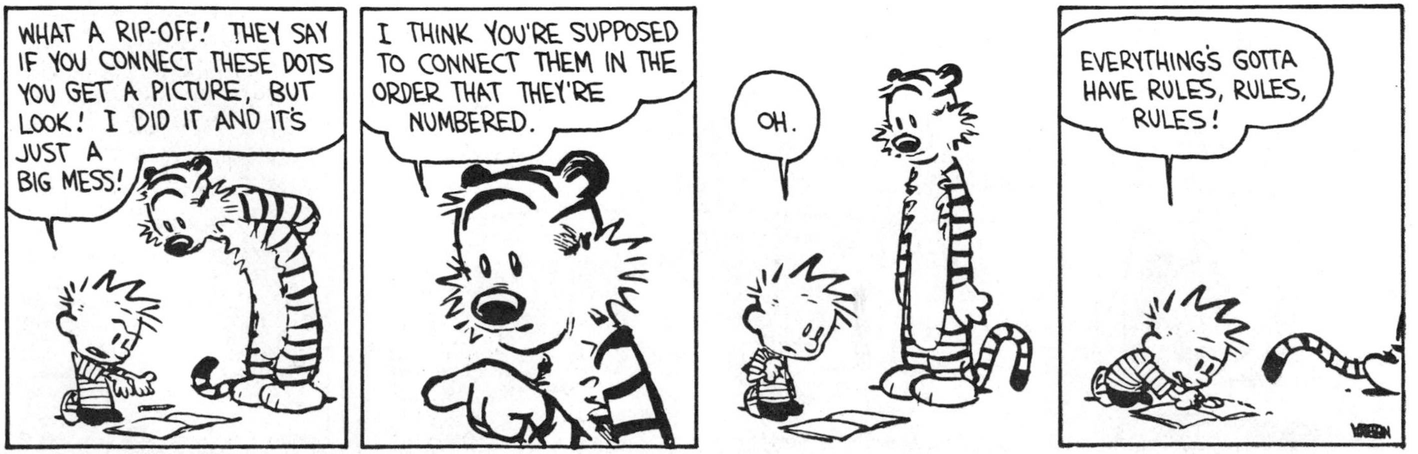
WHAT A RIP-OFF! THEY SAY IF YOU CONNECT THESE DOTS YOU GET A PICTURE, BUT LOOK! I DID IT AND IT'S JUST A BIG MESS!
I THINK YOU'RE SUPPOSED TO CONNECT THEM IN THE ORDER THAT THEY'RE NUMBERED.
OH.
EVERYTHING'S GOTTA HAVE RULES, RULES, RULES!

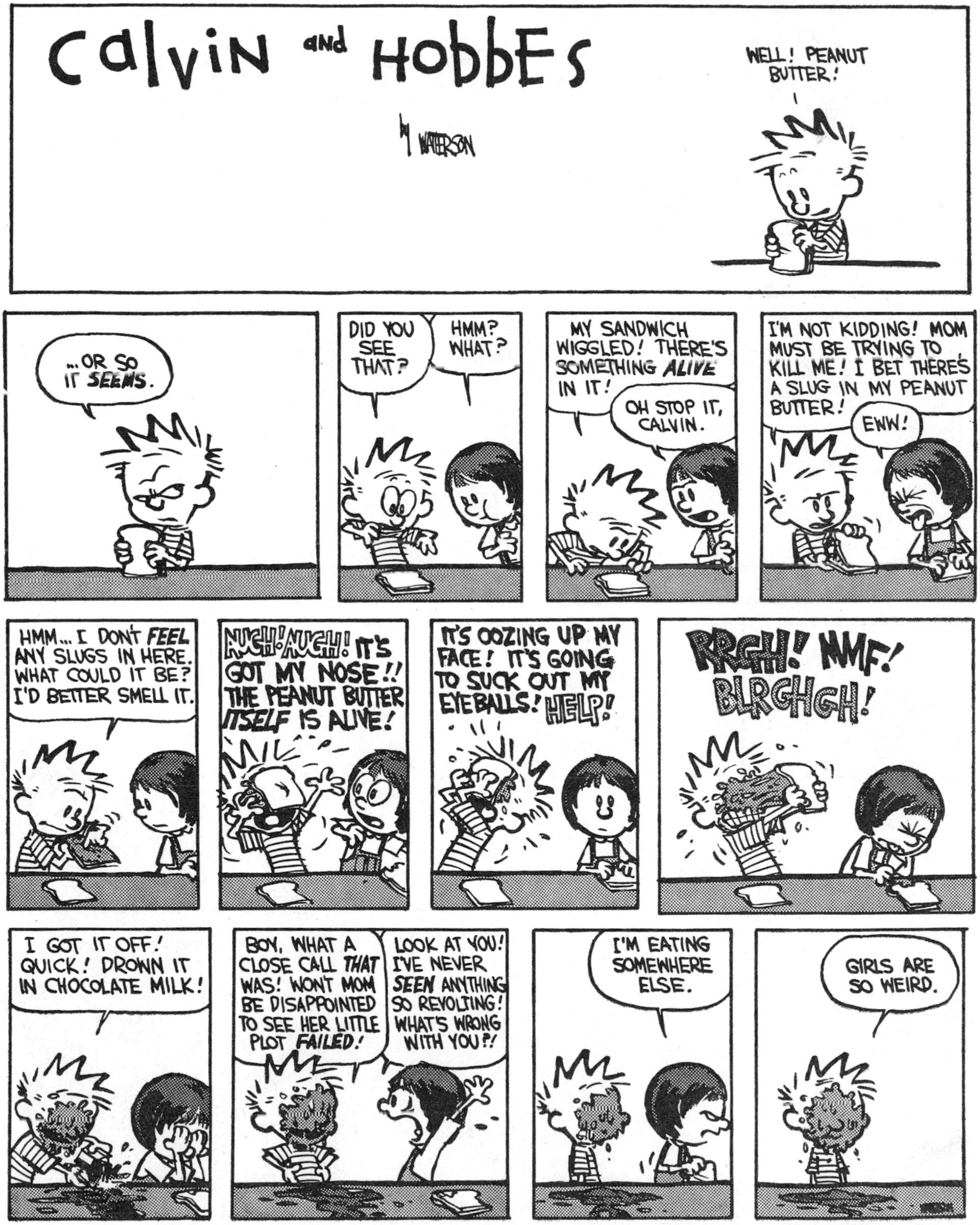
Calvin and HOBBES
by WATTERSON
WELL! PEANUT BUTTER!
...OR SO IT SEEMS.
DID YOU SEE THAT?
HMM? WHAT?
MY SANDWICH WIGGLED! THERE'S SOMETHING ALIVE IN IT!
OH STOP IT, CALVIN.
I'M NOT KIDDING! MOM MUST BE TRYING TO KILL ME! I BET THERE'S A SLUG IN MY PEANUT BUTTER!
EWW!
HMM... I DON'T FEEL ANY SLUGS IN HERE. WHAT COULD IT BE? I'D BETTER SMELL IT.
AUGH! AUGH! IT'S GOT MY NOSE!! THE PEANUT BUTTER ITSELF IS ALIVE!
IT'S OOZING UP MY FACE! IT'S GOING TO SUCK OUT MY EYEBALLS! HELP!
RRGH! MMF! BLRGHGH!
I GOT IT OFF! QUICK! DROWN IT IN CHOCOLATE MILK!
BOY, WHAT A CLOSE CALL THAT WAS! WON'T MOM BE DISAPPOINTED TO SEE HER LITTLE PLOT FAILED!
LOOK AT YOU! I'VE NEVER SEEN ANYTHING SO REVOLTING! WHAT'S WRONG WITH YOU?!
I'M EATING SOMEWHERE ELSE.
GIRLS ARE SO WEIRD.

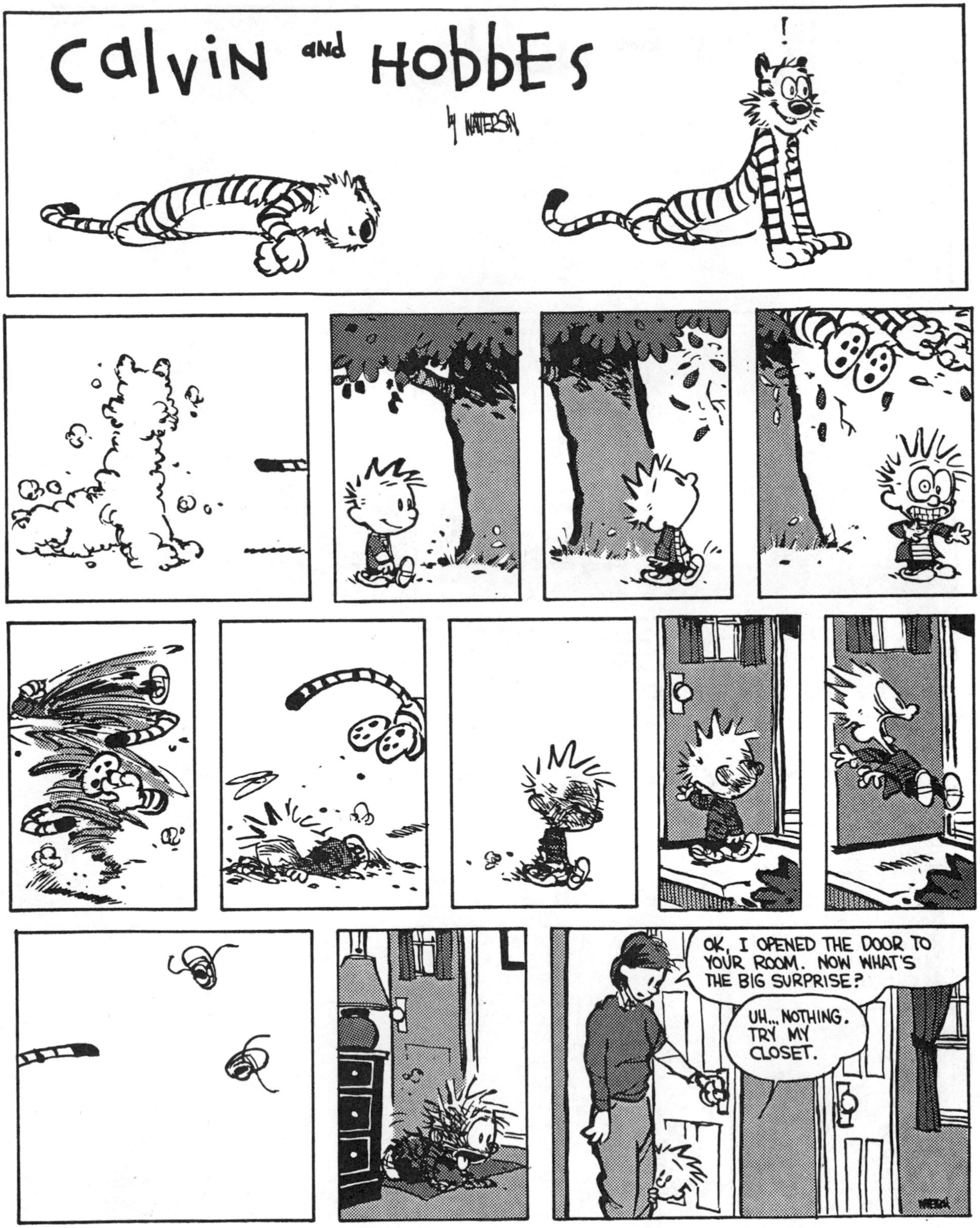
Calvin and HOBBES
by WATERSON
!
OK, I OPENED THE DOOR TO YOUR ROOM. NOW WHAT'S THE BIG SURPRISE?
UH... NOTHING. TRY MY CLOSET.

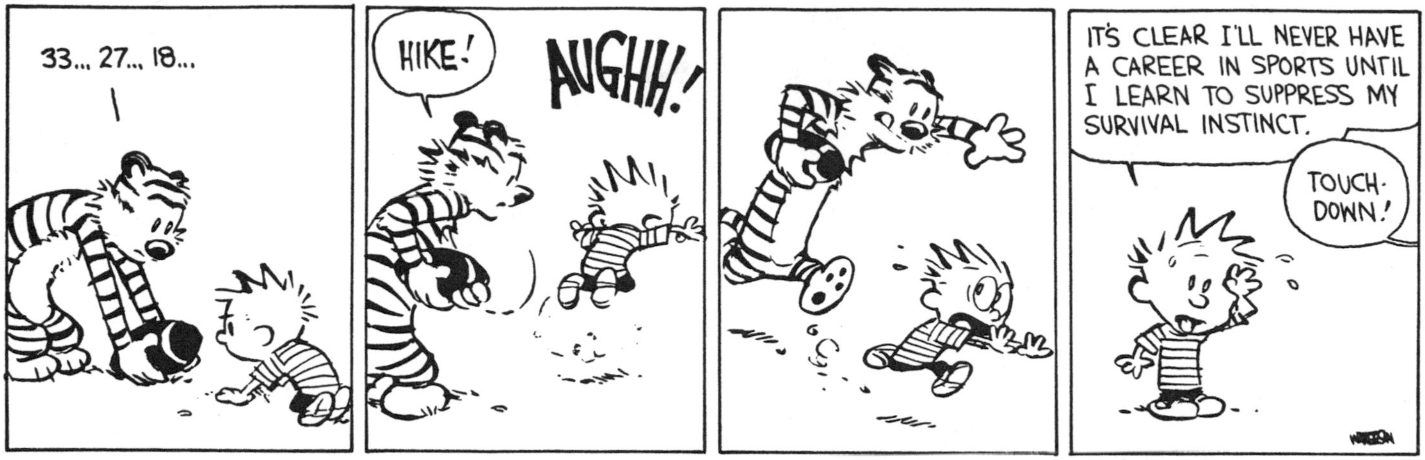
33... 27... 18...
HIKE!
AUGHH!
IT'S CLEAR I'LL NEVER HAVE A CAREER IN SPORTS UNTIL I LEARN TO SUPPRESS MY SURVIVAL INSTINCT.
TOUCH-DOWN!

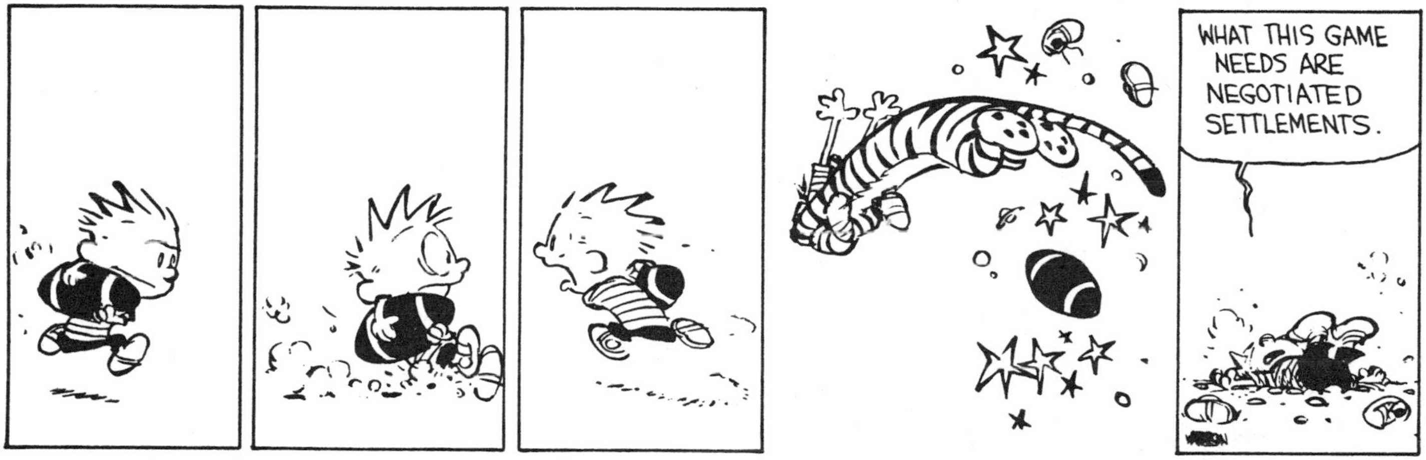
WHAT THIS GAME NEEDS ARE NEGOTIATED SETTLEMENTS.

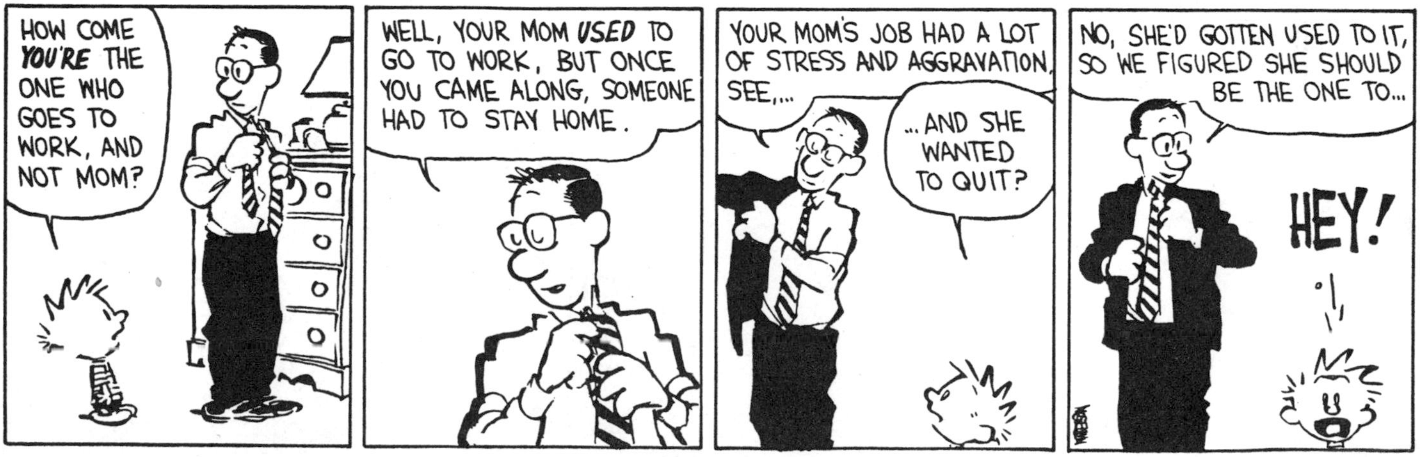
HOW COME *YOU'RE* THE ONE WHO GOES TO WORK, AND NOT MOM?
WELL, YOUR MOM *USED* TO GO TO WORK, BUT ONCE YOU CAME ALONG, SOMEONE HAD TO STAY HOME.
YOUR MOM'S JOB HAD A LOT OF STRESS AND AGGRAVATION, SEE,...
...AND SHE WANTED TO QUIT?
NO, SHE'D GOTTEN USED TO IT, SO WE FIGURED SHE SHOULD BE THE ONE TO...
HEY!

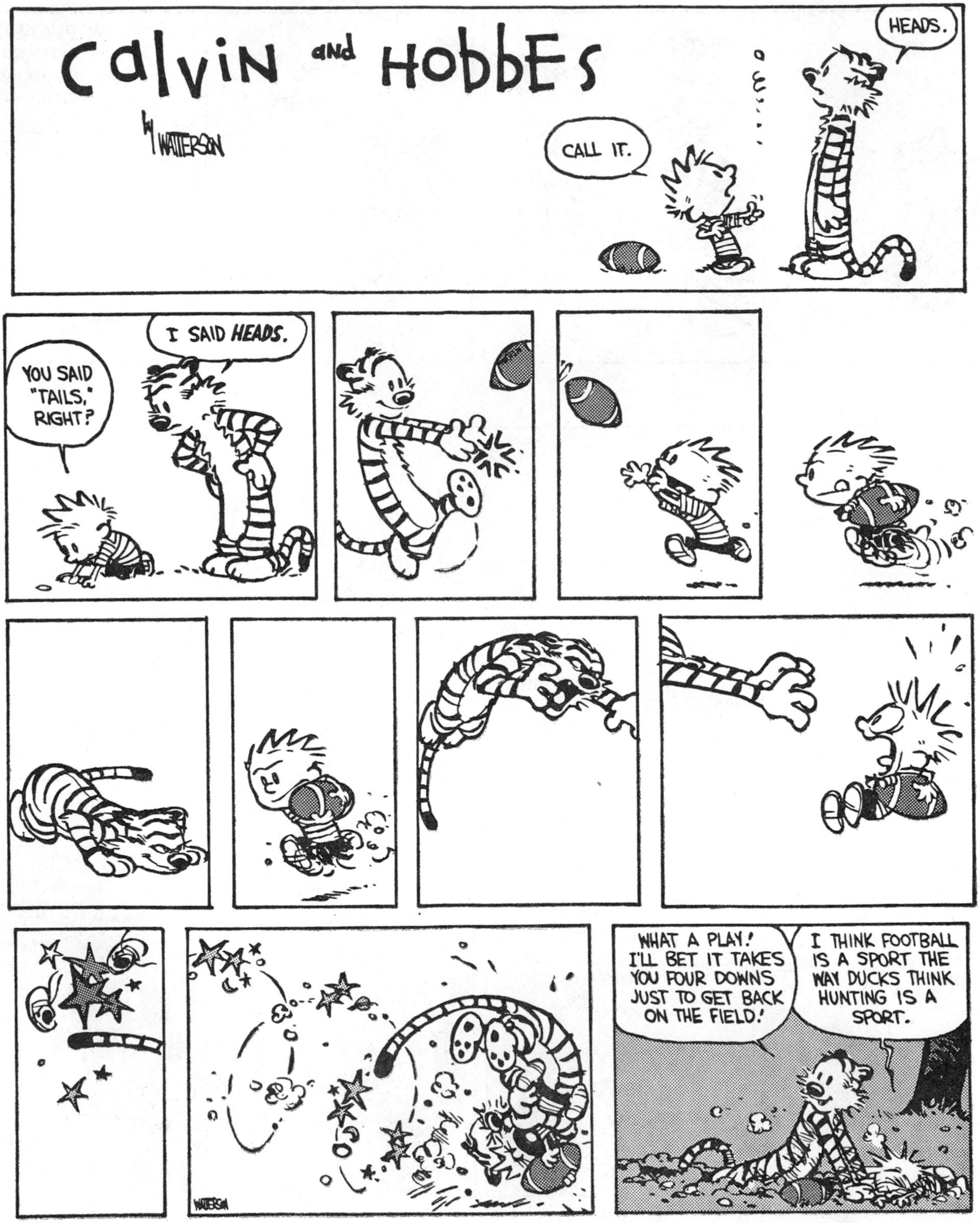
Calvin and Hobbes
by Watterson
CALL IT.
HEADS.
YOU SAID "TAILS," RIGHT?
I SAID HEADS.
WHAT A PLAY! I'LL BET IT TAKES YOU FOUR DOWNS JUST TO GET BACK ON THE FIELD!
I THINK FOOTBALL IS A SPORT THE WAY DUCKS THINK HUNTING IS A SPORT.
WATTERSON

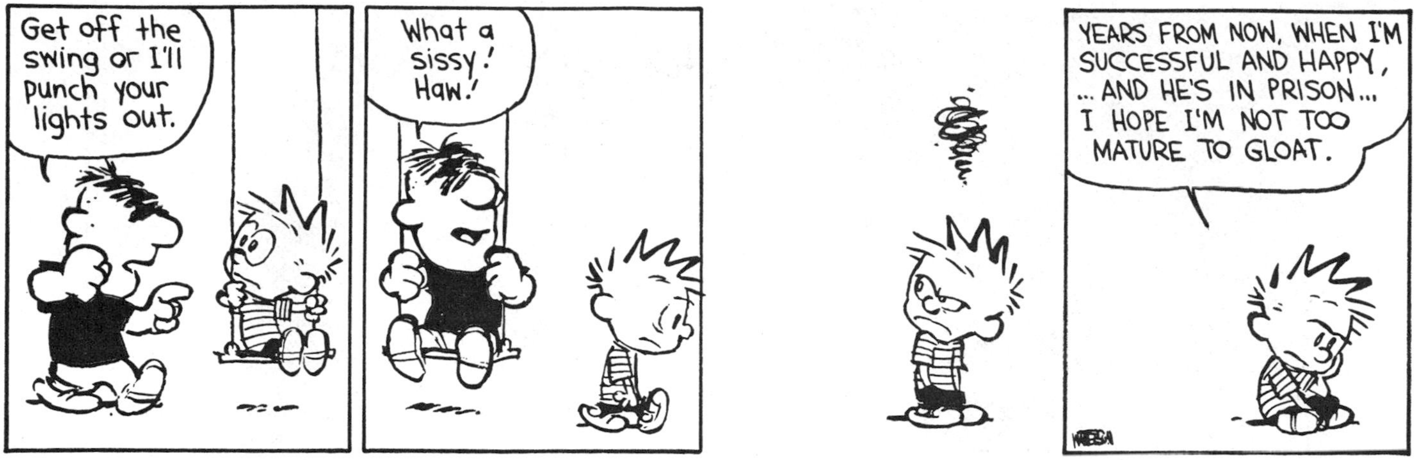
Get off the swing or I'll punch your lights out.
What a sissy! Haw!
YEARS FROM NOW, WHEN I'M SUCCESSFUL AND HAPPY, ... AND HE'S IN PRISON... I HOPE I'M NOT TOO MATURE TO GLOAT.

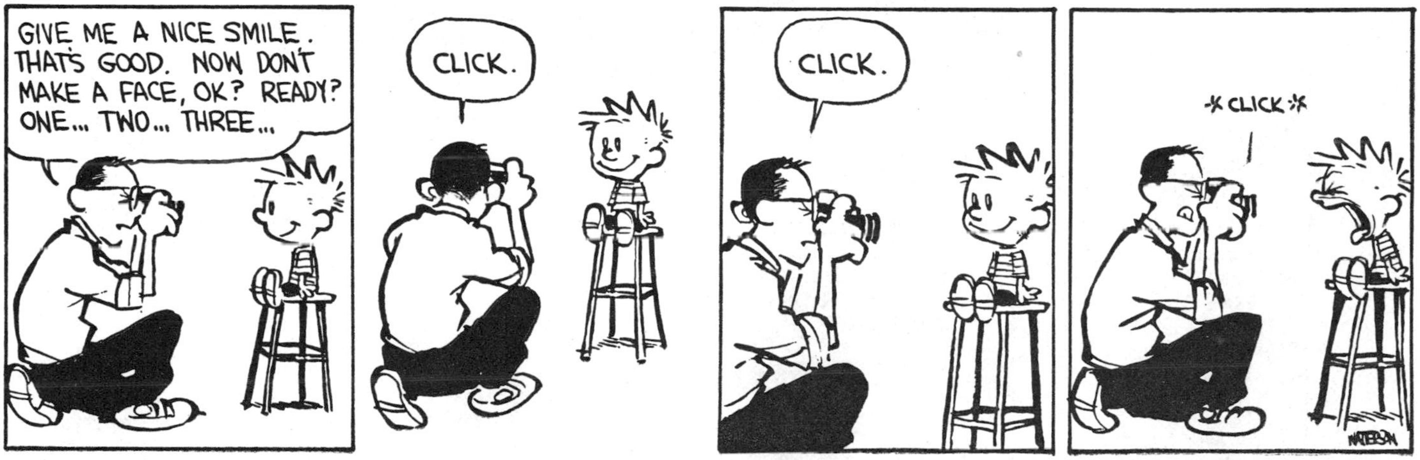
GIVE ME A NICE SMILE. THAT'S GOOD. NOW DON'T MAKE A FACE, OK? READY? ONE... TWO... THREE...
CLICK.
CLICK.
CLICK

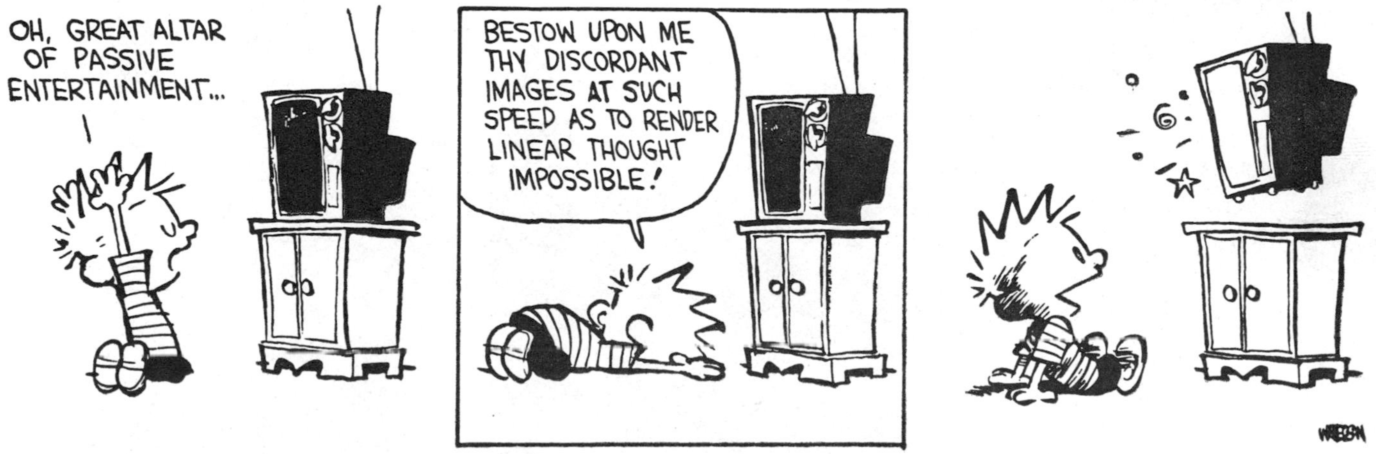
OH, GREAT ALTAR OF PASSIVE ENTERTAINMENT...
BESTOW UPON ME THY DISCORDANT IMAGES AT SUCH SPEED AS TO RENDER LINEAR THOUGHT IMPOSSIBLE!

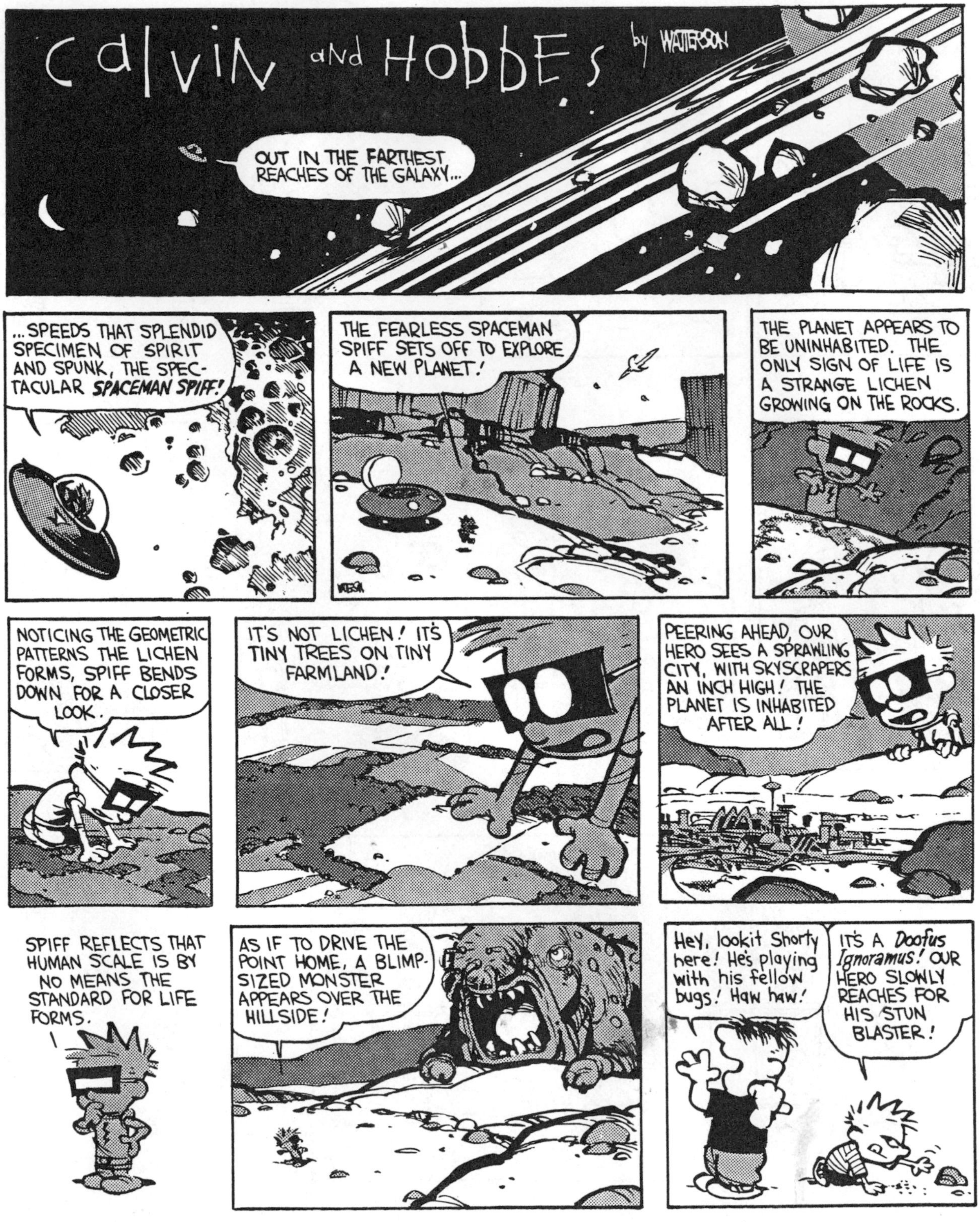
Calvin and HOBBES by WATTERSON
OUT IN THE FARTHEST REACHES OF THE GALAXY...
...SPEEDS THAT SPLENDID SPECIMEN OF SPIRIT AND SPUNK, THE SPECTACULAR SPACEMAN SPIFF!
THE FEARLESS SPACEMAN SPIFF SETS OFF TO EXPLORE A NEW PLANET!
THE PLANET APPEARS TO BE UNINHABITED. THE ONLY SIGN OF LIFE IS A STRANGE LICHEN GROWING ON THE ROCKS.
NOTICING THE GEOMETRIC PATTERNS THE LICHEN FORMS, SPIFF BENDS DOWN FOR A CLOSER LOOK.
IT'S NOT LICHEN! IT'S TINY TREES ON TINY FARMLAND!
PEERING AHEAD, OUR HERO SEES A SPRAWLING CITY, WITH SKYSCRAPERS AN INCH HIGH! THE PLANET IS INHABITED AFTER ALL!
SPIFF REFLECTS THAT HUMAN SCALE IS BY NO MEANS THE STANDARD FOR LIFE FORMS.
AS IF TO DRIVE THE POINT HOME, A BLIMP-SIZED MONSTER APPEARS OVER THE HILLSIDE!
Hey, lookit Shorty here! He's playing with his fellow bugs! Haw haw!
IT'S A *Doofus Ignoramus!* OUR HERO SLOWLY REACHES FOR HIS STUN BLASTER!

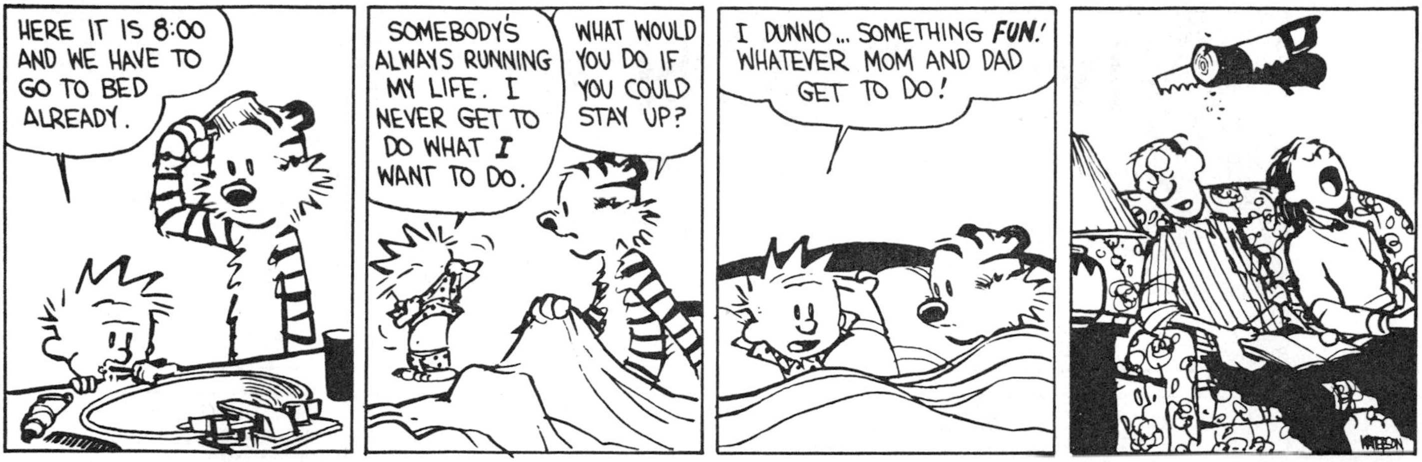
HERE IT IS 8:00 AND WE HAVE TO GO TO BED ALREADY.
SOMEBODY'S ALWAYS RUNNING MY LIFE. I NEVER GET TO DO WHAT I WANT TO DO.
WHAT WOULD YOU DO IF YOU COULD STAY UP?
I DUNNO... SOMETHING FUN! WHATEVER MOM AND DAD GET TO DO!

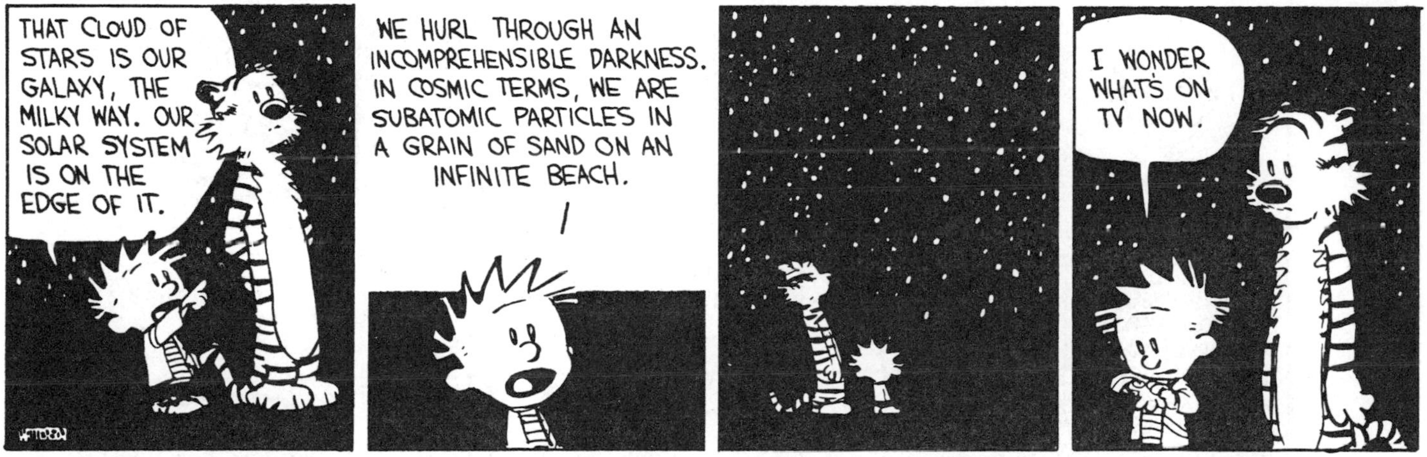
THAT CLOUD OF STARS IS OUR GALAXY, THE MILKY WAY. OUR SOLAR SYSTEM IS ON THE EDGE OF IT.
WE HURL THROUGH AN INCOMPREHENSIBLE DARKNESS. IN COSMIC TERMS, WE ARE SUBATOMIC PARTICLES IN A GRAIN OF SAND ON AN INFINITE BEACH.
I WONDER WHAT'S ON TV NOW.

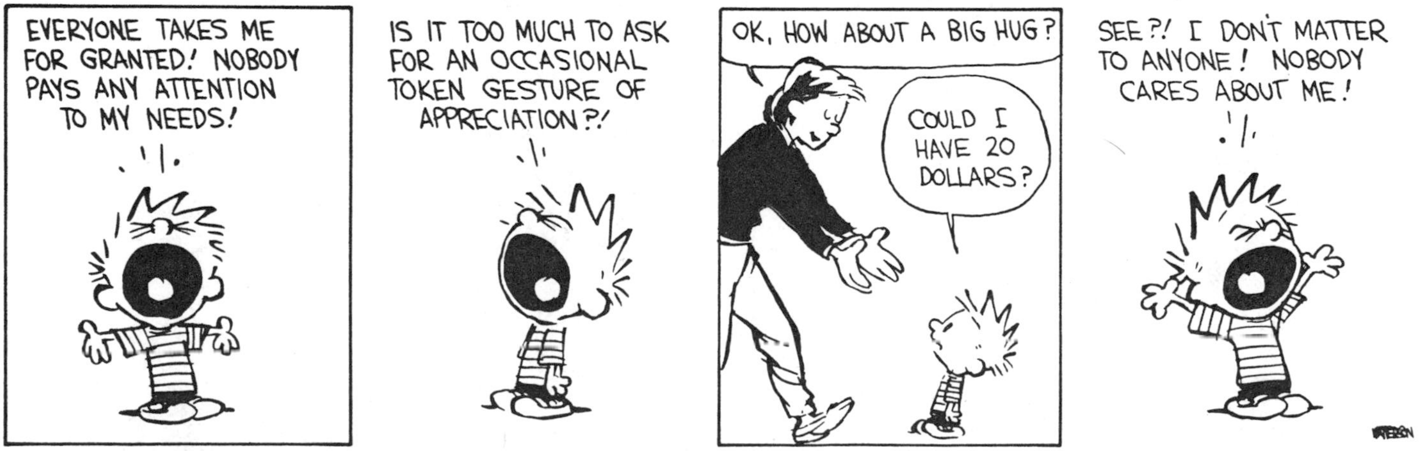
EVERYONE TAKES ME FOR GRANTED! NOBODY PAYS ANY ATTENTION TO MY NEEDS!
IS IT TOO MUCH TO ASK FOR AN OCCASIONAL TOKEN GESTURE OF APPRECIATION?!
OK, HOW ABOUT A BIG HUG?
COULD I HAVE 20 DOLLARS?
SEE?! I DON'T MATTER TO ANYONE! NOBODY CARES ABOUT ME!

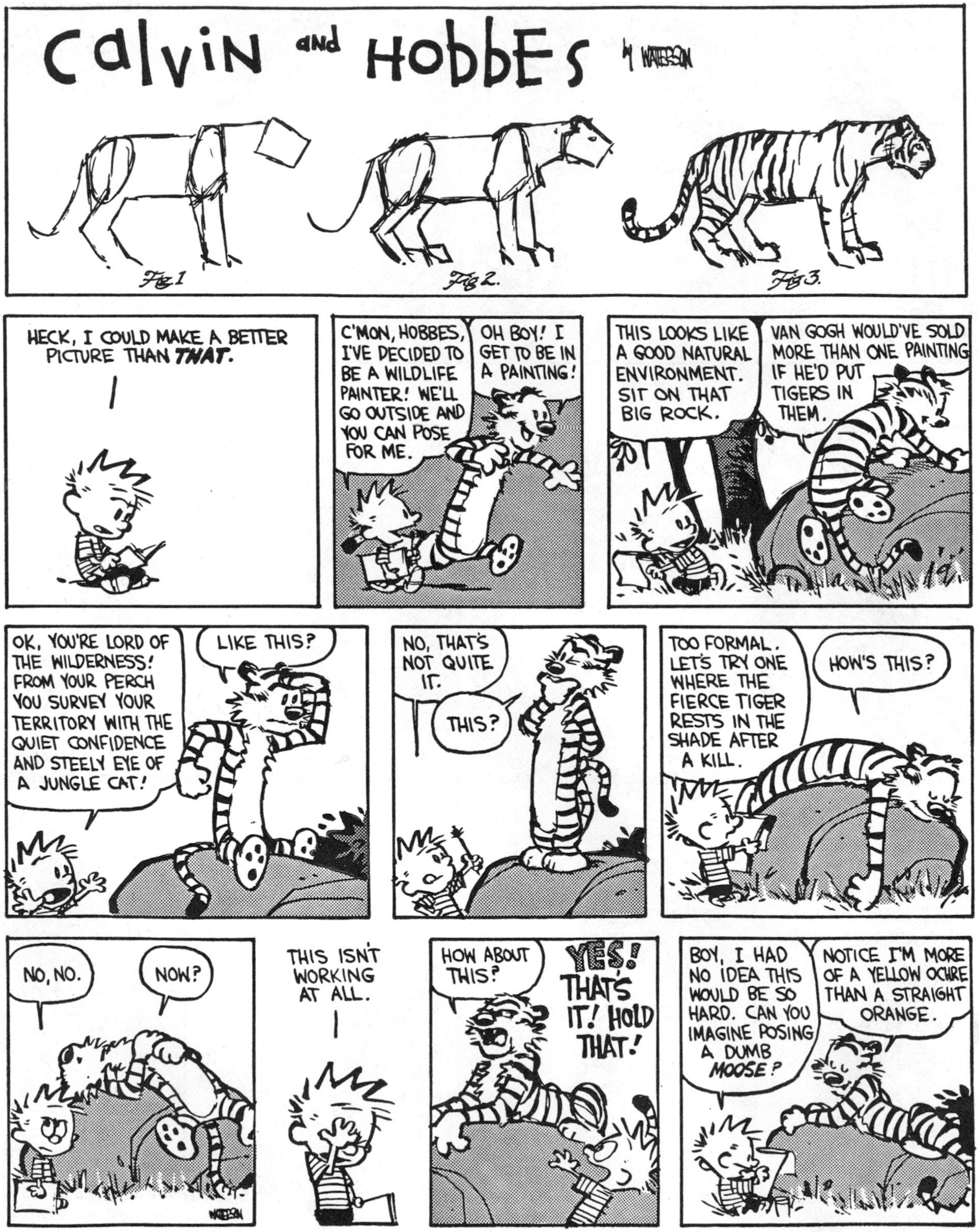
Calvin and HOBBES
by WATERSON
Fig 1
Fig 2.
Fig 3.
HECK, I COULD MAKE A BETTER PICTURE THAN THAT.
C'MON, HOBBES, I'VE DECIDED TO BE A WILDLIFE PAINTER! WE'LL GO OUTSIDE AND YOU CAN POSE FOR ME.
OH BOY! I GET TO BE IN A PAINTING!
THIS LOOKS LIKE A GOOD NATURAL ENVIRONMENT. SIT ON THAT BIG ROCK.
VAN GOGH WOULD'VE SOLD MORE THAN ONE PAINTING IF HE'D PUT TIGERS IN THEM.
OK, YOU'RE LORD OF THE WILDERNESS! FROM YOUR PERCH YOU SURVEY YOUR TERRITORY WITH THE QUIET CONFIDENCE AND STEELY EYE OF A JUNGLE CAT!
LIKE THIS?
NO, THAT'S NOT QUITE IT.
THIS?
TOO FORMAL. LET'S TRY ONE WHERE THE FIERCE TIGER RESTS IN THE SHADE AFTER A KILL.
HOW'S THIS?
NO, NO.
NOW?
WATERSON
THIS ISN'T WORKING AT ALL.
HOW ABOUT THIS?
YES! THAT'S IT! HOLD THAT!
BOY, I HAD NO IDEA THIS WOULD BE SO HARD. CAN YOU IMAGINE POSING A DUMB MOOSE?
NOTICE I'M MORE OF A YELLOW OCHRE THAN A STRAIGHT ORANGE.

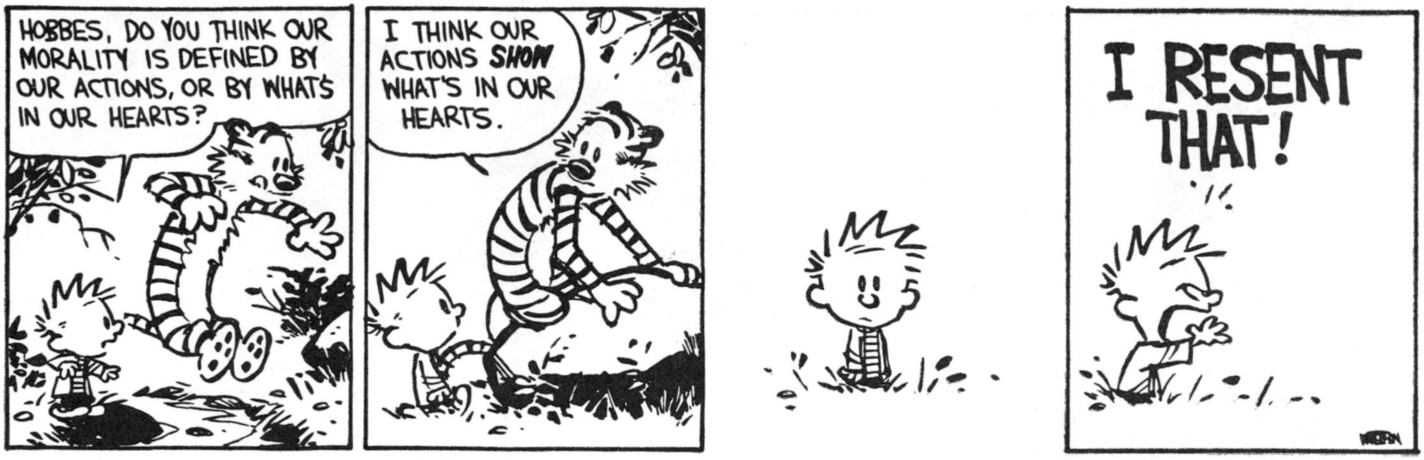
HOBBES, DO YOU THINK OUR MORALITY IS DEFINED BY OUR ACTIONS, OR BY WHAT'S IN OUR HEARTS?
I THINK OUR ACTIONS *SHOW* WHAT'S IN OUR HEARTS.
I RESENT THAT!

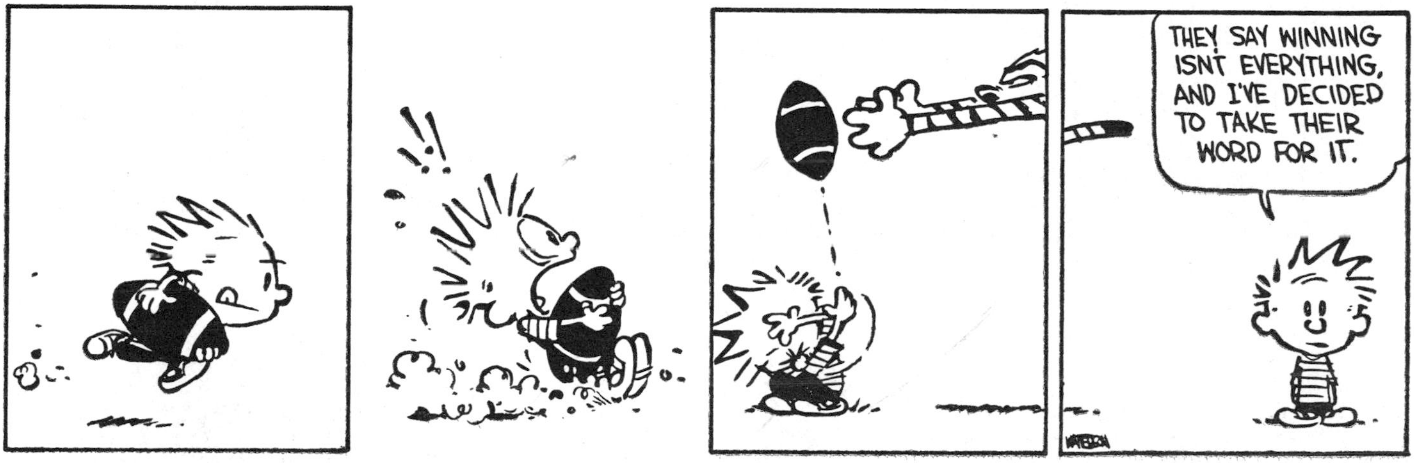
THEY SAY WINNING ISN'T EVERYTHING, AND I'VE DECIDED TO TAKE THEIR WORD FOR IT.

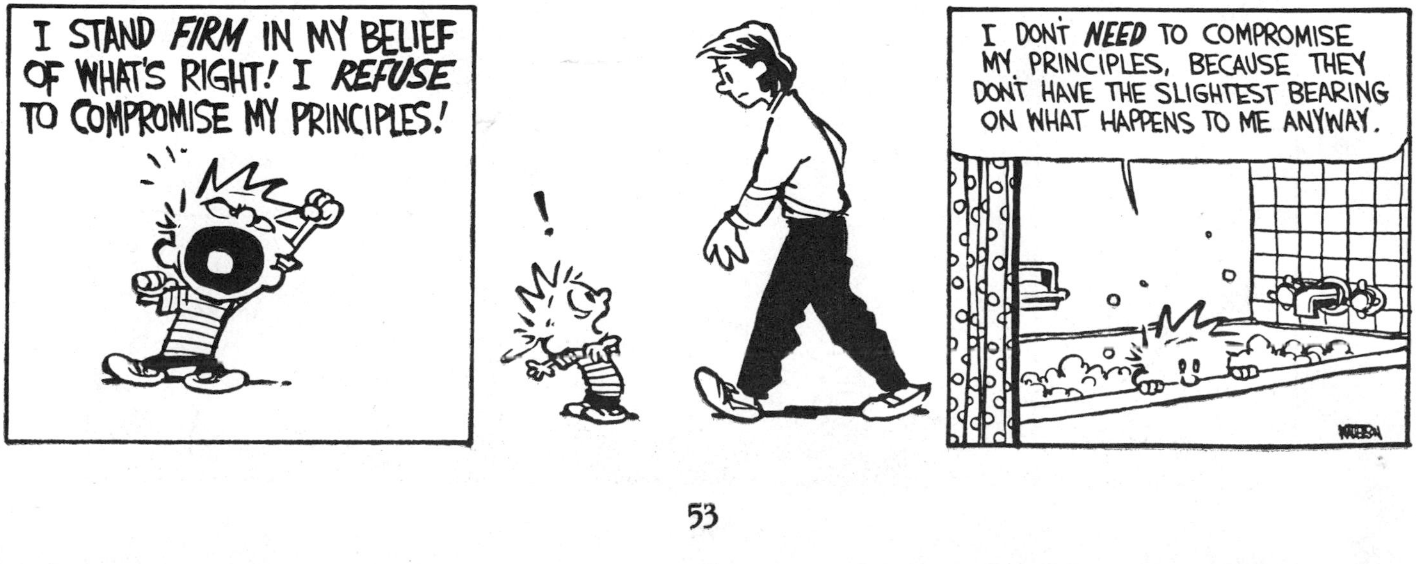
I STAND *FIRM* IN MY BELIEF OF WHAT'S RIGHT! I *REFUSE* TO COMPROMISE MY PRINCIPLES!
I DON'T *NEED* TO COMPROMISE MY PRINCIPLES, BECAUSE THEY DON'T HAVE THE SLIGHTEST BEARING ON WHAT HAPPENS TO ME ANYWAY.

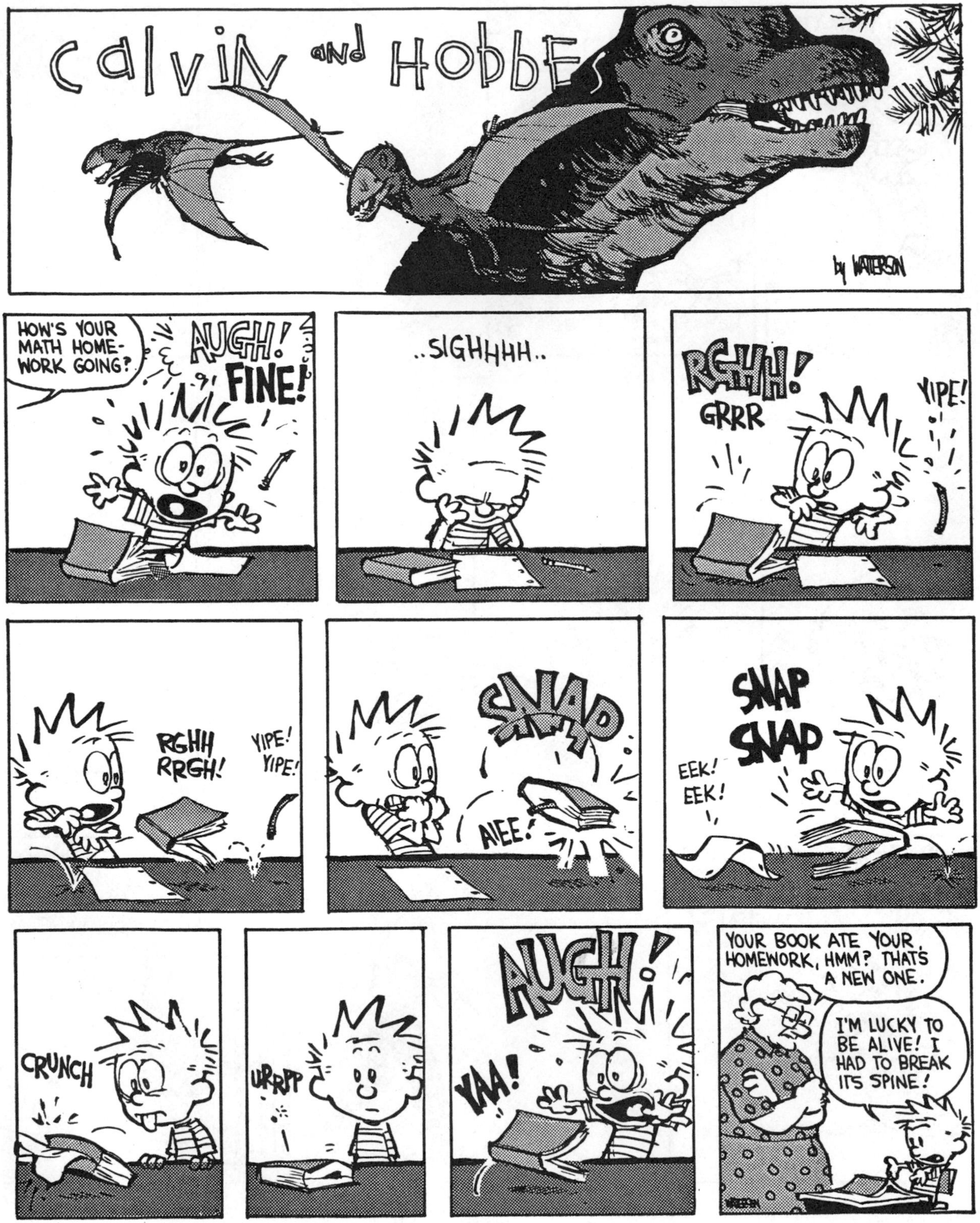
Calvin and Hobbes
by WATTERSON
HOW'S YOUR MATH HOMEWORK GOING?
AUGH! FINE!
..SIGHHHH..
RGHHH! GRRR
YIPE!
RGHH RRGH!
YIPE! YIPE!
SNAP
AIEE!
SNAP SNAP
EEK! EEK!
CRUNCH
URRPP
AUGH!
YAA!
YOUR BOOK ATE YOUR HOMEWORK, HMM? THAT'S A NEW ONE.
I'M LUCKY TO BE ALIVE! I HAD TO BREAK ITS SPINE!

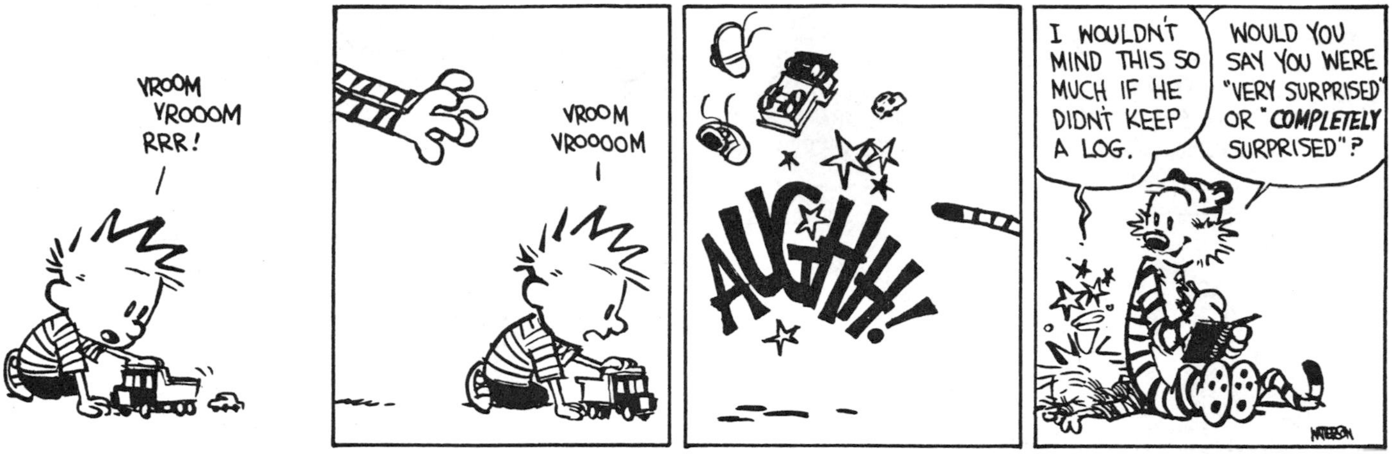
VROOM VROOOM RRR!
VROOM VROOOOM
AUGHH!
I WOULDN'T MIND THIS SO MUCH IF HE DIDN'T KEEP A LOG.
WOULD YOU SAY YOU WERE "VERY SURPRISED" OR "COMPLETELY SURPRISED"?

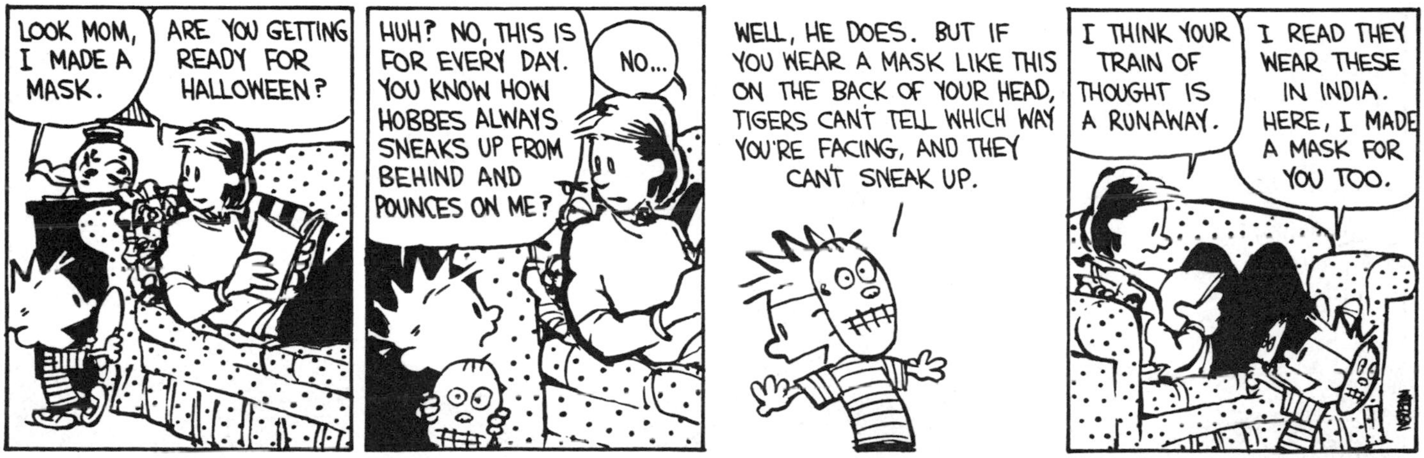
LOOK MOM, I MADE A MASK.
ARE YOU GETTING READY FOR HALLOWEEN?
HUH? NO, THIS IS FOR EVERY DAY. YOU KNOW HOW HOBBES ALWAYS SNEAKS UP FROM BEHIND AND POUNCES ON ME?
NO...
WELL, HE DOES. BUT IF YOU WEAR A MASK LIKE THIS ON THE BACK OF YOUR HEAD, TIGERS CAN'T TELL WHICH WAY YOU'RE FACING, AND THEY CAN'T SNEAK UP.
I THINK YOUR TRAIN OF THOUGHT IS A RUNAWAY.
I READ THEY WEAR THESE IN INDIA. HERE, I MADE A MASK FOR YOU TOO.

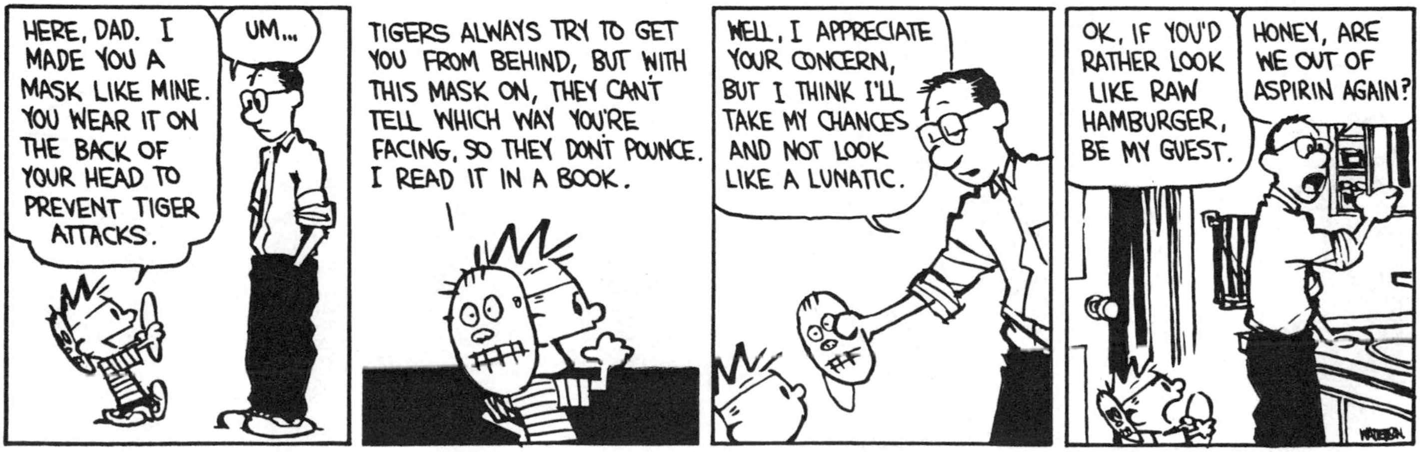
HERE, DAD. I MADE YOU A MASK LIKE MINE. YOU WEAR IT ON THE BACK OF YOUR HEAD TO PREVENT TIGER ATTACKS.
UM...
TIGERS ALWAYS TRY TO GET YOU FROM BEHIND, BUT WITH THIS MASK ON, THEY CAN'T TELL WHICH WAY YOU'RE FACING, SO THEY DON'T POUNCE. I READ IT IN A BOOK.
WELL, I APPRECIATE YOUR CONCERN, BUT I THINK I'LL TAKE MY CHANCES AND NOT LOOK LIKE A LUNATIC.
OK, IF YOU'D RATHER LOOK LIKE RAW HAMBURGER, BE MY GUEST.
HONEY, ARE WE OUT OF ASPIRIN AGAIN?

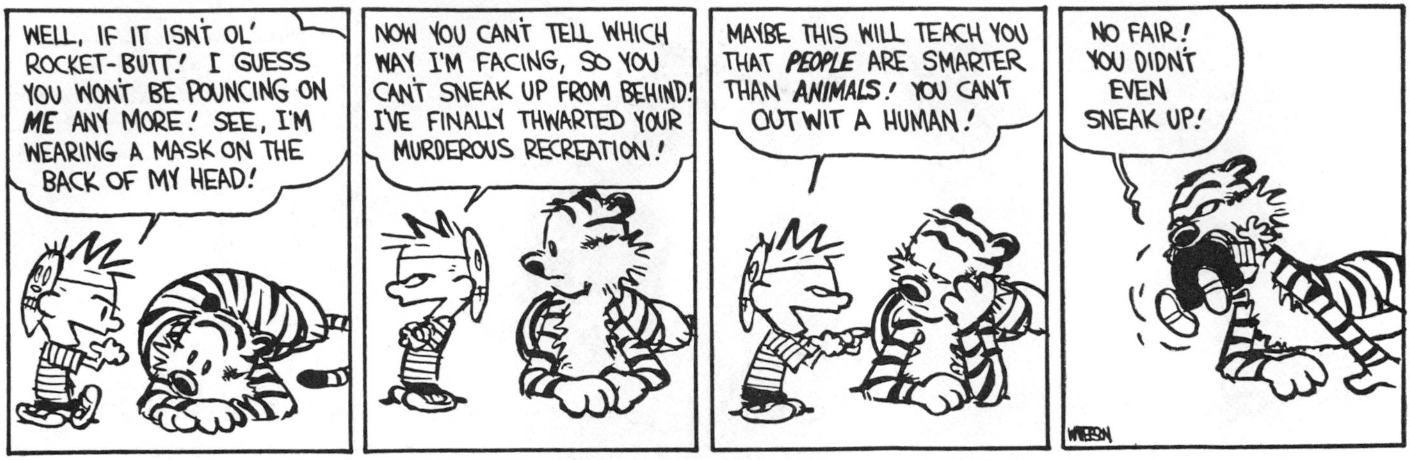
WELL, IF IT ISN'T OL' ROCKET-BUTT! I GUESS YOU WON'T BE POUNCING ON ME ANY MORE! SEE, I'M WEARING A MASK ON THE BACK OF MY HEAD!
NOW YOU CAN'T TELL WHICH WAY I'M FACING, SO YOU CAN'T SNEAK UP FROM BEHIND! I'VE FINALLY THWARTED YOUR MURDEROUS RECREATION!
MAYBE THIS WILL TEACH YOU THAT PEOPLE ARE SMARTER THAN ANIMALS! YOU CAN'T OUTWIT A HUMAN!
NO FAIR! YOU DIDN'T EVEN SNEAK UP!

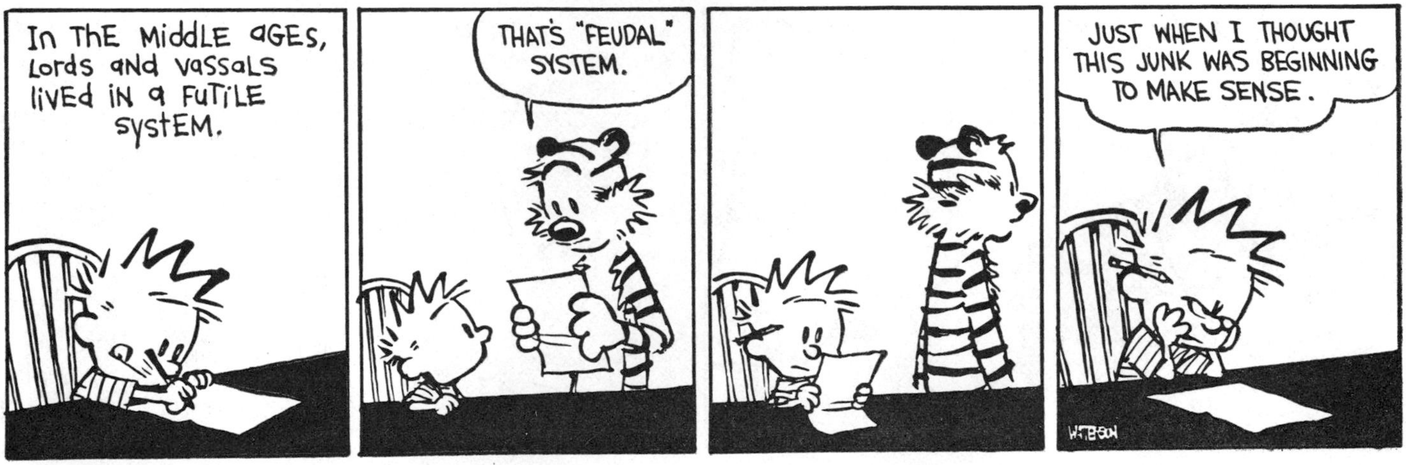
In THE MiddLE aGES, Lords and vassaLs lived in a FUTiLE systEM.
THAT'S "FEUDAL" SYSTEM.
JUST WHEN I THOUGHT THIS JUNK WAS BEGINNING TO MAKE SENSE.

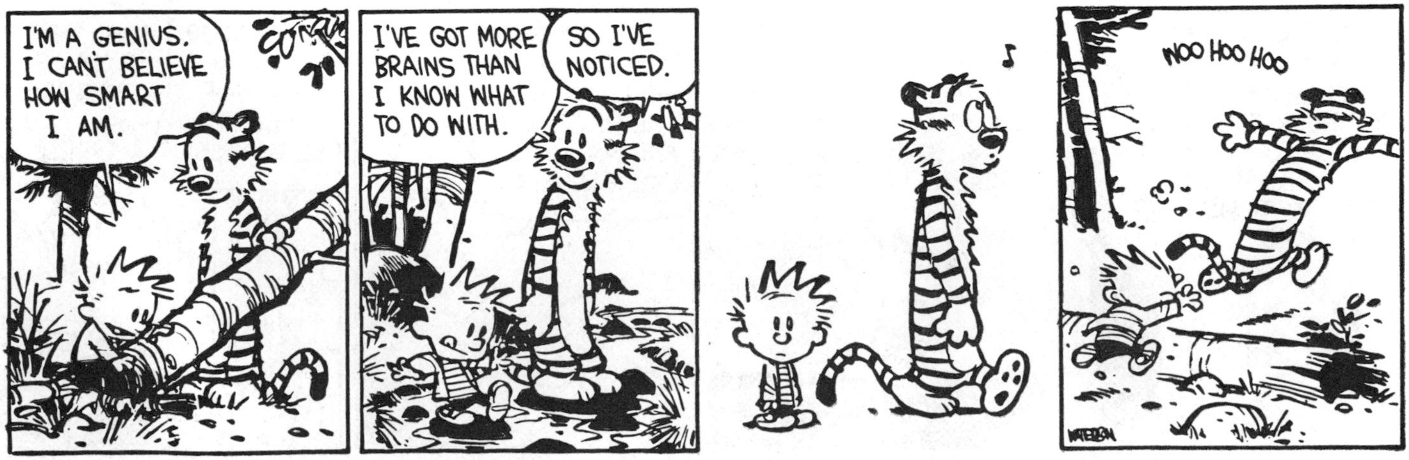
I'M A GENIUS. I CAN'T BELIEVE HOW SMART I AM.
I'VE GOT MORE BRAINS THAN I KNOW WHAT TO DO WITH.
SO I'VE NOTICED.
WOO HOO HOO

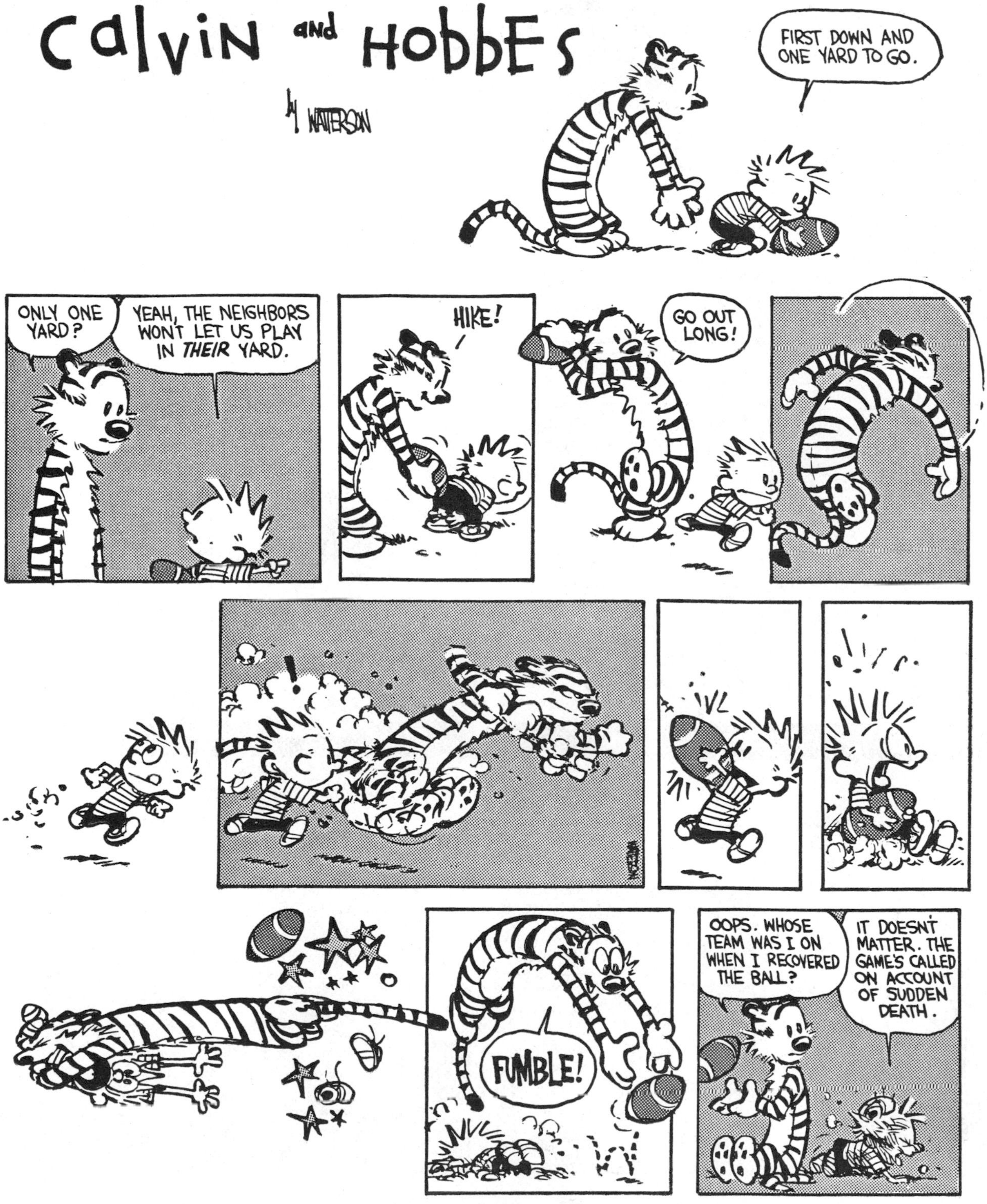
Calvin and HOBBES
by WATTERSON
FIRST DOWN AND ONE YARD TO GO.
ONLY ONE YARD?
YEAH, THE NEIGHBORS WON'T LET US PLAY IN THEIR YARD.
HIKE!
GO OUT LONG!
FUMBLE!
OOPS. WHOSE TEAM WAS I ON WHEN I RECOVERED THE BALL?
IT DOESN'T MATTER. THE GAME'S CALLED ON ACCOUNT OF SUDDEN DEATH.

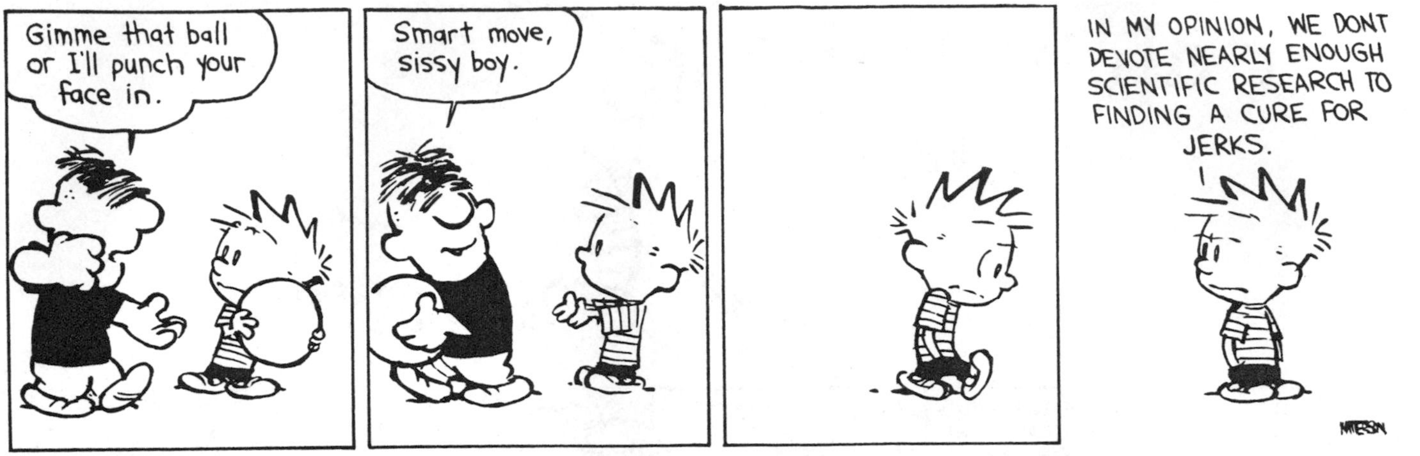
Gimme that ball or I'll punch your face in.
Smart move, sissy boy.
IN MY OPINION, WE DONT DEVOTE NEARLY ENOUGH SCIENTIFIC RESEARCH TO FINDING A CURE FOR JERKS.

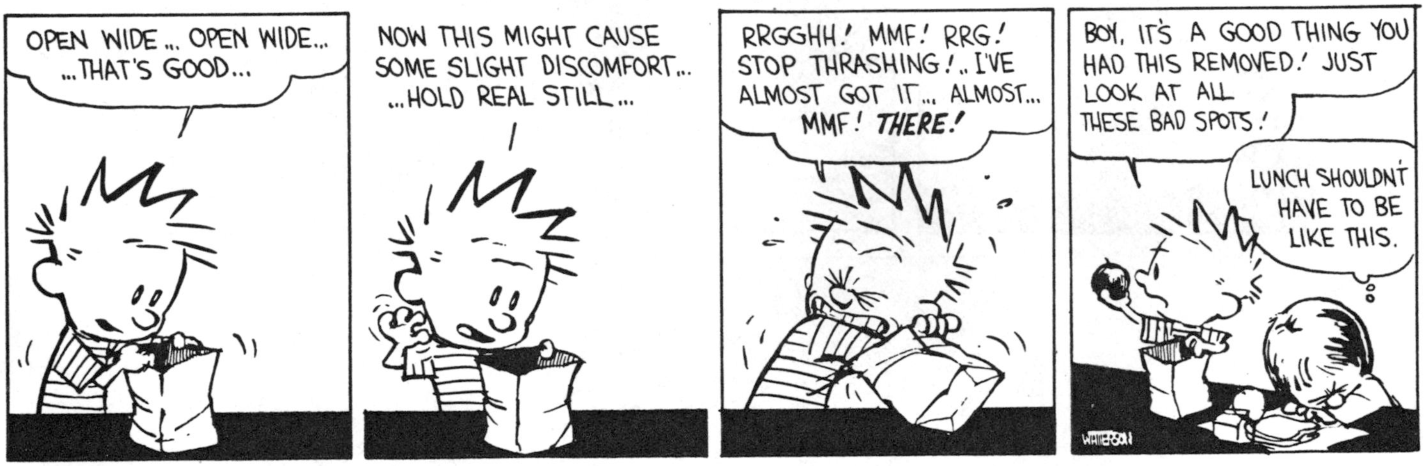
OPEN WIDE... OPEN WIDE... ...THAT'S GOOD...
NOW THIS MIGHT CAUSE SOME SLIGHT DISCOMFORT... ...HOLD REAL STILL...
RRGGHH! MMF! RRG! STOP THRASHING!.. I'VE ALMOST GOT IT... ALMOST... MMF! THERE!
BOY, IT'S A GOOD THING YOU HAD THIS REMOVED! JUST LOOK AT ALL THESE BAD SPOTS!
LUNCH SHOULDN'T HAVE TO BE LIKE THIS.

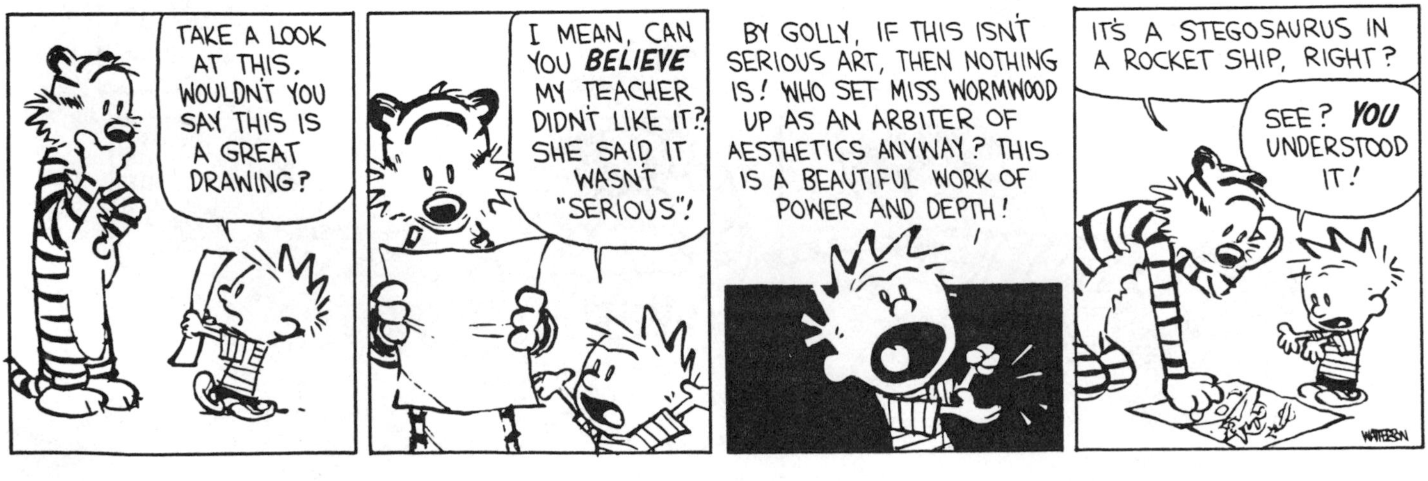
TAKE A LOOK AT THIS. WOULDN'T YOU SAY THIS IS A GREAT DRAWING?
I MEAN, CAN YOU BELIEVE MY TEACHER DIDN'T LIKE IT? SHE SAID IT WASN'T "SERIOUS"!
BY GOLLY, IF THIS ISN'T SERIOUS ART, THEN NOTHING IS! WHO SET MISS WORMWOOD UP AS AN ARBITER OF AESTHETICS ANYWAY? THIS IS A BEAUTIFUL WORK OF POWER AND DEPTH!
IT'S A STEGOSAURUS IN A ROCKET SHIP, RIGHT?
SEE? YOU UNDERSTOOD IT!

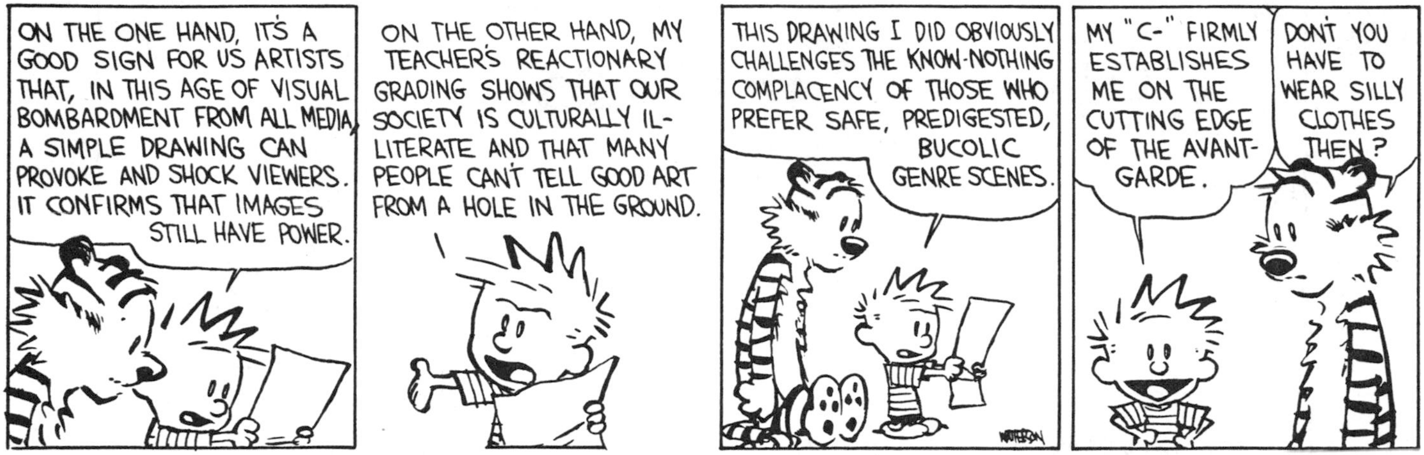
ON THE ONE HAND, IT'S A GOOD SIGN FOR US ARTISTS THAT, IN THIS AGE OF VISUAL BOMBARDMENT FROM ALL MEDIA, A SIMPLE DRAWING CAN PROVOKE AND SHOCK VIEWERS. IT CONFIRMS THAT IMAGES STILL HAVE POWER.
ON THE OTHER HAND, MY TEACHER'S REACTIONARY GRADING SHOWS THAT OUR SOCIETY IS CULTURALLY ILLITERATE AND THAT MANY PEOPLE CAN'T TELL GOOD ART FROM A HOLE IN THE GROUND.
THIS DRAWING I DID OBVIOUSLY CHALLENGES THE KNOW-NOTHING COMPLACENCY OF THOSE WHO PREFER SAFE, PREDIGESTED, BUCOLIC GENRE SCENES.
MY "C-" FIRMLY ESTABLISHES ME ON THE CUTTING EDGE OF THE AVANT-GARDE.
DON'T YOU HAVE TO WEAR SILLY CLOTHES THEN?

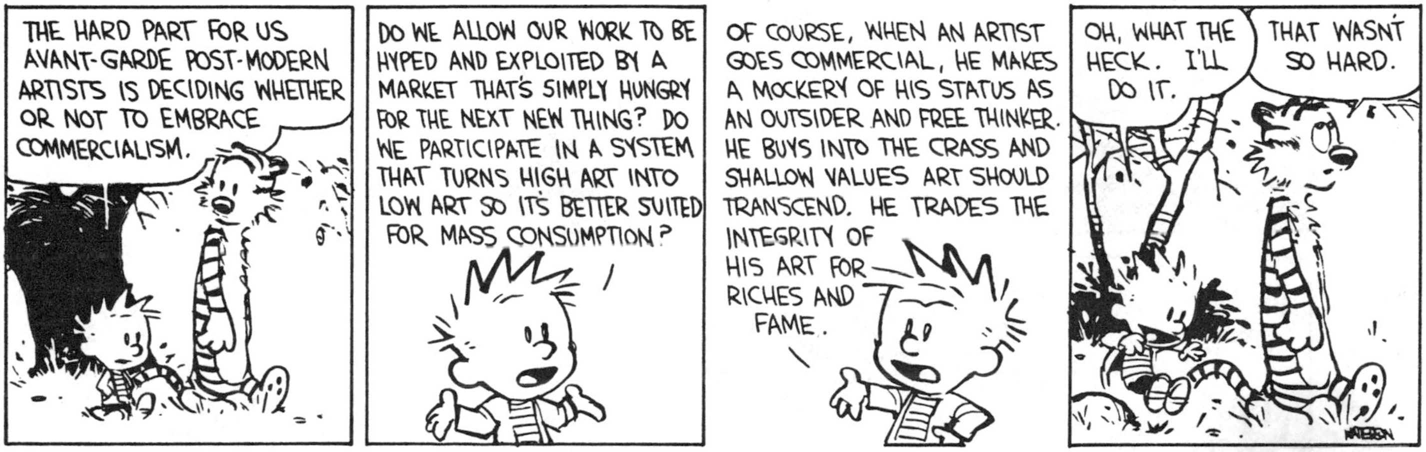
THE HARD PART FOR US AVANT-GARDE POST-MODERN ARTISTS IS DECIDING WHETHER OR NOT TO EMBRACE COMMERCIALISM.
DO WE ALLOW OUR WORK TO BE HYPED AND EXPLOITED BY A MARKET THAT'S SIMPLY HUNGRY FOR THE NEXT NEW THING? DO WE PARTICIPATE IN A SYSTEM THAT TURNS HIGH ART INTO LOW ART SO IT'S BETTER SUITED FOR MASS CONSUMPTION?
OF COURSE, WHEN AN ARTIST GOES COMMERCIAL, HE MAKES A MOCKERY OF HIS STATUS AS AN OUTSIDER AND FREE THINKER. HE BUYS INTO THE CRASS AND SHALLOW VALUES ART SHOULD TRANSCEND. HE TRADES THE INTEGRITY OF HIS ART FOR RICHES AND FAME.
OH, WHAT THE HECK. I'LL DO IT.
THAT WASN'T SO HARD.

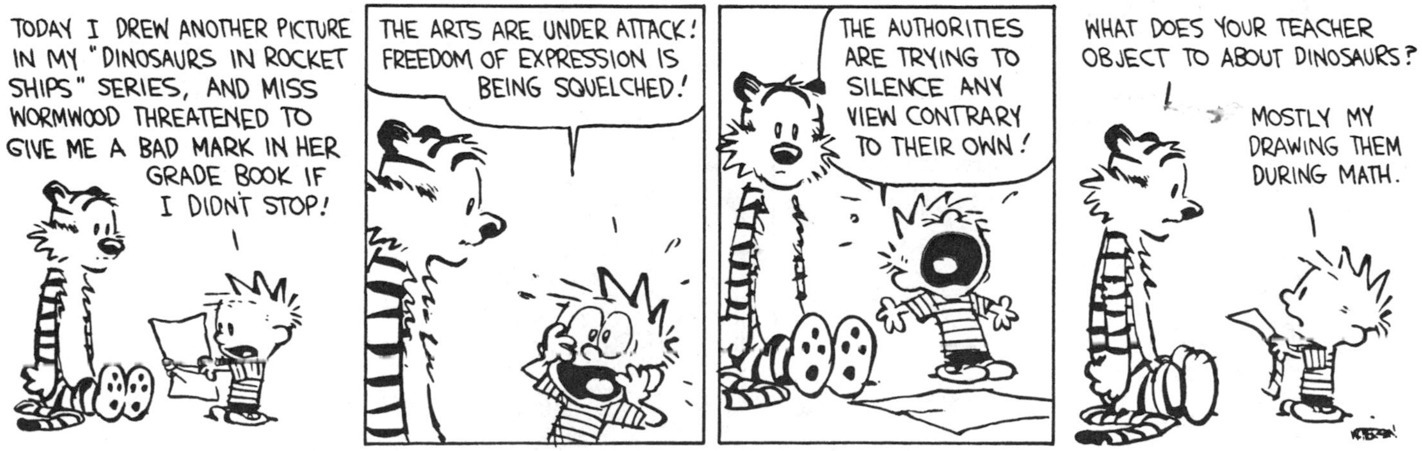
TODAY I DREW ANOTHER PICTURE IN MY "DINOSAURS IN ROCKET SHIPS" SERIES, AND MISS WORMWOOD THREATENED TO GIVE ME A BAD MARK IN HER GRADE BOOK IF I DIDN'T STOP!
THE ARTS ARE UNDER ATTACK! FREEDOM OF EXPRESSION IS BEING SQUELCHED!
THE AUTHORITIES ARE TRYING TO SILENCE ANY VIEW CONTRARY TO THEIR OWN!
WHAT DOES YOUR TEACHER OBJECT TO ABOUT DINOSAURS?
MOSTLY MY DRAWING THEM DURING MATH.

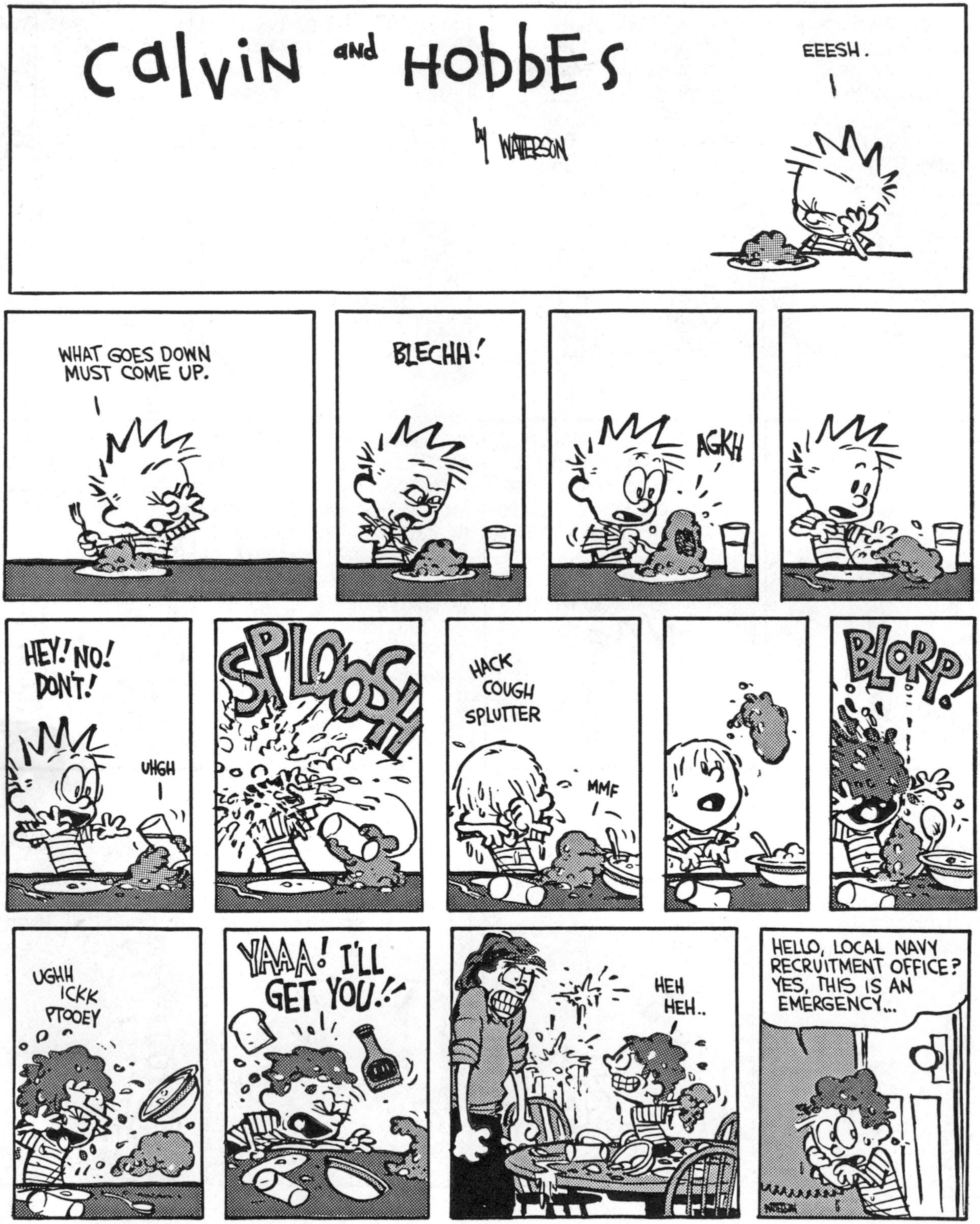
Calvin and HOBBES
by WATTERSON
EEESH.
WHAT GOES DOWN MUST COME UP.
BLECHH!
AGKH
HEY! NO! DON'T!
UHGH
SPLOOSH
HACK COUGH SPLUTTER
MMF
BLORP!
UGHH ICKK PTOOEY
YAAA! I'LL GET YOU!!
HEH HEH..
HELLO, LOCAL NAVY RECRUITMENT OFFICE? YES, THIS IS AN EMERGENCY...

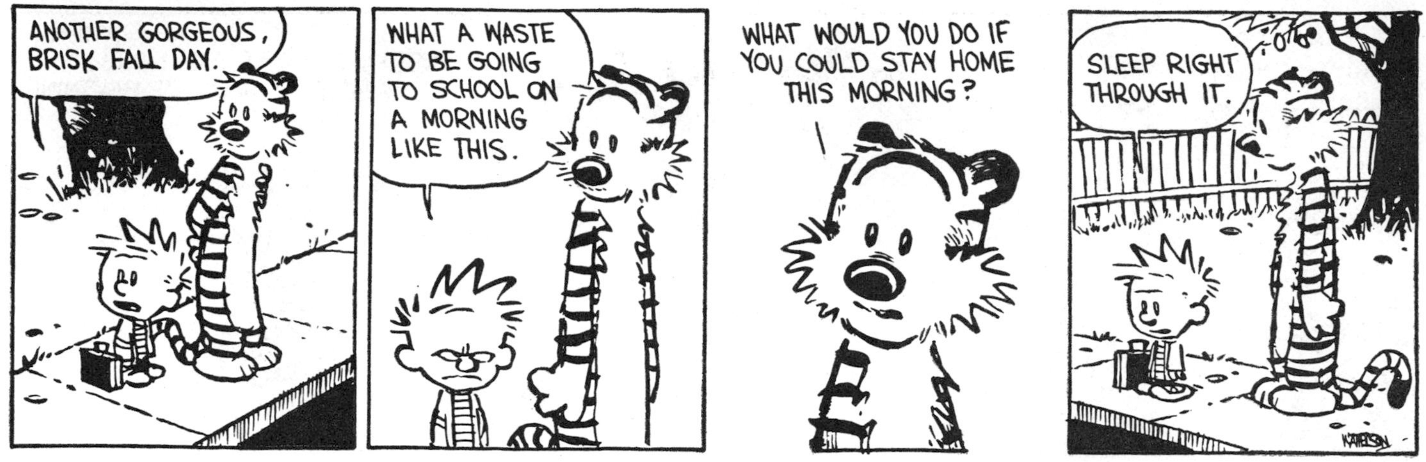
ANOTHER GORGEOUS, BRISK FALL DAY.
WHAT A WASTE TO BE GOING TO SCHOOL ON A MORNING LIKE THIS.
WHAT WOULD YOU DO IF YOU COULD STAY HOME THIS MORNING?
SLEEP RIGHT THROUGH IT.

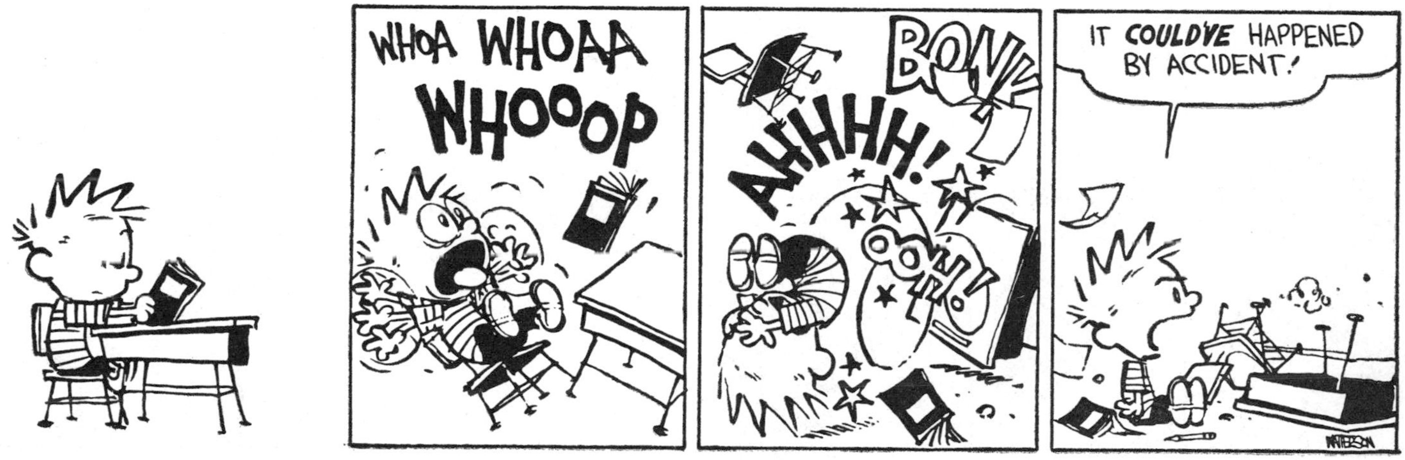
WHOA WHOAA
WHOOOP
AHHHH!
IT COULD'VE HAPPENED BY ACCIDENT!

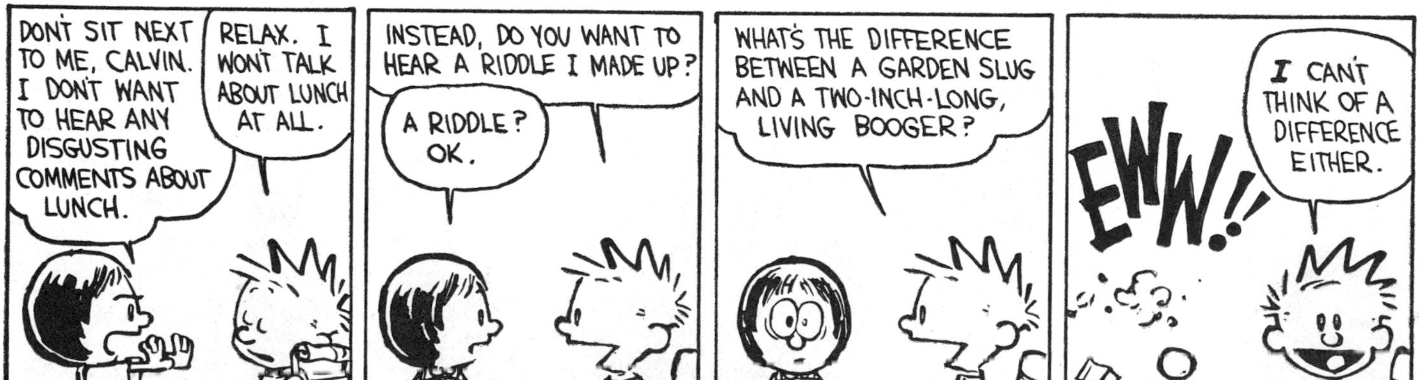
DON'T SIT NEXT TO ME, CALVIN. I DON'T WANT TO HEAR ANY DISGUSTING COMMENTS ABOUT LUNCH.
RELAX. I WON'T TALK ABOUT LUNCH AT ALL.
INSTEAD, DO YOU WANT TO HEAR A RIDDLE I MADE UP?
A RIDDLE? OK.
WHAT'S THE DIFFERENCE BETWEEN A GARDEN SLUG AND A TWO-INCH-LONG, LIVING BOOGER?
EWW!!
I CAN'T THINK OF A DIFFERENCE EITHER.

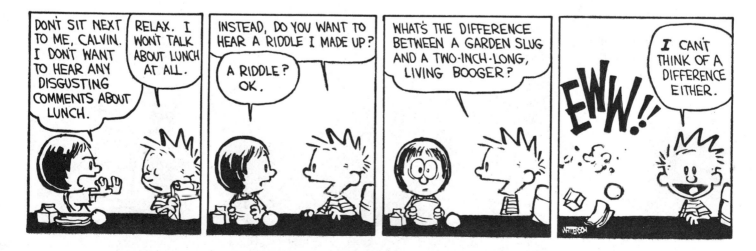

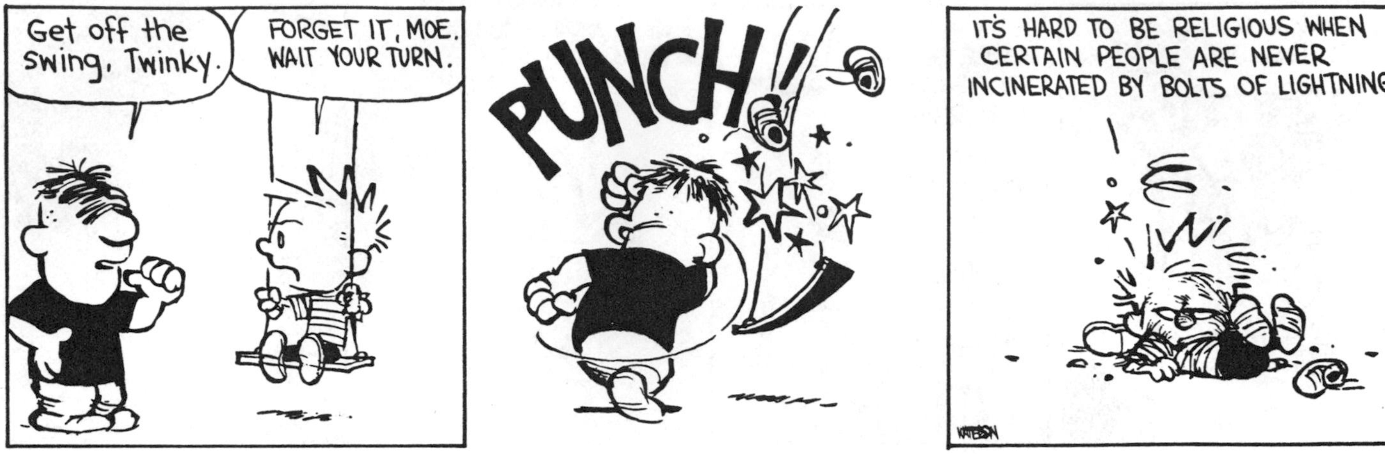
Get off the swing, Twinky.
FORGET IT, MOE. WAIT YOUR TURN.
PUNCH!!
IT'S HARD TO BE RELIGIOUS WHEN CERTAIN PEOPLE ARE NEVER INCINERATED BY BOLTS OF LIGHTNING.

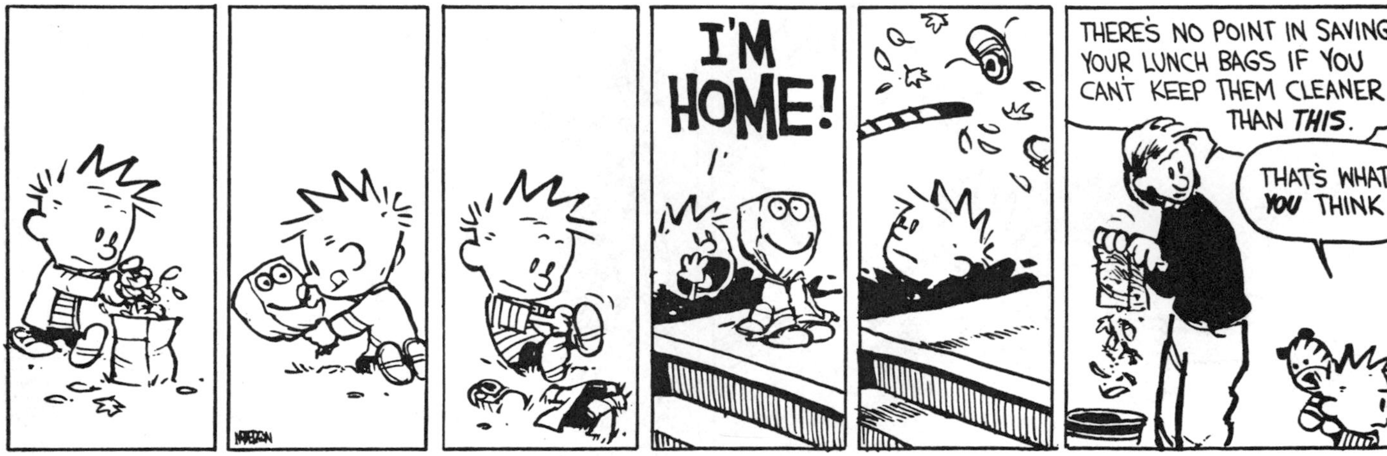
I'M HOME!
THERE'S NO POINT IN SAVING YOUR LUNCH BAGS IF YOU CAN'T KEEP THEM CLEANER THAN *THIS*.
THAT'S WHAT *YOU* THINK.

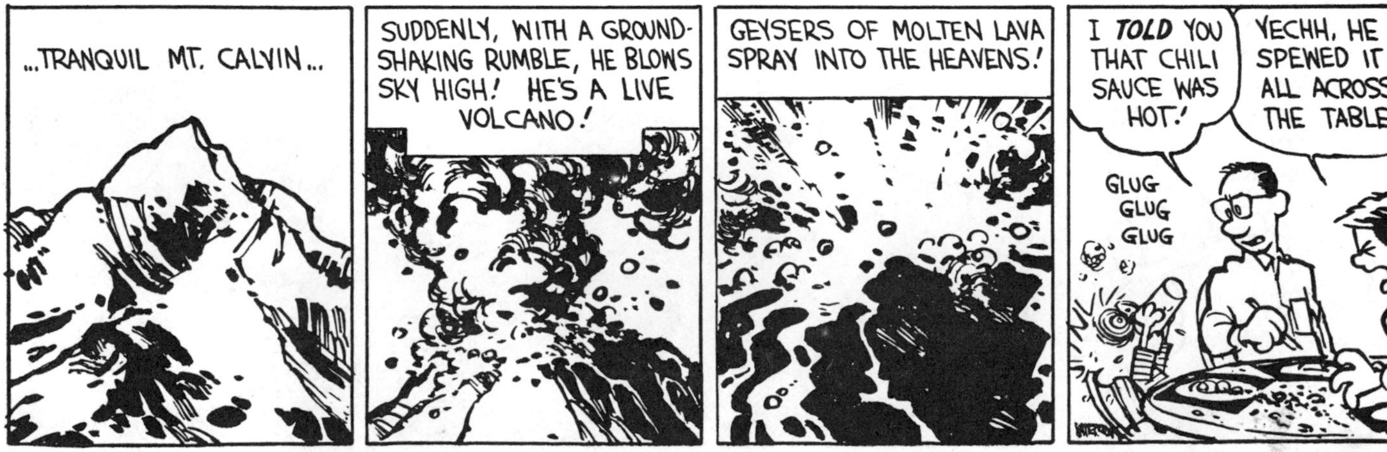
...TRANQUIL MT. CALVIN...
SUDDENLY, WITH A GROUND-SHAKING RUMBLE, HE BLOWS SKY HIGH! HE'S A LIVE VOLCANO!
GEYSERS OF MOLTEN LAVA SPRAY INTO THE HEAVENS!
I *TOLD* YOU THAT CHILI SAUCE WAS HOT!
YECHH, HE SPEWED IT ALL ACROSS THE TABLE!
GLUG GLUG GLUG

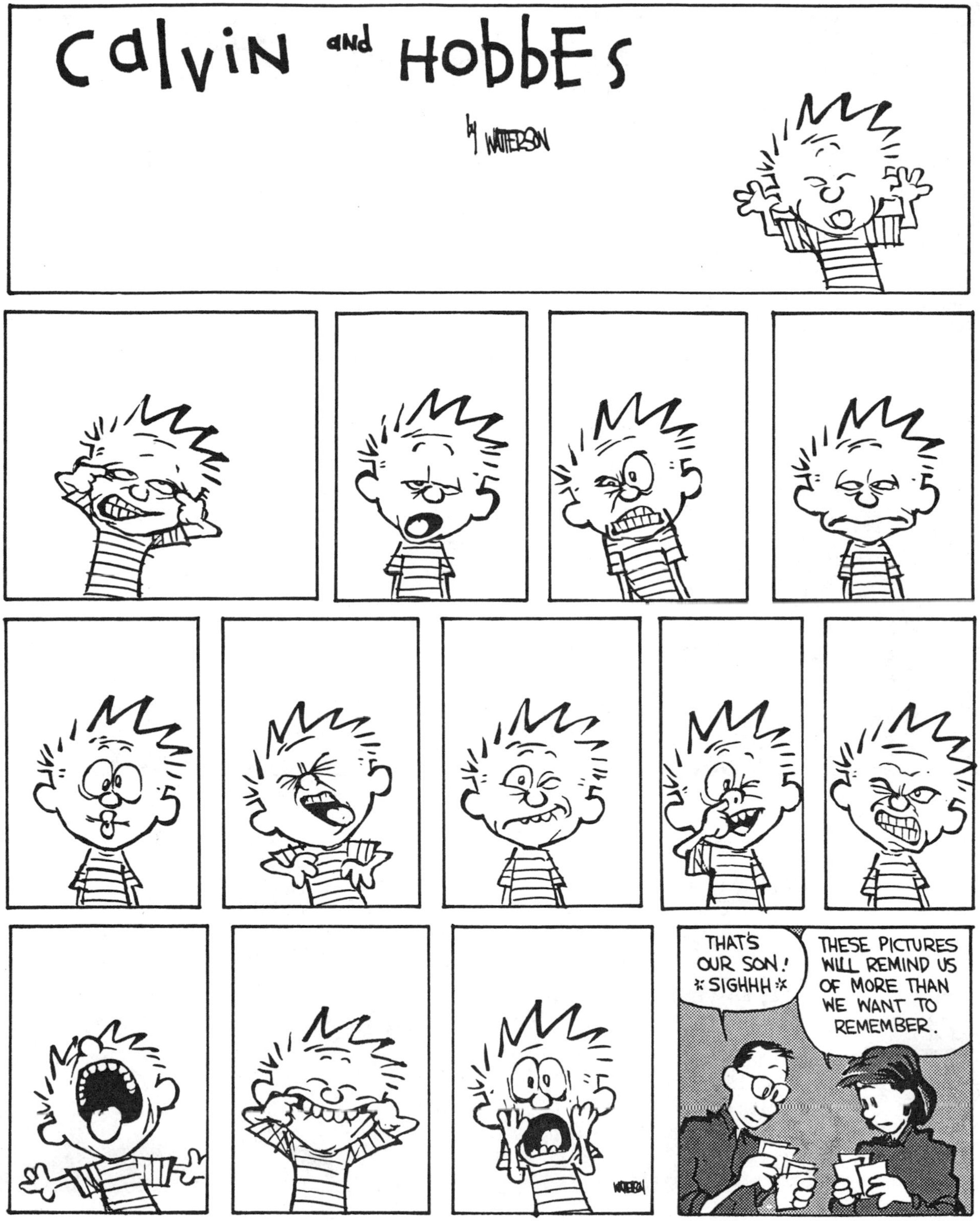
Calvin and HOBBES
by WATTERSON
THAT'S OUR SON! *SIGHHH*
THESE PICTURES WILL REMIND US OF MORE THAN WE WANT TO REMEMBER.
WATTERSON

65

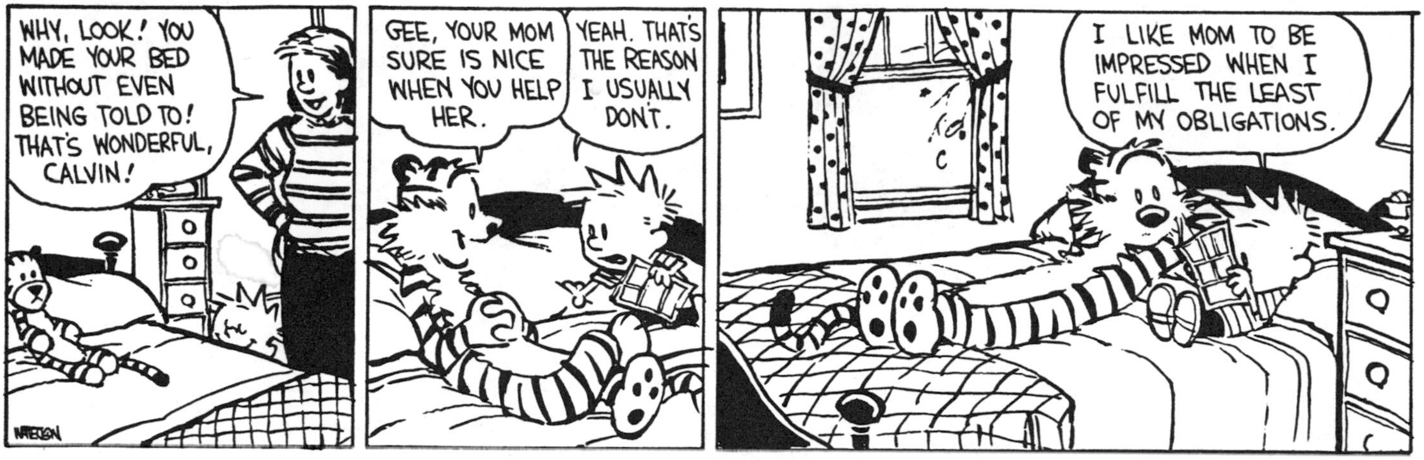
WHY, LOOK! YOU MADE YOUR BED WITHOUT EVEN BEING TOLD TO! THAT'S WONDERFUL, CALVIN!
GEE, YOUR MOM SURE IS NICE WHEN YOU HELP HER.
YEAH. THAT'S THE REASON I USUALLY DON'T.
I LIKE MOM TO BE IMPRESSED WHEN I FULFILL THE LEAST OF MY OBLIGATIONS.

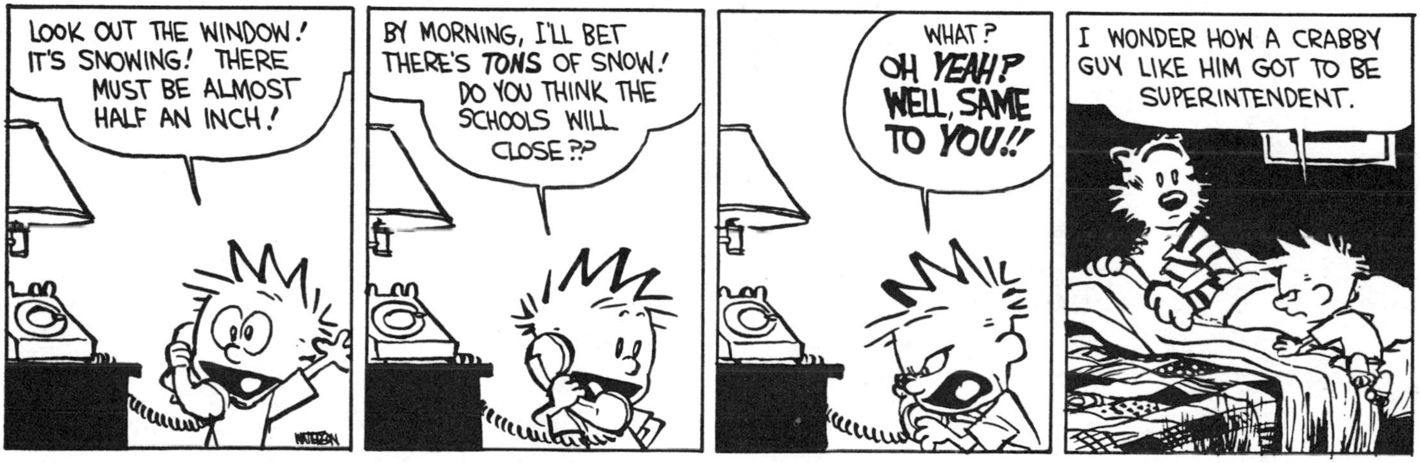
LOOK OUT THE WINDOW! IT'S SNOWING! THERE MUST BE ALMOST HALF AN INCH!
BY MORNING, I'LL BET THERE'S TONS OF SNOW! DO YOU THINK THE SCHOOLS WILL CLOSE?!?
WHAT? OH YEAH?! WELL, SAME TO YOU!!
I WONDER HOW A CRABBY GUY LIKE HIM GOT TO BE SUPERINTENDENT.

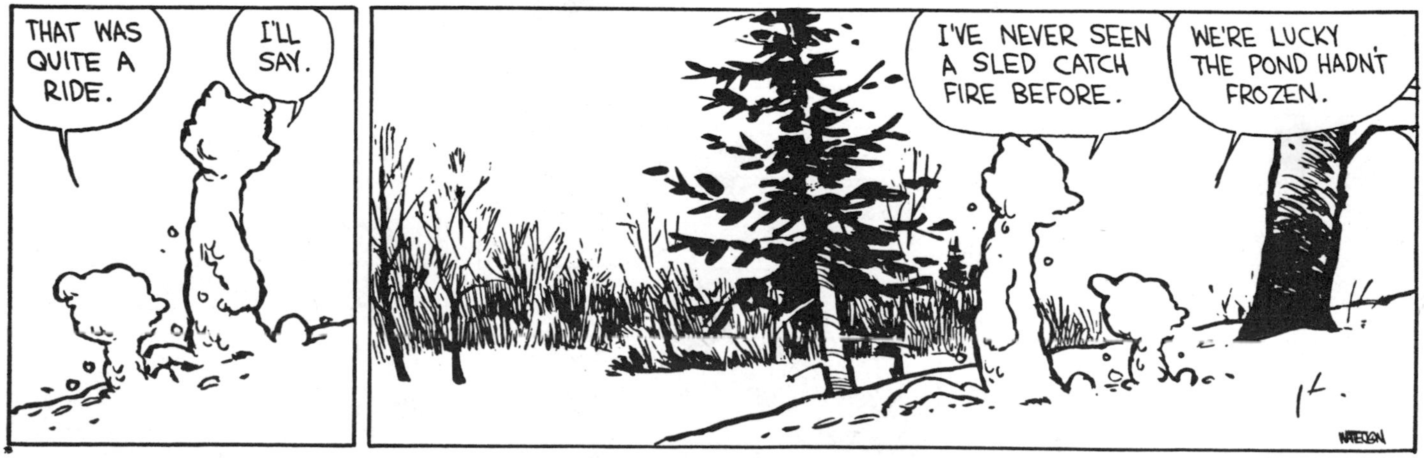
THAT WAS QUITE A RIDE.
I'LL SAY.
I'VE NEVER SEEN A SLED CATCH FIRE BEFORE.
WE'RE LUCKY THE POND HADN'T FROZEN.

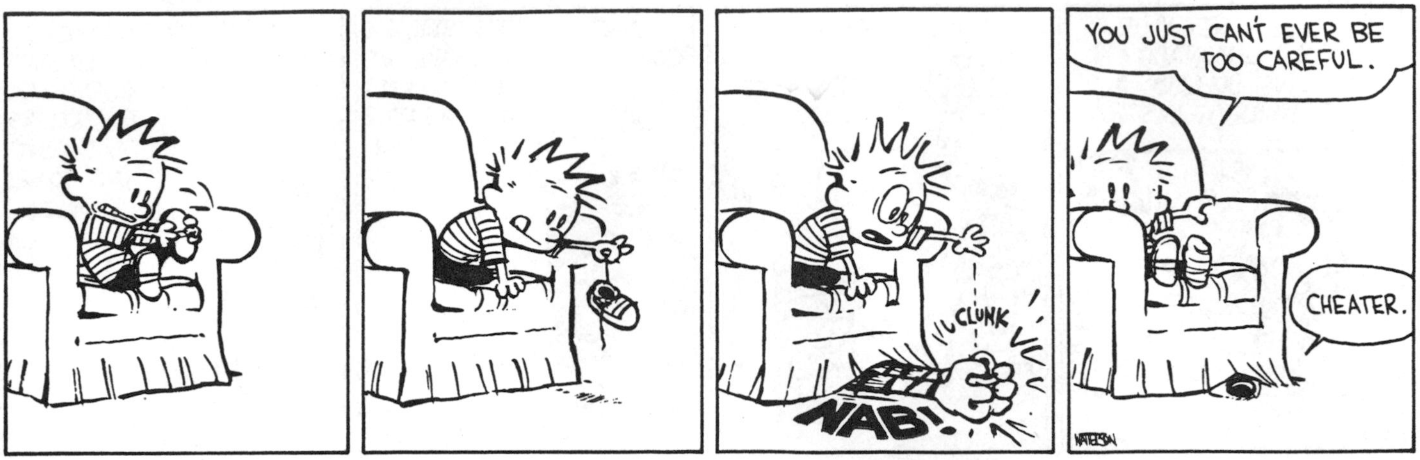
CLUNK
NAB!
YOU JUST CAN'T EVER BE TOO CAREFUL.
CHEATER.

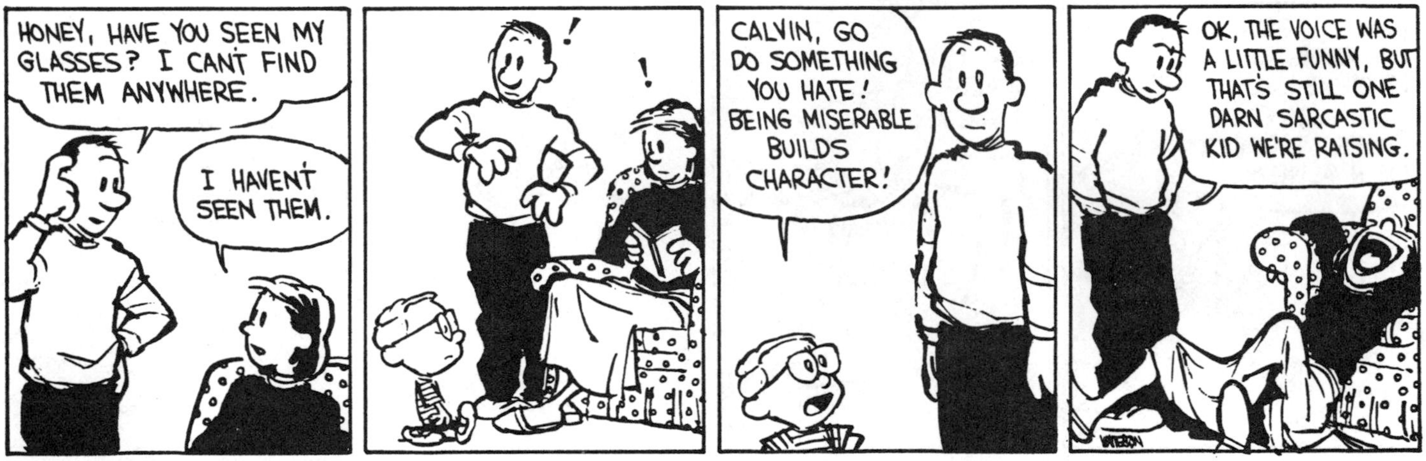
HONEY, HAVE YOU SEEN MY GLASSES? I CAN'T FIND THEM ANYWHERE.
I HAVEN'T SEEN THEM.
!
!
CALVIN, GO DO SOMETHING YOU HATE! BEING MISERABLE BUILDS CHARACTER!
OK, THE VOICE WAS A LITTLE FUNNY, BUT THAT'S STILL ONE DARN SARCASTIC KID WE'RE RAISING.

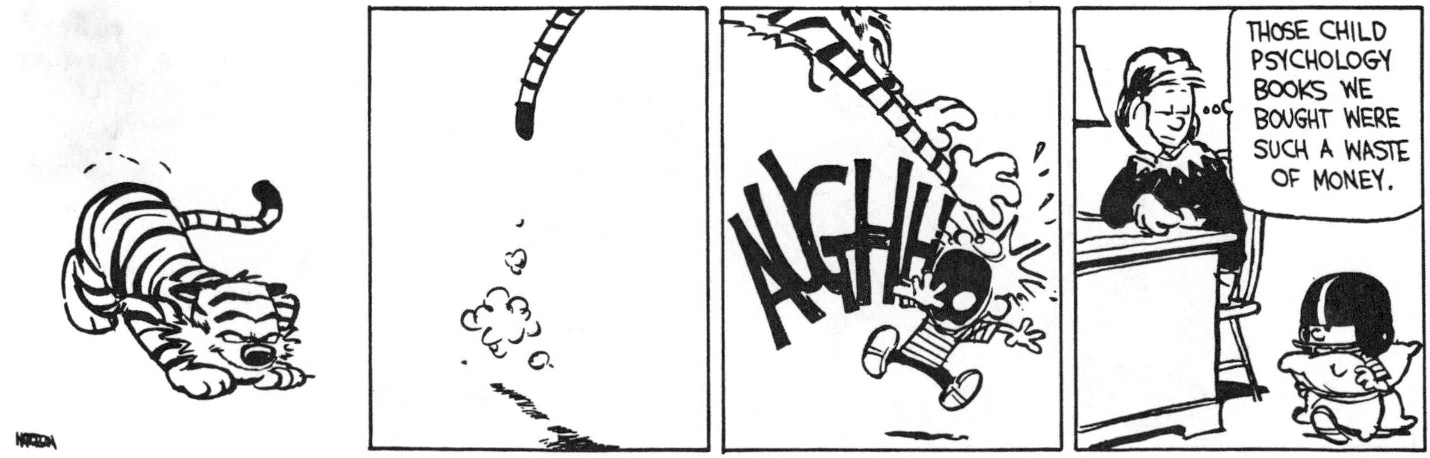
AGHH!
THOSE CHILD PSYCHOLOGY BOOKS WE BOUGHT WERE SUCH A WASTE OF MONEY.

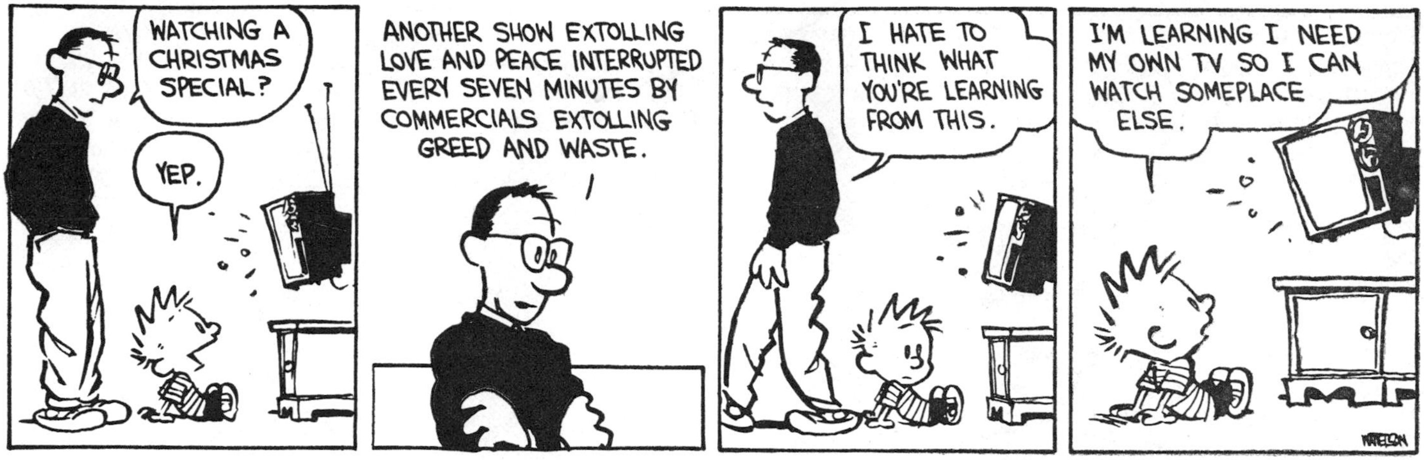
WATCHING A CHRISTMAS SPECIAL?
YEP.
ANOTHER SHOW EXTOLLING LOVE AND PEACE INTERRUPTED EVERY SEVEN MINUTES BY COMMERCIALS EXTOLLING GREED AND WASTE.
I HATE TO THINK WHAT YOU'RE LEARNING FROM THIS.
I'M LEARNING I NEED MY OWN TV SO I CAN WATCH SOMEPLACE ELSE.

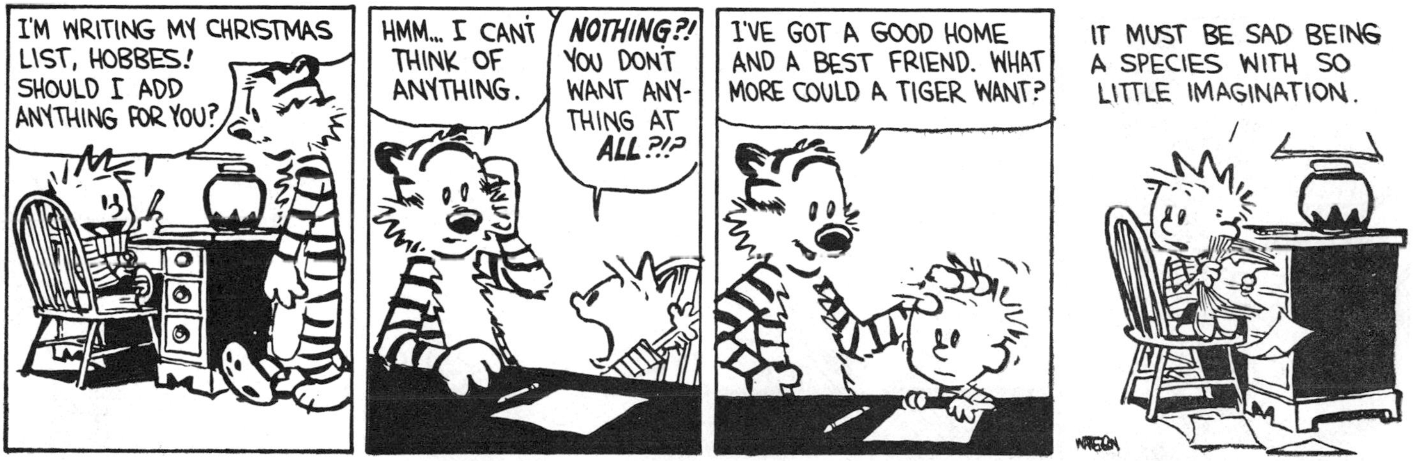
I'M WRITING MY CHRISTMAS LIST, HOBBES! SHOULD I ADD ANYTHING FOR YOU?
HMM... I CAN'T THINK OF ANYTHING.
NOTHING?! YOU DON'T WANT ANY-THING AT ALL?!?
I'VE GOT A GOOD HOME AND A BEST FRIEND. WHAT MORE COULD A TIGER WANT?
IT MUST BE SAD BEING A SPECIES WITH SO LITTLE IMAGINATION.

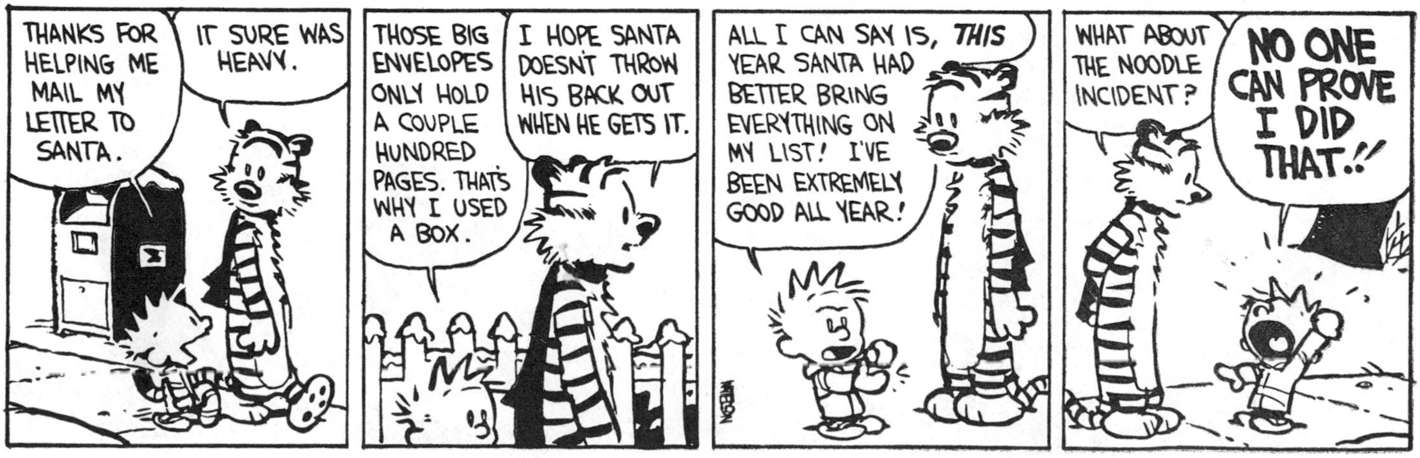
THANKS FOR HELPING ME MAIL MY LETTER TO SANTA.
IT SURE WAS HEAVY.
THOSE BIG ENVELOPES ONLY HOLD A COUPLE HUNDRED PAGES. THAT'S WHY I USED A BOX.
I HOPE SANTA DOESN'T THROW HIS BACK OUT WHEN HE GETS IT.
ALL I CAN SAY IS, THIS YEAR SANTA HAD BETTER BRING EVERYTHING ON MY LIST! I'VE BEEN EXTREMELY GOOD ALL YEAR!
WHAT ABOUT THE NOODLE INCIDENT?
NO ONE CAN PROVE I DID THAT!!

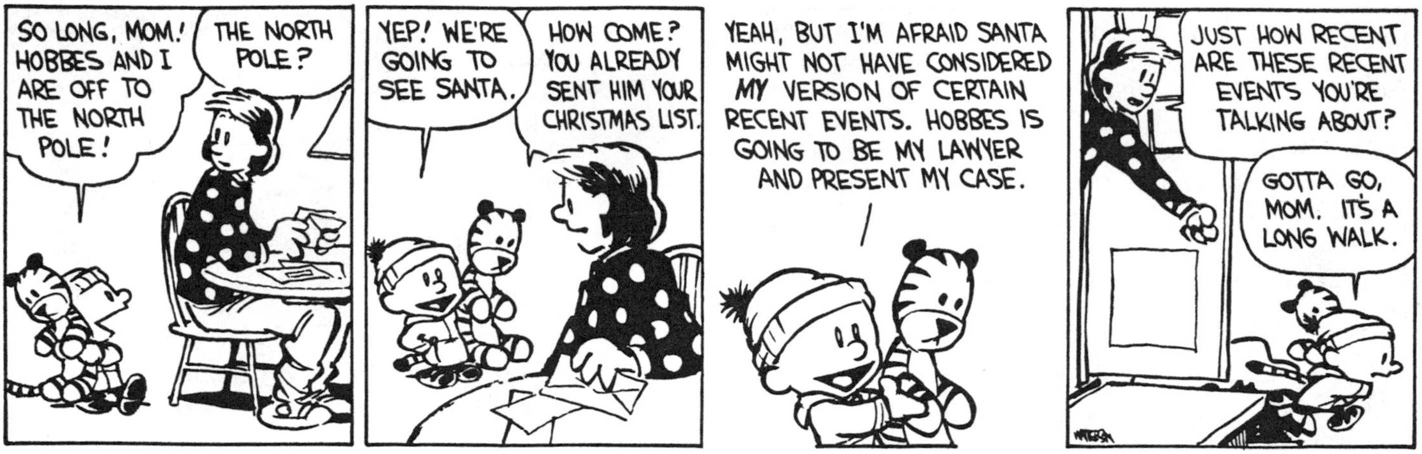
SO LONG, MOM! HOBBES AND I ARE OFF TO THE NORTH POLE!
THE NORTH POLE?
YEP! WE'RE GOING TO SEE SANTA.
HOW COME? YOU ALREADY SENT HIM YOUR CHRISTMAS LIST.
YEAH, BUT I'M AFRAID SANTA MIGHT NOT HAVE CONSIDERED MY VERSION OF CERTAIN RECENT EVENTS. HOBBES IS GOING TO BE MY LAWYER AND PRESENT MY CASE.
JUST HOW RECENT ARE THESE RECENT EVENTS YOU'RE TALKING ABOUT?
GOTTA GO, MOM. IT'S A LONG WALK.

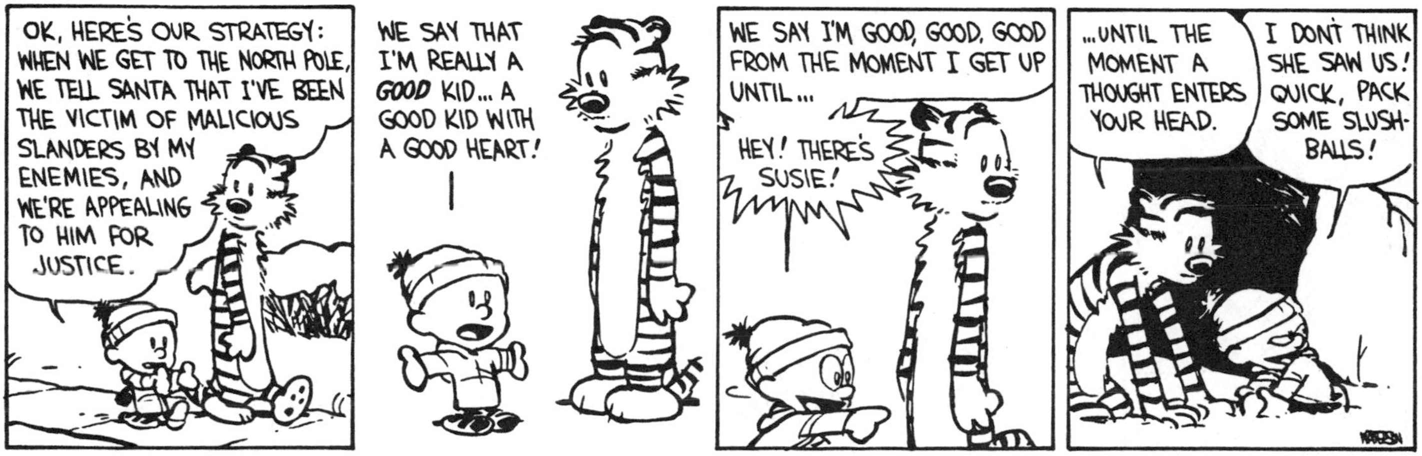
OK, HERE'S OUR STRATEGY: WHEN WE GET TO THE NORTH POLE, WE TELL SANTA THAT I'VE BEEN THE VICTIM OF MALICIOUS SLANDERS BY MY ENEMIES, AND WE'RE APPEALING TO HIM FOR JUSTICE.
WE SAY THAT I'M REALLY A GOOD KID... A GOOD KID WITH A GOOD HEART!
WE SAY I'M GOOD, GOOD, GOOD FROM THE MOMENT I GET UP UNTIL...
HEY! THERE'S SUSIE!
...UNTIL THE MOMENT A THOUGHT ENTERS YOUR HEAD.
I DON'T THINK SHE SAW US! QUICK, PACK SOME SLUSH-BALLS!

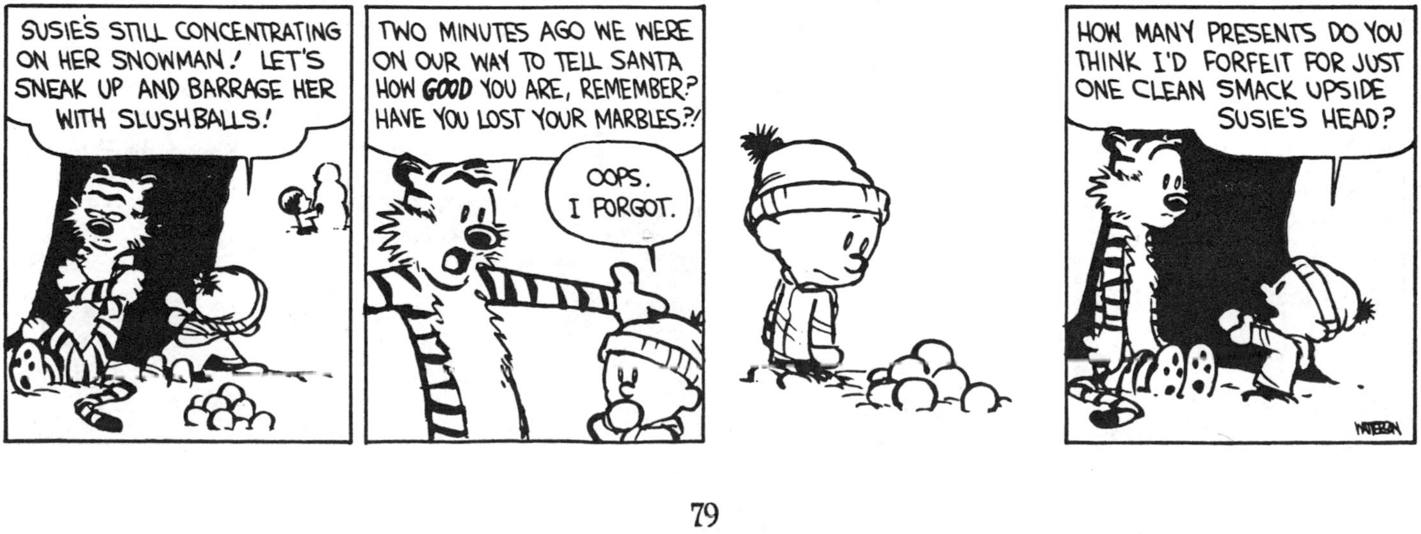
SUSIE'S STILL CONCENTRATING ON HER SNOWMAN! LET'S SNEAK UP AND BARRAGE HER WITH SLUSHBALLS!
TWO MINUTES AGO WE WERE ON OUR WAY TO TELL SANTA HOW GOOD YOU ARE, REMEMBER? HAVE YOU LOST YOUR MARBLES?!
OOPS. I FORGOT.
HOW MANY PRESENTS DO YOU THINK I'D FORFEIT FOR JUST ONE CLEAN SMACK UPSIDE SUSIE'S HEAD?

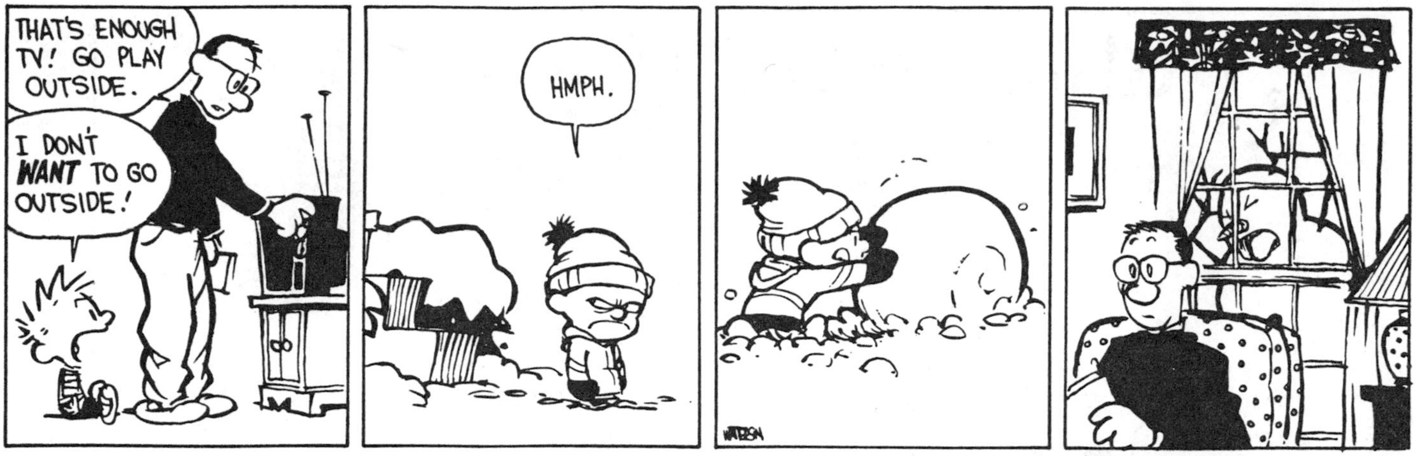
THAT'S ENOUGH TV! GO PLAY OUTSIDE.
I DON'T **WANT** TO GO OUTSIDE!
HMPH.

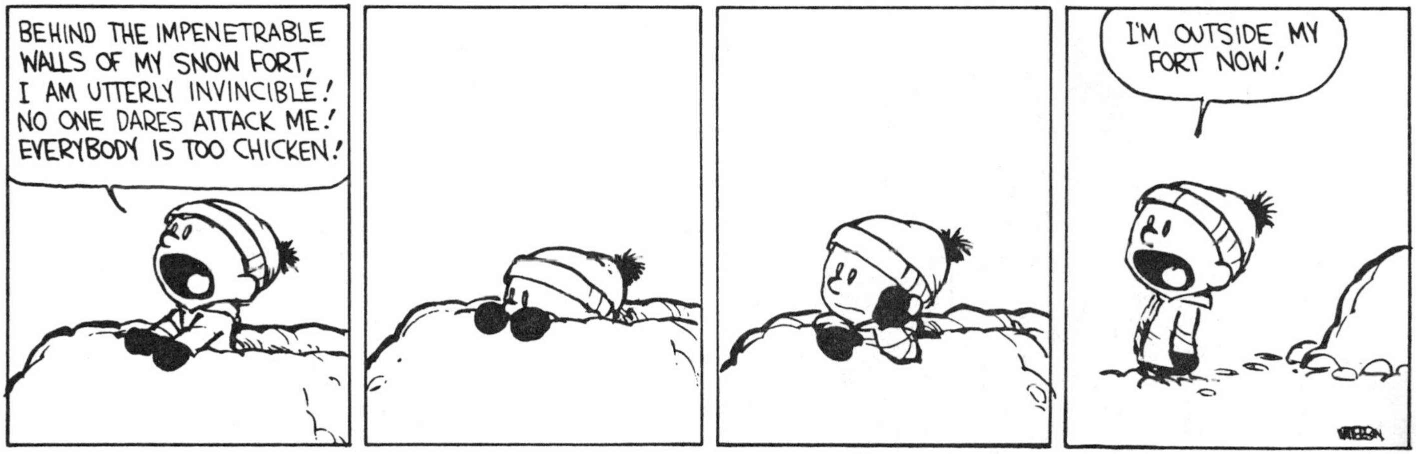
BEHIND THE IMPENETRABLE WALLS OF MY SNOW FORT, I AM UTTERLY INVINCIBLE! NO ONE DARES ATTACK ME! EVERYBODY IS TOO CHICKEN!
I'M OUTSIDE MY FORT NOW!

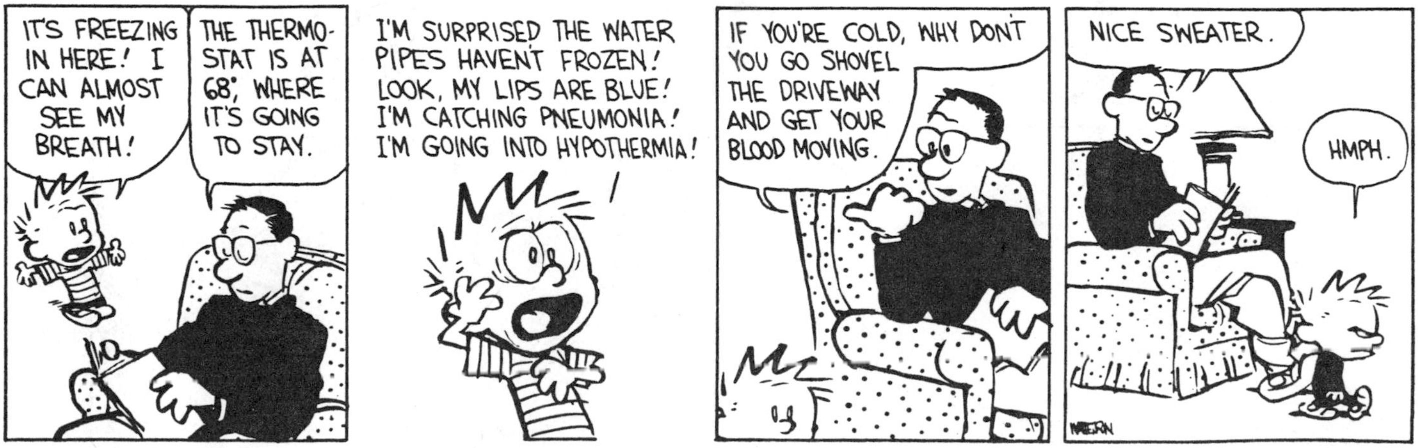
IT'S FREEZING IN HERE! I CAN ALMOST SEE MY BREATH!
THE THERMOSTAT IS AT 68°, WHERE IT'S GOING TO STAY.
I'M SURPRISED THE WATER PIPES HAVEN'T FROZEN! LOOK, MY LIPS ARE BLUE! I'M CATCHING PNEUMONIA! I'M GOING INTO HYPOTHERMIA!
IF YOU'RE COLD, WHY DON'T YOU GO SHOVEL THE DRIVEWAY AND GET YOUR BLOOD MOVING.
NICE SWEATER.
HMPH.

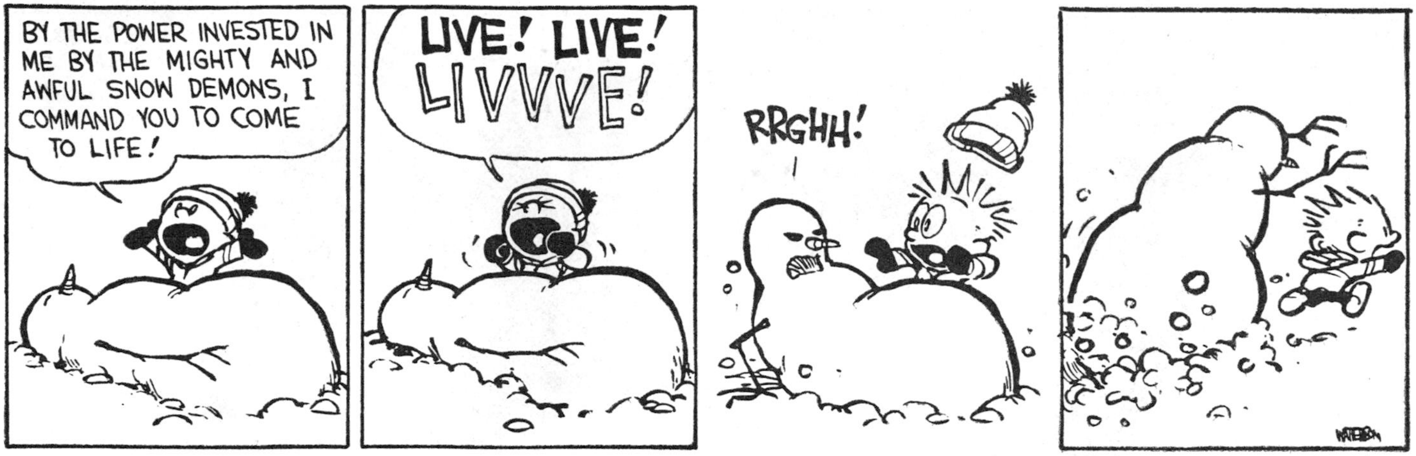
BY THE POWER INVESTED IN ME BY THE MIGHTY AND AWFUL SNOW DEMONS, I COMMAND YOU TO COME TO LIFE!
LIVE! LIVE! LIVVVE!
RRGHH!

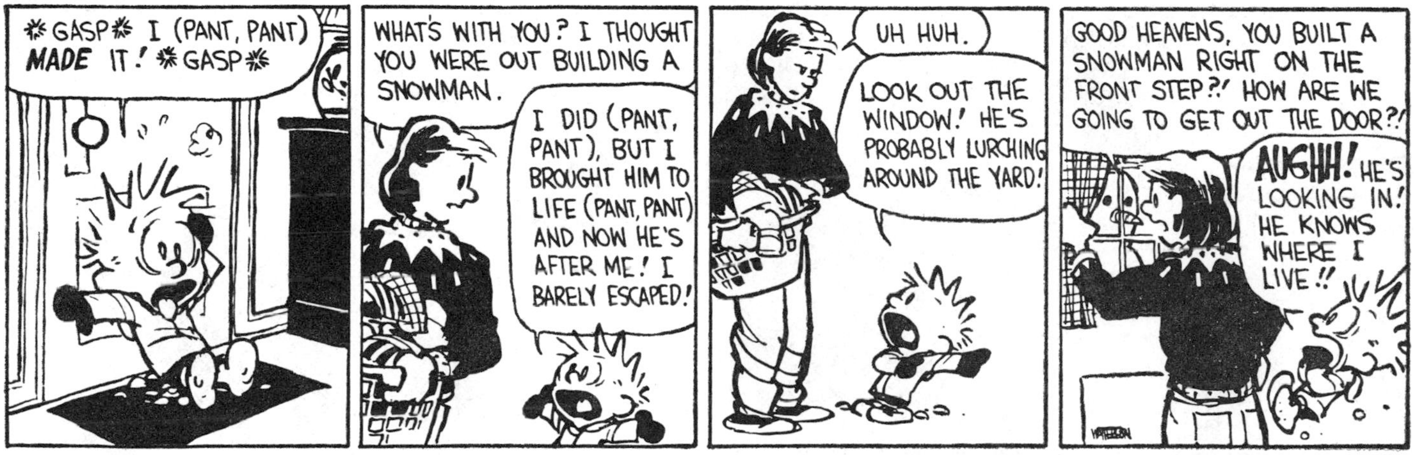
GASP I (PANT, PANT) MADE IT! *GASP*
WHAT'S WITH YOU? I THOUGHT YOU WERE OUT BUILDING A SNOWMAN.
I DID (PANT, PANT), BUT I BROUGHT HIM TO LIFE (PANT, PANT) AND NOW HE'S AFTER ME! I BARELY ESCAPED!
UH HUH.
LOOK OUT THE WINDOW! HE'S PROBABLY LURCHING AROUND THE YARD!
GOOD HEAVENS, YOU BUILT A SNOWMAN RIGHT ON THE FRONT STEP?! HOW ARE WE GOING TO GET OUT THE DOOR?!
AUGHH! HE'S LOOKING IN! HE KNOWS WHERE I LIVE!!

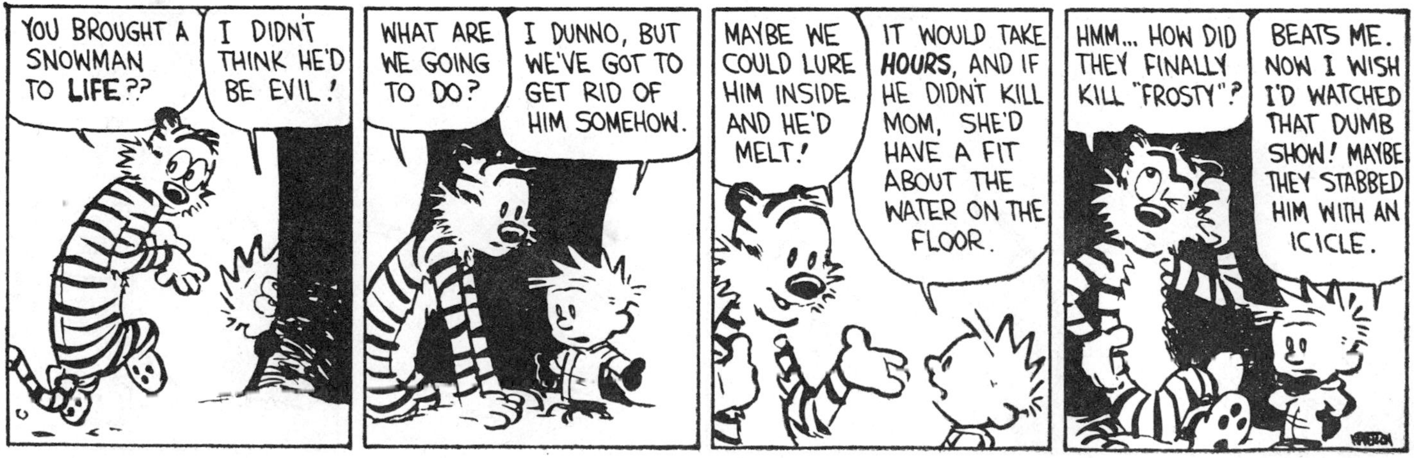
YOU BROUGHT A SNOWMAN TO LIFE??
I DIDN'T THINK HE'D BE EVIL!
WHAT ARE WE GOING TO DO?
I DUNNO, BUT WE'VE GOT TO GET RID OF HIM SOMEHOW.
MAYBE WE COULD LURE HIM INSIDE AND HE'D MELT!
IT WOULD TAKE HOURS, AND IF HE DIDN'T KILL MOM, SHE'D HAVE A FIT ABOUT THE WATER ON THE FLOOR.
HMM... HOW DID THEY FINALLY KILL "FROSTY"?
BEATS ME. NOW I WISH I'D WATCHED THAT DUMB SHOW! MAYBE THEY STABBED HIM WITH AN ICICLE.

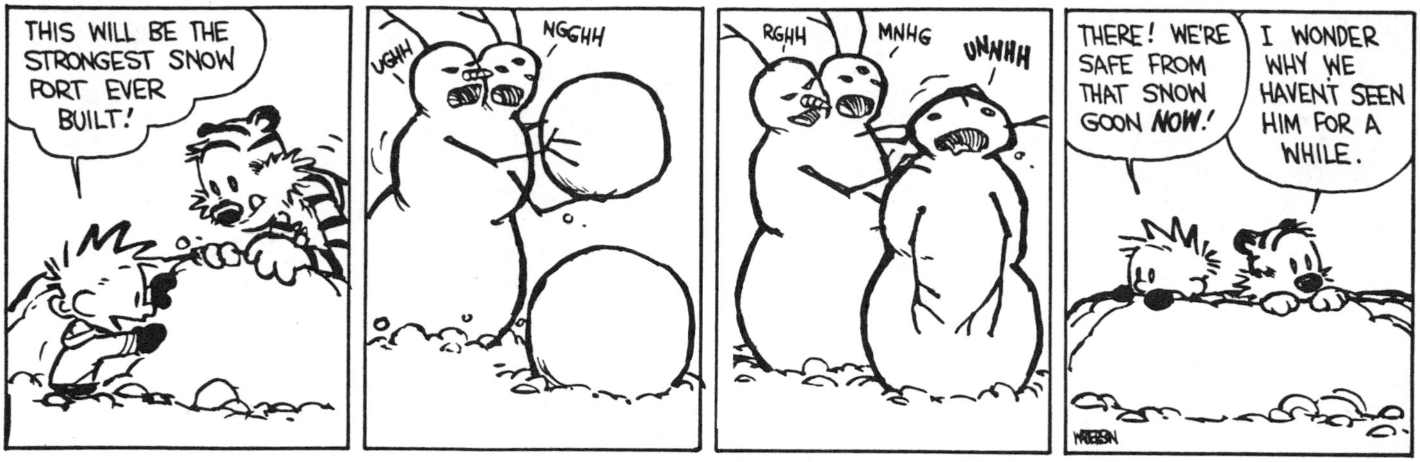
THIS WILL BE THE STRONGEST SNOW FORT EVER BUILT!
UGHH
NGGHH
RGHH
MNHG
UNNHH
THERE! WE'RE SAFE FROM THAT SNOW GOON NOW!
I WONDER WHY WE HAVEN'T SEEN HIM FOR A WHILE.

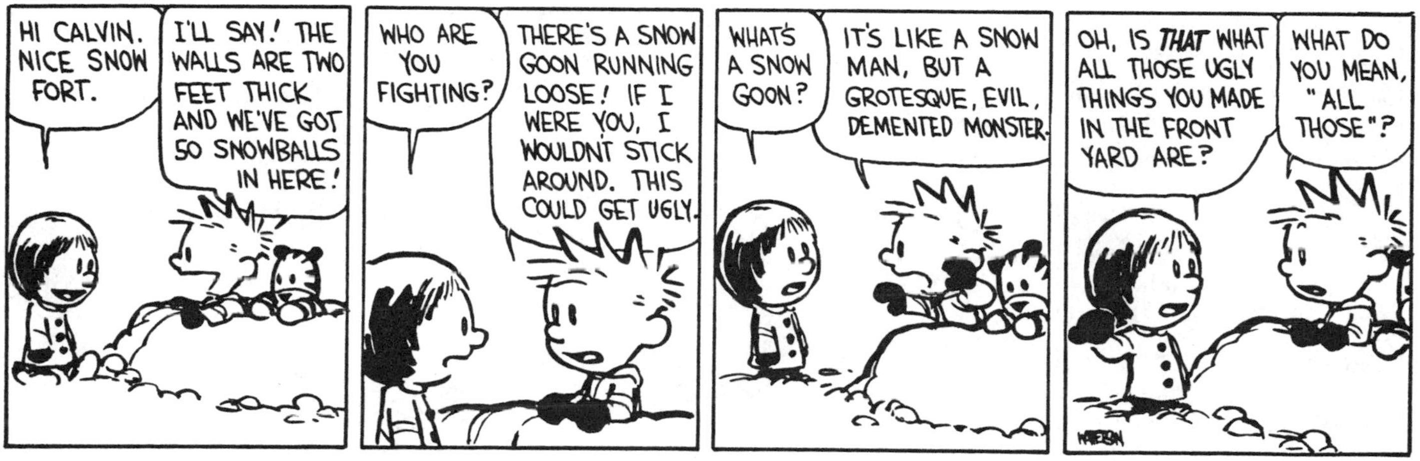
HI CALVIN. NICE SNOW FORT.
I'LL SAY! THE WALLS ARE TWO FEET THICK AND WE'VE GOT 50 SNOWBALLS IN HERE!
WHO ARE YOU FIGHTING?
THERE'S A SNOW GOON RUNNING LOOSE! IF I WERE YOU, I WOULDN'T STICK AROUND. THIS COULD GET UGLY.
WHAT'S A SNOW GOON?
IT'S LIKE A SNOW MAN, BUT A GROTESQUE, EVIL, DEMENTED MONSTER.
OH, IS THAT WHAT ALL THOSE UGLY THINGS YOU MADE IN THE FRONT YARD ARE?
WHAT DO YOU MEAN, "ALL THOSE"?

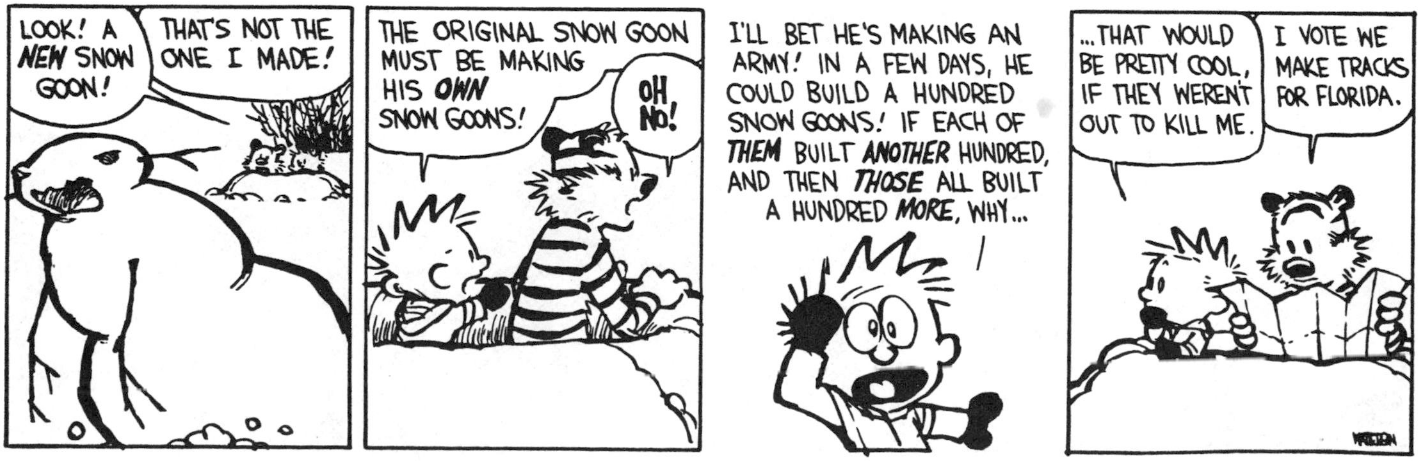
LOOK! A NEW SNOW GOON!
THAT'S NOT THE ONE I MADE!
THE ORIGINAL SNOW GOON MUST BE MAKING HIS OWN SNOW GOONS!
OH NO!
I'LL BET HE'S MAKING AN ARMY! IN A FEW DAYS, HE COULD BUILD A HUNDRED SNOW GOONS! IF EACH OF THEM BUILT ANOTHER HUNDRED, AND THEN THOSE ALL BUILT A HUNDRED MORE, WHY...
...THAT WOULD BE PRETTY COOL, IF THEY WEREN'T OUT TO KILL ME.
I VOTE WE MAKE TRACKS FOR FLORIDA.

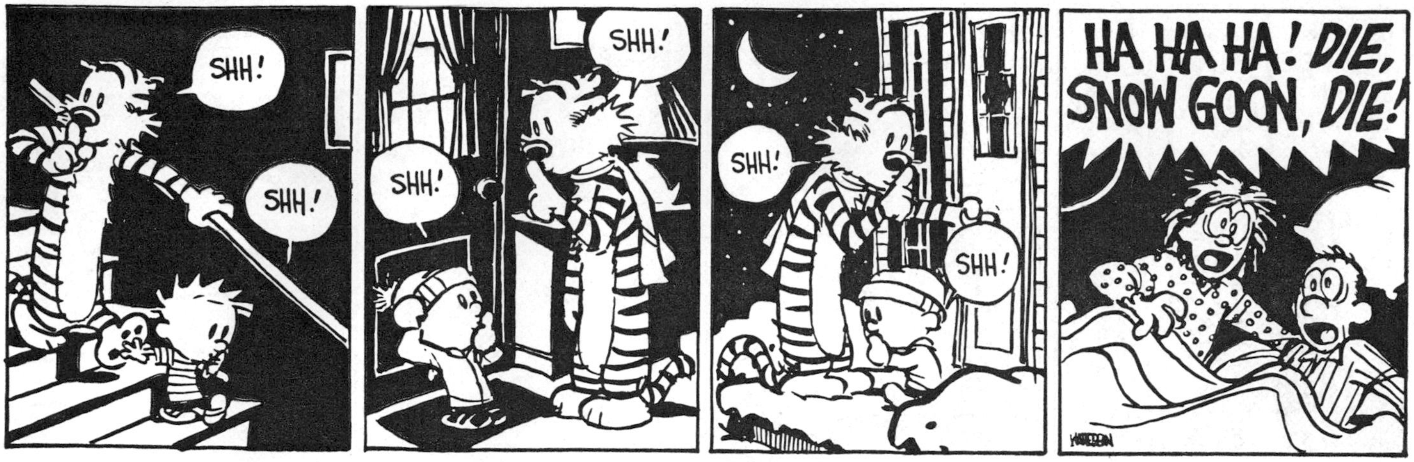
SHH!
SHH!
SHH!
SHH!
SHH!
SHH!
HA HA HA! DIE, SNOW GOON, DIE!

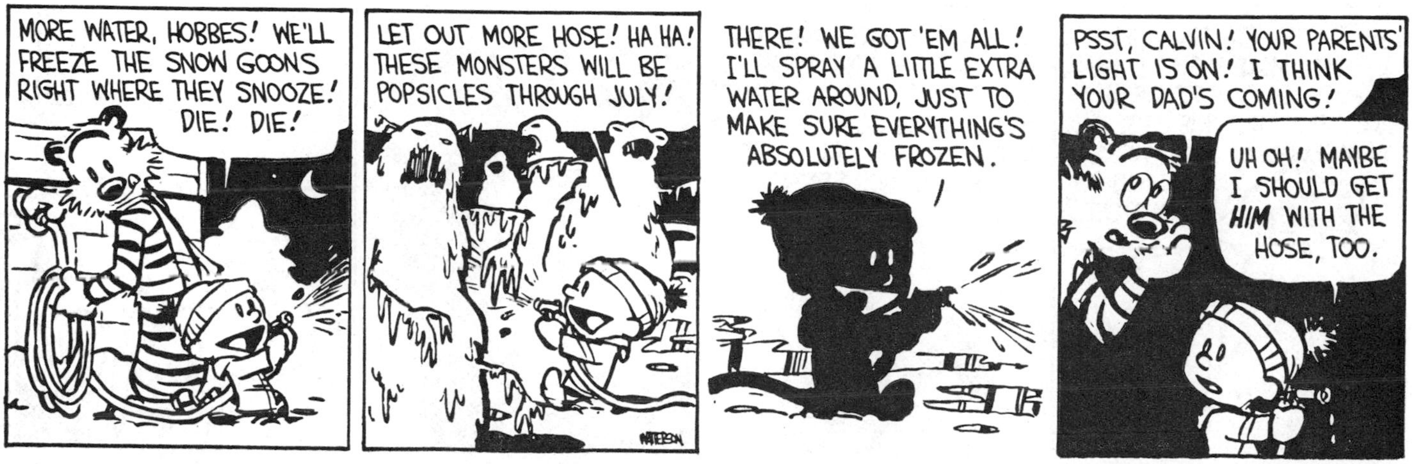
MORE WATER, HOBBES! WE'LL FREEZE THE SNOW GOONS RIGHT WHERE THEY SNOOZE! DIE! DIE!
LET OUT MORE HOSE! HA HA! THESE MONSTERS WILL BE POPSICLES THROUGH JULY!
THERE! WE GOT 'EM ALL! I'LL SPRAY A LITTLE EXTRA WATER AROUND, JUST TO MAKE SURE EVERYTHING'S ABSOLUTELY FROZEN.
PSST, CALVIN! YOUR PARENTS' LIGHT IS ON! I THINK YOUR DAD'S COMING!
UH OH! MAYBE I SHOULD GET HIM WITH THE HOSE, TOO.

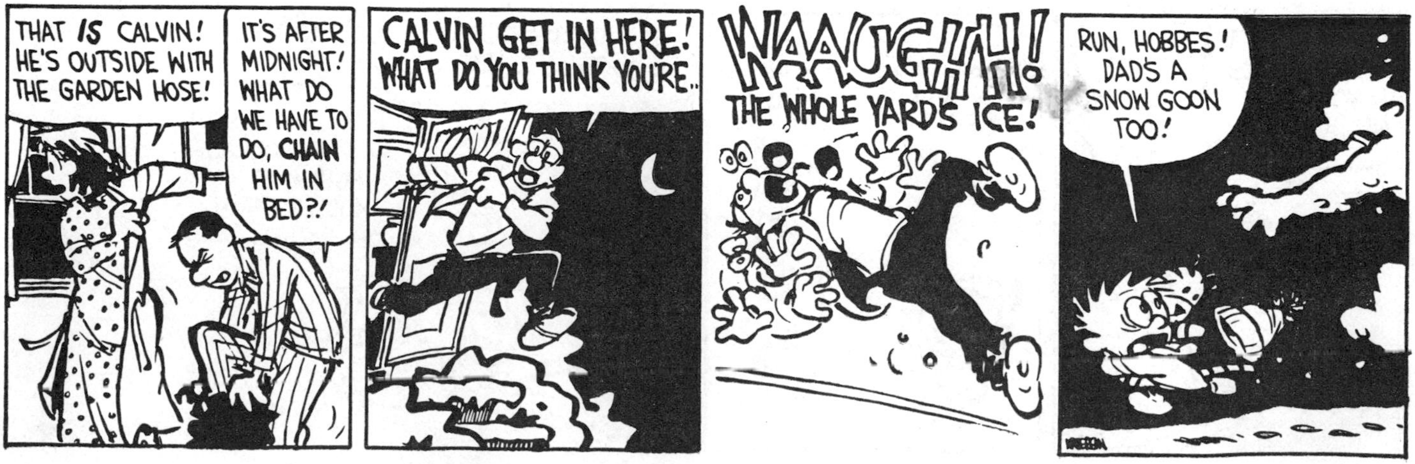
THAT IS CALVIN! HE'S OUTSIDE WITH THE GARDEN HOSE!
IT'S AFTER MIDNIGHT! WHAT DO WE HAVE TO DO, CHAIN HIM IN BED?!
CALVIN GET IN HERE! WHAT DO YOU THINK YOU'RE..
WAAUGHH!
THE WHOLE YARD'S ICE!
RUN, HOBBES! DAD'S A SNOW GOON TOO!

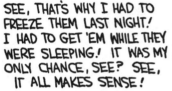

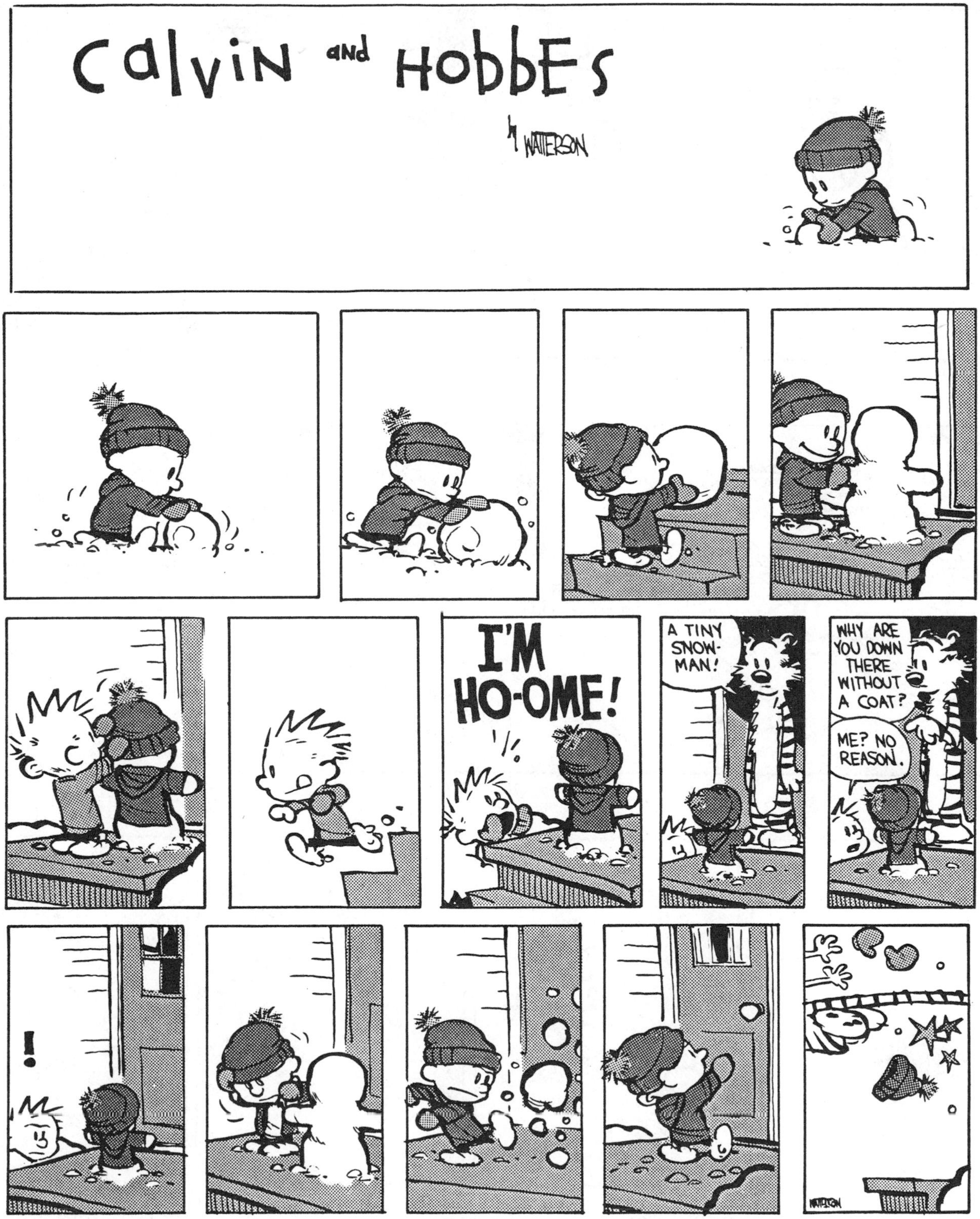
Calvin and HOBBES
by WATTERSON
I'M HO-OME!
A TINY SNOW-MAN!
WHY ARE YOU DOWN THERE WITHOUT A COAT?
ME? NO REASON.
!
WATTERSON

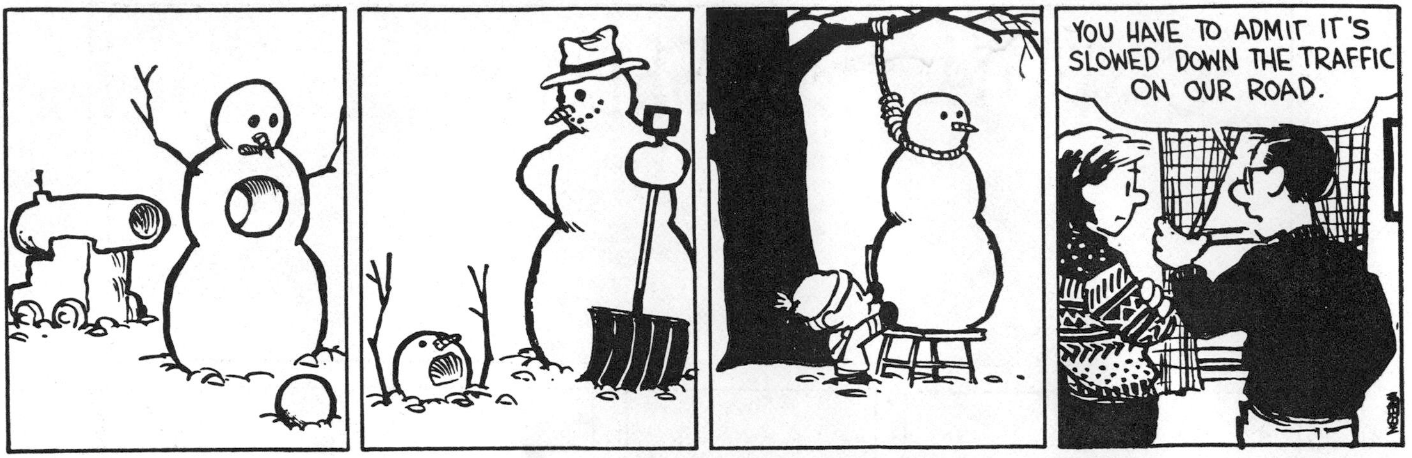
YOU HAVE TO ADMIT IT'S SLOWED DOWN THE TRAFFIC ON OUR ROAD.

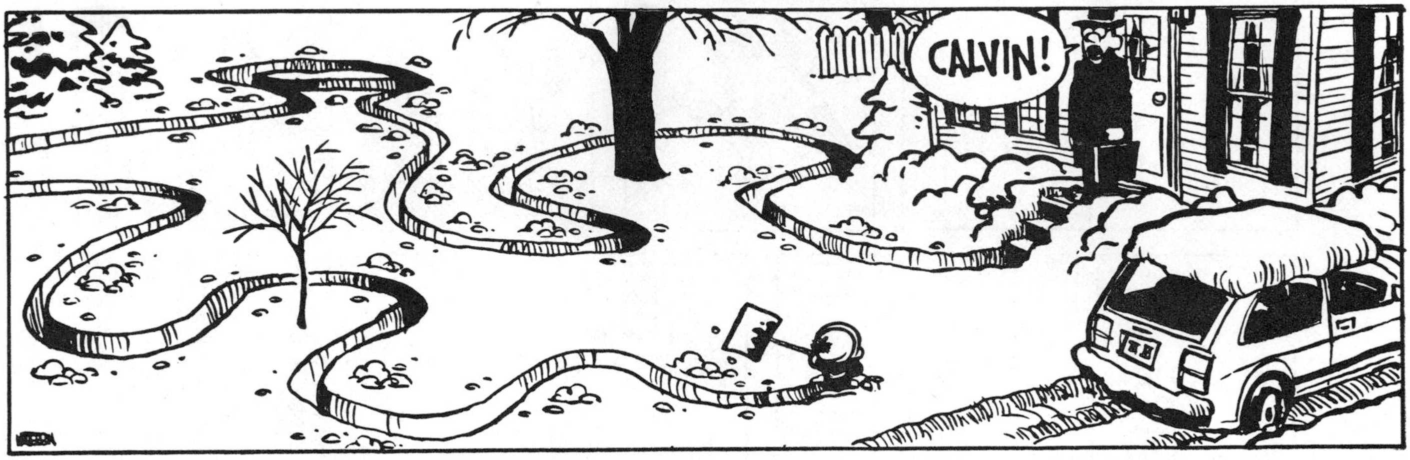
CALVIN!

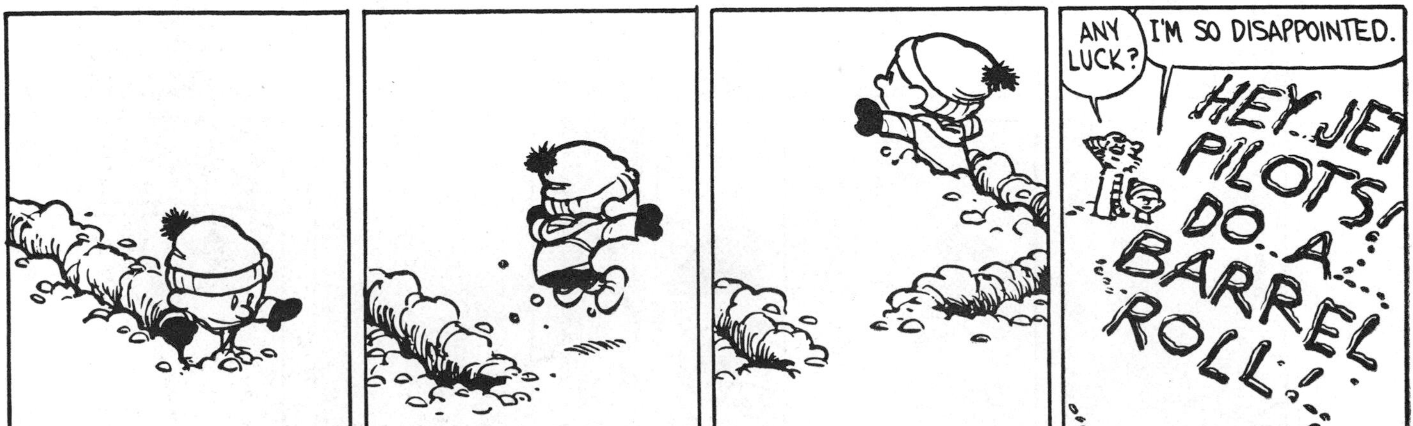
ANY LUCK?
I'M SO DISAPPOINTED.
HEY JET PILOTS! DO A BARREL ROLL!

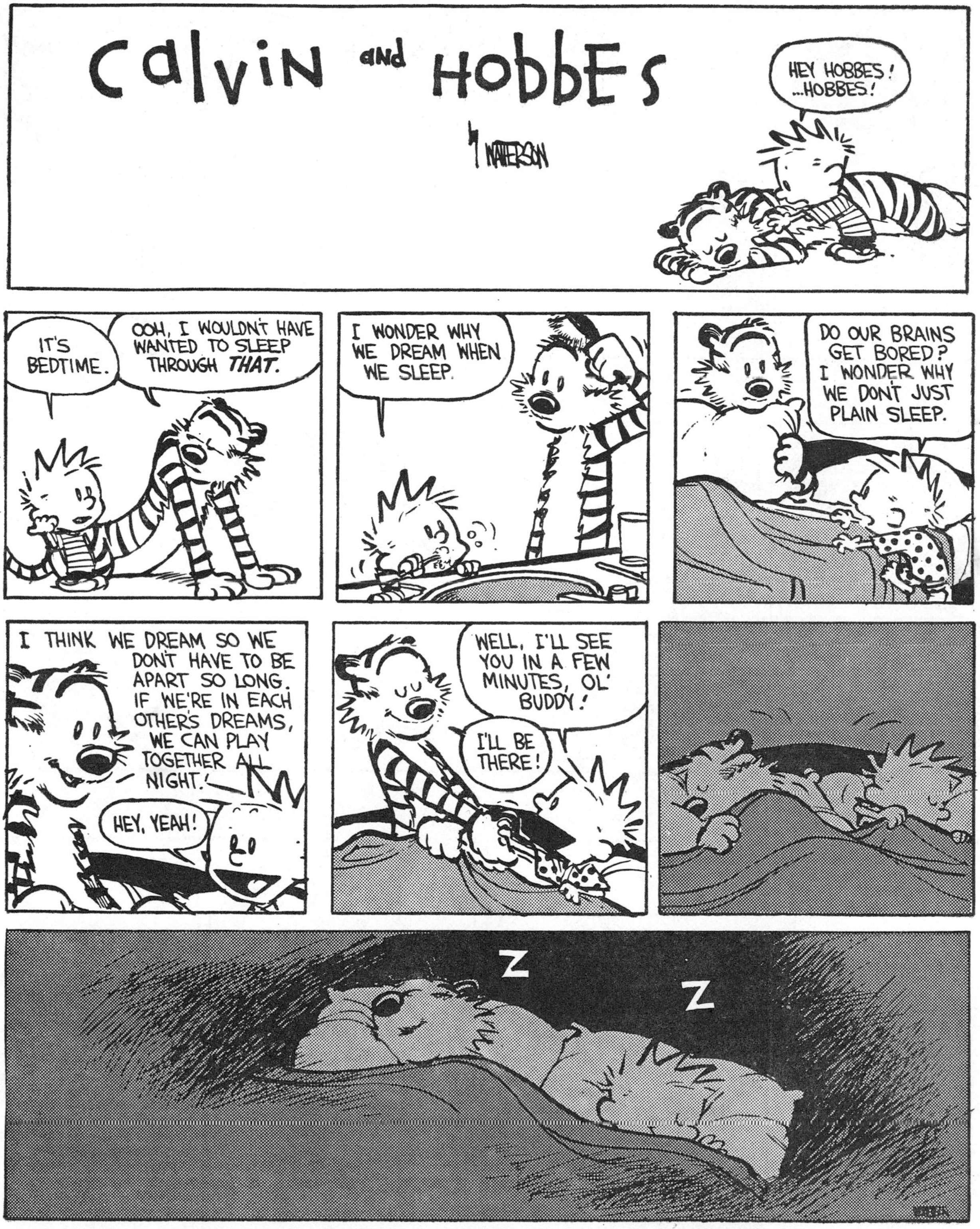
Calvin and HOBBES
by WATTERSON
HEY HOBBES! ...HOBBES!
IT'S BEDTIME.
OOH, I WOULDN'T HAVE WANTED TO SLEEP THROUGH THAT.
I WONDER WHY WE DREAM WHEN WE SLEEP.
DO OUR BRAINS GET BORED? I WONDER WHY WE DON'T JUST PLAIN SLEEP.
I THINK WE DREAM SO WE DON'T HAVE TO BE APART SO LONG. IF WE'RE IN EACH OTHER'S DREAMS, WE CAN PLAY TOGETHER ALL NIGHT.
HEY, YEAH!
WELL, I'LL SEE YOU IN A FEW MINUTES, OL' BUDDY!
I'LL BE THERE!
Z
Z

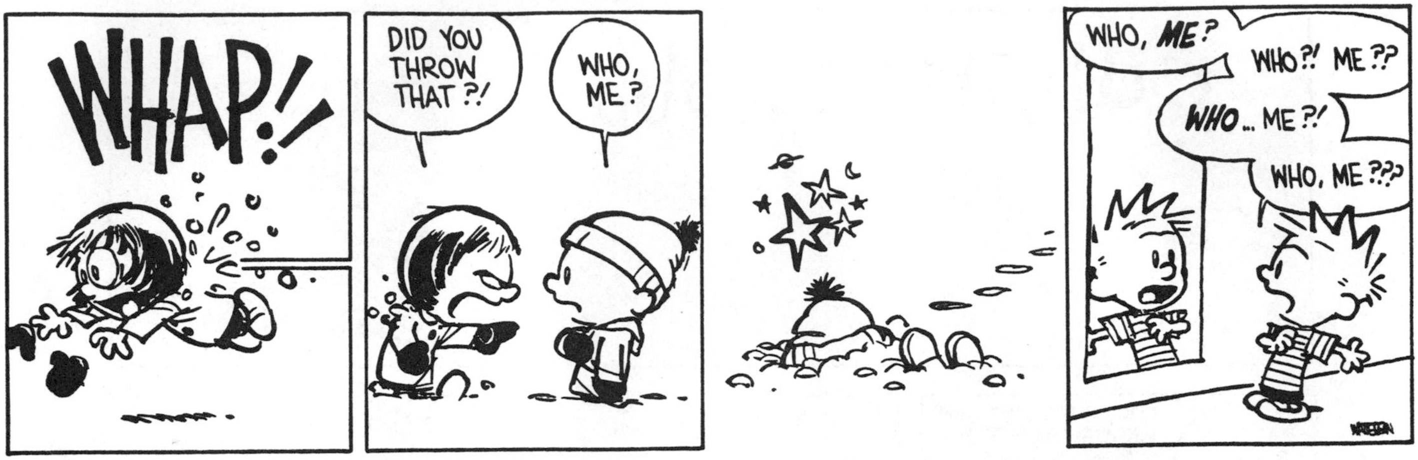
WHAP!!
DID YOU THROW THAT?!
WHO, ME?
WHO, ME?
WHO?! ME??
WHO... ME?!
WHO, ME???

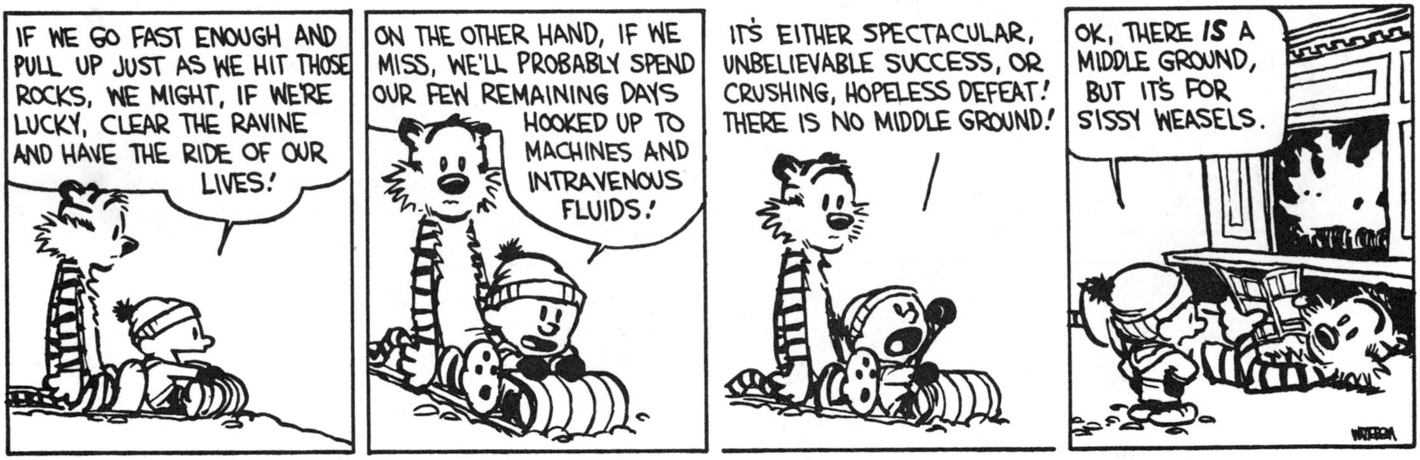
IF WE GO FAST ENOUGH AND PULL UP JUST AS WE HIT THOSE ROCKS, WE MIGHT, IF WE'RE LUCKY, CLEAR THE RAVINE AND HAVE THE RIDE OF OUR LIVES!
ON THE OTHER HAND, IF WE MISS, WE'LL PROBABLY SPEND OUR FEW REMAINING DAYS HOOKED UP TO MACHINES AND INTRAVENOUS FLUIDS!
IT'S EITHER SPECTACULAR, UNBELIEVABLE SUCCESS, OR CRUSHING, HOPELESS DEFEAT! THERE IS NO MIDDLE GROUND!
OK, THERE IS A MIDDLE GROUND, BUT IT'S FOR SISSY WEASELS.

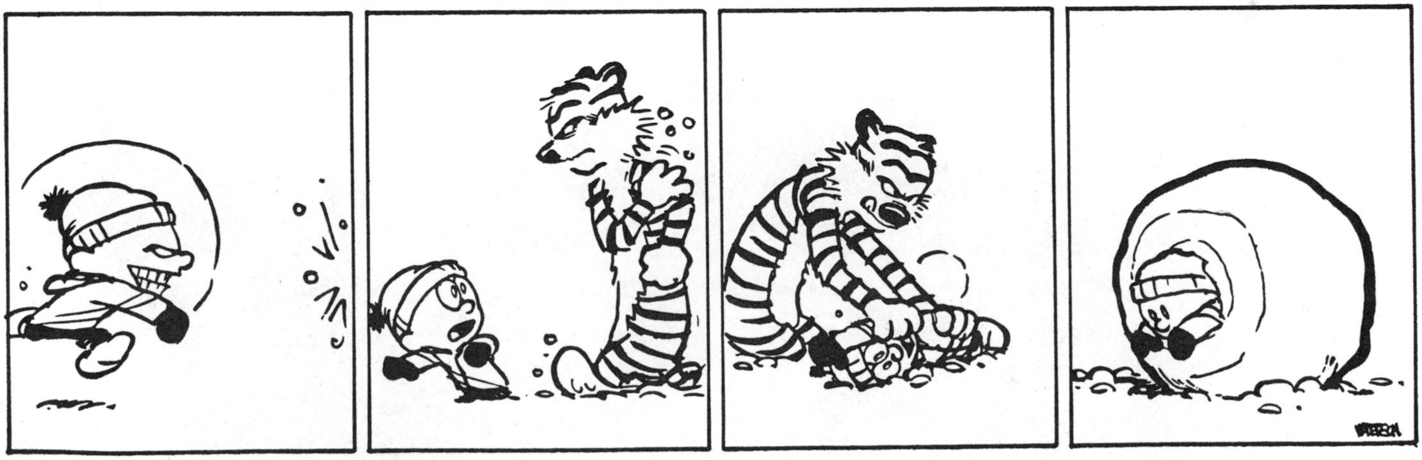

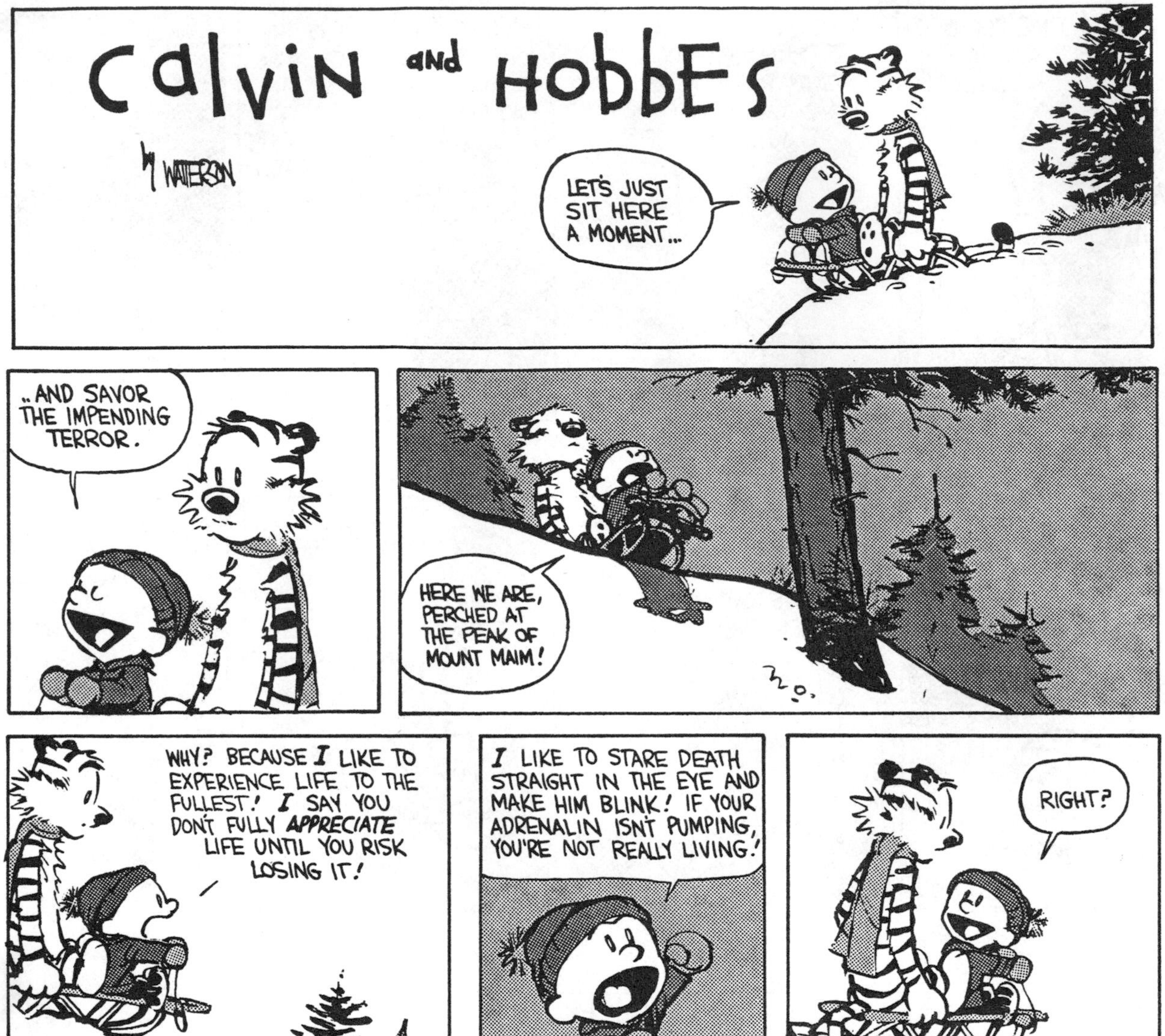
Calvin and HOBBES
by WATTERSON
LET'S JUST SIT HERE A MOMENT...
..AND SAVOR THE IMPENDING TERROR.
HERE WE ARE, PERCHED AT THE PEAK OF MOUNT MAIM!
WHY? BECAUSE I LIKE TO EXPERIENCE LIFE TO THE FULLEST! I SAY YOU DON'T FULLY APPRECIATE LIFE UNTIL YOU RISK LOSING IT!
I LIKE TO STARE DEATH STRAIGHT IN THE EYE AND MAKE HIM BLINK! IF YOUR ADRENALIN ISN'T PUMPING, YOU'RE NOT REALLY LIVING!
RIGHT?
ACTUALLY, I THINK REAL LIVING IS SITTING BY A FIRE, SLURPING MARSH-MALLOWS FROM THE BOTTOM OF A MUG OF HOT COCOA.
SLURRP

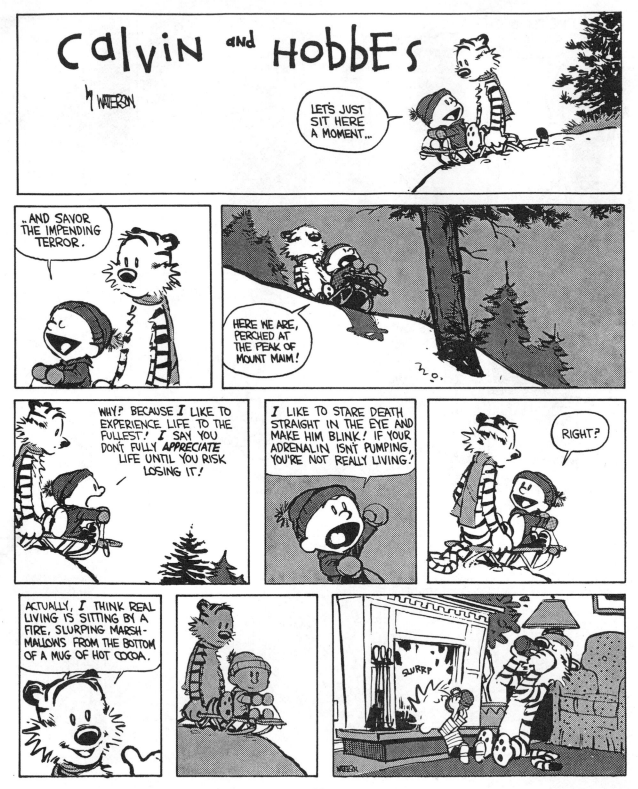

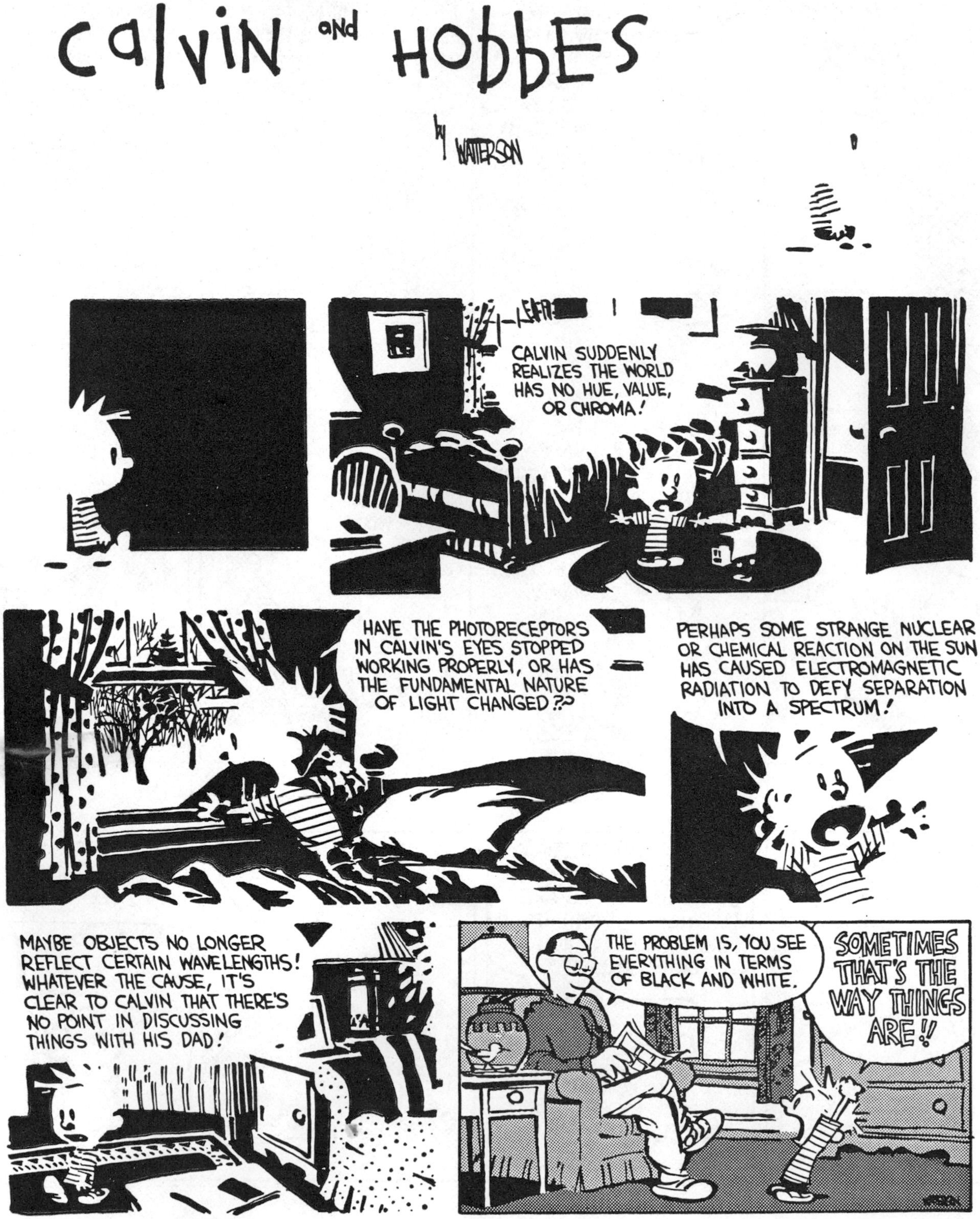
Calvin and Hobbes
by Watterson
CALVIN SUDDENLY REALIZES THE WORLD HAS NO HUE, VALUE, OR CHROMA!
HAVE THE PHOTORECEPTORS IN CALVIN'S EYES STOPPED WORKING PROPERLY, OR HAS THE FUNDAMENTAL NATURE OF LIGHT CHANGED?!
PERHAPS SOME STRANGE NUCLEAR OR CHEMICAL REACTION ON THE SUN HAS CAUSED ELECTROMAGNETIC RADIATION TO DEFY SEPARATION INTO A SPECTRUM!
MAYBE OBJECTS NO LONGER REFLECT CERTAIN WAVELENGTHS! WHATEVER THE CAUSE, IT'S CLEAR TO CALVIN THAT THERE'S NO POINT IN DISCUSSING THINGS WITH HIS DAD!
THE PROBLEM IS, YOU SEE EVERYTHING IN TERMS OF BLACK AND WHITE.
SOMETIMES THAT'S THE WAY THINGS ARE!!
WATTERSON

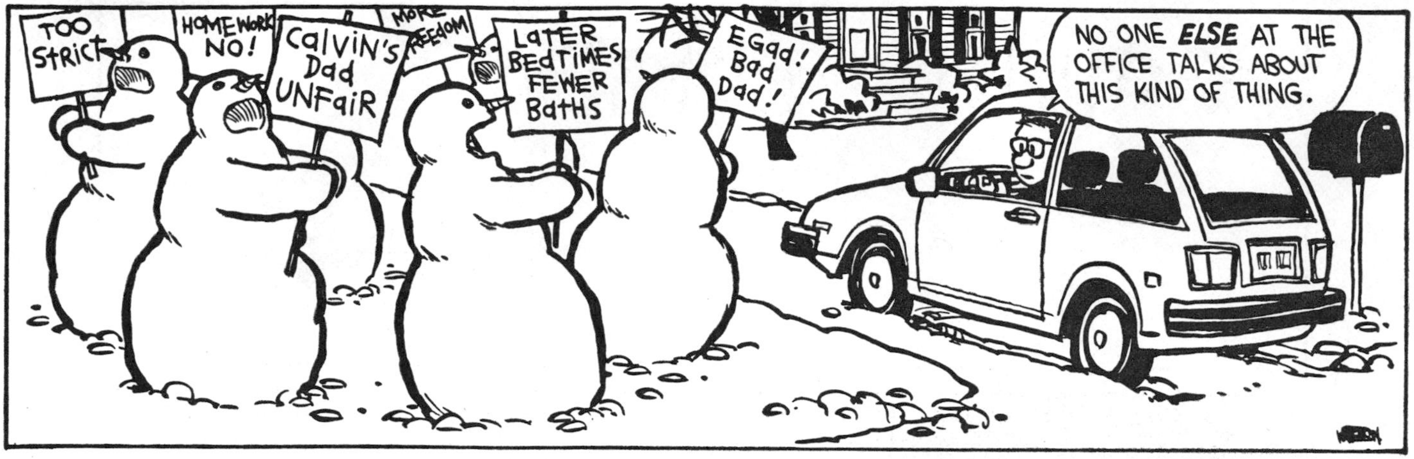
TOO Strict
HOMEWORK NO!
Calvin's Dad UNFair
Later Bedtimes Fewer Baths
Egad! Bad Dad!
NO ONE **ELSE** AT THE OFFICE TALKS ABOUT THIS KIND OF THING.

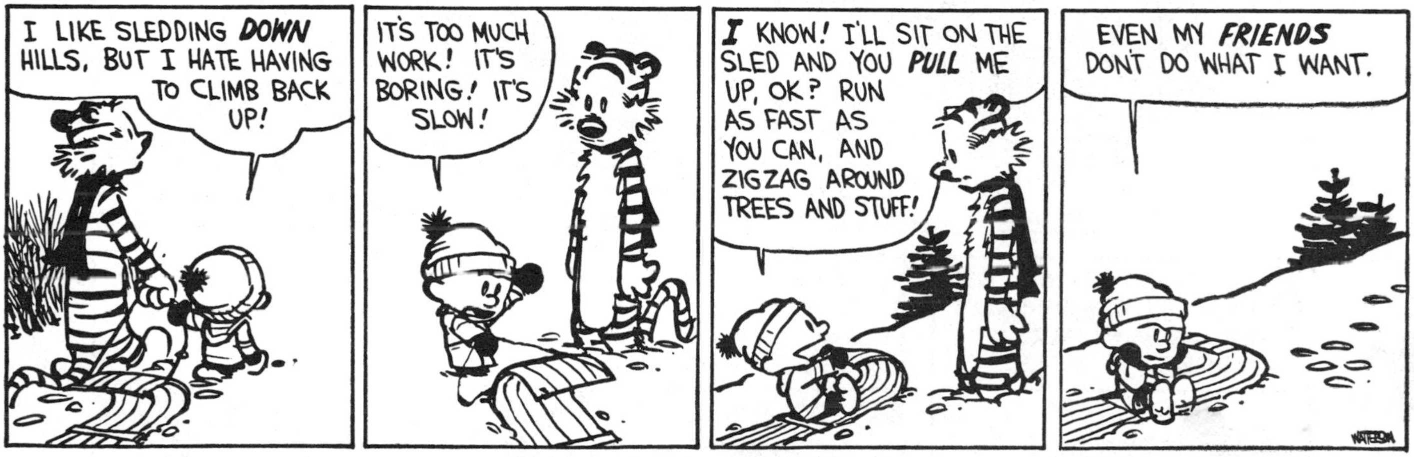
I LIKE SLEDDING **DOWN** HILLS, BUT I HATE HAVING TO CLIMB BACK UP!
IT'S TOO MUCH WORK! IT'S BORING! IT'S SLOW!
I KNOW! I'LL SIT ON THE SLED AND YOU **PULL** ME UP, OK? RUN AS FAST AS YOU CAN, AND ZIGZAG AROUND TREES AND STUFF!
EVEN MY **FRIENDS** DON'T DO WHAT I WANT.

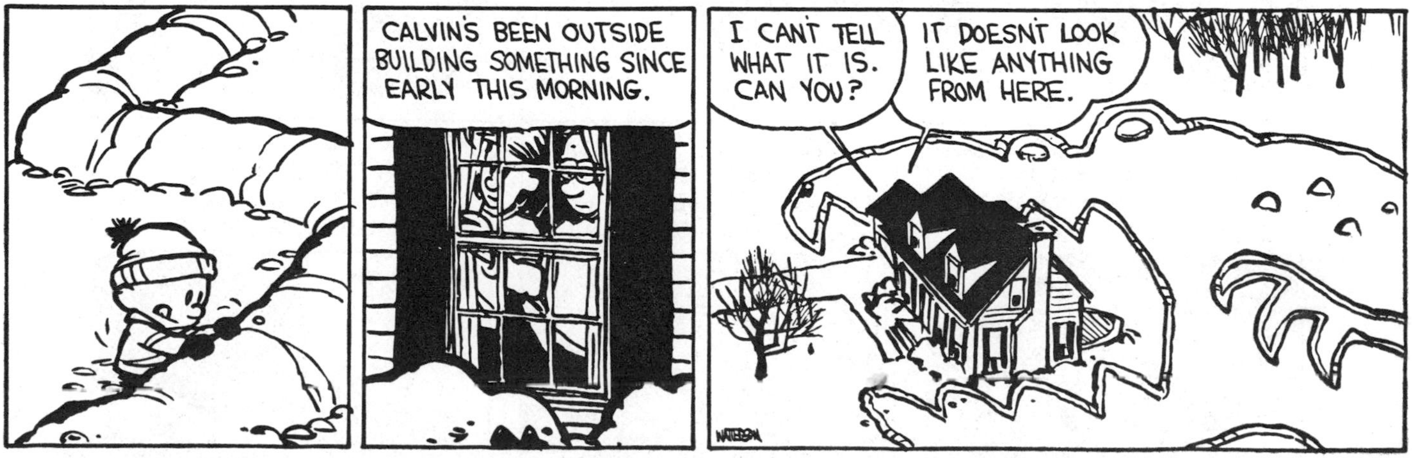
CALVIN'S BEEN OUTSIDE BUILDING SOMETHING SINCE EARLY THIS MORNING.
I CAN'T TELL WHAT IT IS. CAN YOU?
IT DOESN'T LOOK LIKE ANYTHING FROM HERE.

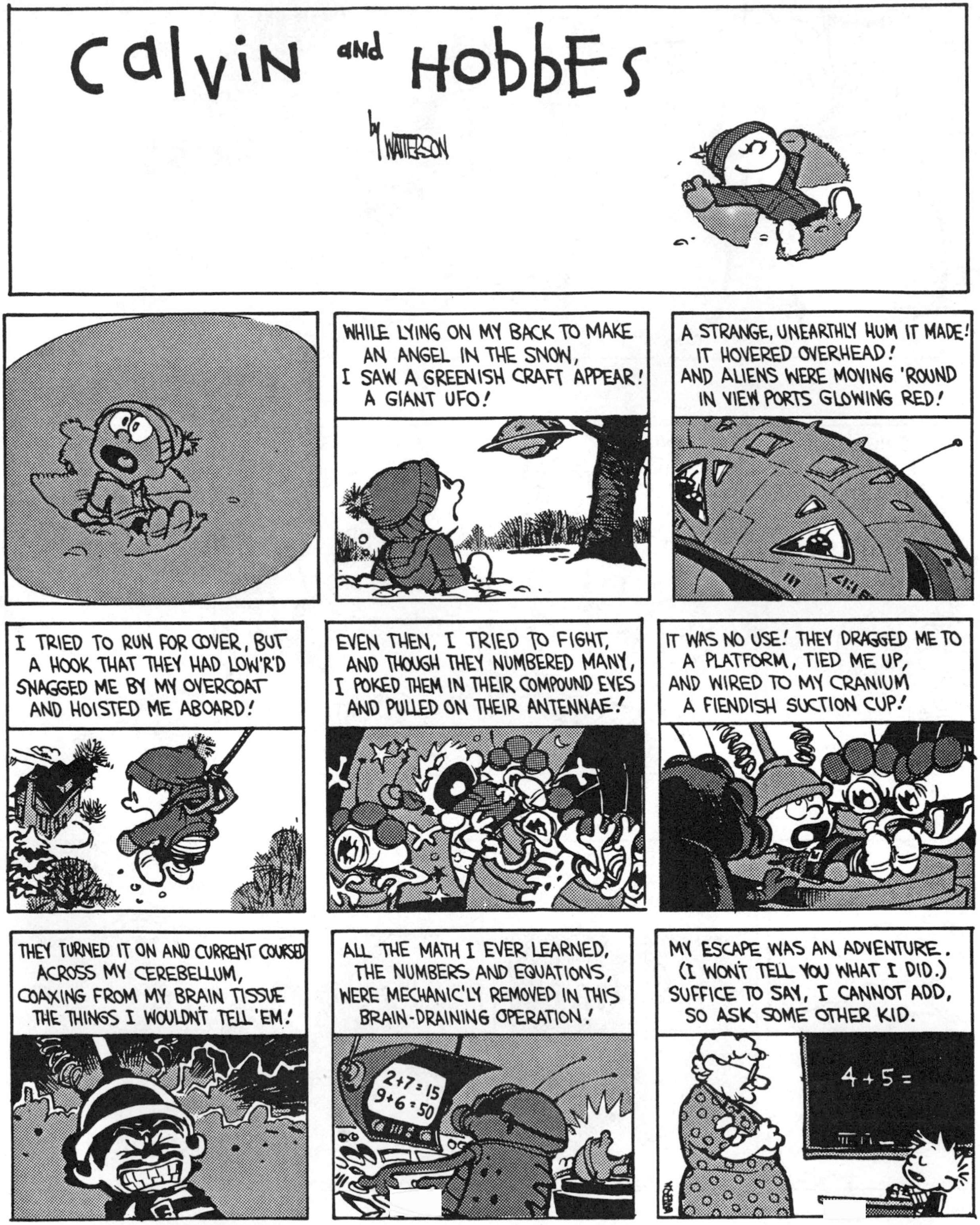
Calvin and HOBBES
by WATTERSON
WHILE LYING ON MY BACK TO MAKE AN ANGEL IN THE SNOW, I SAW A GREENISH CRAFT APPEAR! A GIANT UFO!
A STRANGE, UNEARTHLY HUM IT MADE! IT HOVERED OVERHEAD! AND ALIENS WERE MOVING 'ROUND IN VIEW PORTS GLOWING RED!
I TRIED TO RUN FOR COVER, BUT A HOOK THAT THEY HAD LOW'R'D SNAGGED ME BY MY OVERCOAT AND HOISTED ME ABOARD!
EVEN THEN, I TRIED TO FIGHT, AND THOUGH THEY NUMBERED MANY, I POKED THEM IN THEIR COMPOUND EYES AND PULLED ON THEIR ANTENNAE!
IT WAS NO USE! THEY DRAGGED ME TO A PLATFORM, TIED ME UP, AND WIRED TO MY CRANIUM A FIENDISH SUCTION CUP!
THEY TURNED IT ON AND CURRENT COURSED ACROSS MY CEREBELLUM, COAXING FROM MY BRAIN TISSUE THE THINGS I WOULDN'T TELL 'EM!
ALL THE MATH I EVER LEARNED, THE NUMBERS AND EQUATIONS, WERE MECHANIC'LY REMOVED IN THIS BRAIN-DRAINING OPERATION!
2+7=15
9+6=50
MY ESCAPE WAS AN ADVENTURE. (I WON'T TELL YOU WHAT I DID.) SUFFICE TO SAY, I CANNOT ADD, SO ASK SOME OTHER KID.
4+5=

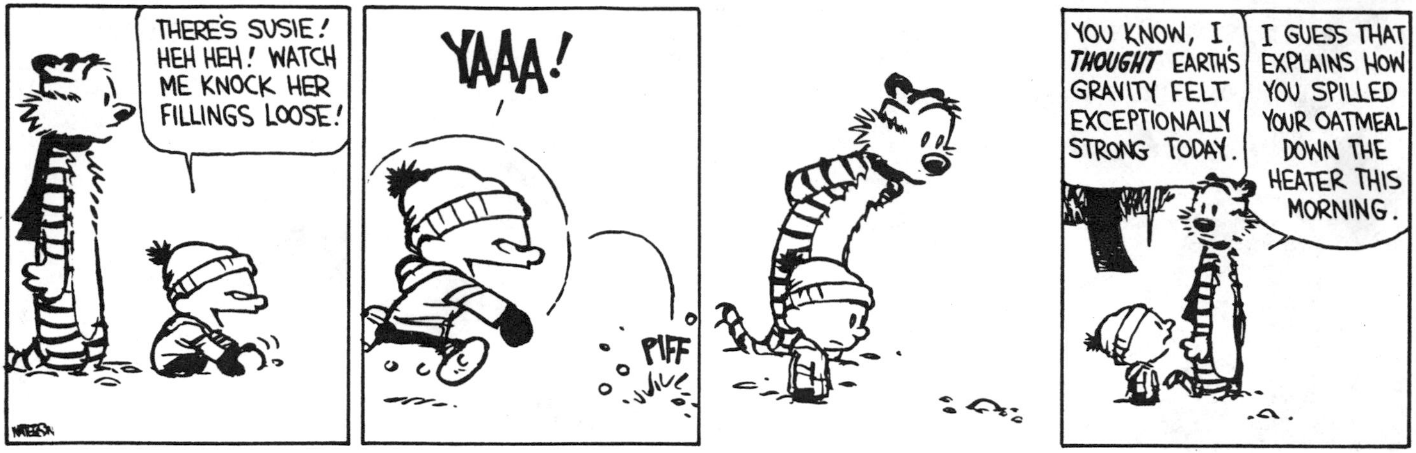
THERE'S SUSIE! HEH HEH! WATCH ME KNOCK HER FILLINGS LOOSE!
YAAA!
PIFF
YOU KNOW, I *THOUGHT* EARTH'S GRAVITY FELT EXCEPTIONALLY STRONG TODAY.
I GUESS THAT EXPLAINS HOW YOU SPILLED YOUR OATMEAL DOWN THE HEATER THIS MORNING.

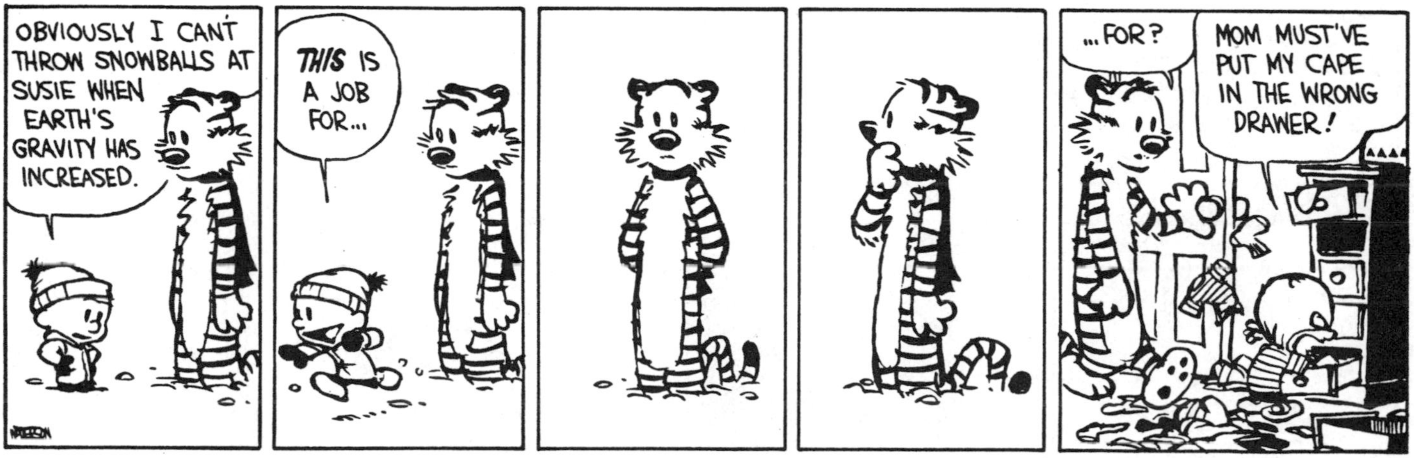
OBVIOUSLY I CAN'T THROW SNOWBALLS AT SUSIE WHEN EARTH'S GRAVITY HAS INCREASED.
THIS IS A JOB FOR...
...FOR?
MOM MUST'VE PUT MY CAPE IN THE WRONG DRAWER!

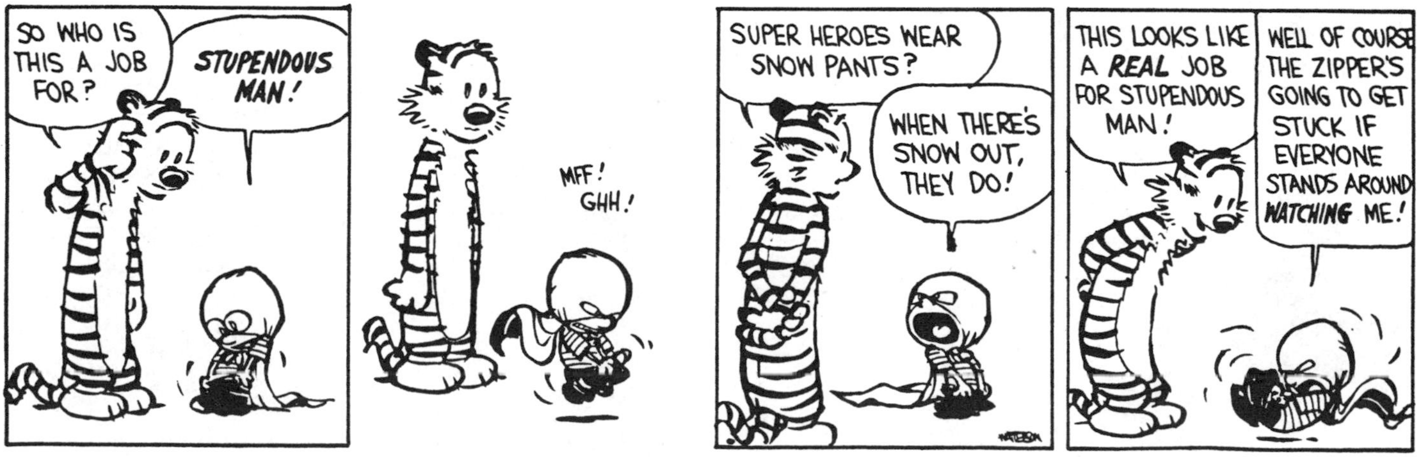
SO WHO IS THIS A JOB FOR?
STUPENDOUS MAN!
MFF! GHH!
SUPER HEROES WEAR SNOW PANTS?
WHEN THERE'S SNOW OUT, THEY DO!
THIS LOOKS LIKE A *REAL* JOB FOR STUPENDOUS MAN!
WELL OF COURSE THE ZIPPER'S GOING TO GET STUCK IF EVERYONE STANDS AROUND *WATCHING* ME!

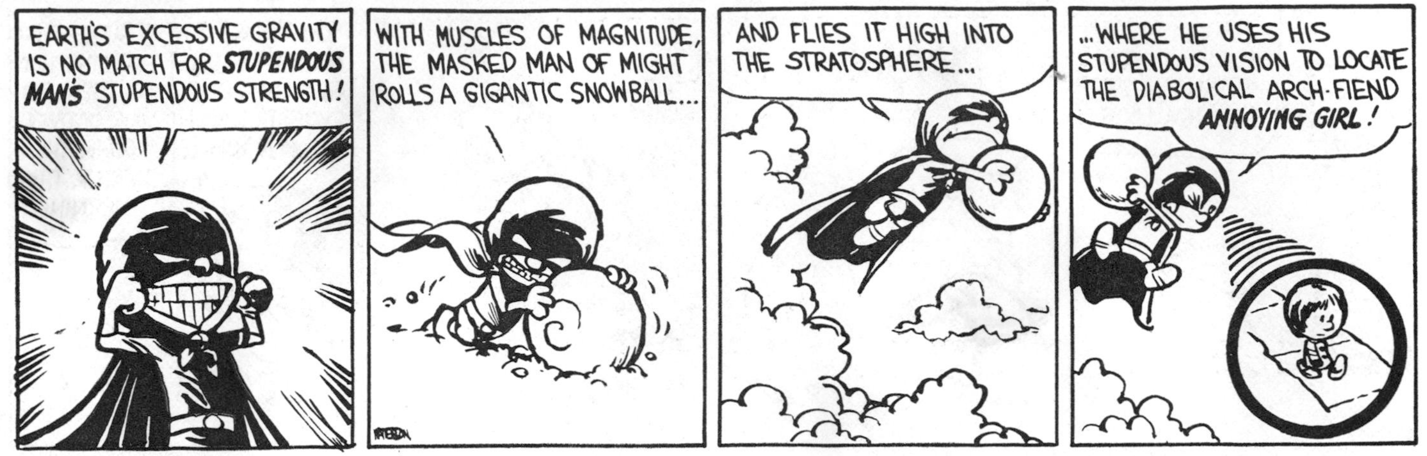
EARTH'S EXCESSIVE GRAVITY IS NO MATCH FOR STUPENDOUS MAN'S STUPENDOUS STRENGTH!
WITH MUSCLES OF MAGNITUDE, THE MASKED MAN OF MIGHT ROLLS A GIGANTIC SNOWBALL...
AND FLIES IT HIGH INTO THE STRATOSPHERE...
...WHERE HE USES HIS STUPENDOUS VISION TO LOCATE THE DIABOLICAL ARCH-FIEND ANNOYING GIRL!

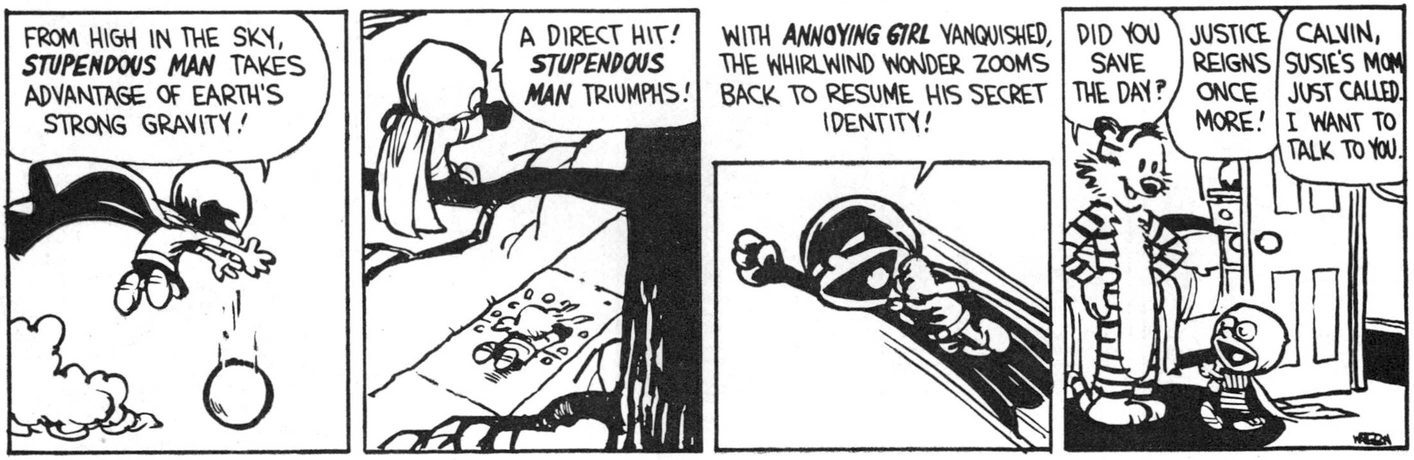
FROM HIGH IN THE SKY, STUPENDOUS MAN TAKES ADVANTAGE OF EARTH'S STRONG GRAVITY!
A DIRECT HIT! STUPENDOUS MAN TRIUMPHS!
WITH ANNOYING GIRL VANQUISHED, THE WHIRLWIND WONDER ZOOMS BACK TO RESUME HIS SECRET IDENTITY!
DID YOU SAVE THE DAY?
JUSTICE REIGNS ONCE MORE!
CALVIN, SUSIE'S MOM JUST CALLED. I WANT TO TALK TO YOU.

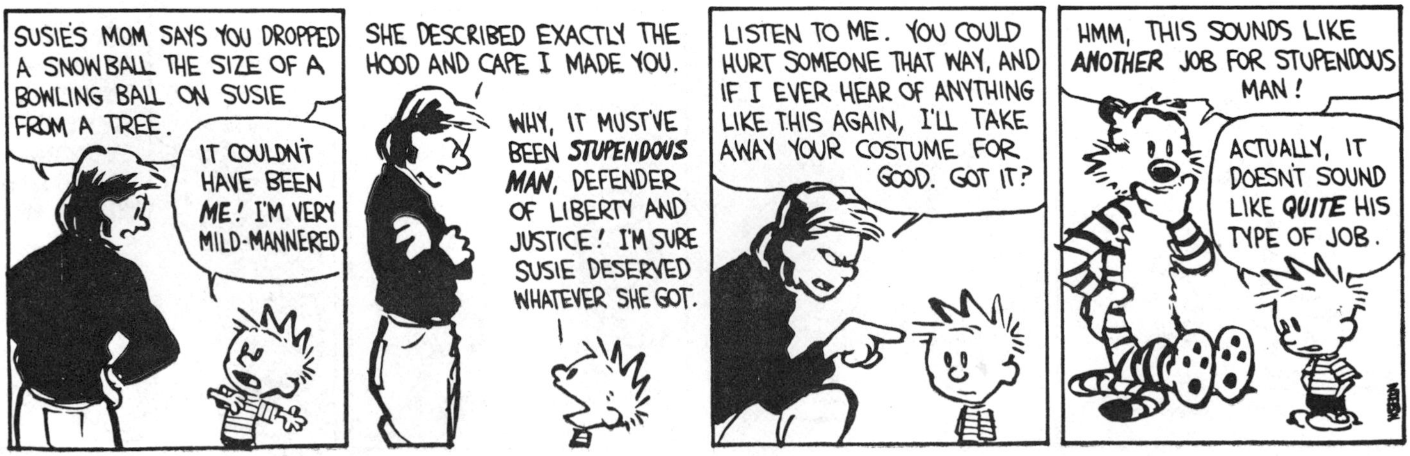
SUSIE'S MOM SAYS YOU DROPPED A SNOWBALL THE SIZE OF A BOWLING BALL ON SUSIE FROM A TREE.
IT COULDN'T HAVE BEEN ME! I'M VERY MILD-MANNERED.
SHE DESCRIBED EXACTLY THE HOOD AND CAPE I MADE YOU.
WHY, IT MUST'VE BEEN STUPENDOUS MAN, DEFENDER OF LIBERTY AND JUSTICE! I'M SURE SUSIE DESERVED WHATEVER SHE GOT.
LISTEN TO ME. YOU COULD HURT SOMEONE THAT WAY, AND IF I EVER HEAR OF ANYTHING LIKE THIS AGAIN, I'LL TAKE AWAY YOUR COSTUME FOR GOOD. GOT IT?
HMM, THIS SOUNDS LIKE ANOTHER JOB FOR STUPENDOUS MAN!
ACTUALLY, IT DOESN'T SOUND LIKE QUITE HIS TYPE OF JOB.

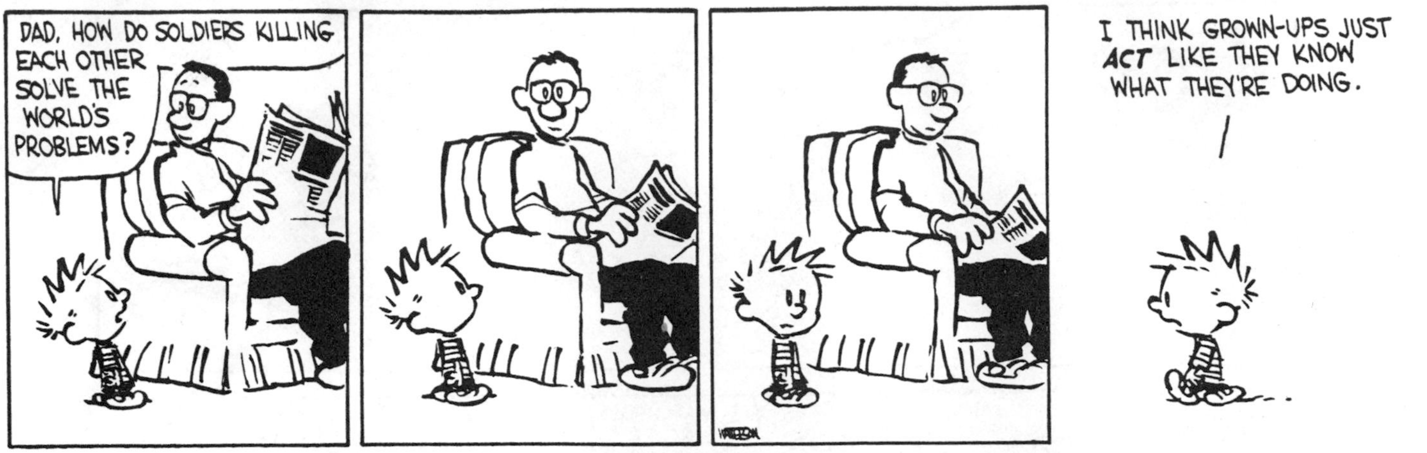
DAD, HOW DO SOLDIERS KILLING EACH OTHER SOLVE THE WORLD'S PROBLEMS?
I THINK GROWN-UPS JUST ACT LIKE THEY KNOW WHAT THEY'RE DOING.

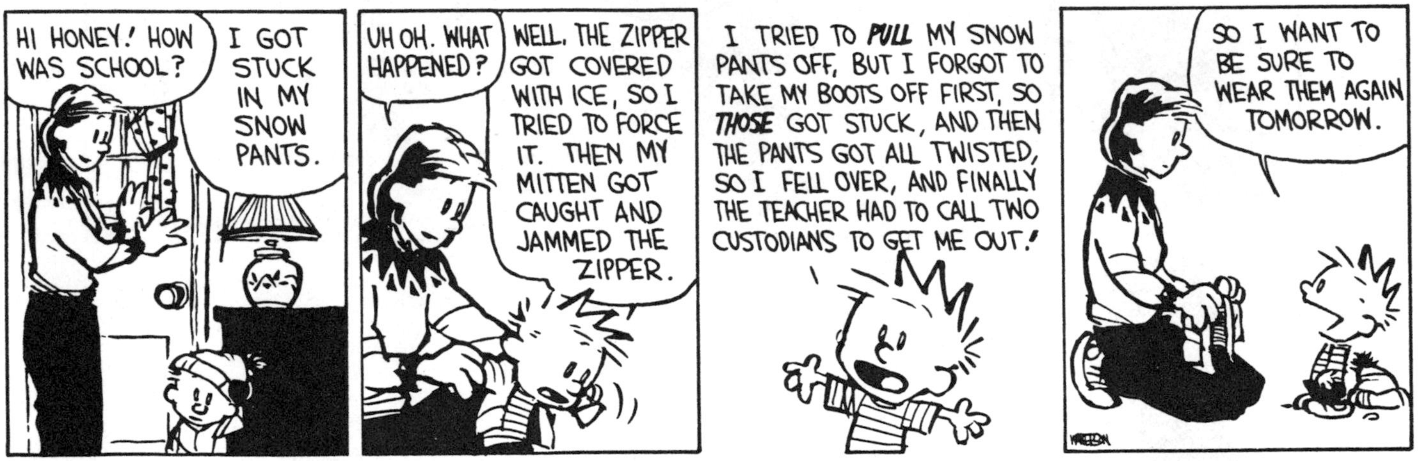
HI HONEY! HOW WAS SCHOOL?
I GOT STUCK IN MY SNOW PANTS.
UH OH. WHAT HAPPENED?
WELL, THE ZIPPER GOT COVERED WITH ICE, SO I TRIED TO FORCE IT. THEN MY MITTEN GOT CAUGHT AND JAMMED THE ZIPPER.
I TRIED TO PULL MY SNOW PANTS OFF, BUT I FORGOT TO TAKE MY BOOTS OFF FIRST, SO THOSE GOT STUCK, AND THEN THE PANTS GOT ALL TWISTED, SO I FELL OVER, AND FINALLY THE TEACHER HAD TO CALL TWO CUSTODIANS TO GET ME OUT!
SO I WANT TO BE SURE TO WEAR THEM AGAIN TOMORROW.

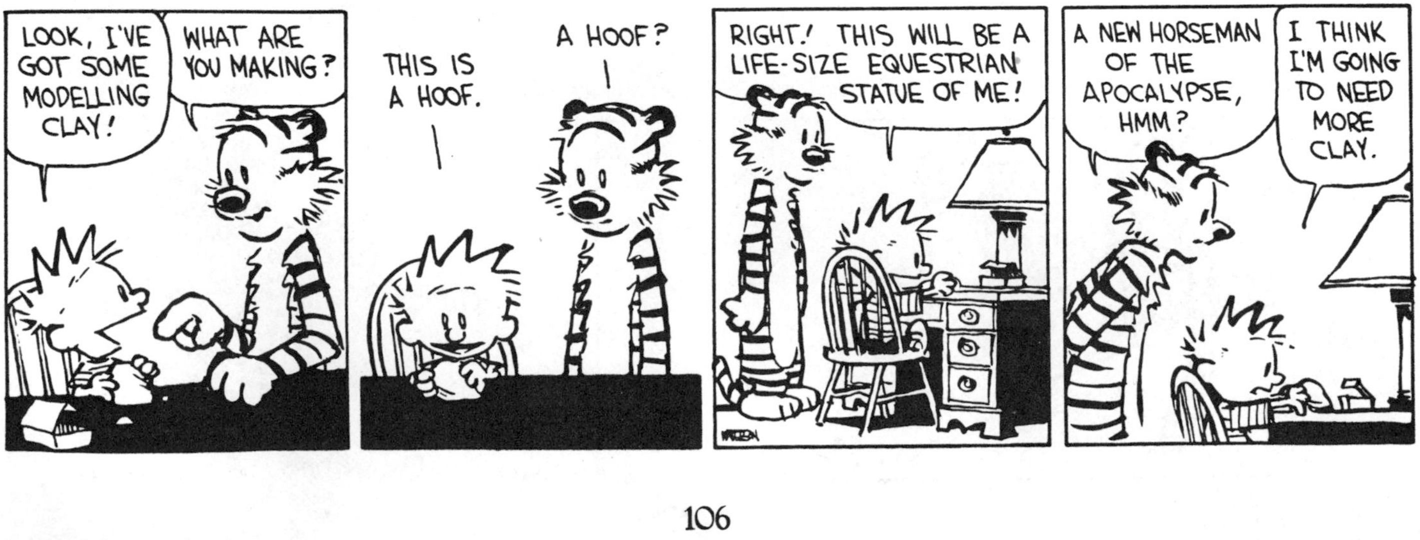
LOOK, I'VE GOT SOME MODELLING CLAY!
WHAT ARE YOU MAKING?
THIS IS A HOOF.
A HOOF?
RIGHT! THIS WILL BE A LIFE-SIZE EQUESTRIAN STATUE OF ME!
A NEW HORSEMAN OF THE APOCALYPSE, HMM?
I THINK I'M GOING TO NEED MORE CLAY.

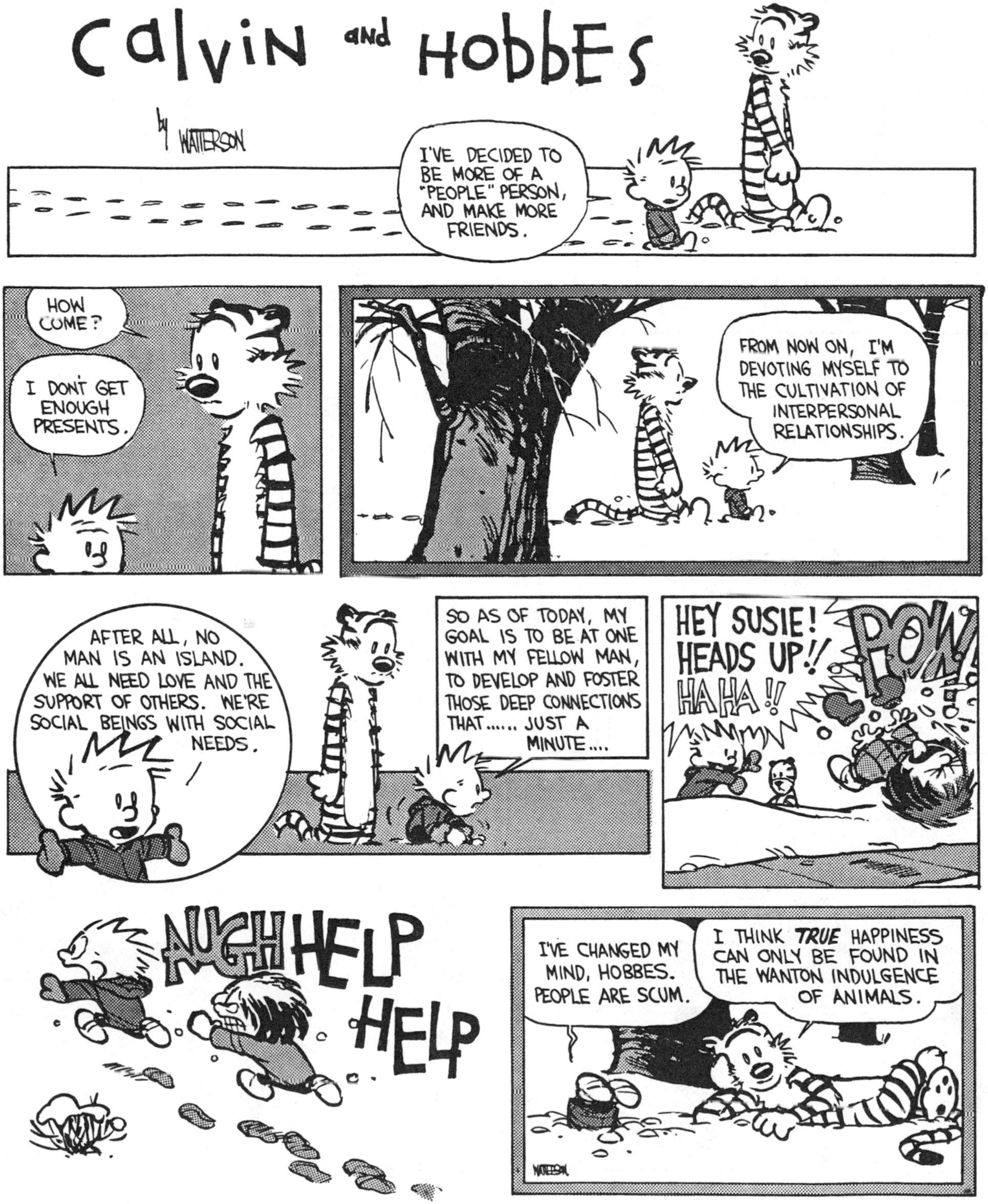
Calvin and HOBBES
by WATTERSON
I'VE DECIDED TO BE MORE OF A "PEOPLE" PERSON, AND MAKE MORE FRIENDS.
HOW COME?
I DON'T GET ENOUGH PRESENTS.
FROM NOW ON, I'M DEVOTING MYSELF TO THE CULTIVATION OF INTERPERSONAL RELATIONSHIPS.
AFTER ALL, NO MAN IS AN ISLAND. WE ALL NEED LOVE AND THE SUPPORT OF OTHERS. WE'RE SOCIAL BEINGS WITH SOCIAL NEEDS.
SO AS OF TODAY, MY GOAL IS TO BE AT ONE WITH MY FELLOW MAN, TO DEVELOP AND FOSTER THOSE DEEP CONNECTIONS THAT...... JUST A MINUTE....
HEY SUSIE! HEADS UP!!
HAHA!!
POW
AUGH
HELP
HELP
I'VE CHANGED MY MIND, HOBBES. PEOPLE ARE SCUM.
I THINK TRUE HAPPINESS CAN ONLY BE FOUND IN THE WANTON INDULGENCE OF ANIMALS.
WATTERSON

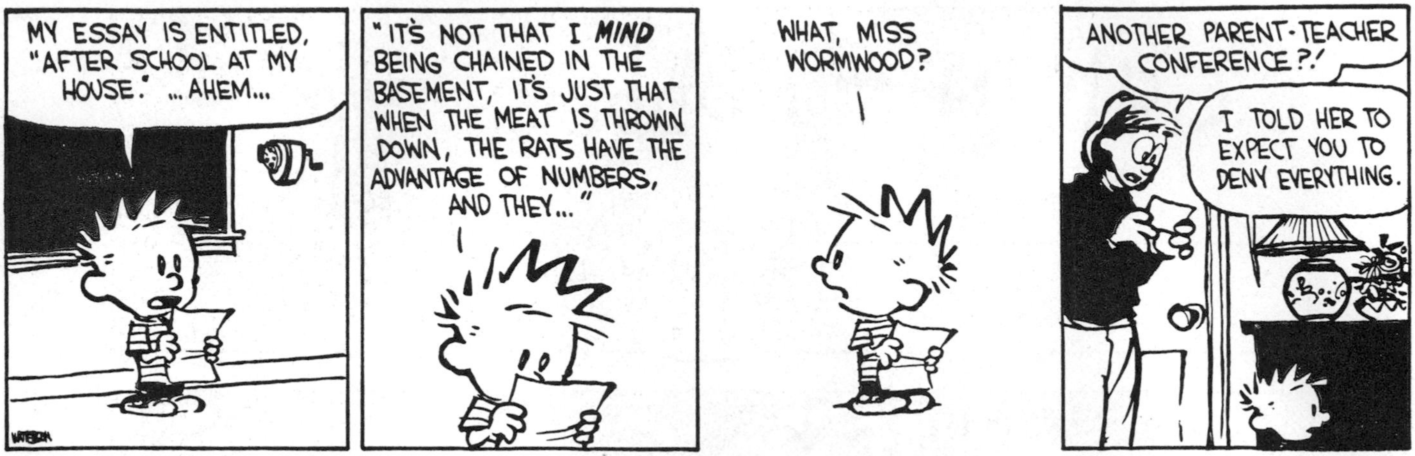
MY ESSAY IS ENTITLED, "AFTER SCHOOL AT MY HOUSE." ...AHEM...
"IT'S NOT THAT I MIND BEING CHAINED IN THE BASEMENT, IT'S JUST THAT WHEN THE MEAT IS THROWN DOWN, THE RATS HAVE THE ADVANTAGE OF NUMBERS, AND THEY..."
WHAT, MISS WORMWOOD?
ANOTHER PARENT-TEACHER CONFERENCE?!
I TOLD HER TO EXPECT YOU TO DENY EVERYTHING.

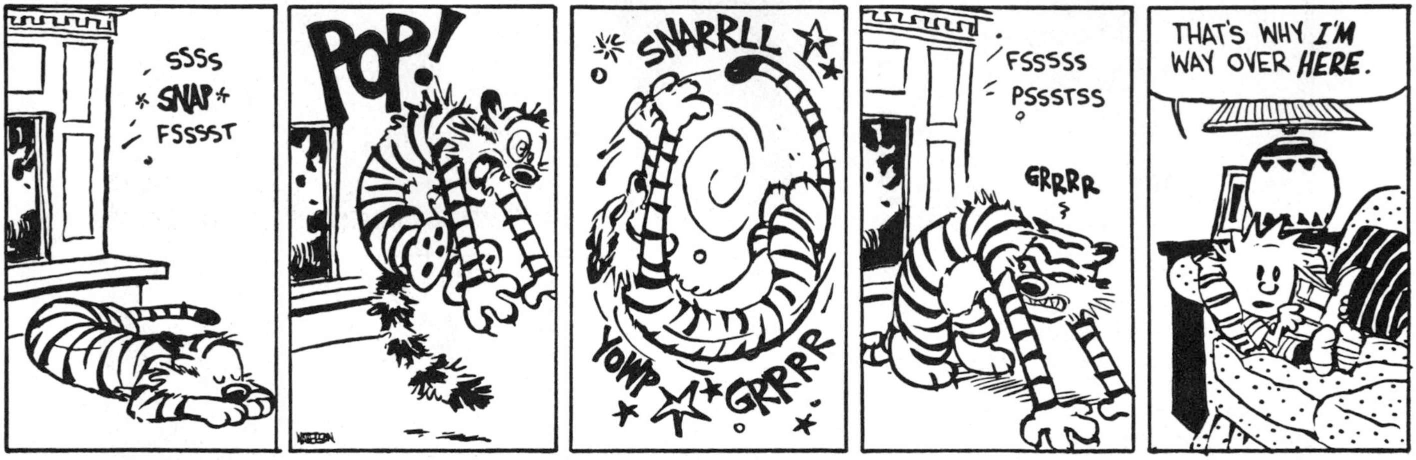
SSSS
SNAP
FSSSST
POP!
SNARRLL
YOWP
GRRRR
FSSSSS
PSSSTSS
GRRRR
THAT'S WHY I'M WAY OVER HERE.

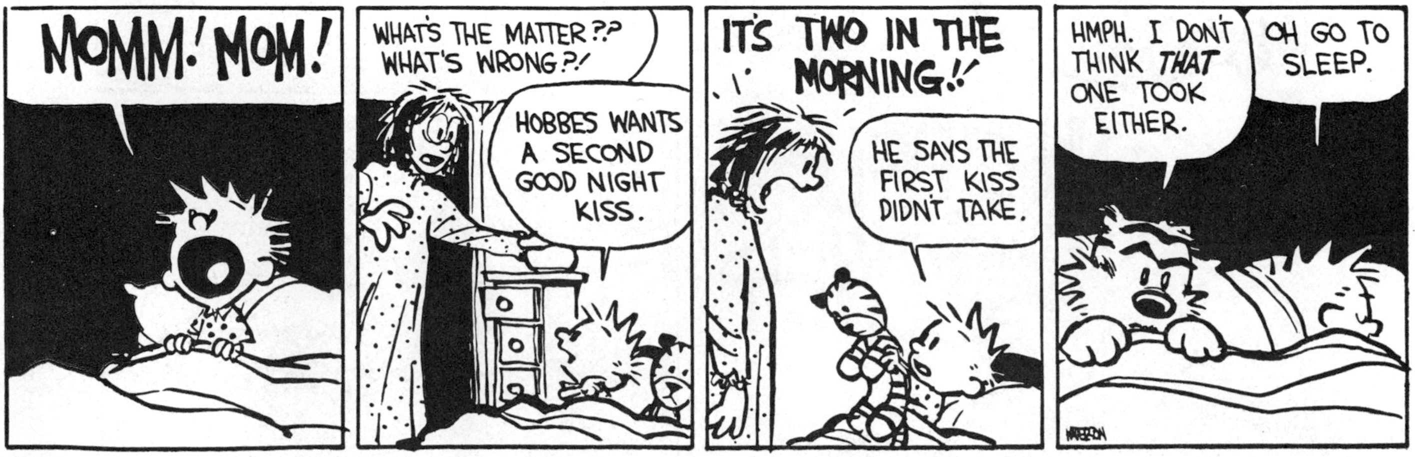
MOMM! MOM!
WHAT'S THE MATTER?? WHAT'S WRONG?!
HOBBES WANTS A SECOND GOOD NIGHT KISS.
IT'S TWO IN THE MORNING!!
HE SAYS THE FIRST KISS DIDN'T TAKE.
HMPH. I DON'T THINK THAT ONE TOOK EITHER.
OH GO TO SLEEP.

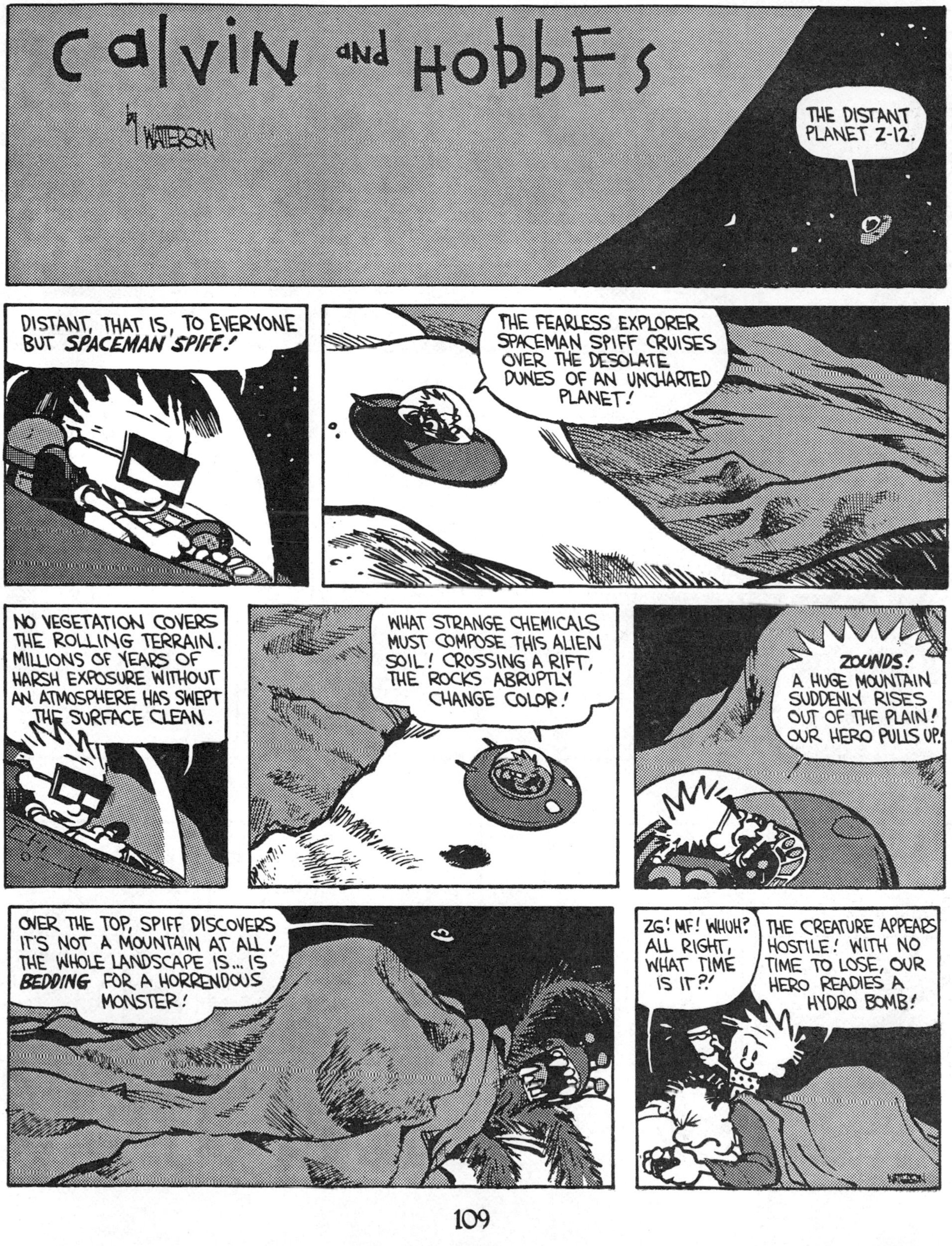

Calvin and HobbEs
by WATTERSON
THE DISTANT PLANET Z-12.
DISTANT, THAT IS, TO EVERYONE BUT SPACEMAN SPIFF!
THE FEARLESS EXPLORER SPACEMAN SPIFF CRUISES OVER THE DESOLATE DUNES OF AN UNCHARTED PLANET!
NO VEGETATION COVERS THE ROLLING TERRAIN. MILLIONS OF YEARS OF HARSH EXPOSURE WITHOUT AN ATMOSPHERE HAS SWEPT THE SURFACE CLEAN.
WHAT STRANGE CHEMICALS MUST COMPOSE THIS ALIEN SOIL! CROSSING A RIFT, THE ROCKS ABRUPTLY CHANGE COLOR!
ZOUNDS! A HUGE MOUNTAIN SUDDENLY RISES OUT OF THE PLAIN! OUR HERO PULLS UP!
OVER THE TOP, SPIFF DISCOVERS IT'S NOT A MOUNTAIN AT ALL! THE WHOLE LANDSCAPE IS... IS BEDDING FOR A HORRENDOUS MONSTER!
ZG! MF! WHUH? ALL RIGHT, WHAT TIME IS IT?!
THE CREATURE APPEARS HOSTILE! WITH NO TIME TO LOSE, OUR HERO READIES A HYDRO BOMB!

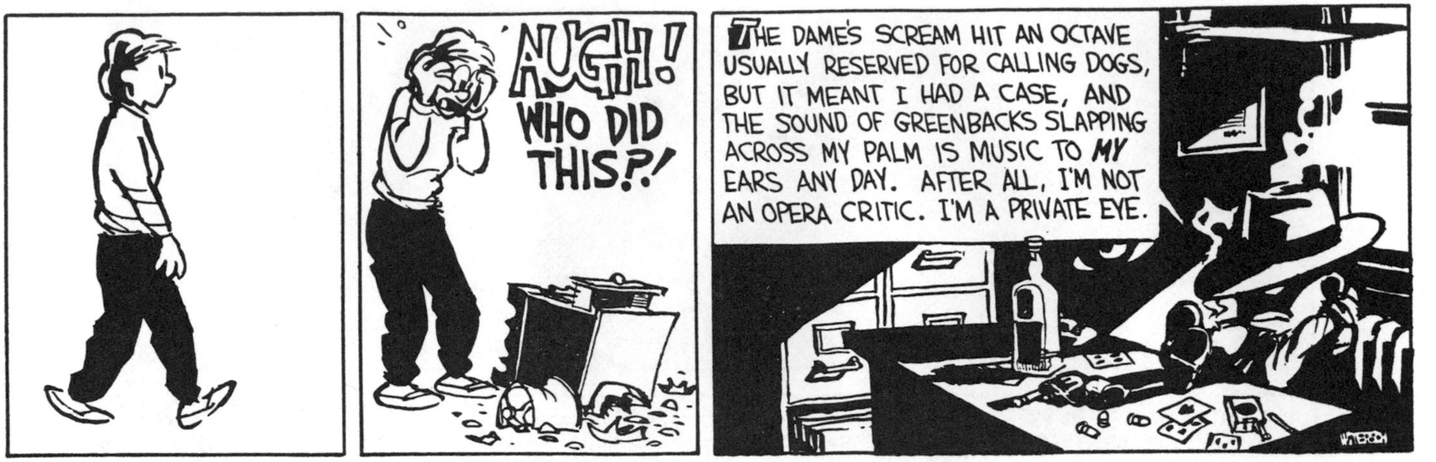
AUGH! WHO DID THIS?!
THE DAME'S SCREAM HIT AN OCTAVE USUALLY RESERVED FOR CALLING DOGS, BUT IT MEANT I HAD A CASE, AND THE SOUND OF GREENBACKS SLAPPING ACROSS MY PALM IS MUSIC TO MY EARS ANY DAY. AFTER ALL, I'M NOT AN OPERA CRITIC. I'M A PRIVATE EYE.
WATTERSON

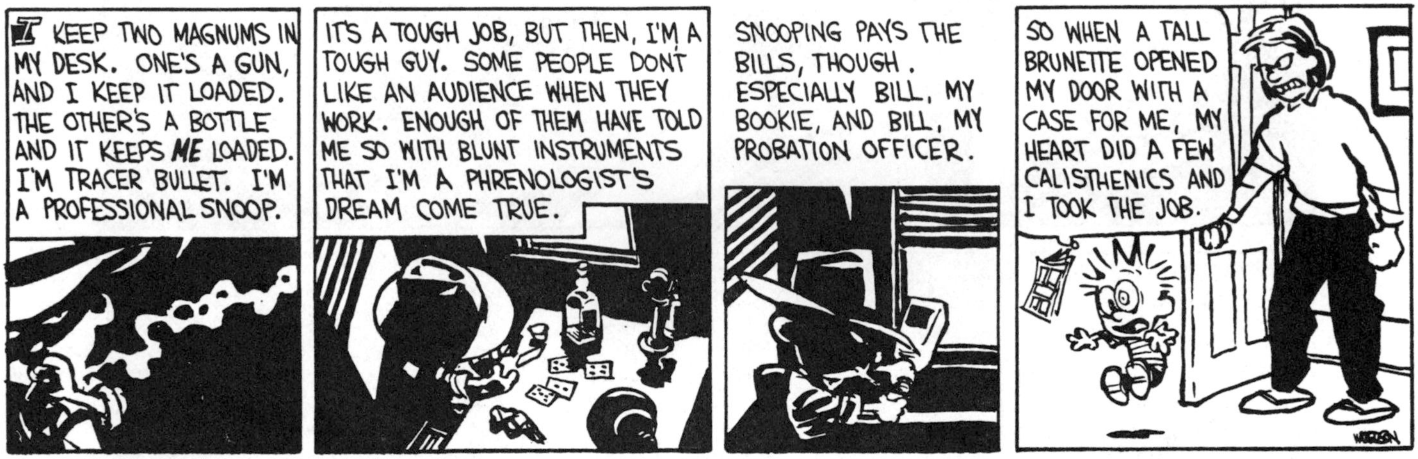
I KEEP TWO MAGNUMS IN MY DESK. ONE'S A GUN, AND I KEEP IT LOADED. THE OTHER'S A BOTTLE AND IT KEEPS ME LOADED. I'M TRACER BULLET. I'M A PROFESSIONAL SNOOP.
IT'S A TOUGH JOB, BUT THEN, I'M A TOUGH GUY. SOME PEOPLE DON'T LIKE AN AUDIENCE WHEN THEY WORK. ENOUGH OF THEM HAVE TOLD ME SO WITH BLUNT INSTRUMENTS THAT I'M A PHRENOLOGIST'S DREAM COME TRUE.
SNOOPING PAYS THE BILLS, THOUGH. ESPECIALLY BILL, MY BOOKIE, AND BILL, MY PROBATION OFFICER.
SO WHEN A TALL BRUNETTE OPENED MY DOOR WITH A CASE FOR ME, MY HEART DID A FEW CALISTHENICS AND I TOOK THE JOB.
WATTERSON

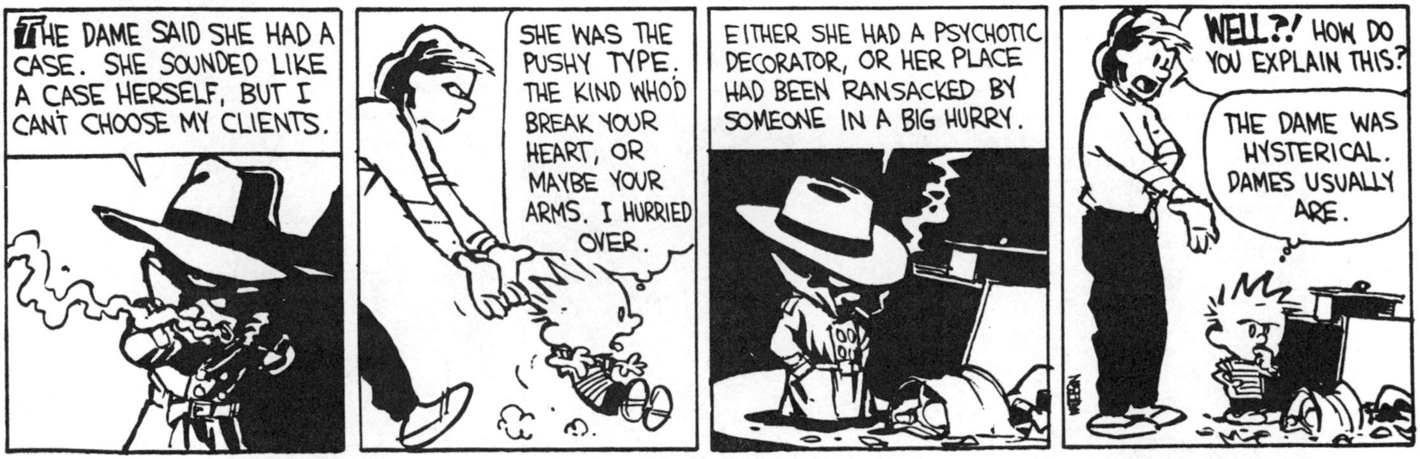
THE DAME SAID SHE HAD A CASE. SHE SOUNDED LIKE A CASE HERSELF, BUT I CAN'T CHOOSE MY CLIENTS.
SHE WAS THE PUSHY TYPE. THE KIND WHO'D BREAK YOUR HEART, OR MAYBE YOUR ARMS. I HURRIED OVER.
EITHER SHE HAD A PSYCHOTIC DECORATOR, OR HER PLACE HAD BEEN RANSACKED BY SOMEONE IN A BIG HURRY.
WELL?! HOW DO YOU EXPLAIN THIS?
THE DAME WAS HYSTERICAL. DAMES USUALLY ARE.
WATTERSON

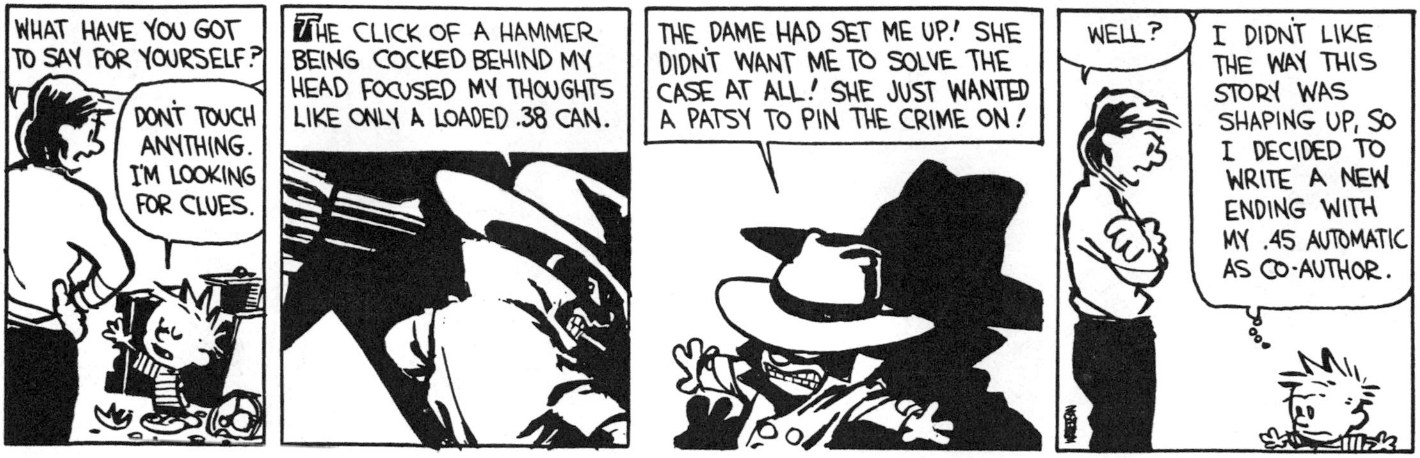
WHAT HAVE YOU GOT TO SAY FOR YOURSELF?
DON'T TOUCH ANYTHING. I'M LOOKING FOR CLUES.
THE CLICK OF A HAMMER BEING COCKED BEHIND MY HEAD FOCUSED MY THOUGHTS LIKE ONLY A LOADED .38 CAN.
THE DAME HAD SET ME UP! SHE DIDN'T WANT ME TO SOLVE THE CASE AT ALL! SHE JUST WANTED A PATSY TO PIN THE CRIME ON!
WELL?
I DIDN'T LIKE THE WAY THIS STORY WAS SHAPING UP, SO I DECIDED TO WRITE A NEW ENDING WITH MY .45 AUTOMATIC AS CO-AUTHOR.

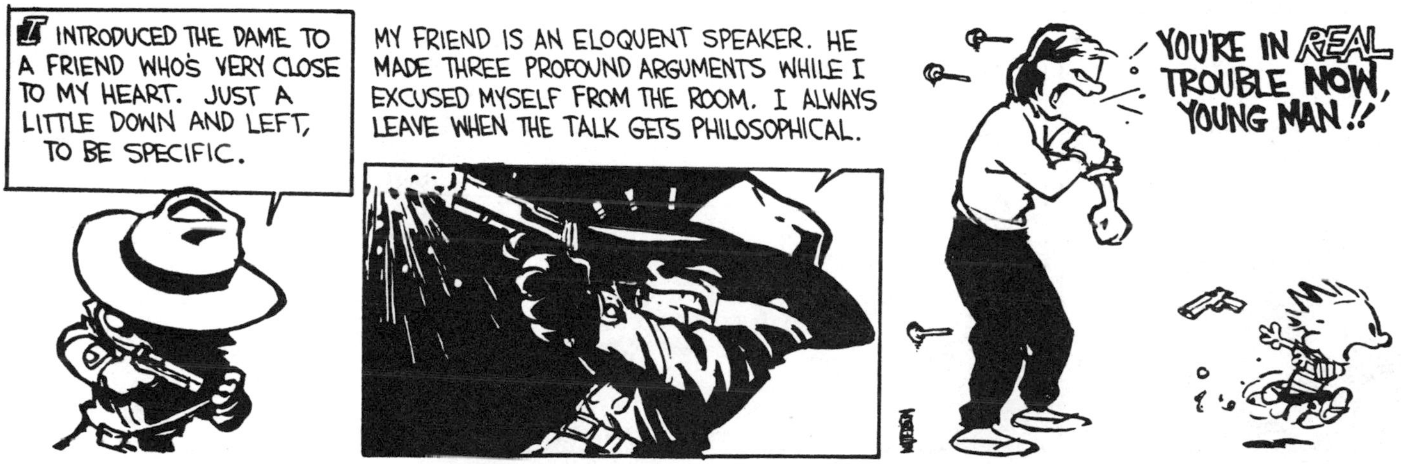
I INTRODUCED THE DAME TO A FRIEND WHO'S VERY CLOSE TO MY HEART. JUST A LITTLE DOWN AND LEFT, TO BE SPECIFIC.
MY FRIEND IS AN ELOQUENT SPEAKER. HE MADE THREE PROFOUND ARGUMENTS WHILE I EXCUSED MYSELF FROM THE ROOM. I ALWAYS LEAVE WHEN THE TALK GETS PHILOSOPHICAL.
YOU'RE IN REAL TROUBLE NOW, YOUNG MAN!!

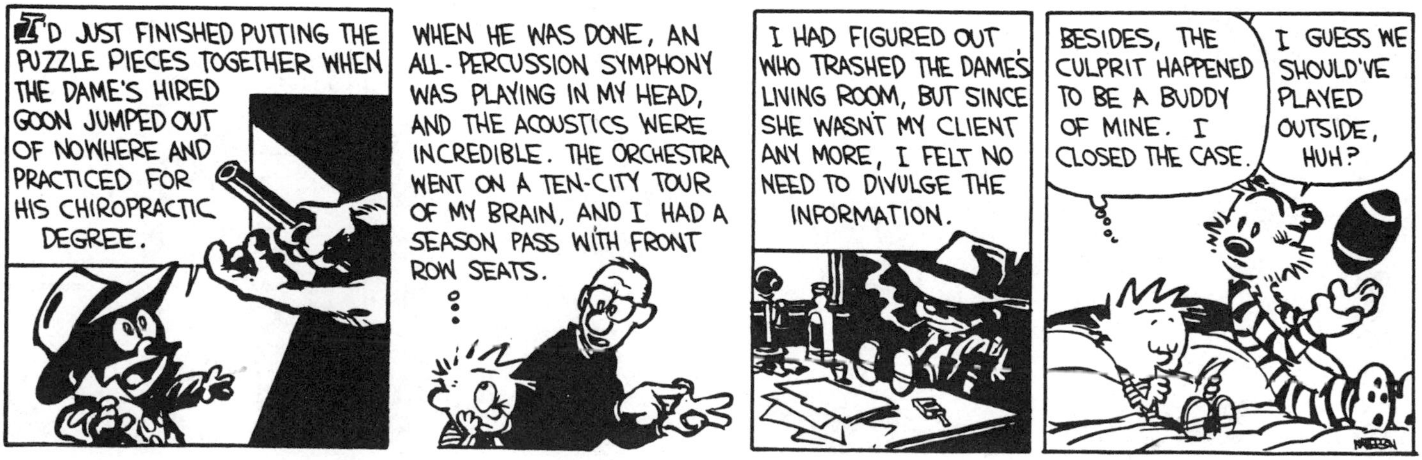
I'D JUST FINISHED PUTTING THE PUZZLE PIECES TOGETHER WHEN THE DAME'S HIRED GOON JUMPED OUT OF NOWHERE AND PRACTICED FOR HIS CHIROPRACTIC DEGREE.
WHEN HE WAS DONE, AN ALL-PERCUSSION SYMPHONY WAS PLAYING IN MY HEAD, AND THE ACOUSTICS WERE INCREDIBLE. THE ORCHESTRA WENT ON A TEN-CITY TOUR OF MY BRAIN, AND I HAD A SEASON PASS WITH FRONT ROW SEATS.
I HAD FIGURED OUT WHO TRASHED THE DAME'S LIVING ROOM, BUT SINCE SHE WASN'T MY CLIENT ANY MORE, I FELT NO NEED TO DIVULGE THE INFORMATION.
BESIDES, THE CULPRIT HAPPENED TO BE A BUDDY OF MINE. I CLOSED THE CASE.
I GUESS WE SHOULD'VE PLAYED OUTSIDE, HUH?

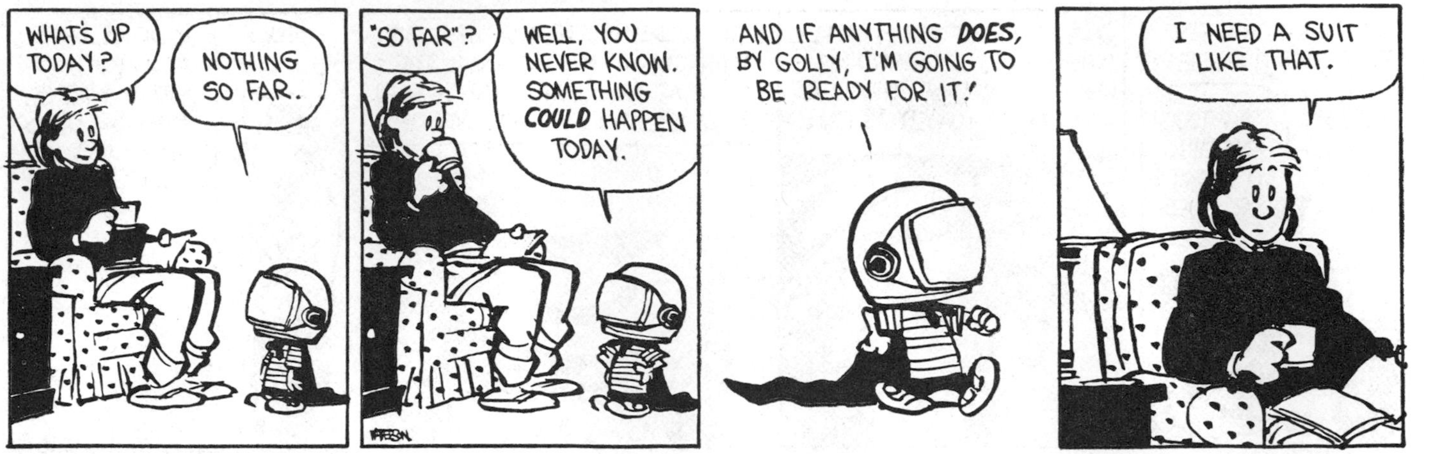
WHAT'S UP TODAY?
NOTHING SO FAR.
"SO FAR"?
WELL, YOU NEVER KNOW. SOMETHING **COULD** HAPPEN TODAY.
AND IF ANYTHING **DOES**, BY GOLLY, I'M GOING TO BE READY FOR IT!
I NEED A SUIT LIKE THAT.

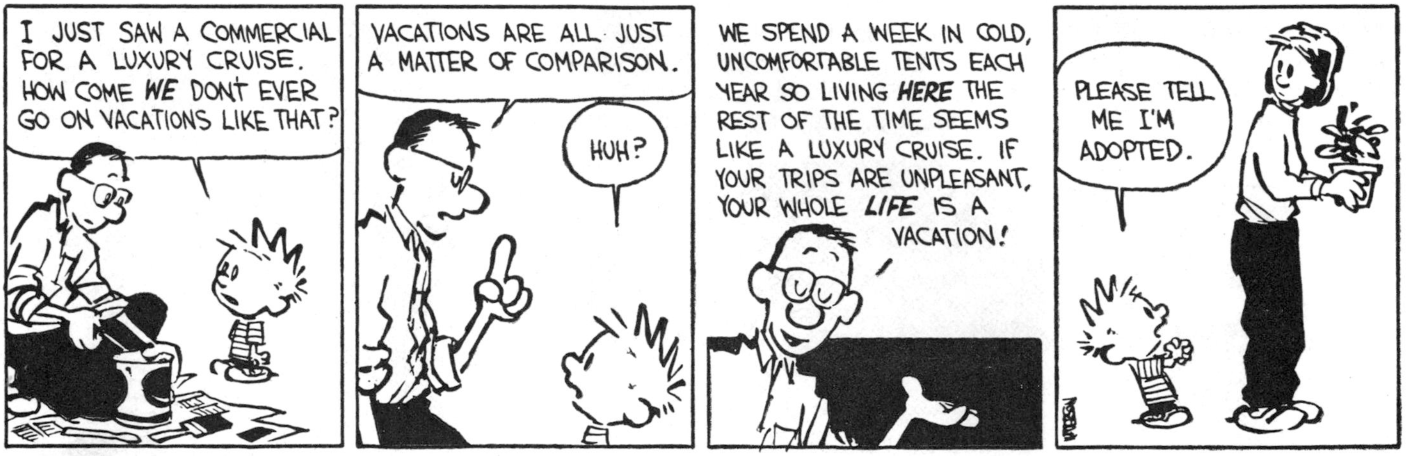
I JUST SAW A COMMERCIAL FOR A LUXURY CRUISE. HOW COME **WE** DON'T EVER GO ON VACATIONS LIKE THAT?
VACATIONS ARE ALL JUST A MATTER OF COMPARISON.
HUH?
WE SPEND A WEEK IN COLD, UNCOMFORTABLE TENTS EACH YEAR SO LIVING **HERE** THE REST OF THE TIME SEEMS LIKE A LUXURY CRUISE. IF YOUR TRIPS ARE UNPLEASANT, YOUR WHOLE **LIFE** IS A VACATION!
PLEASE TELL ME I'M ADOPTED.

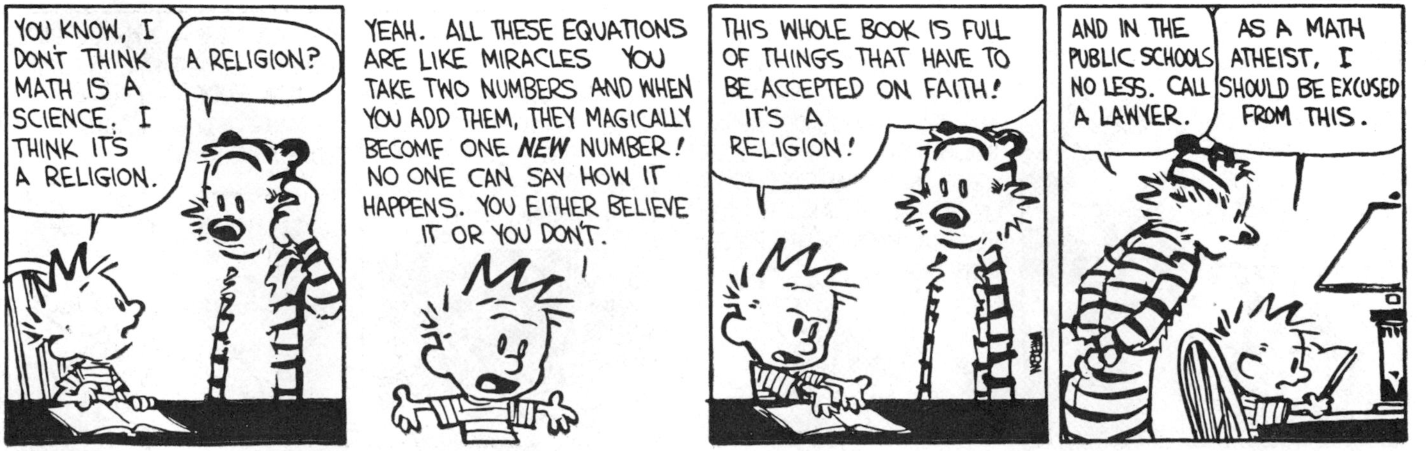
YOU KNOW, I DON'T THINK MATH IS A SCIENCE. I THINK IT'S A RELIGION.
A RELIGION?
YEAH. ALL THESE EQUATIONS ARE LIKE MIRACLES. YOU TAKE TWO NUMBERS AND WHEN YOU ADD THEM, THEY MAGICALLY BECOME ONE **NEW** NUMBER! NO ONE CAN SAY HOW IT HAPPENS. YOU EITHER BELIEVE IT OR YOU DON'T.
THIS WHOLE BOOK IS FULL OF THINGS THAT HAVE TO BE ACCEPTED ON FAITH! IT'S A RELIGION!
AND IN THE PUBLIC SCHOOLS NO LESS. CALL A LAWYER.
AS A MATH ATHEIST, I SHOULD BE EXCUSED FROM THIS.

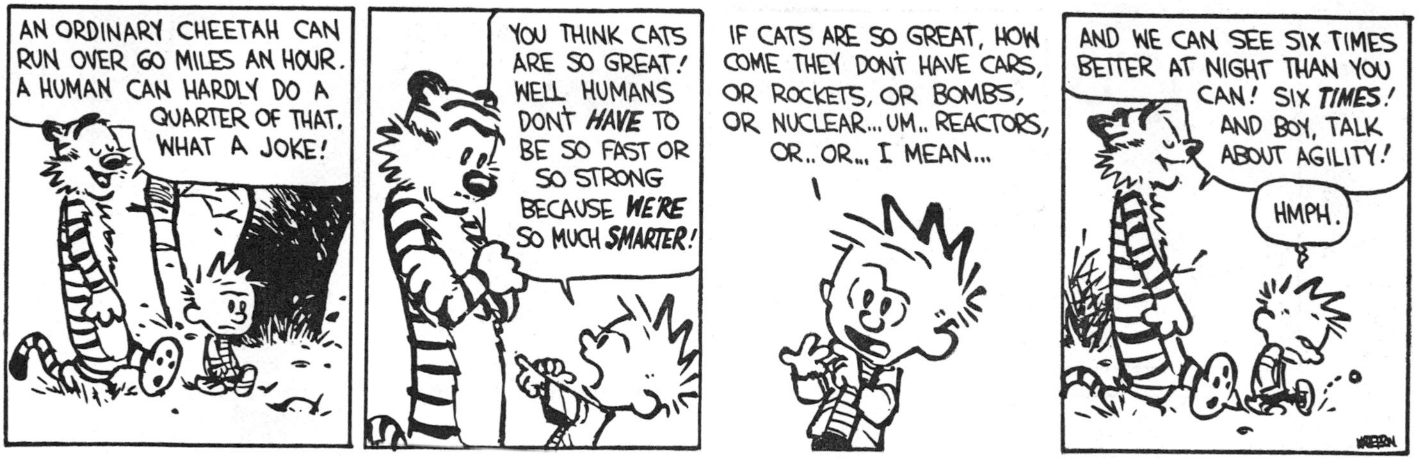
AN ORDINARY CHEETAH CAN RUN OVER 60 MILES AN HOUR. A HUMAN CAN HARDLY DO A QUARTER OF THAT. WHAT A JOKE!
YOU THINK CATS ARE SO GREAT! WELL HUMANS DON'T HAVE TO BE SO FAST OR SO STRONG BECAUSE WE'RE SO MUCH SMARTER!
IF CATS ARE SO GREAT, HOW COME THEY DON'T HAVE CARS, OR ROCKETS, OR BOMBS, OR NUCLEAR... UM.. REACTORS, OR.. OR... I MEAN...
AND WE CAN SEE SIX TIMES BETTER AT NIGHT THAN YOU CAN! SIX TIMES! AND BOY, TALK ABOUT AGILITY!
HMPH.

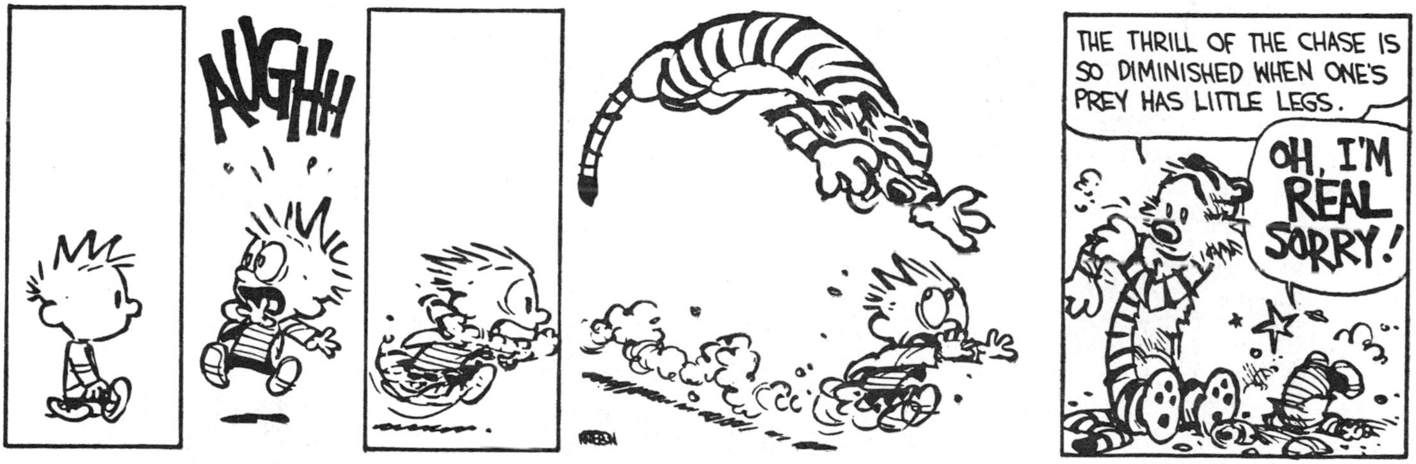
AUGHHH
THE THRILL OF THE CHASE IS SO DIMINISHED WHEN ONE'S PREY HAS LITTLE LEGS.
OH, I'M REAL SORRY!

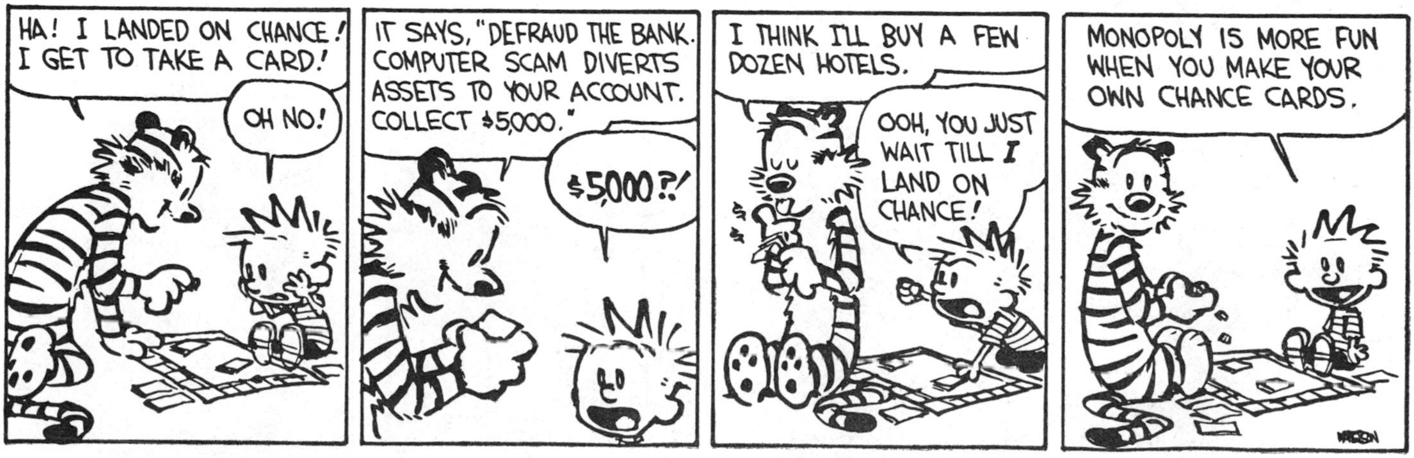
HA! I LANDED ON CHANCE! I GET TO TAKE A CARD!
OH NO!
IT SAYS, "DEFRAUD THE BANK. COMPUTER SCAM DIVERTS ASSETS TO YOUR ACCOUNT. COLLECT $5,000."
$5,000?!
I THINK I'LL BUY A FEW DOZEN HOTELS.
OOH, YOU JUST WAIT TILL I LAND ON CHANCE!
MONOPOLY IS MORE FUN WHEN YOU MAKE YOUR OWN CHANCE CARDS.

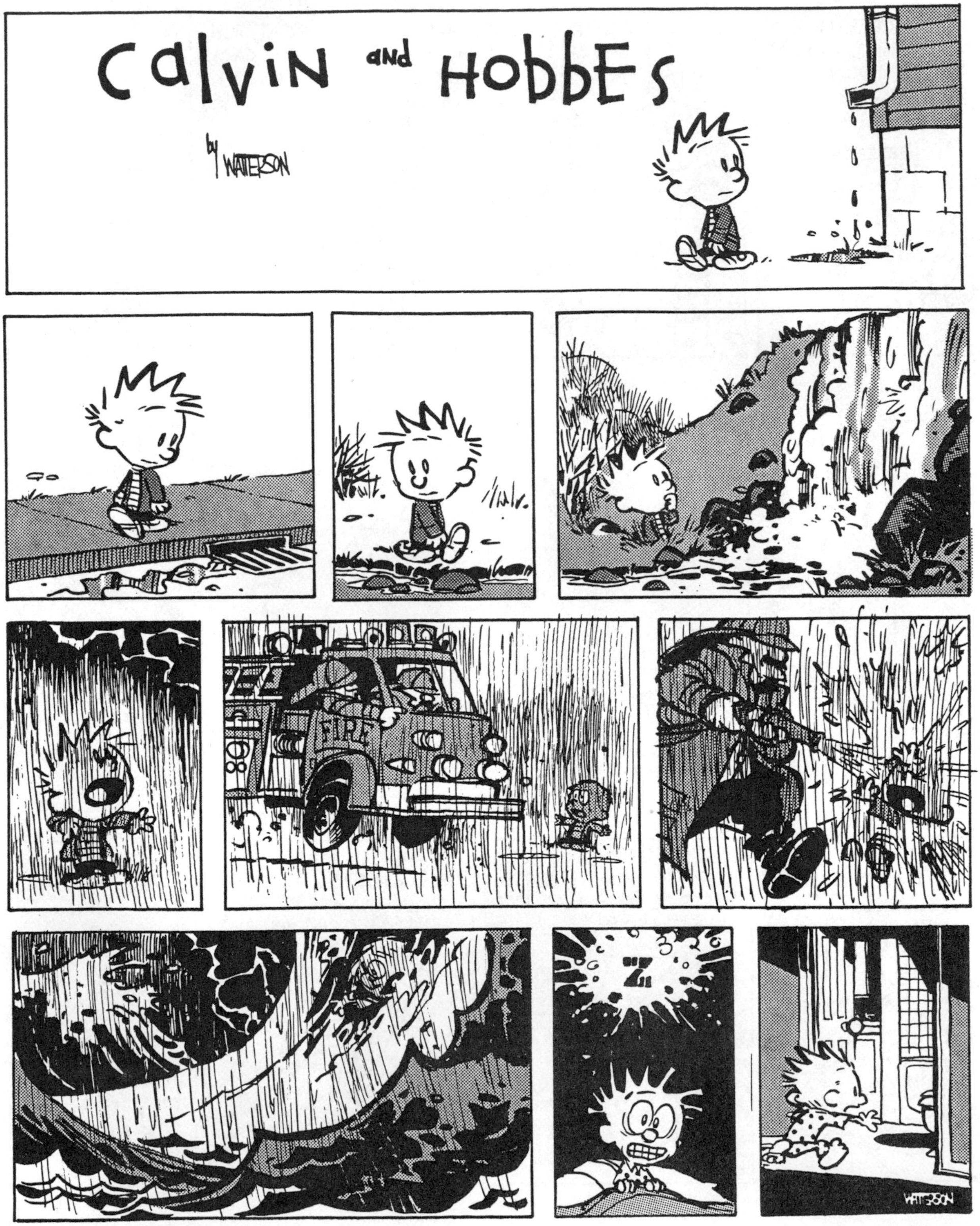
Calvin and HOBBES
by WATTERSON
FIRE
WATTERSON

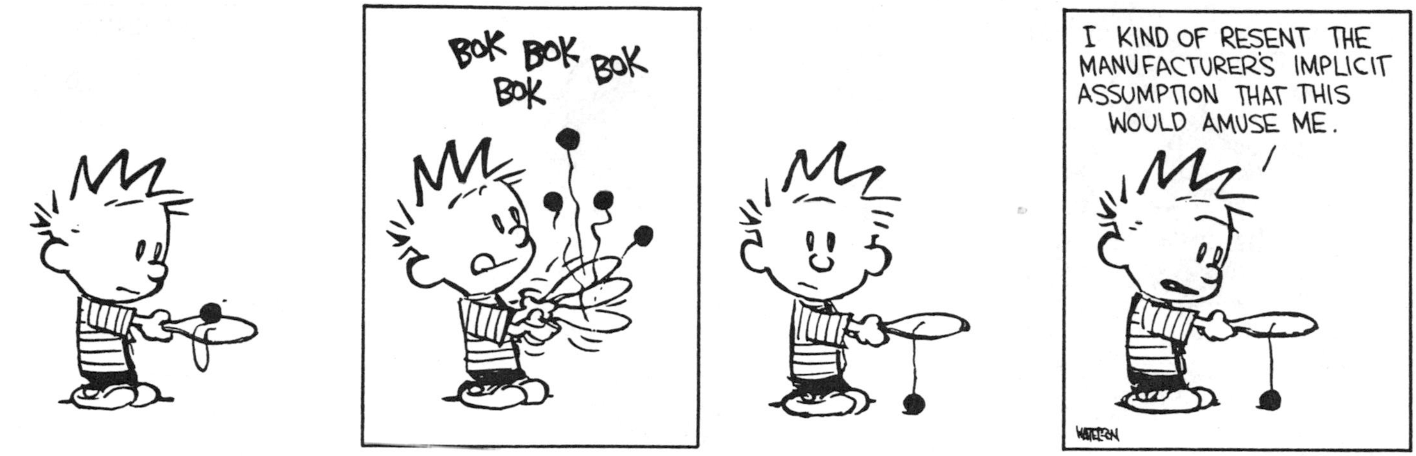
BOK BOK BOK BOK
I KIND OF RESENT THE MANUFACTURER'S IMPLICIT ASSUMPTION THAT THIS WOULD AMUSE ME.

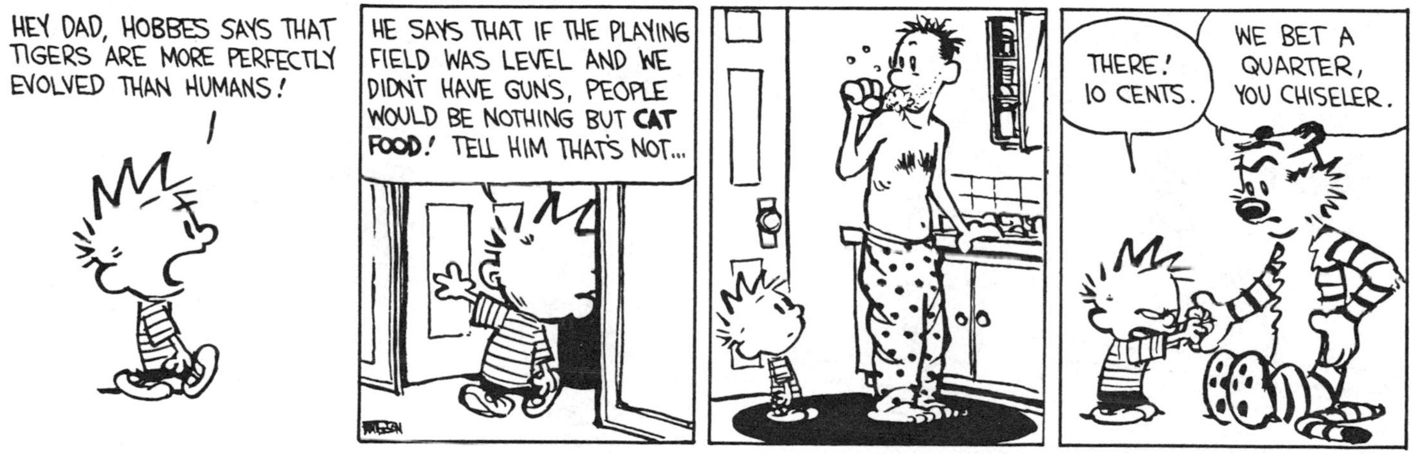
HEY DAD, HOBBES SAYS THAT TIGERS ARE MORE PERFECTLY EVOLVED THAN HUMANS!
HE SAYS THAT IF THE PLAYING FIELD WAS LEVEL AND WE DIDN'T HAVE GUNS, PEOPLE WOULD BE NOTHING BUT **CAT FOOD**! TELL HIM THAT'S NOT...
THERE! 10 CENTS.
WE BET A QUARTER, YOU CHISELER.

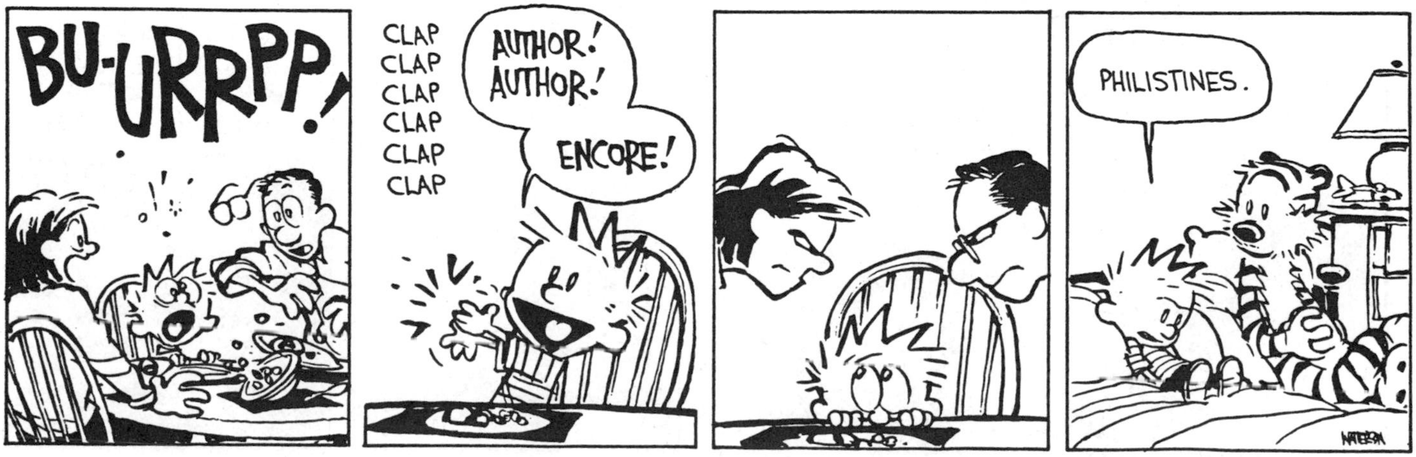
BU-URRPP!
CLAP CLAP CLAP CLAP CLAP CLAP
AUTHOR! AUTHOR!
ENCORE!
PHILISTINES.

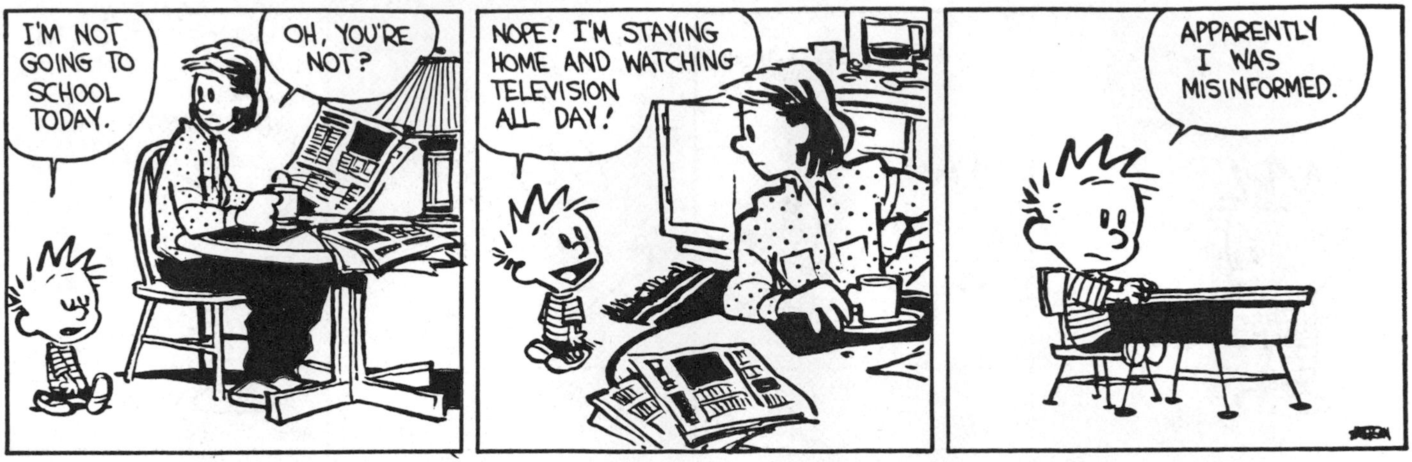
I'M NOT GOING TO SCHOOL TODAY.
OH, YOU'RE NOT?
NOPE! I'M STAYING HOME AND WATCHING TELEVISION ALL DAY!
APPARENTLY I WAS MISINFORMED.

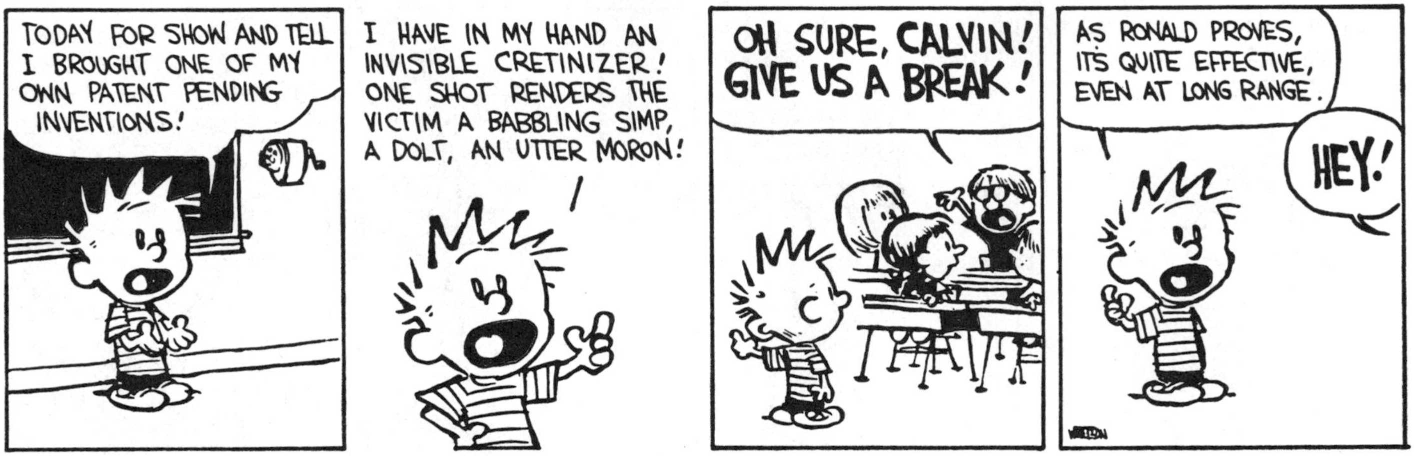
TODAY FOR SHOW AND TELL I BROUGHT ONE OF MY OWN PATENT PENDING INVENTIONS!
I HAVE IN MY HAND AN INVISIBLE CRETINIZER! ONE SHOT RENDERS THE VICTIM A BABBLING SIMP, A DOLT, AN UTTER MORON!
OH SURE, CALVIN! GIVE US A BREAK!
AS RONALD PROVES, IT'S QUITE EFFECTIVE, EVEN AT LONG RANGE.
HEY!

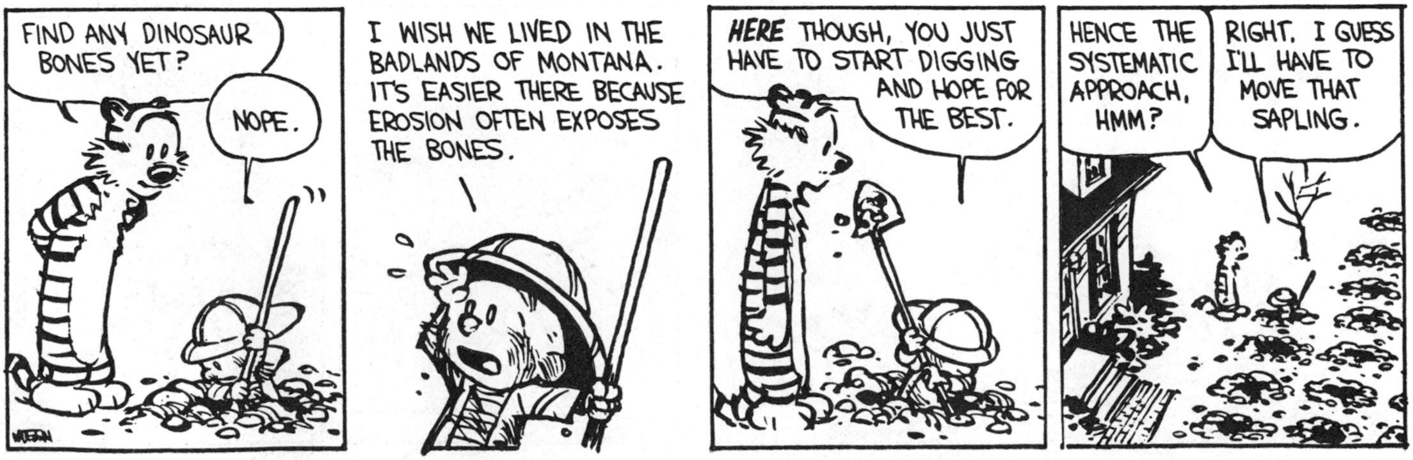
FIND ANY DINOSAUR BONES YET?
NOPE.
I WISH WE LIVED IN THE BADLANDS OF MONTANA. IT'S EASIER THERE BECAUSE EROSION OFTEN EXPOSES THE BONES.
HERE THOUGH, YOU JUST HAVE TO START DIGGING AND HOPE FOR THE BEST.
HENCE THE SYSTEMATIC APPROACH, HMM?
RIGHT. I GUESS I'LL HAVE TO MOVE THAT SAPLING.

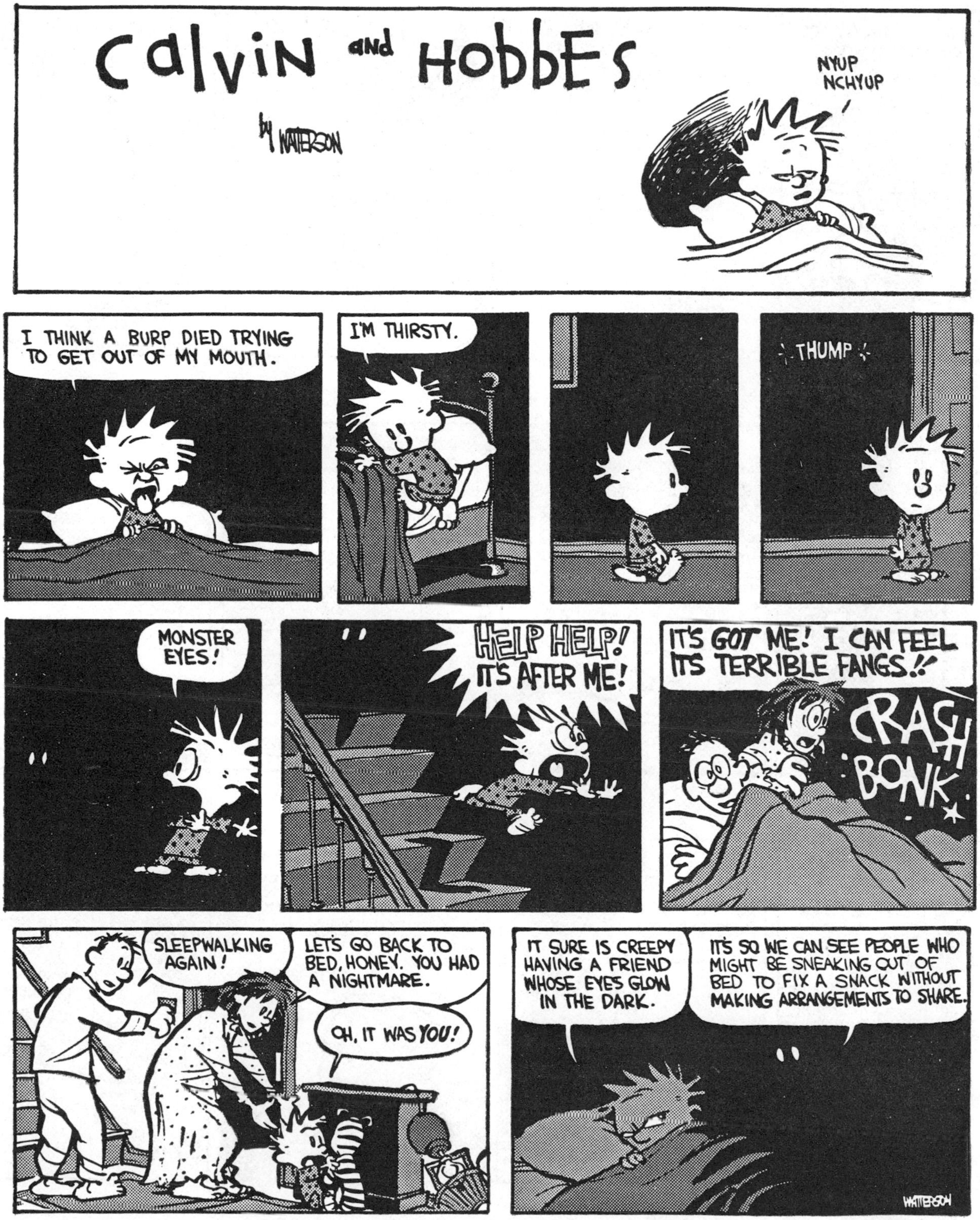
Calvin and HOBBES
by WATTERSON
NYUP NCHYUP
I THINK A BURP DIED TRYING TO GET OUT OF MY MOUTH.
I'M THIRSTY.
THUMP
MONSTER EYES!
HELP HELP! IT'S AFTER ME!
IT'S GOT ME! I CAN FEEL ITS TERRIBLE FANGS!!
CRASH
BONK
SLEEPWALKING AGAIN!
LET'S GO BACK TO BED, HONEY. YOU HAD A NIGHTMARE.
OH, IT WAS YOU!
IT SURE IS CREEPY HAVING A FRIEND WHOSE EYES GLOW IN THE DARK.
IT'S SO WE CAN SEE PEOPLE WHO MIGHT BE SNEAKING OUT OF BED TO FIX A SNACK WITHOUT MAKING ARRANGEMENTS TO SHARE.
WATTERSON

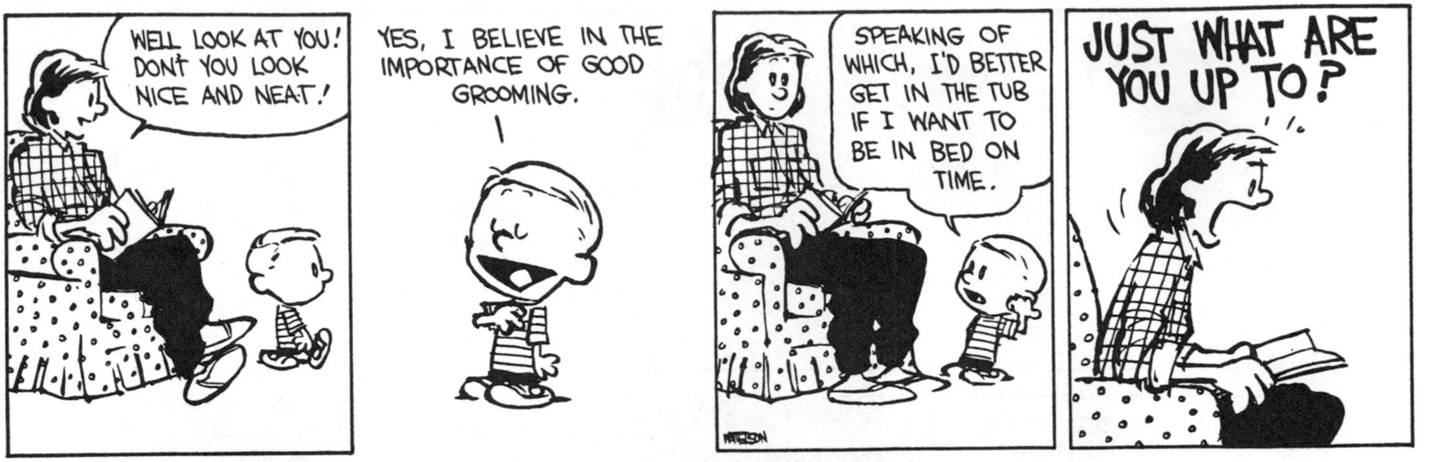
WELL LOOK AT YOU! DON'T YOU LOOK NICE AND NEAT!
YES, I BELIEVE IN THE IMPORTANCE OF GOOD GROOMING.
SPEAKING OF WHICH, I'D BETTER GET IN THE TUB IF I WANT TO BE IN BED ON TIME.
JUST WHAT ARE YOU UP TO?

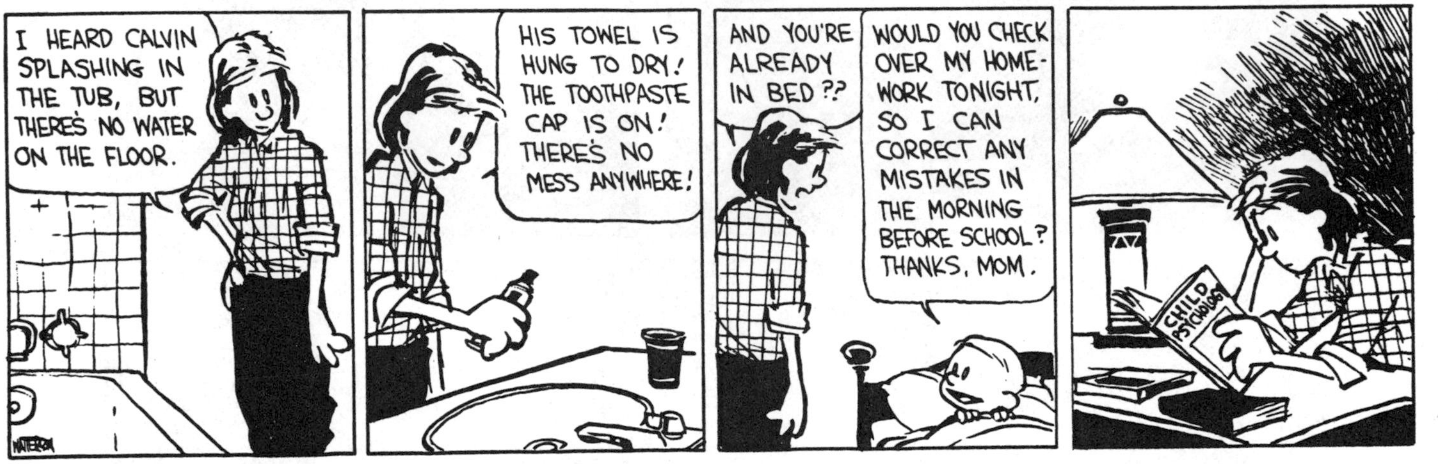
I HEARD CALVIN SPLASHING IN THE TUB, BUT THERE'S NO WATER ON THE FLOOR.
HIS TOWEL IS HUNG TO DRY! THE TOOTHPASTE CAP IS ON! THERE'S NO MESS ANYWHERE!
AND YOU'RE ALREADY IN BED??
WOULD YOU CHECK OVER MY HOME-WORK TONIGHT, SO I CAN CORRECT ANY MISTAKES IN THE MORNING BEFORE SCHOOL? THANKS, MOM.
CHILD PSYCHOLOGY

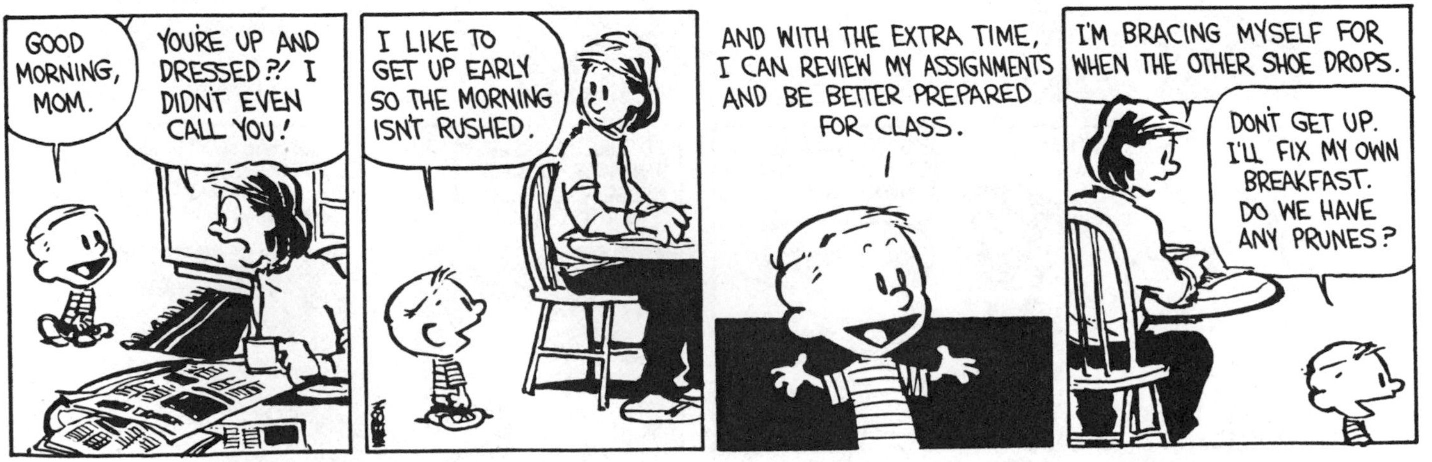
GOOD MORNING, MOM.
YOU'RE UP AND DRESSED?! I DIDN'T EVEN CALL YOU!
I LIKE TO GET UP EARLY SO THE MORNING ISN'T RUSHED.
AND WITH THE EXTRA TIME, I CAN REVIEW MY ASSIGNMENTS AND BE BETTER PREPARED FOR CLASS.
I'M BRACING MYSELF FOR WHEN THE OTHER SHOE DROPS.
DON'T GET UP. I'LL FIX MY OWN BREAKFAST. DO WE HAVE ANY PRUNES?

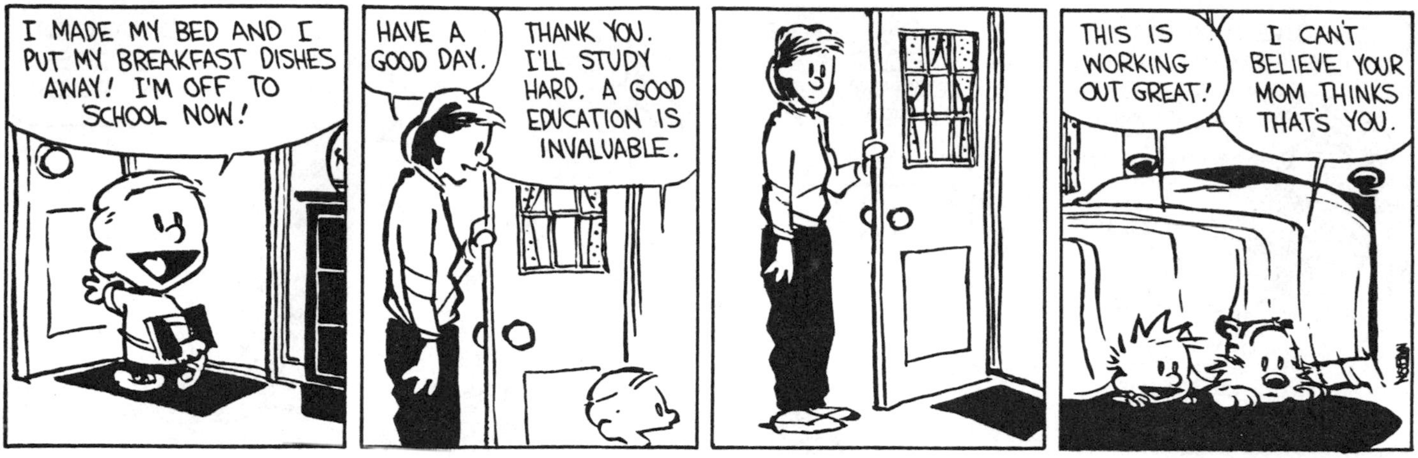
I MADE MY BED AND I PUT MY BREAKFAST DISHES AWAY! I'M OFF TO SCHOOL NOW!
HAVE A GOOD DAY.
THANK YOU. I'LL STUDY HARD. A GOOD EDUCATION IS INVALUABLE.
THIS IS WORKING OUT GREAT!
I CAN'T BELIEVE YOUR MOM THINKS THAT'S YOU.

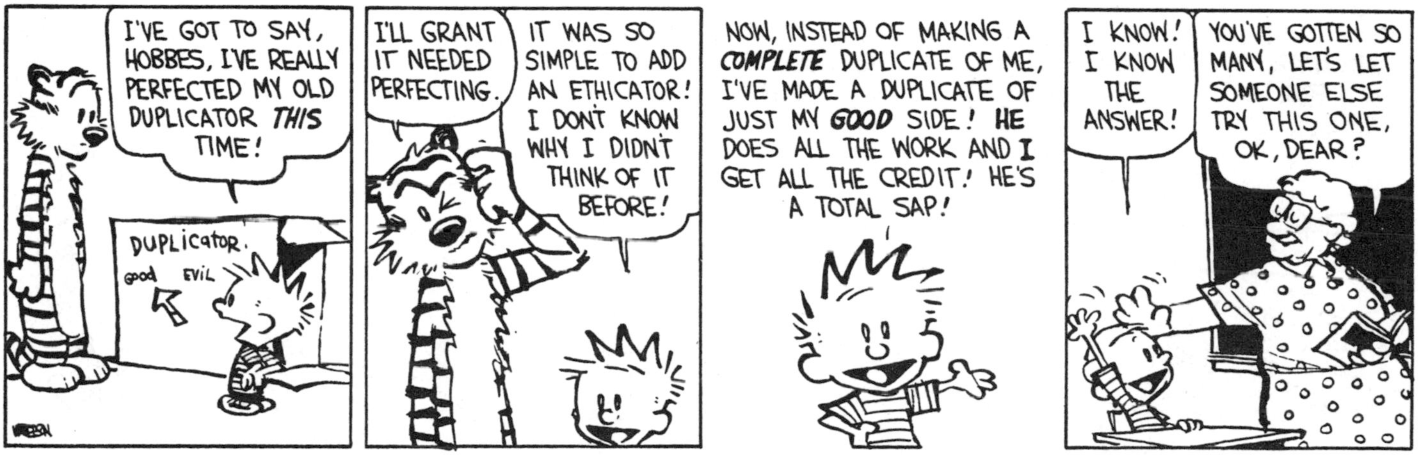
I'VE GOT TO SAY, HOBBES, I'VE REALLY PERFECTED MY OLD DUPLICATOR THIS TIME!
DUPLicator
Good
EVIL
I'LL GRANT IT NEEDED PERFECTING.
IT WAS SO SIMPLE TO ADD AN ETHICATOR! I DON'T KNOW WHY I DIDN'T THINK OF IT BEFORE!
NOW, INSTEAD OF MAKING A COMPLETE DUPLICATE OF ME, I'VE MADE A DUPLICATE OF JUST MY GOOD SIDE! HE DOES ALL THE WORK AND I GET ALL THE CREDIT! HE'S A TOTAL SAP!
I KNOW! I KNOW THE ANSWER!
YOU'VE GOTTEN SO MANY, LET'S LET SOMEONE ELSE TRY THIS ONE, OK, DEAR?

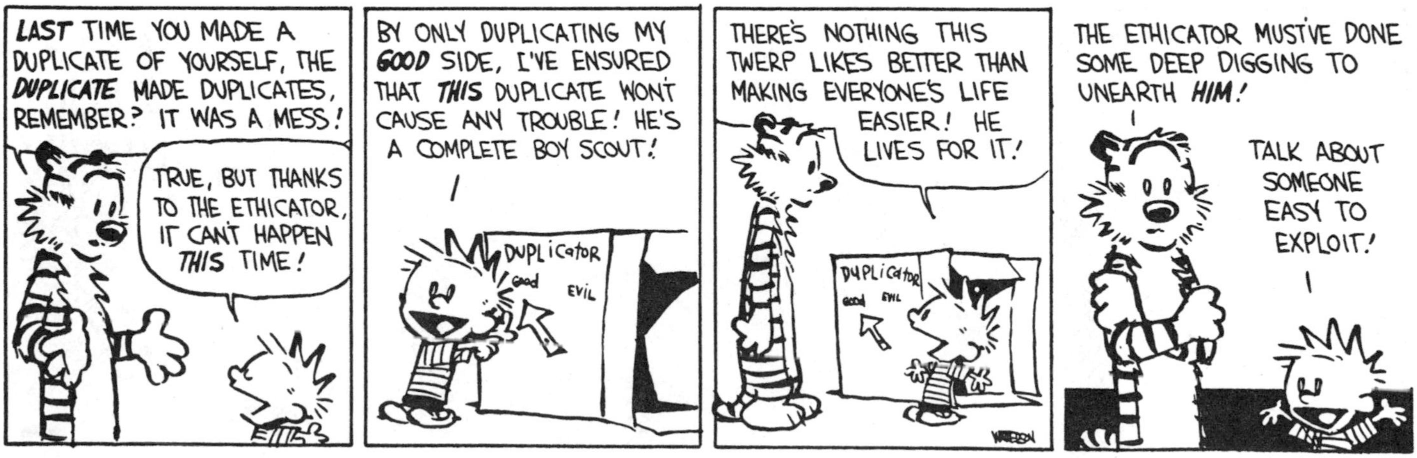
LAST TIME YOU MADE A DUPLICATE OF YOURSELF, THE DUPLICATE MADE DUPLICATES, REMEMBER? IT WAS A MESS!
TRUE, BUT THANKS TO THE ETHICATOR, IT CAN'T HAPPEN THIS TIME!
BY ONLY DUPLICATING MY GOOD SIDE, I'VE ENSURED THAT THIS DUPLICATE WON'T CAUSE ANY TROUBLE! HE'S A COMPLETE BOY SCOUT!
DUPLicator
Good
EVIL
THERE'S NOTHING THIS TWERP LIKES BETTER THAN MAKING EVERYONE'S LIFE EASIER! HE LIVES FOR IT!
DUPLicator
Good
EVIL
THE ETHICATOR MUST'VE DONE SOME DEEP DIGGING TO UNEARTH HIM!
TALK ABOUT SOMEONE EASY TO EXPLOIT!

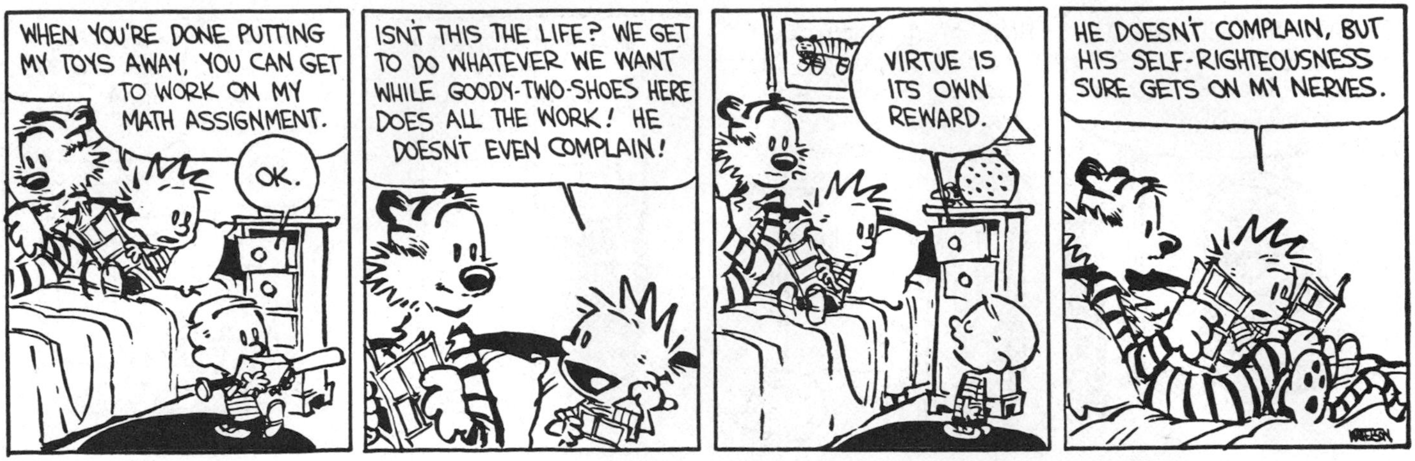
WHEN YOU'RE DONE PUTTING MY TOYS AWAY, YOU CAN GET TO WORK ON MY MATH ASSIGNMENT.
OK.
ISN'T THIS THE LIFE? WE GET TO DO WHATEVER WE WANT WHILE GOODY-TWO-SHOES HERE DOES ALL THE WORK! HE DOESN'T EVEN COMPLAIN!
VIRTUE IS ITS OWN REWARD.
HE DOESN'T COMPLAIN, BUT HIS SELF-RIGHTEOUSNESS SURE GETS ON MY NERVES.

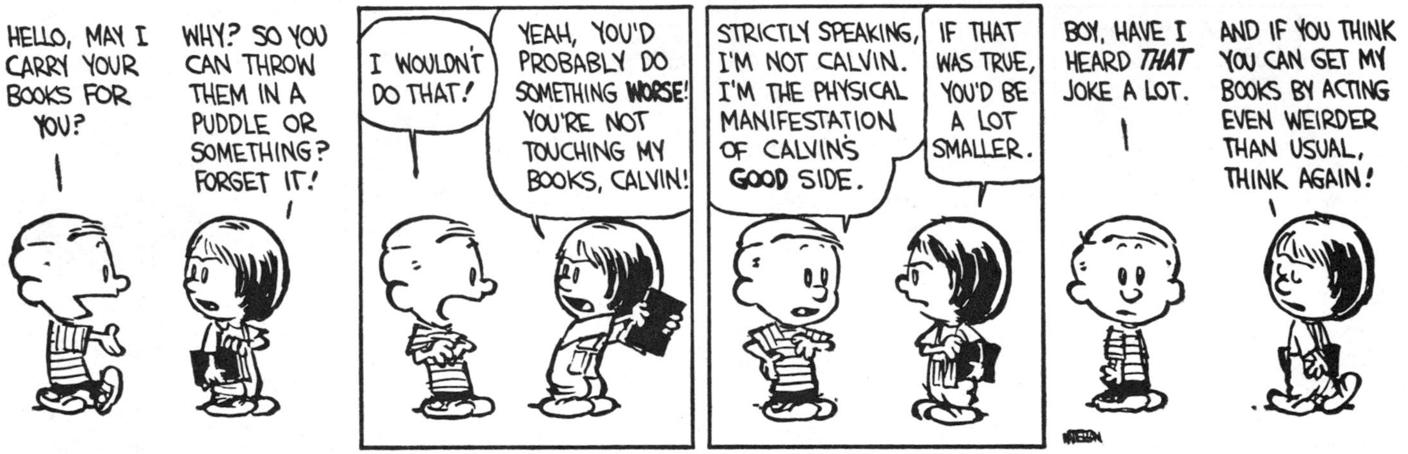
HELLO, MAY I CARRY YOUR BOOKS FOR YOU?
WHY? SO YOU CAN THROW THEM IN A PUDDLE OR SOMETHING? FORGET IT!
I WOULDN'T DO THAT!
YEAH, YOU'D PROBABLY DO SOMETHING WORSE! YOU'RE NOT TOUCHING MY BOOKS, CALVIN!
STRICTLY SPEAKING, I'M NOT CALVIN. I'M THE PHYSICAL MANIFESTATION OF CALVIN'S GOOD SIDE.
IF THAT WAS TRUE, YOU'D BE A LOT SMALLER.
BOY, HAVE I HEARD THAT JOKE A LOT.
AND IF YOU THINK YOU CAN GET MY BOOKS BY ACTING EVEN WEIRDER THAN USUAL, THINK AGAIN!

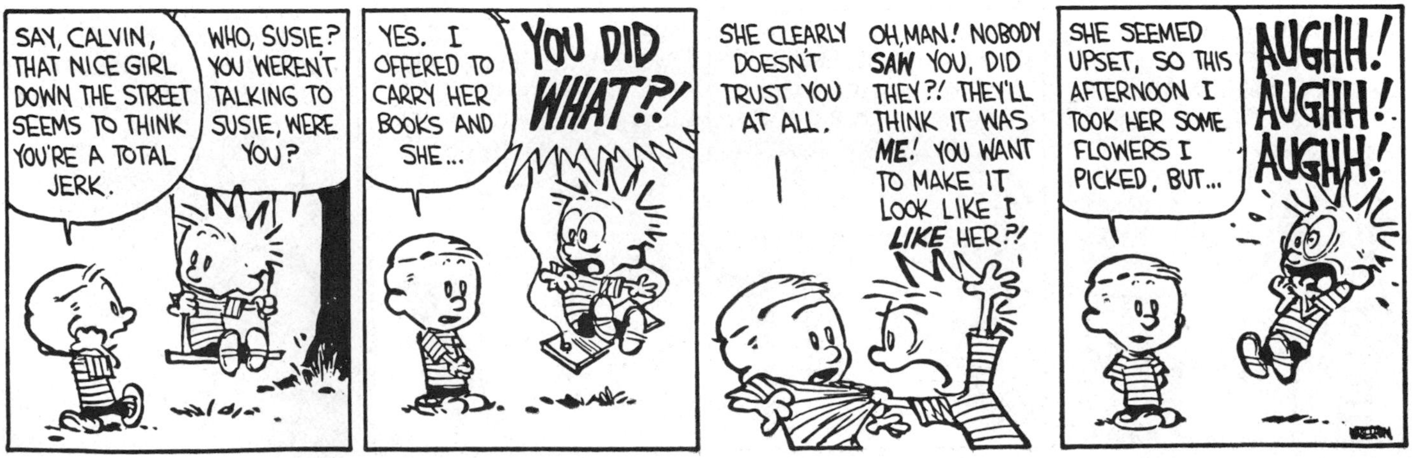
SAY, CALVIN, THAT NICE GIRL DOWN THE STREET SEEMS TO THINK YOU'RE A TOTAL JERK.
WHO, SUSIE? YOU WEREN'T TALKING TO SUSIE, WERE YOU?
YES. I OFFERED TO CARRY HER BOOKS AND SHE...
YOU DID WHAT?!
SHE CLEARLY DOESN'T TRUST YOU AT ALL.
OH, MAN! NOBODY SAW YOU, DID THEY?! THEY'LL THINK IT WAS ME! YOU WANT TO MAKE IT LOOK LIKE I LIKE HER?!
SHE SEEMED UPSET, SO THIS AFTERNOON I TOOK HER SOME FLOWERS I PICKED, BUT...
AUGHH! AUGHH! AUGHH!

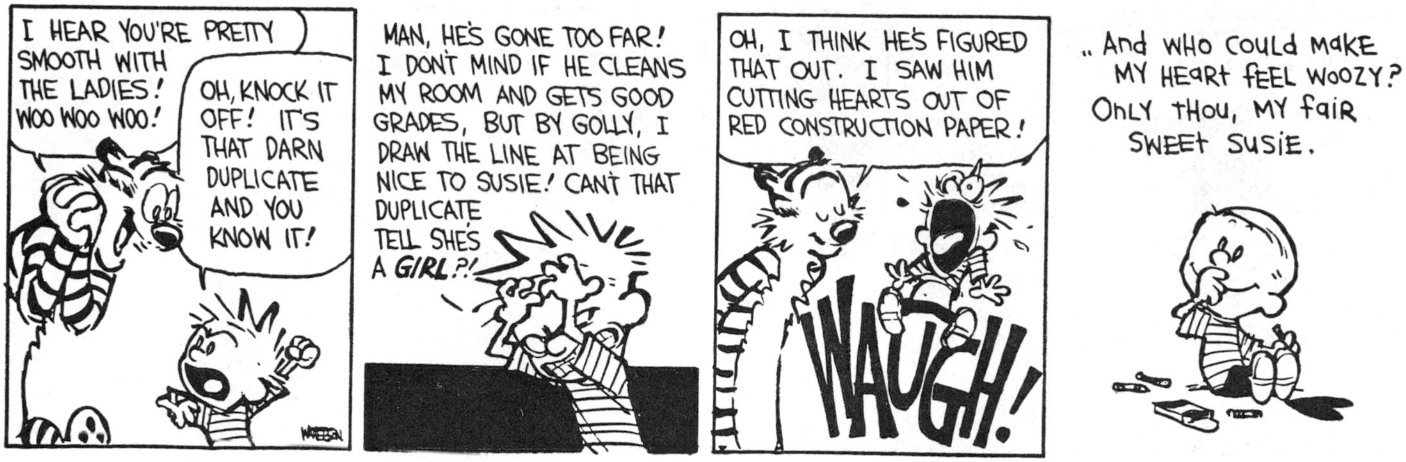
I HEAR YOU'RE PRETTY SMOOTH WITH THE LADIES! WOO WOO WOO!
OH, KNOCK IT OFF! IT'S THAT DARN DUPLICATE AND YOU KNOW IT!
MAN, HE'S GONE TOO FAR! I DON'T MIND IF HE CLEANS MY ROOM AND GETS GOOD GRADES, BUT BY GOLLY, I DRAW THE LINE AT BEING NICE TO SUSIE! CAN'T THAT DUPLICATE TELL SHE'S A GIRL?!
OH, I THINK HE'S FIGURED THAT OUT. I SAW HIM CUTTING HEARTS OUT OF RED CONSTRUCTION PAPER!
WAUGH!
.. And who could make my heart feel woozy? Only thou, my fair sweet Susie.
WATTERSON

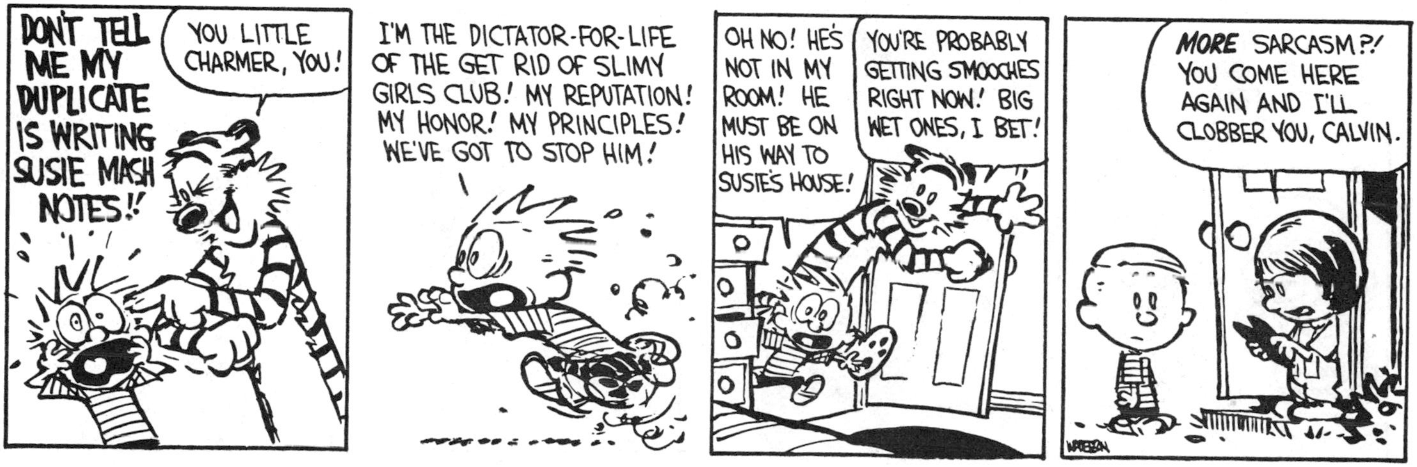
DON'T TELL ME MY DUPLICATE IS WRITING SUSIE MASH NOTES?!
YOU LITTLE CHARMER, YOU!
I'M THE DICTATOR-FOR-LIFE OF THE GET RID OF SLIMY GIRLS CLUB! MY REPUTATION! MY HONOR! MY PRINCIPLES! WE'VE GOT TO STOP HIM!
OH NO! HE'S NOT IN MY ROOM! HE MUST BE ON HIS WAY TO SUSIE'S HOUSE!
YOU'RE PROBABLY GETTING SMOOCHES RIGHT NOW! BIG WET ONES, I BET!
MORE SARCASM?! YOU COME HERE AGAIN AND I'LL CLOBBER YOU, CALVIN.
WATTERSON

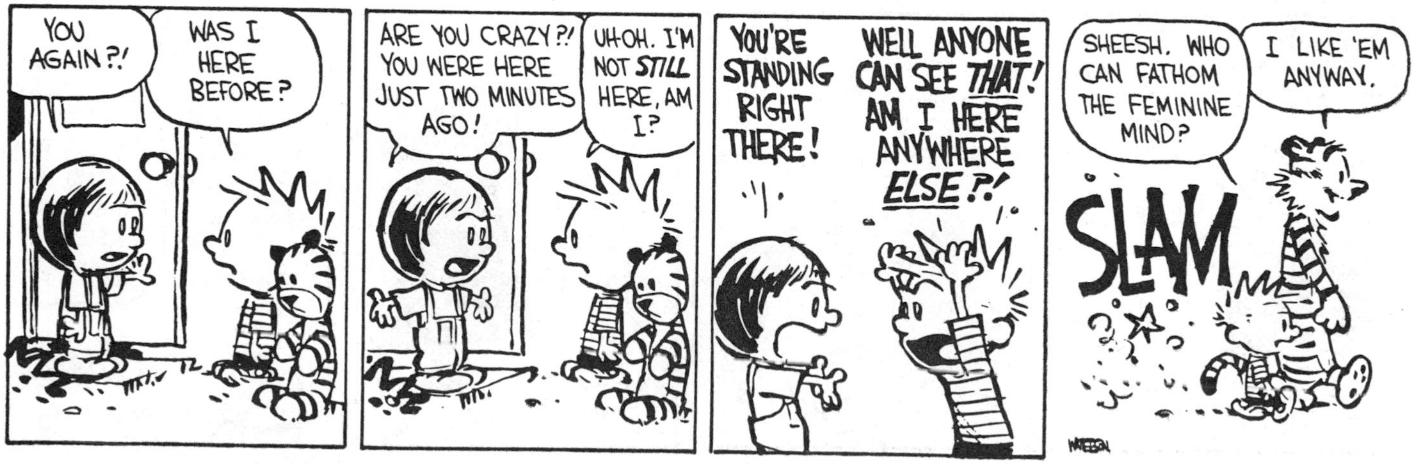
YOU AGAIN?!
WAS I HERE BEFORE?
ARE YOU CRAZY?! YOU WERE HERE JUST TWO MINUTES AGO!
UH-OH. I'M NOT STILL HERE, AM I?
YOU'RE STANDING RIGHT THERE!
WELL ANYONE CAN SEE THAT! AM I HERE ANYWHERE ELSE?!
SHEESH. WHO CAN FATHOM THE FEMININE MIND?
I LIKE 'EM ANYWAY.
SLAM
WATTERSON

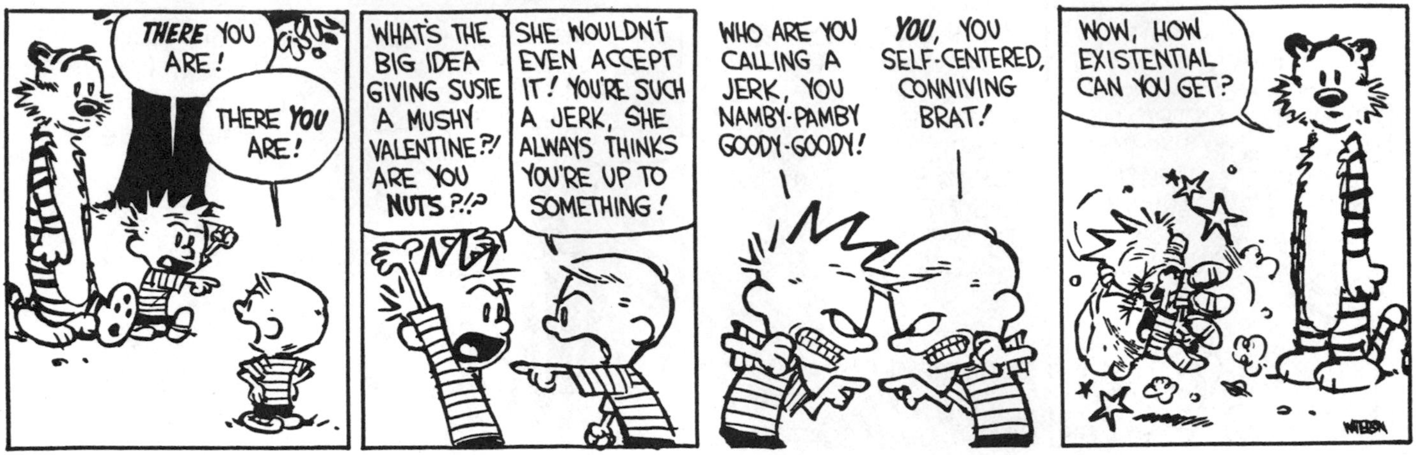
THERE YOU ARE!
THERE YOU ARE!
WHAT'S THE BIG IDEA GIVING SUSIE A MUSHY VALENTINE?! ARE YOU NUTS?!?
SHE WOULDN'T EVEN ACCEPT IT! YOU'RE SUCH A JERK, SHE ALWAYS THINKS YOU'RE UP TO SOMETHING!
WHO ARE YOU CALLING A JERK, YOU NAMBY-PAMBY GOODY-GOODY!
YOU, YOU SELF-CENTERED, CONNIVING BRAT!
WOW, HOW EXISTENTIAL CAN YOU GET?

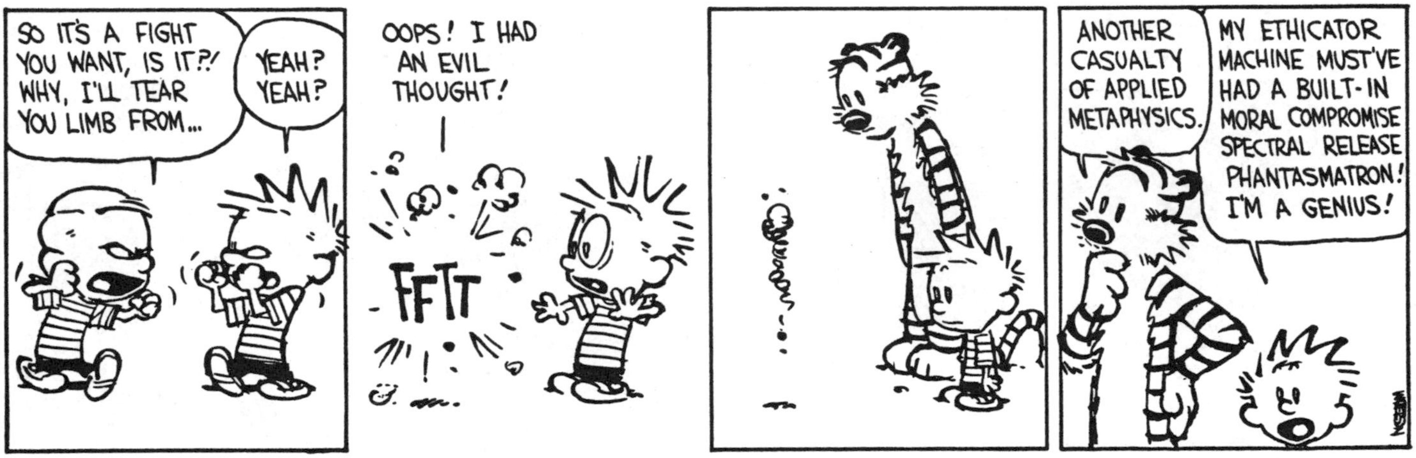
SO IT'S A FIGHT YOU WANT, IS IT?! WHY, I'LL TEAR YOU LIMB FROM...
YEAH? YEAH?
OOPS! I HAD AN EVIL THOUGHT!
FFT
ANOTHER CASUALTY OF APPLIED METAPHYSICS.
MY ETHICATOR MACHINE MUST'VE HAD A BUILT-IN MORAL COMPROMISE SPECTRAL RELEASE PHANTASMATRON! I'M A GENIUS!

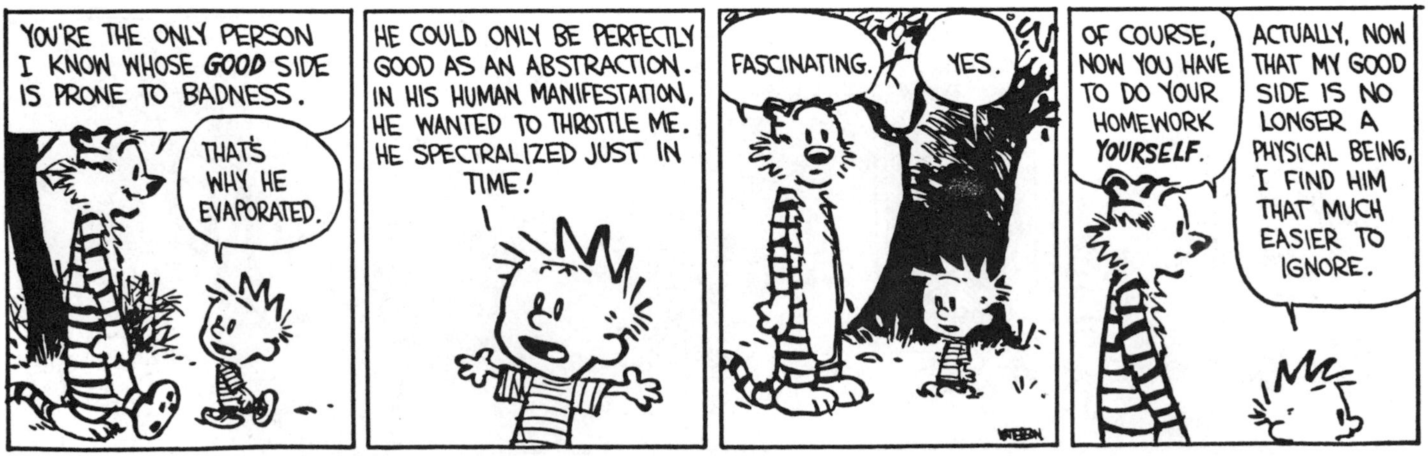
YOU'RE THE ONLY PERSON I KNOW WHOSE GOOD SIDE IS PRONE TO BADNESS.
THAT'S WHY HE EVAPORATED.
HE COULD ONLY BE PERFECTLY GOOD AS AN ABSTRACTION. IN HIS HUMAN MANIFESTATION, HE WANTED TO THROTTLE ME. HE SPECTRALIZED JUST IN TIME!
FASCINATING.
YES.
OF COURSE, NOW YOU HAVE TO DO YOUR HOMEWORK YOURSELF.
ACTUALLY, NOW THAT MY GOOD SIDE IS NO LONGER A PHYSICAL BEING, I FIND HIM THAT MUCH EASIER TO IGNORE.

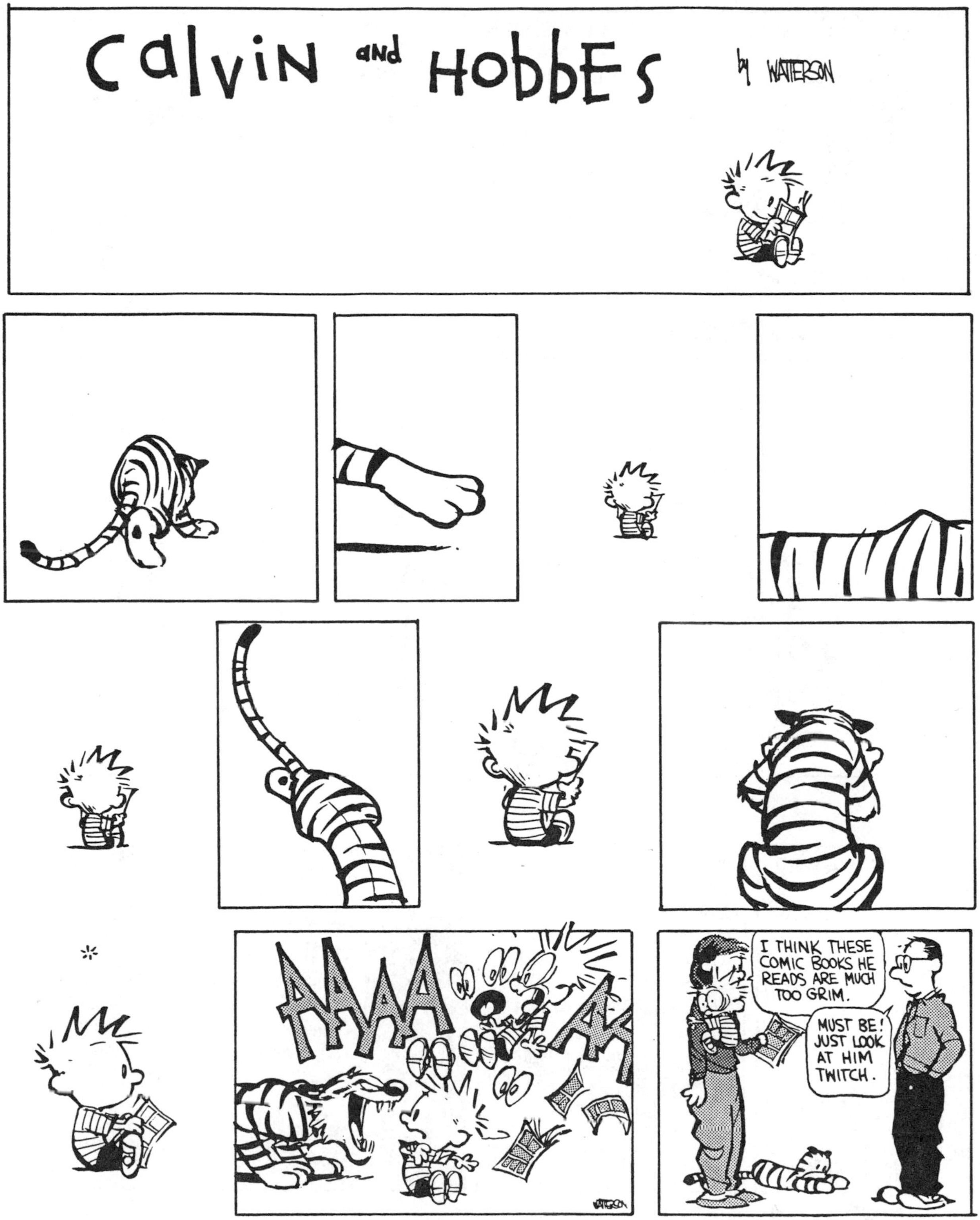
Calvin and HOBBES
by WATTERSON
I THINK THESE COMIC BOOKS HE READS ARE MUCH TOO GRIM.
MUST BE! JUST LOOK AT HIM TWITCH.

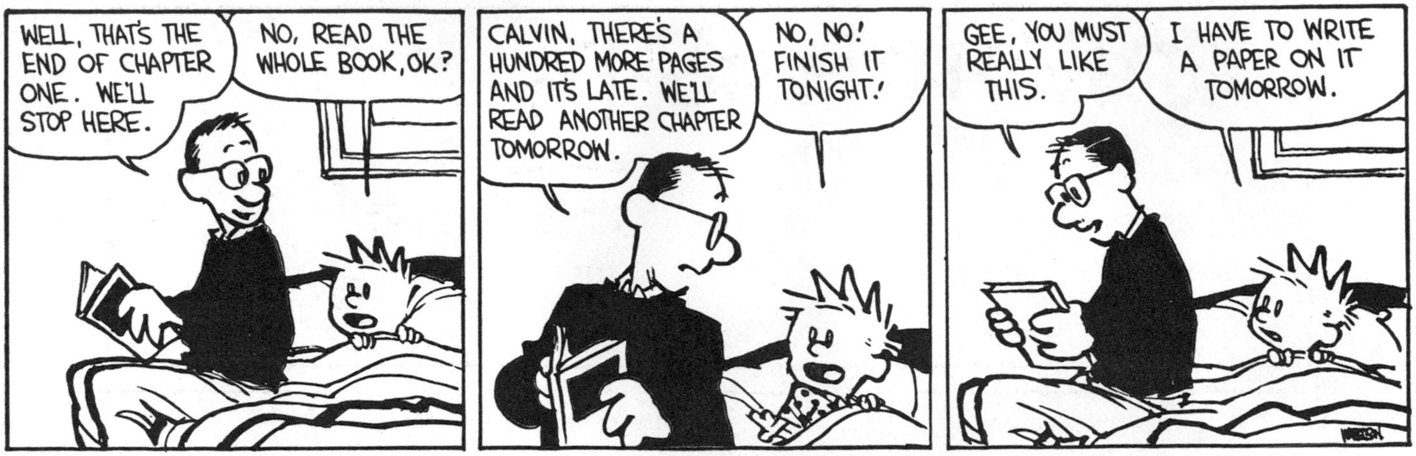
WELL, THAT'S THE END OF CHAPTER ONE. WE'LL STOP HERE.
NO, READ THE WHOLE BOOK, OK?
CALVIN, THERE'S A HUNDRED MORE PAGES AND IT'S LATE. WE'LL READ ANOTHER CHAPTER TOMORROW.
NO, NO! FINISH IT TONIGHT!
GEE, YOU MUST REALLY LIKE THIS.
I HAVE TO WRITE A PAPER ON IT TOMORROW.

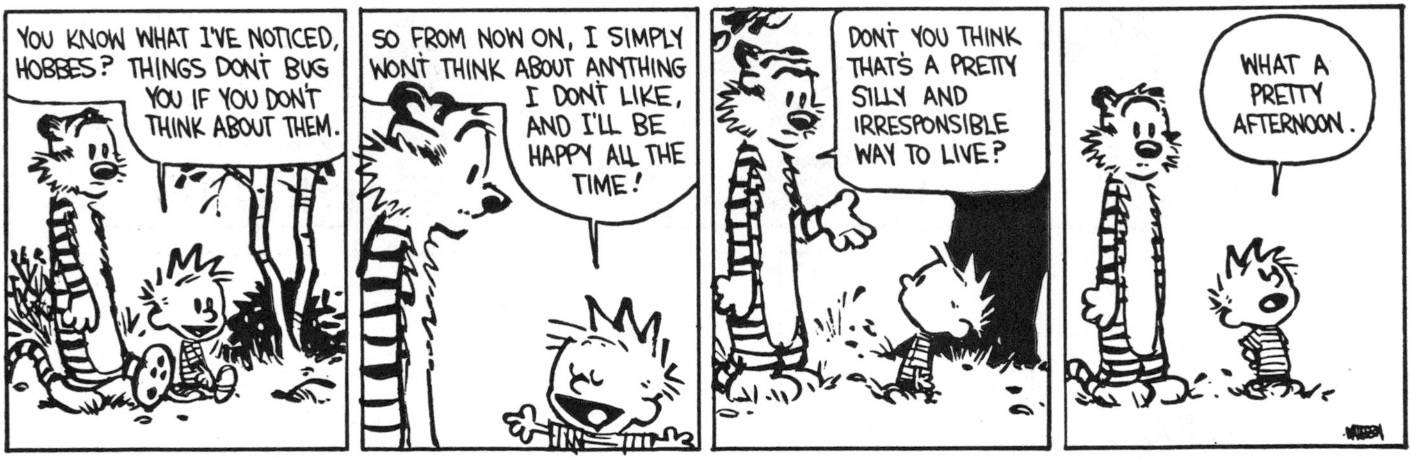
YOU KNOW WHAT I'VE NOTICED, HOBBES? THINGS DON'T BUG YOU IF YOU DON'T THINK ABOUT THEM.
SO FROM NOW ON, I SIMPLY WON'T THINK ABOUT ANYTHING I DON'T LIKE, AND I'LL BE HAPPY ALL THE TIME!
DON'T YOU THINK THAT'S A PRETTY SILLY AND IRRESPONSIBLE WAY TO LIVE?
WHAT A PRETTY AFTERNOON.

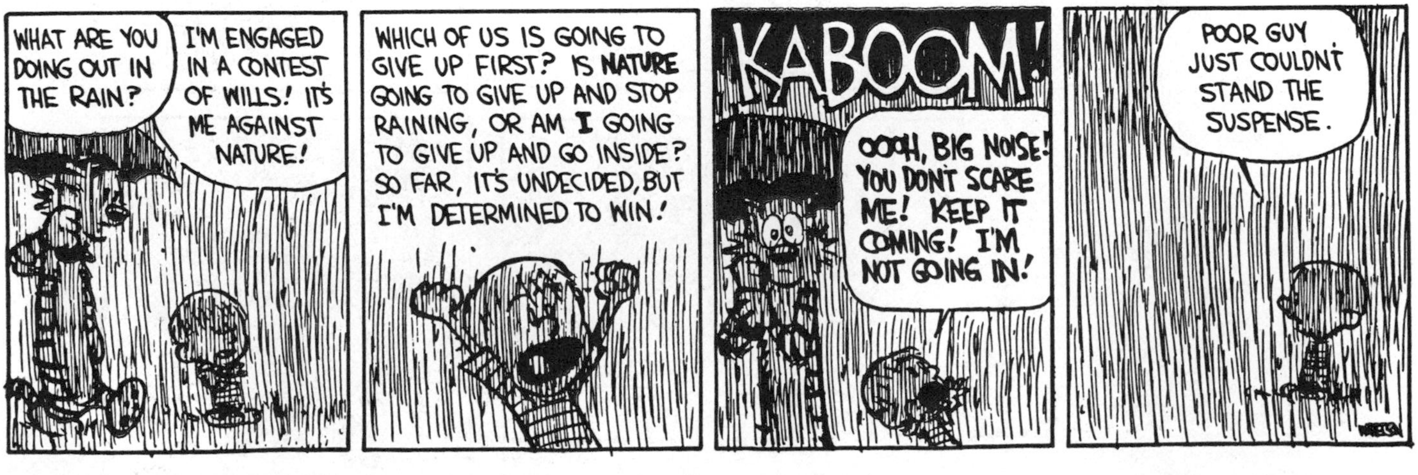
WHAT ARE YOU DOING OUT IN THE RAIN?
I'M ENGAGED IN A CONTEST OF WILLS! IT'S ME AGAINST NATURE!
WHICH OF US IS GOING TO GIVE UP FIRST? IS NATURE GOING TO GIVE UP AND STOP RAINING, OR AM I GOING TO GIVE UP AND GO INSIDE? SO FAR, IT'S UNDECIDED, BUT I'M DETERMINED TO WIN!
KABOOM!
OOOH, BIG NOISE! YOU DON'T SCARE ME! KEEP IT COMING! I'M NOT GOING IN!
POOR GUY JUST COULDN'T STAND THE SUSPENSE.

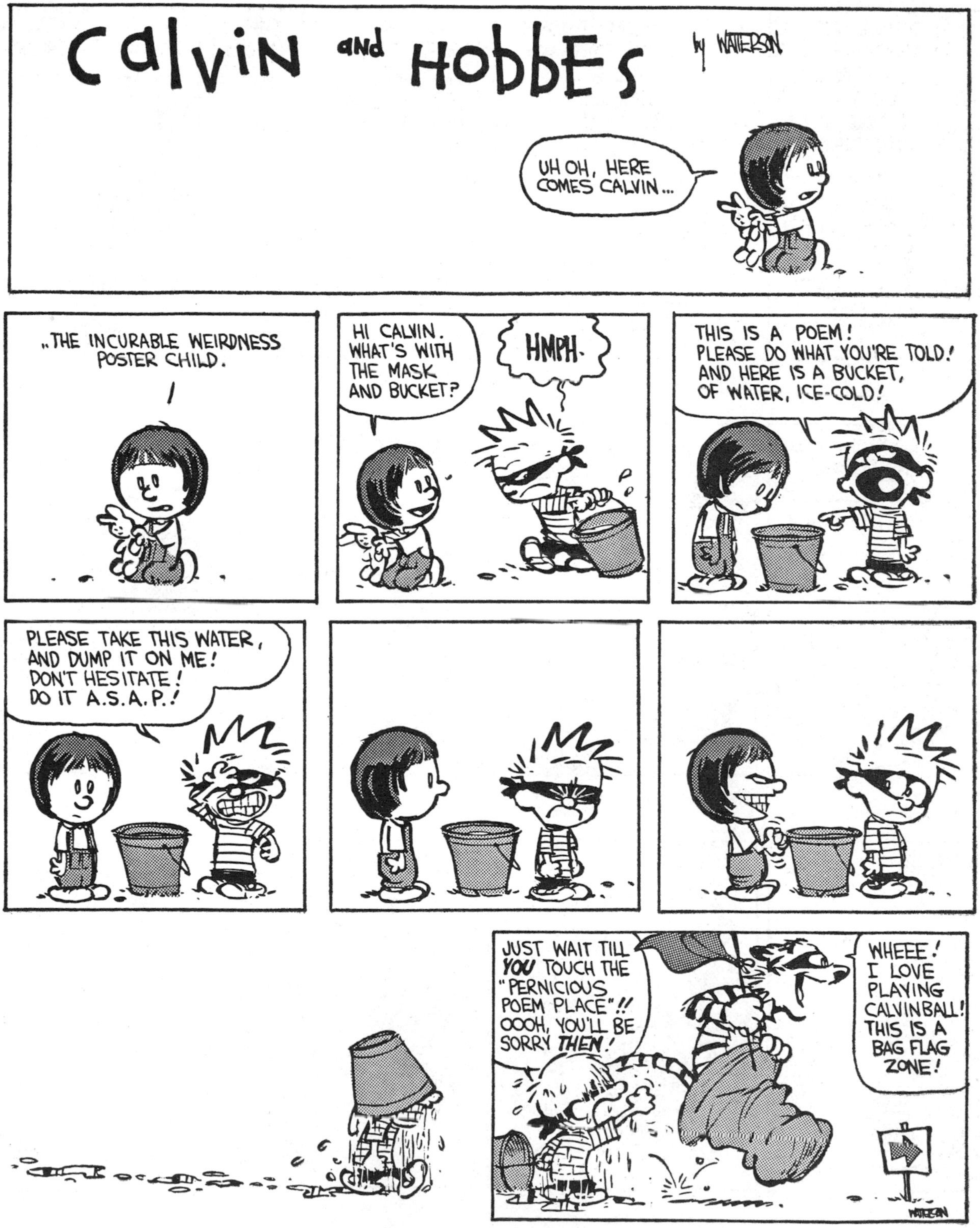
Calvin and HOBBES
by WATTERSON
UH OH, HERE COMES CALVIN...
...THE INCURABLE WEIRDNESS POSTER CHILD.
HI CALVIN. WHAT'S WITH THE MASK AND BUCKET?
HMPH.
THIS IS A POEM! PLEASE DO WHAT YOU'RE TOLD! AND HERE IS A BUCKET, OF WATER, ICE-COLD!
PLEASE TAKE THIS WATER, AND DUMP IT ON ME! DON'T HESITATE! DO IT A.S.A.P.!
JUST WAIT TILL YOU TOUCH THE "PERNICIOUS POEM PLACE"!! OOOH, YOU'LL BE SORRY THEN!
WHEEE! I LOVE PLAYING CALVINBALL! THIS IS A BAG FLAG ZONE!
WATTERSON

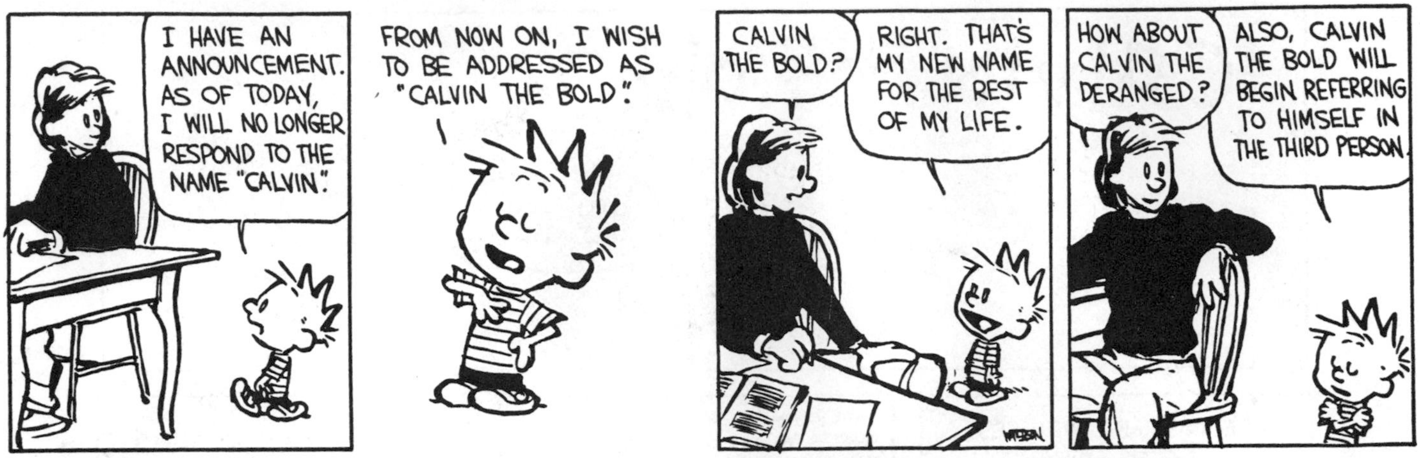
I HAVE AN ANNOUNCEMENT. AS OF TODAY, I WILL NO LONGER RESPOND TO THE NAME "CALVIN."
FROM NOW ON, I WISH TO BE ADDRESSED AS "CALVIN THE BOLD."
CALVIN THE BOLD?
RIGHT. THAT'S MY NEW NAME FOR THE REST OF MY LIFE.
HOW ABOUT CALVIN THE DERANGED?
ALSO, CALVIN THE BOLD WILL BEGIN REFERRING TO HIMSELF IN THE THIRD PERSON.

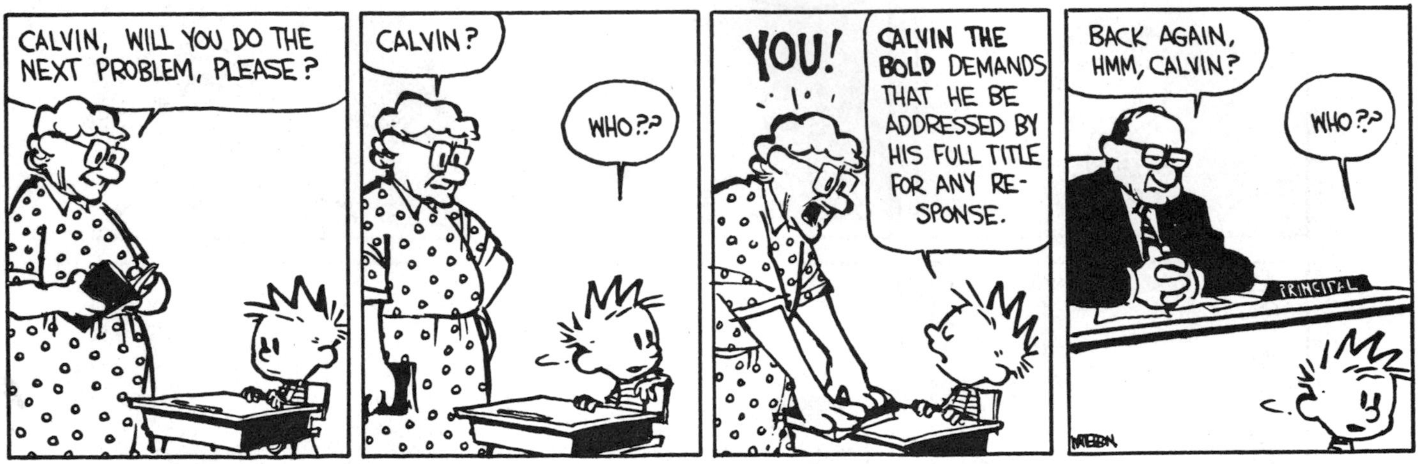
CALVIN, WILL YOU DO THE NEXT PROBLEM, PLEASE?
CALVIN?
WHO?
YOU!
CALVIN THE BOLD DEMANDS THAT HE BE ADDRESSED BY HIS FULL TITLE FOR ANY RESPONSE.
BACK AGAIN, HMM, CALVIN?
WHO?
PRINCIPAL

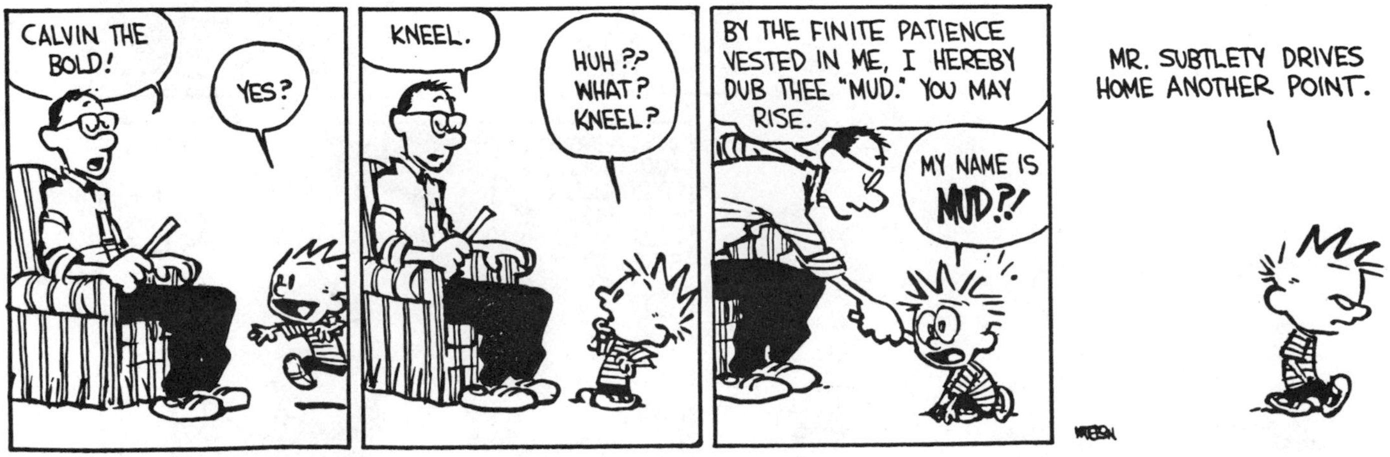
CALVIN THE BOLD!
YES?
KNEEL.
HUH?? WHAT? KNEEL?
BY THE FINITE PATIENCE VESTED IN ME, I HEREBY DUB THEE "MUD." YOU MAY RISE.
MY NAME IS MUD?!
MR. SUBTLETY DRIVES HOME ANOTHER POINT.

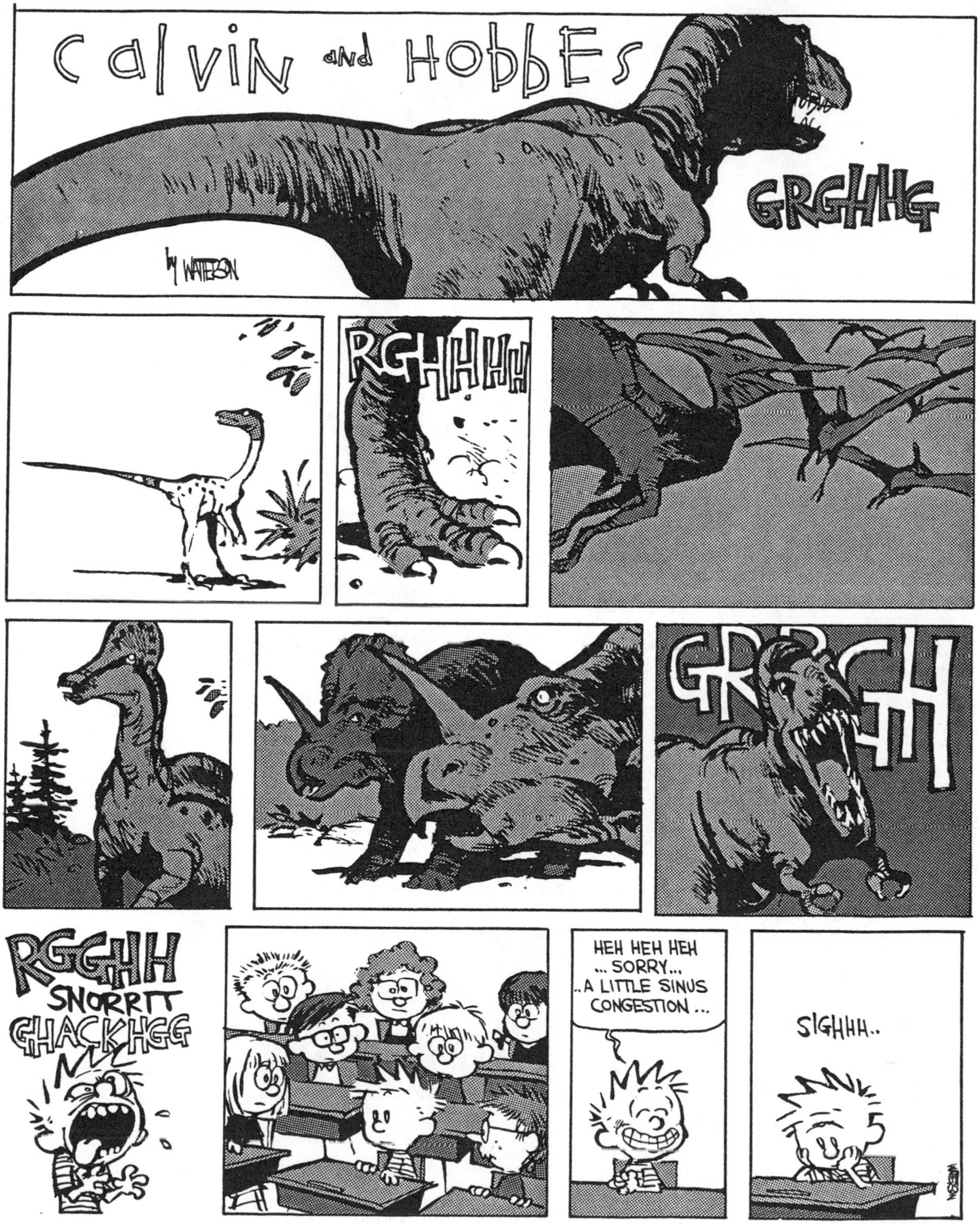
Calvin and HOBBES
by WATTERSON
GRGHHG
RGHHHH
GRRRCH
RGGHH
SNORRTT
GHACKHGG
HEH HEH HEH
... SORRY...
..A LITTLE SINUS CONGESTION ...
SIGHHH..

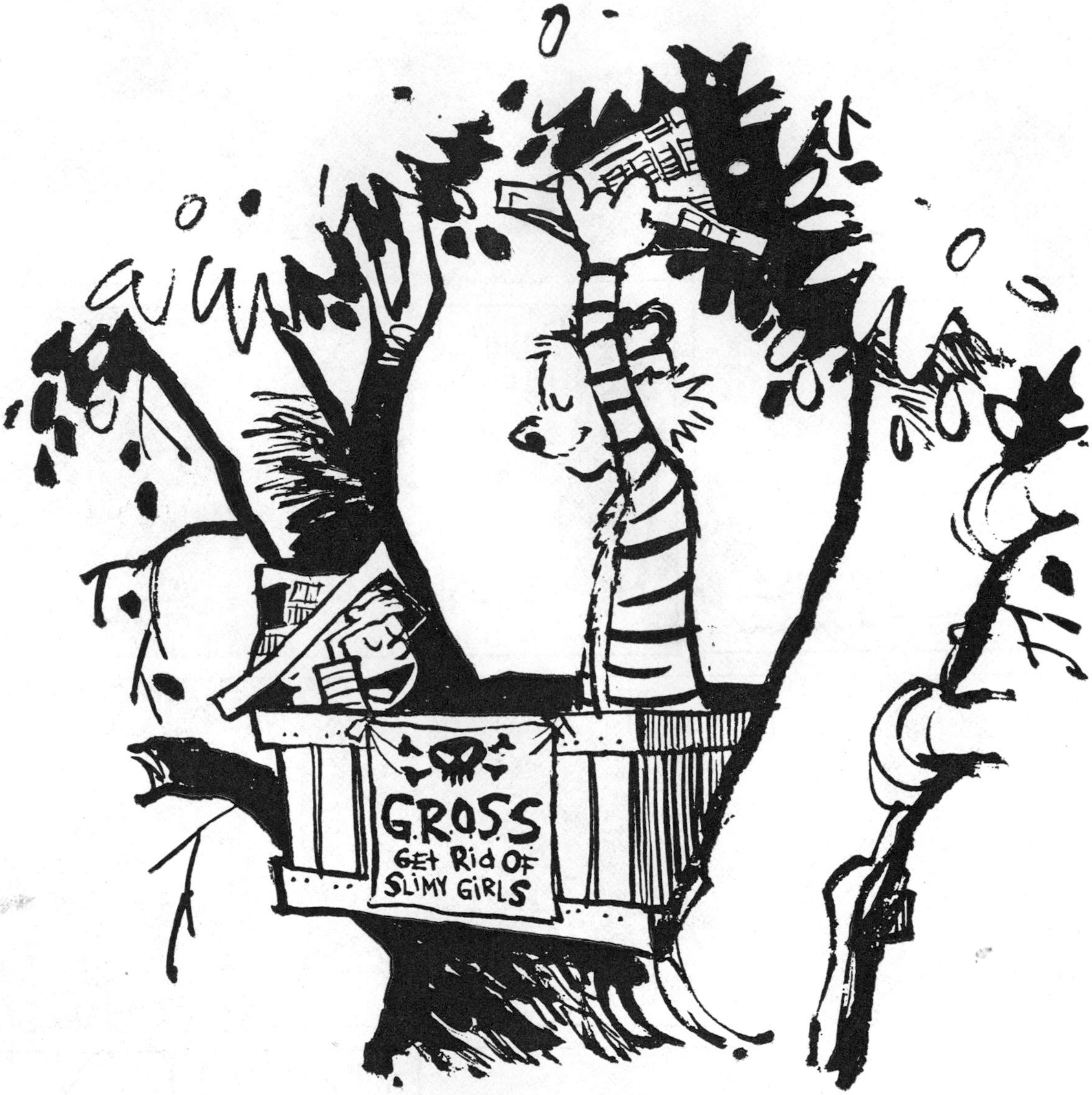
G.R.O.S.S
GET RID OF
SLIMY GIRLS

The End